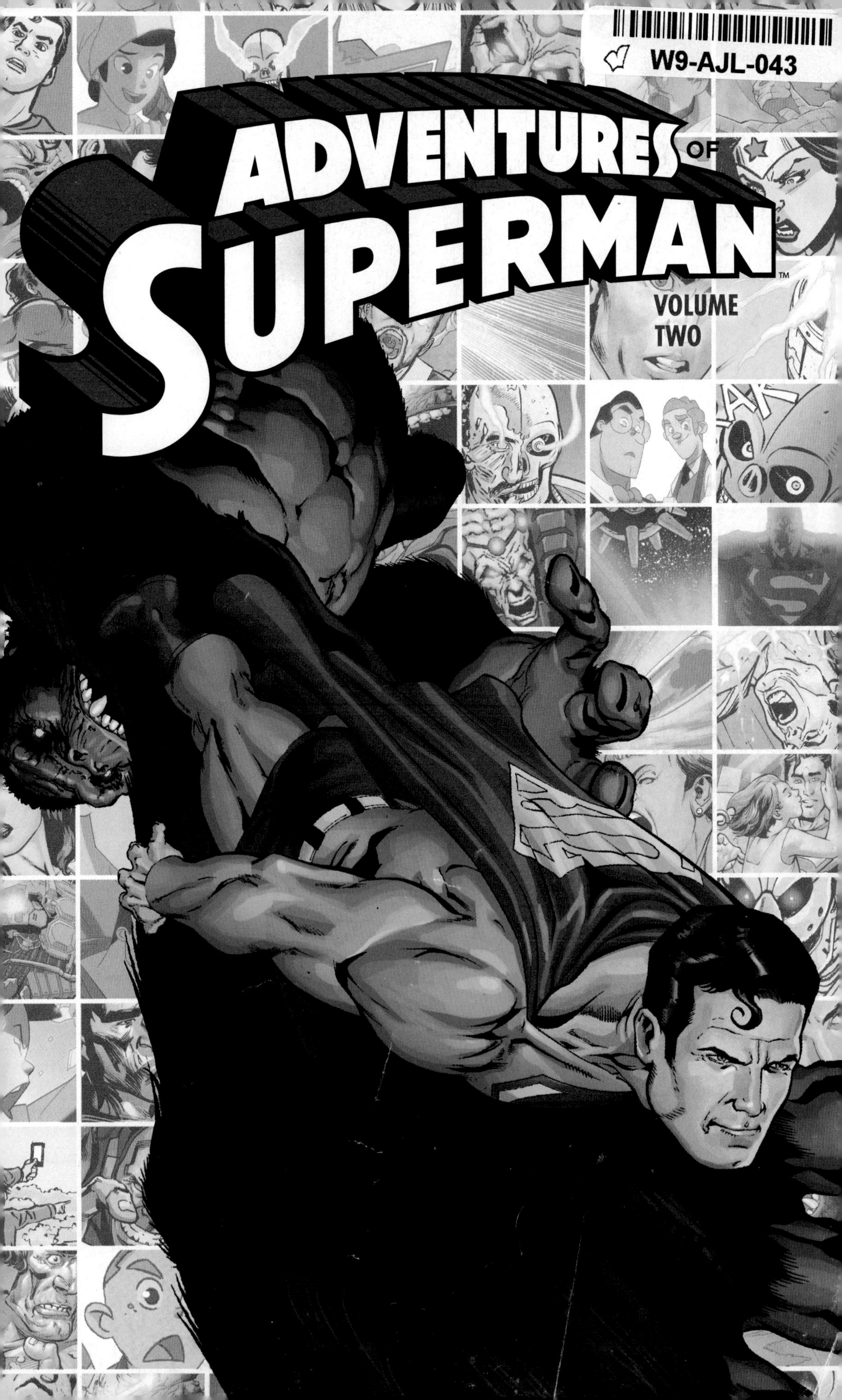
ADVENTURES OF
SUPERMAN™
VOLUME TWO

WRITTEN

BY J.T. Krul · David Lapham · Tim Seeley
Marc Guggenheim · Christos Gage
Derek Fridolfs · Josh Elder

ART

BY Marcus To · David Lapham · Mike Norton
Joe Bennett · Belardino Brabo · Eduardo Francisco
Sean Galloway · Victor Ibáñez

COLORS

BY Ian Herring · Lee Loughridge
Jordie Bellaire · Jason Wright · Stefani Rennee
Sean Galloway · Matthew Wilson

LETTERS

BY Wes Abbott

COVER ART

BY Chris Sprouse, Karl Story and Guy Major

ORIGINAL SERIES COVERS

BY Mitch Breitweiser · Elizabeth Breitweiser
Chris Sprouse · Karl Story · Guy Major
Joe Bennett · Belardino Brabo · Jason Wright
Dan Panosian · Sean Galloway

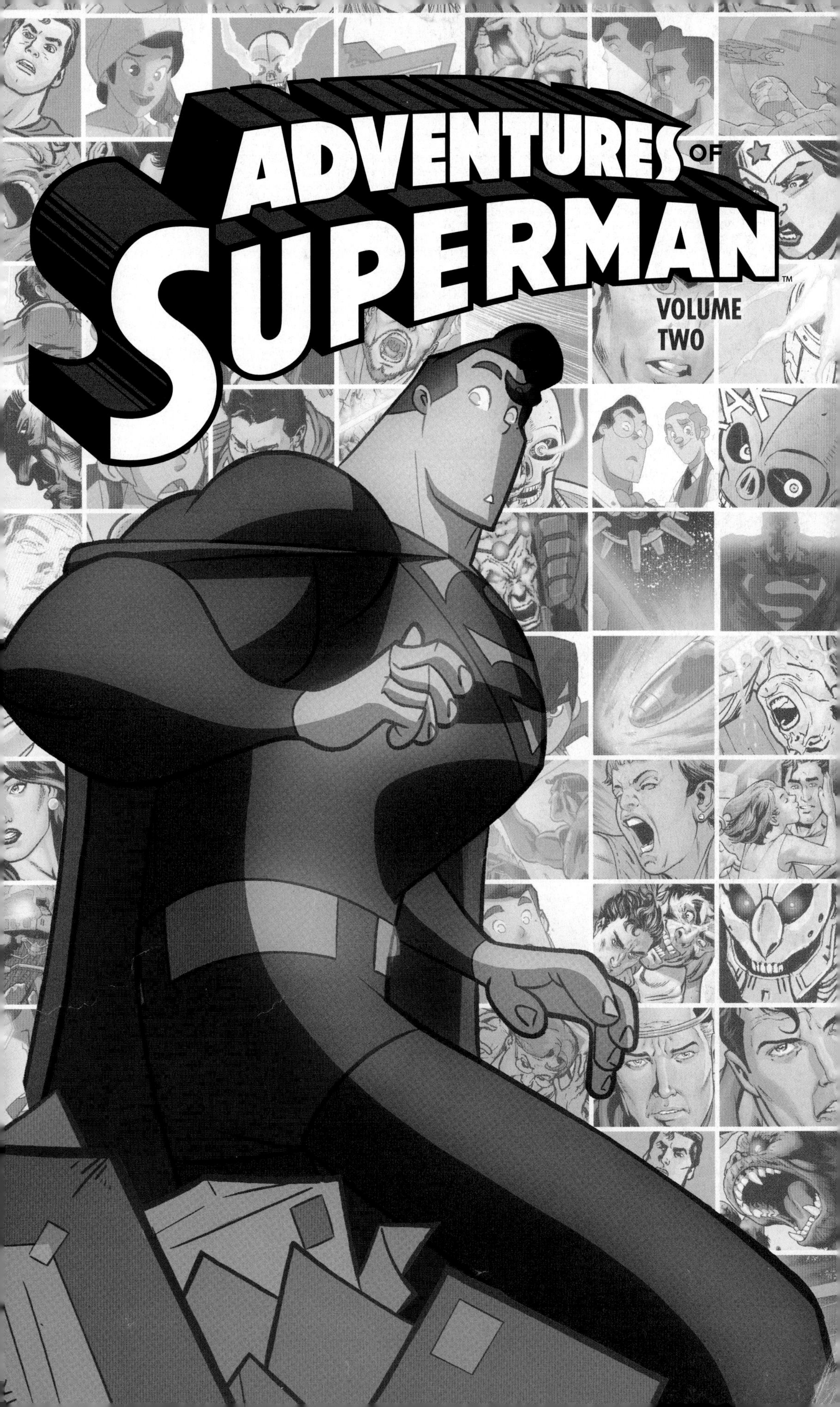
ADVENTURES OF
SUPERMAN™
VOLUME
TWO

ALEX ANTONE EDITOR – ORIGINAL SERIES SCOTT NYBAKKEN EDITOR
ROBBIN BROSTERMAN DESIGN DIRECTOR – BOOKS DAMIAN RYLAND PUBLICATION DESIGN

HANK KANALZ SENIOR VP – VERTIGO & INTEGRATED PUBLISHING

DIANE NELSON PRESIDENT DAN DIDIO AND JIM LEE CO-PUBLISHERS GEOFF JOHNS CHIEF CREATIVE OFFICER
AMIT DESAI SENIOR VP – MARKETING & FRANCHISE MANAGEMENT AMY GENKINS SENIOR VP – BUSINESS & LEGAL AFFAIRS
NAIRI GARDINER SENIOR VP – FINANCE JEFF BOISON VP – PUBLISHING PLANNING MARK CHIARELLO VP – ART DIRECTION & DESIGN
JOHN CUNNINGHAM VP – MARKETING TERRI CUNNINGHAM VP – EDITORIAL ADMINISTRATION
LARRY GANEM VP – TALENT RELATIONS & SERVICES ALISON GILL SENIOR VP – MANUFACTURING & OPERATIONS
JAY KOGAN VP – BUSINESS & LEGAL AFFAIRS, PUBLISHING JACK MAHAN VP – BUSINESS AFFAIRS, TALENT
NICK NAPOLITANO VP – MANUFACTURING ADMINISTRATION SUE POHJA VP – BOOK SALES
FRED RUIZ VP – MANUFACTURING OPERATIONS COURTNEY SIMMONS SENIOR VP – PUBLICITY BOB WAYNE SENIOR VP – SALES

ADVENTURES OF SUPERMAN VOL. 2

PUBLISHED BY DC COMICS. COPYRIGHT © 2014 DC COMICS. ALL RIGHTS RESERVED. ORIGINALLY PUBLISHED IN SINGLE MAGAZINE FORM
AS ADVENTURES OF SUPERMAN 6-10 AND ONLINE AS ADVENTURES OF SUPERMAN CHAPTERS 16-30. COPYRIGHT © 2013, 2014 DC COMICS.
ALL RIGHTS RESERVED. ALL CHARACTERS, THEIR DISTINCTIVE LIKENESSES AND RELATED ELEMENTS FEATURED IN THIS PUBLICATION ARE
TRADEMARKS OF DC COMICS. THE STORIES, CHARACTERS AND INCIDENTS FEATURED IN THIS PUBLICATION ARE ENTIRELY FICTIONAL.
DC COMICS DOES NOT READ OR ACCEPT UNSOLICITED SUBMISSIONS OF IDEAS, STORIES OR ARTWORK.

DC COMICS
1700 BROADWAY, NEW YORK, NY 10019
A WARNER BROS. ENTERTAINMENT COMPANY.
PRINTED BY RR DONNELLEY, SALEM, VA, USA. 9/12/14. FIRST PRINTING.
ISBN: 978-1-4012-5036-2

LIBRARY OF CONGRESS CATALOGING-IN-PUBLICATION DATA

KRUL, J.T., AUTHOR.
  ADVENTURES OF SUPERMAN VOLUME 2 / J.T. KRUL, MARCUS TO, DAVID LAPHAM.
      PAGES CM
  ISBN 978-1-4012-5036-2 (PAPERBACK)
  1. GRAPHIC NOVELS. I. TO, MARCUS, ILLUSTRATOR. II. LAPHAM, DAVID, ILLUSTRATOR. III. TITLE.
  PN6728.S9K76 2014
  741.5'973—DC23
                          2014014887

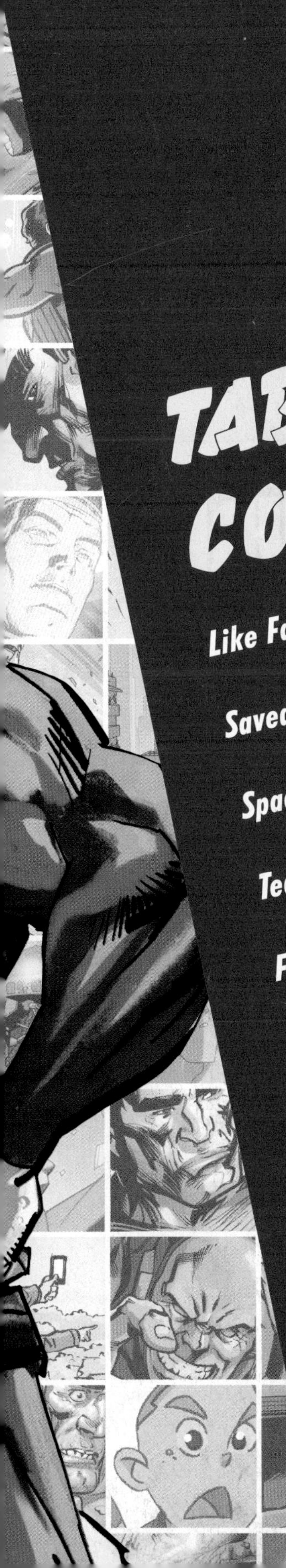

TABLE OF CONTENTS

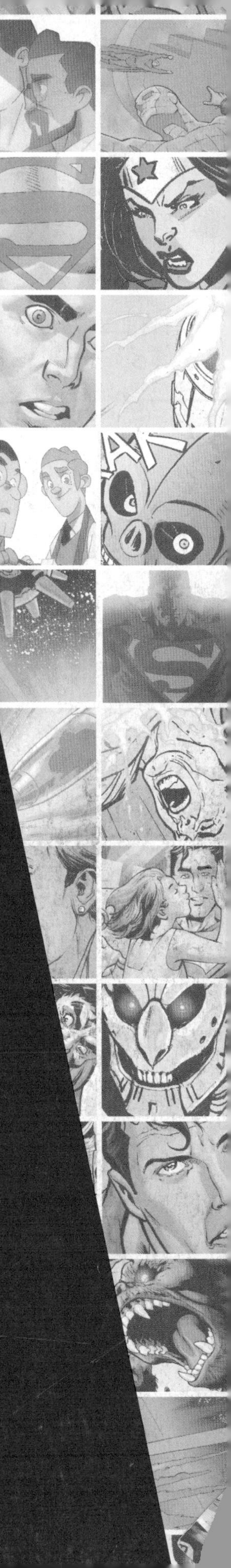

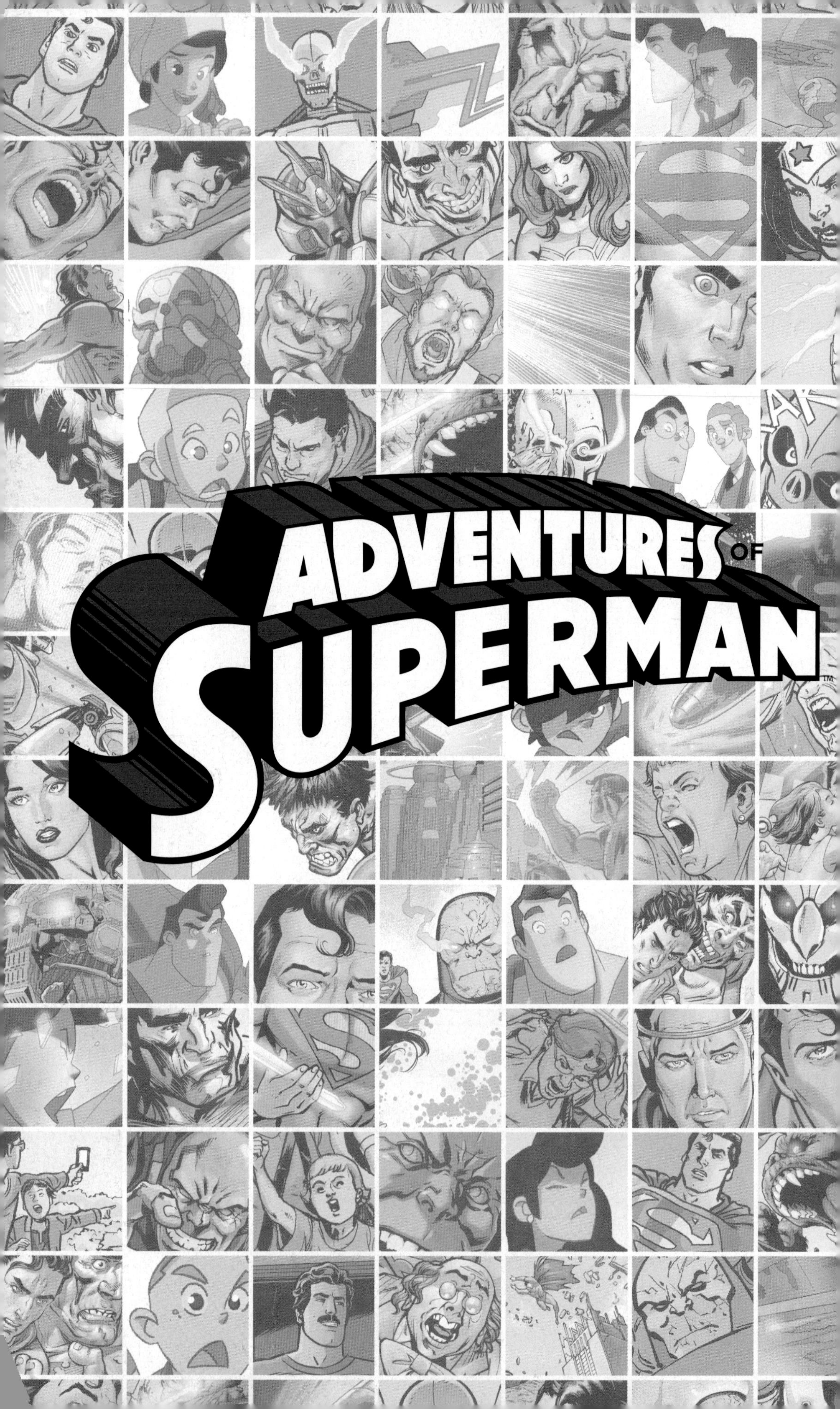
ADVENTURES OF
SUPERMAN™

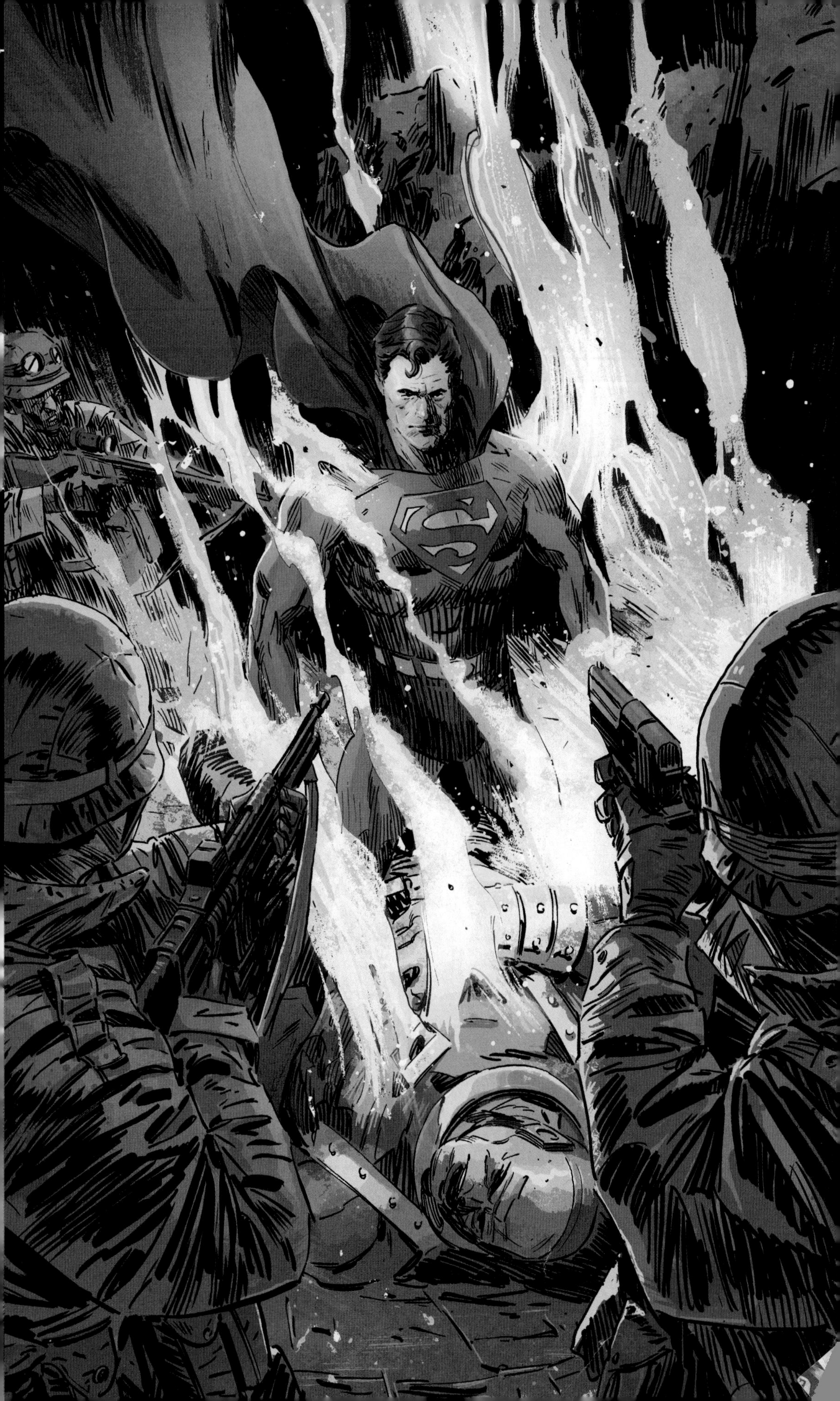

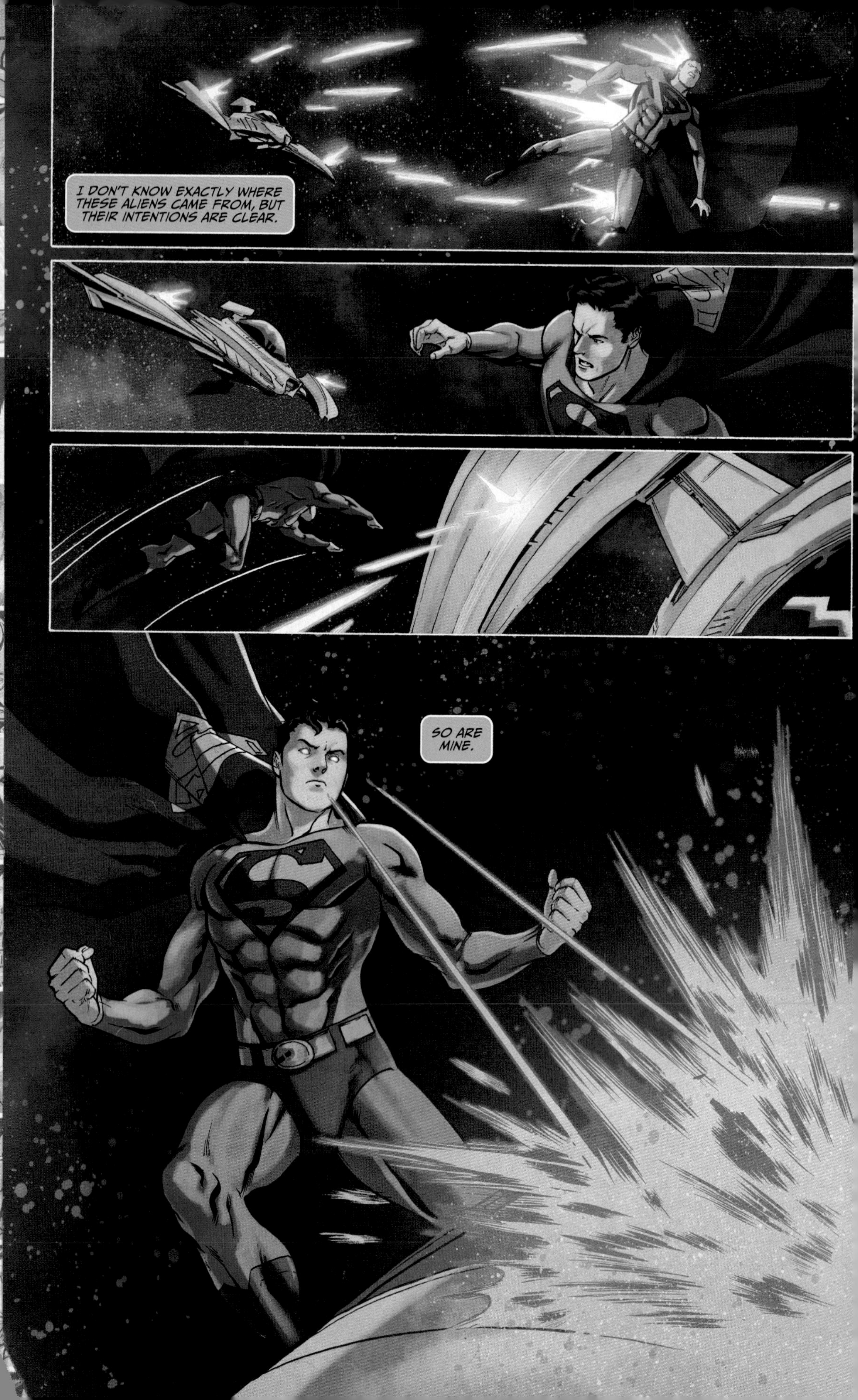
I DON'T KNOW EXACTLY WHERE THESE ALIENS CAME FROM, BUT THEIR INTENTIONS ARE CLEAR.
SO ARE MINE.

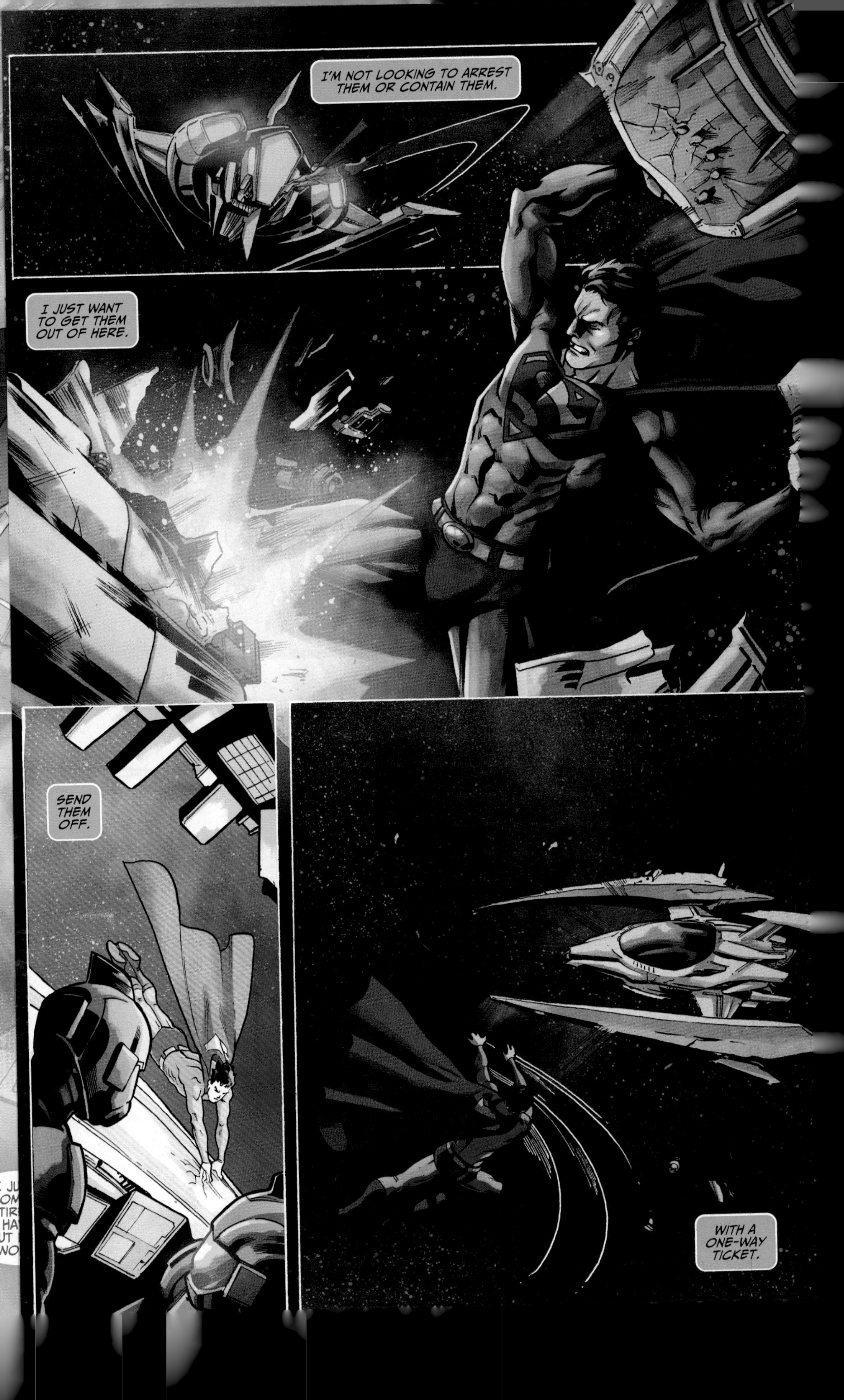
I'M NOT LOOKING TO ARREST THEM OR CONTAIN THEM.
I JUST WANT TO GET THEM OUT OF HERE.
SEND THEM OFF.
WITH A ONE-WAY TICKET.

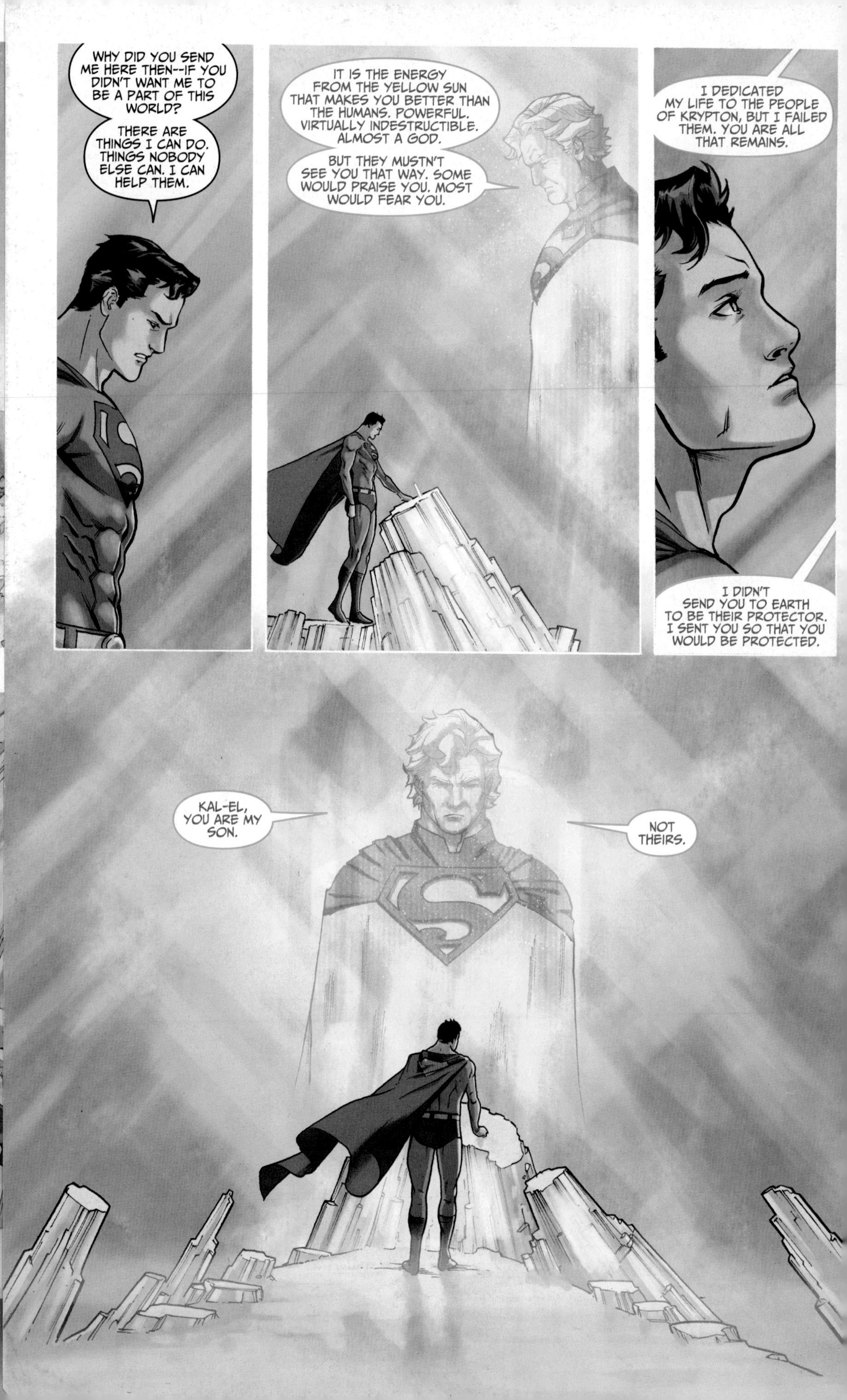
WHY DID YOU SEND ME HERE THEN--IF YOU DIDN'T WANT ME TO BE A PART OF THIS WORLD?
THERE ARE THINGS I CAN DO. THINGS NOBODY ELSE CAN. I CAN HELP THEM.
IT IS THE ENERGY FROM THE YELLOW SUN THAT MAKES YOU BETTER THAN THE HUMANS. POWERFUL. VIRTUALLY INDESTRUCTIBLE. ALMOST A GOD.
BUT THEY MUSTN'T SEE YOU THAT WAY. SOME WOULD PRAISE YOU. MOST WOULD FEAR YOU.
I DEDICATED MY LIFE TO THE PEOPLE OF KRYPTON, BUT I FAILED THEM. YOU ARE ALL THAT REMAINS.
I DIDN'T SEND YOU TO EARTH TO BE THEIR PROTECTOR. I SENT YOU SO THAT YOU WOULD BE PROTECTED.
KAL-EL, YOU ARE MY SON.
NOT THEIRS.

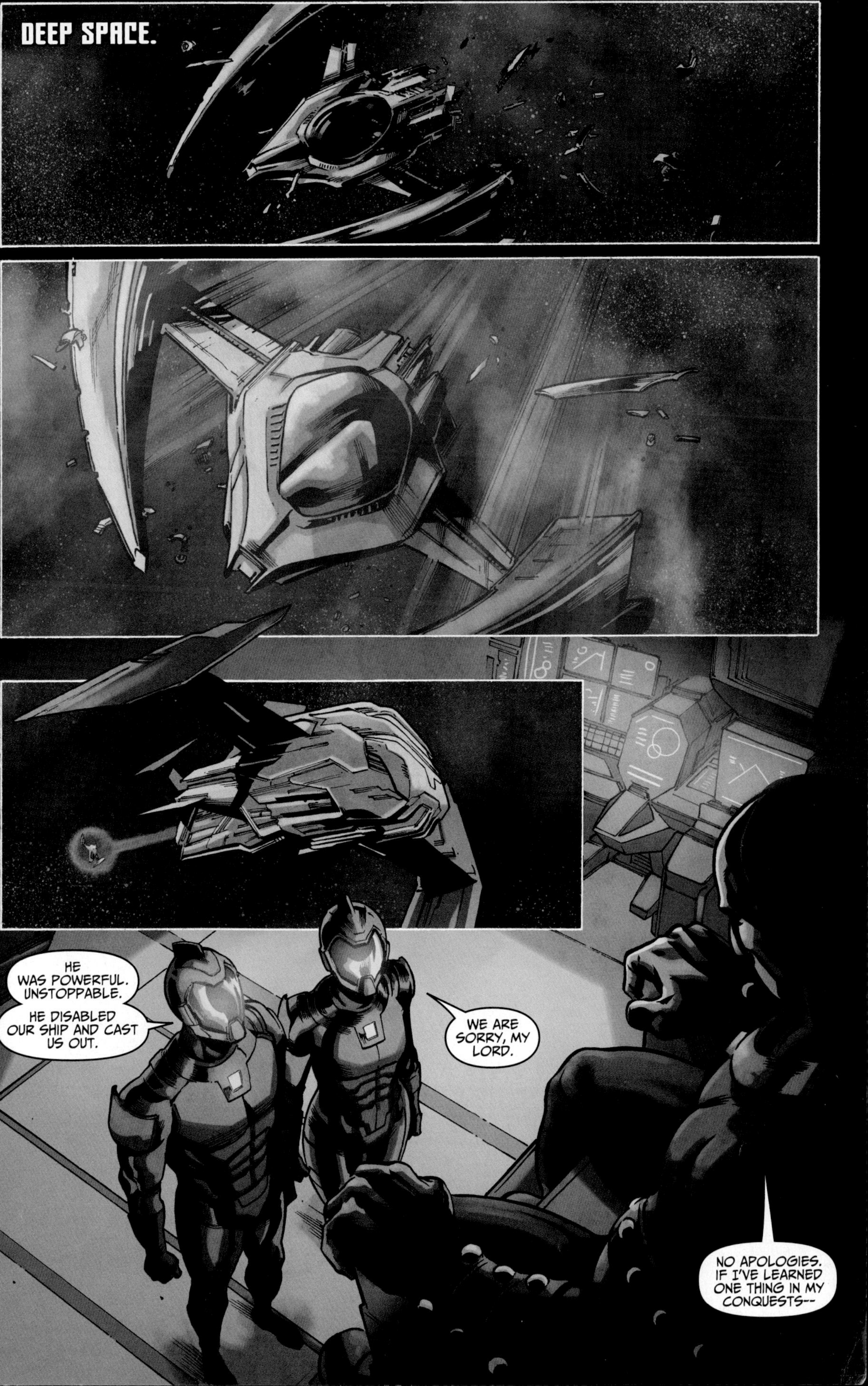
DEEP SPACE.
HE WAS POWERFUL. UNSTOPPABLE.
HE DISABLED OUR SHIP AND CAST US OUT.
WE ARE SORRY, MY LORD.
NO APOLOGIES. IF I'VE LEARNED ONE THING IN MY CONQUESTS--

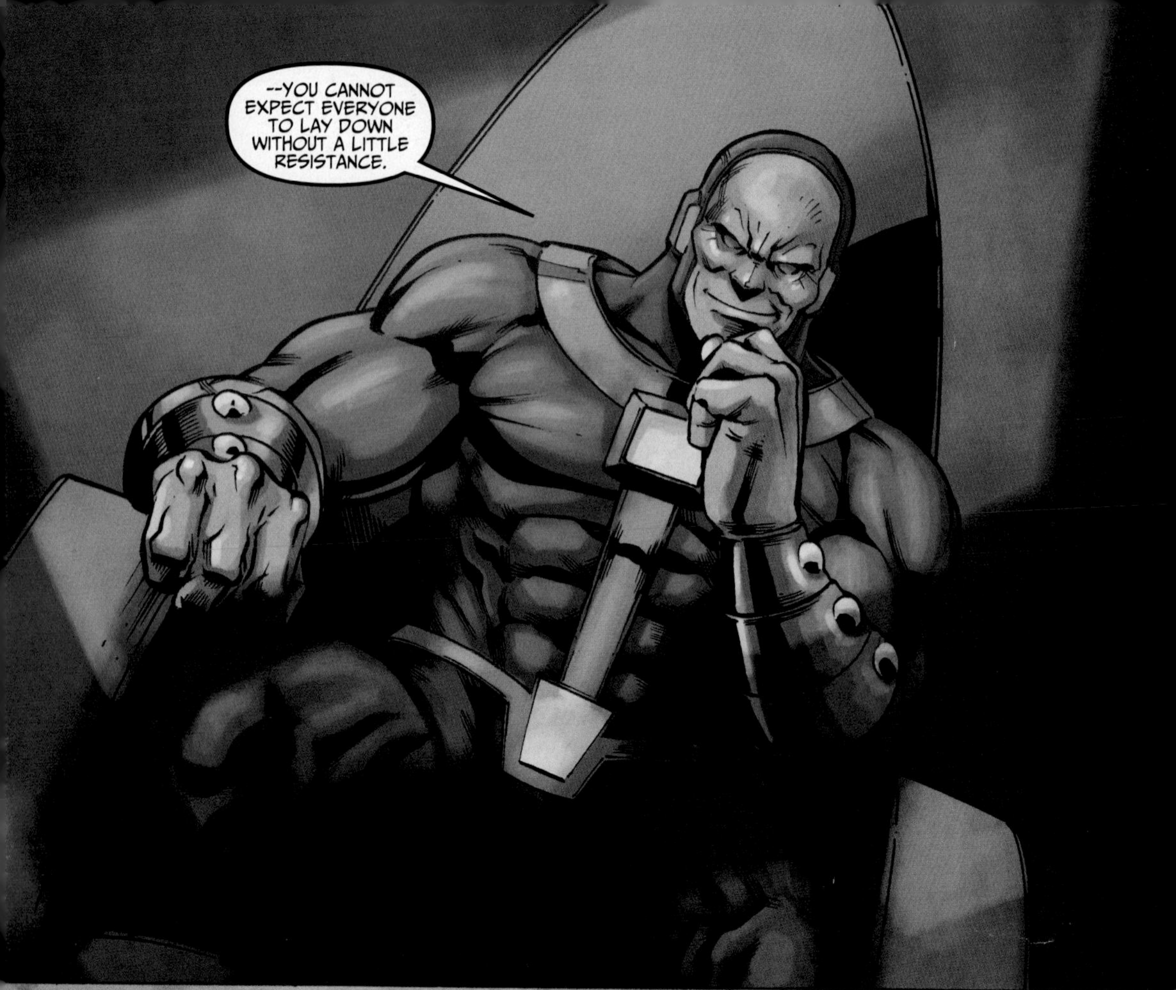
--YOU CANNOT EXPECT EVERYONE TO LAY DOWN WITHOUT A LITTLE RESISTANCE.

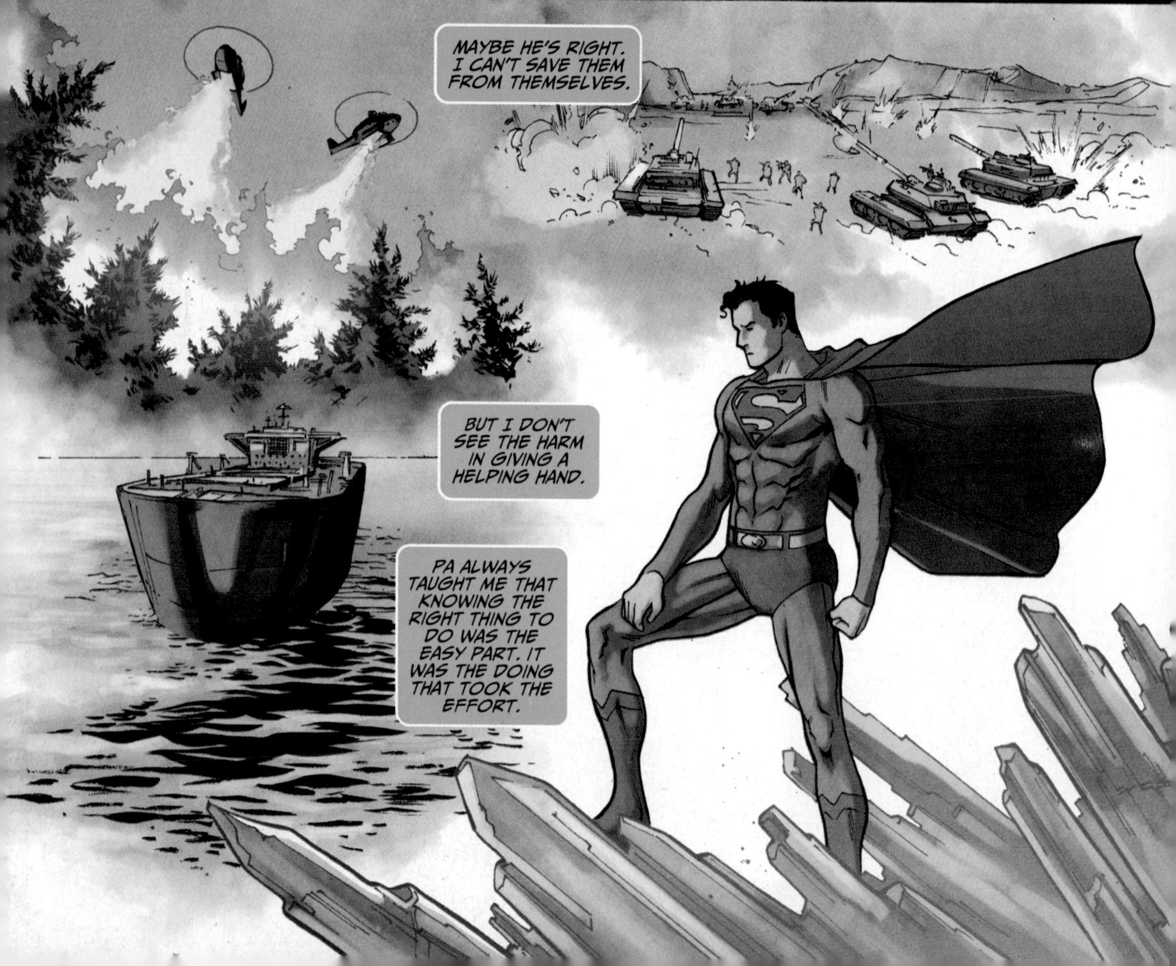
MAYBE HE'S RIGHT. I CAN'T SAVE THEM FROM THEMSELVES.
BUT I DON'T SEE THE HARM IN GIVING A HELPING HAND.
PA ALWAYS TAUGHT ME THAT KNOWING THE RIGHT THING TO DO WAS THE EASY PART. IT WAS THE DOING THAT TOOK THE EFFORT.

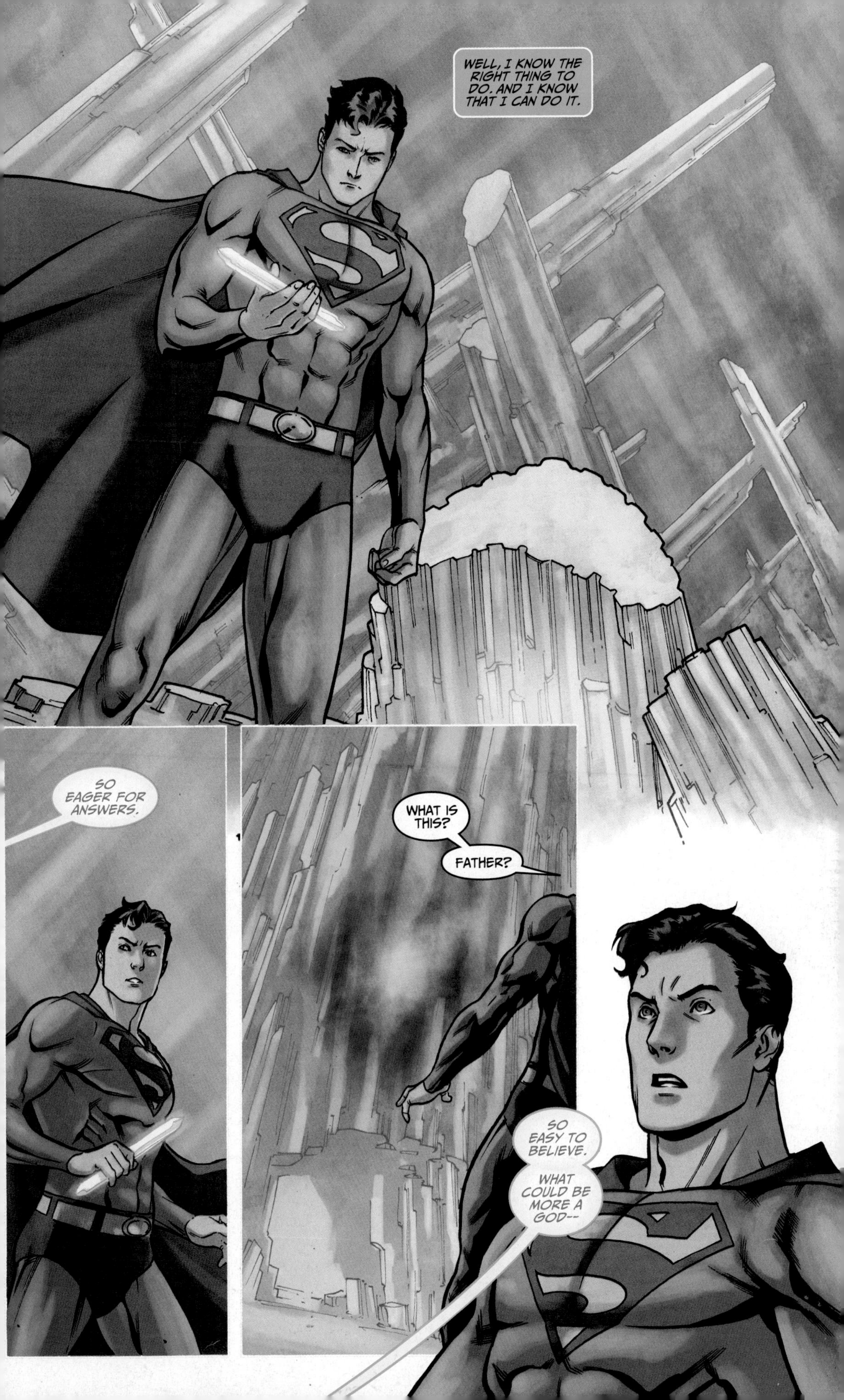
WELL, I KNOW THE RIGHT THING TO DO. AND I KNOW THAT I CAN DO IT.
SO EAGER FOR ANSWERS.
WHAT IS THIS?
FATHER?
SO EASY TO BELIEVE.
WHAT COULD BE MORE A GOD--

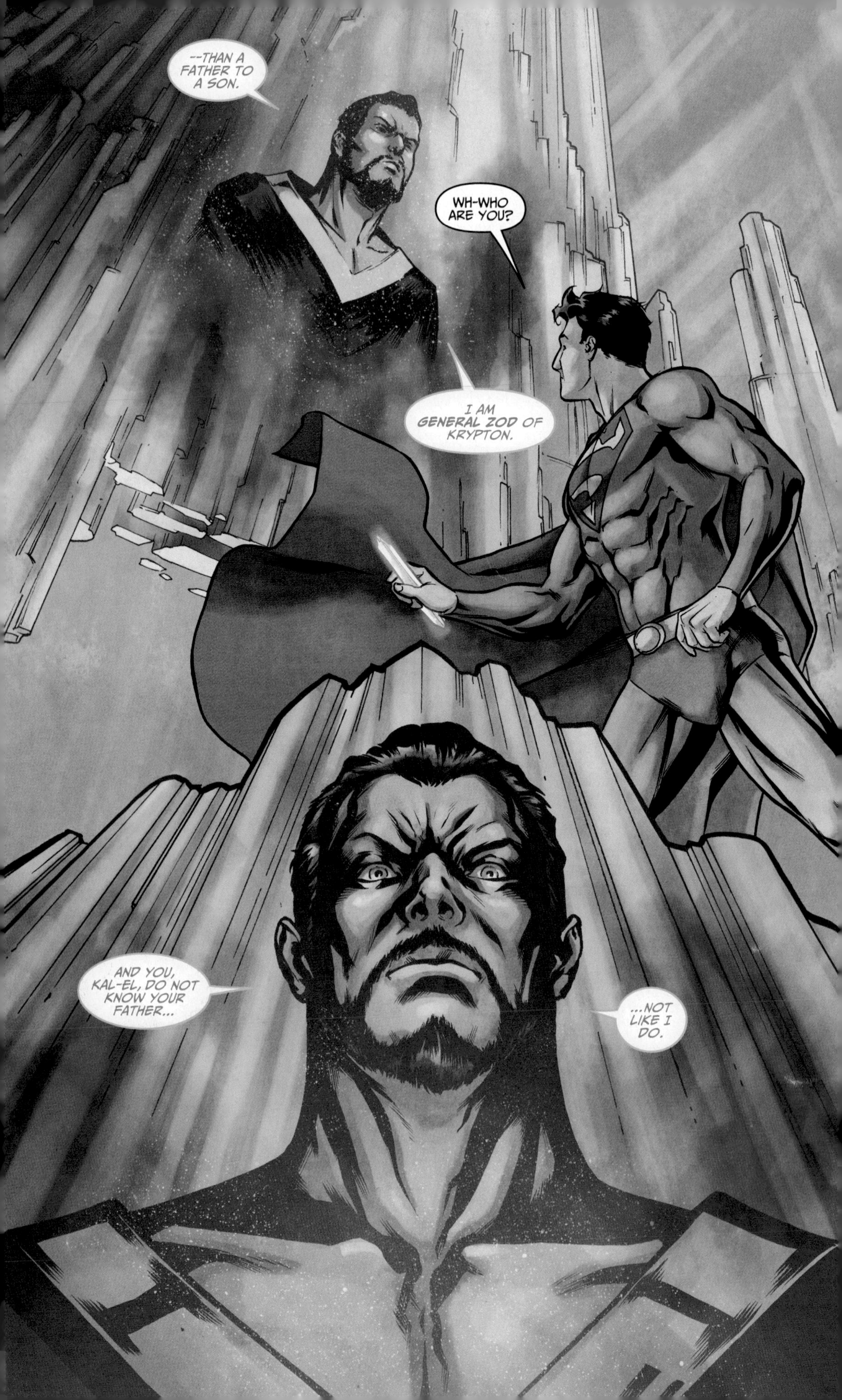
--THAN A FATHER TO A SON.
WH-WHO ARE YOU?
I AM GENERAL ZOD OF KRYPTON.
AND YOU, KAL-EL, DO NOT KNOW YOUR FATHER...
...NOT LIKE I DO.

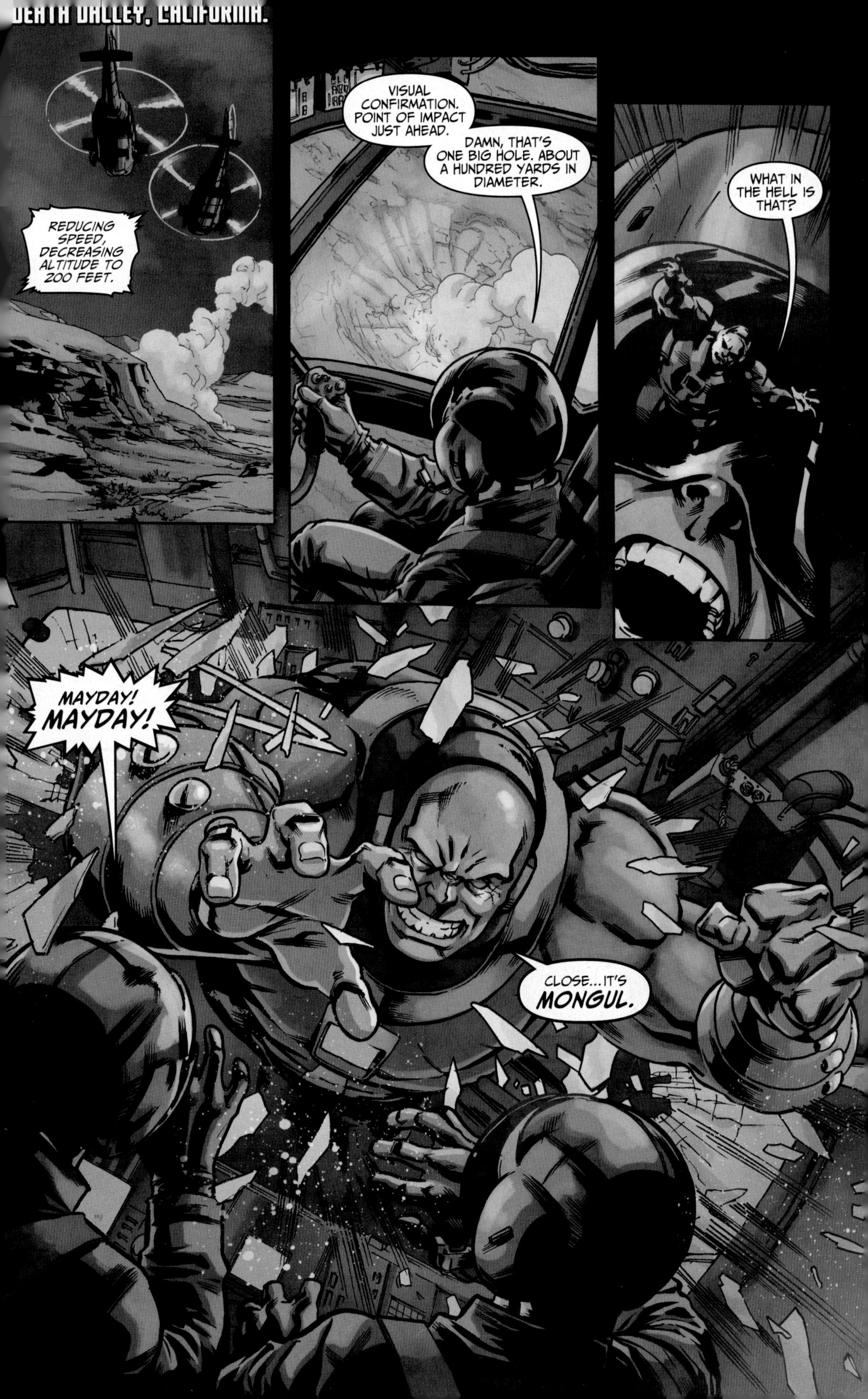
DEATH VALLEY, CALIFORNIA.
REDUCING SPEED, DECREASING ALTITUDE TO 200 FEET.
VISUAL CONFIRMATION. POINT OF IMPACT JUST AHEAD.
DAMN, THAT'S ONE BIG HOLE. ABOUT A HUNDRED YARDS IN DIAMETER.
WHAT IN THE HELL IS THAT?
MAYDAY! MAYDAY!
CLOSE...IT'S MONGUL.

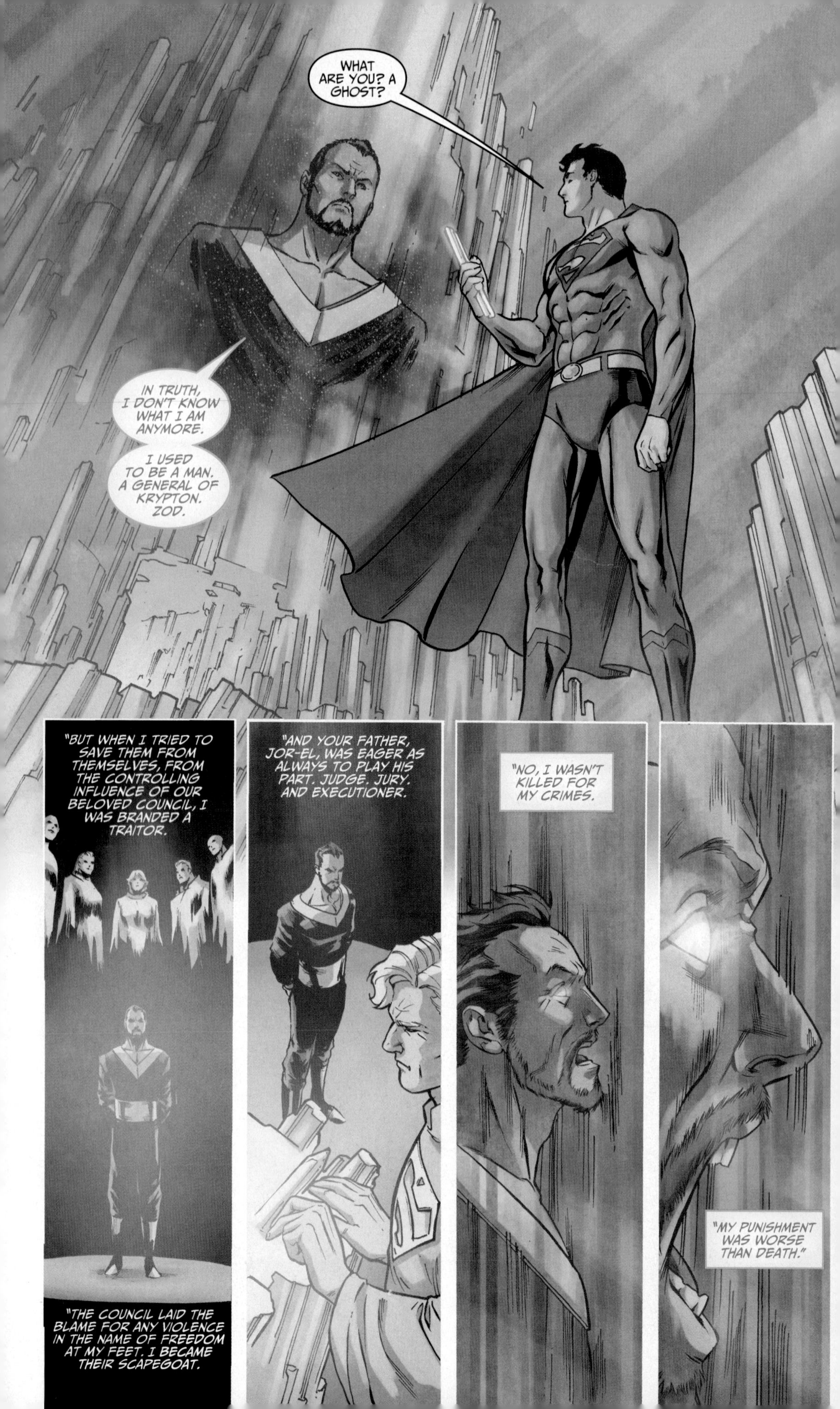

WHAT ARE YOU? A GHOST?
IN TRUTH, I DON'T KNOW WHAT I AM ANYMORE.
I USED TO BE A MAN. A GENERAL OF KRYPTON. ZOD.
"BUT WHEN I TRIED TO SAVE THEM FROM THEMSELVES, FROM THE CONTROLLING INFLUENCE OF OUR BELOVED COUNCIL, I WAS BRANDED A TRAITOR.
"THE COUNCIL LAID THE BLAME FOR ANY VIOLENCE IN THE NAME OF FREEDOM AT MY FEET. I BECAME THEIR SCAPEGOAT.
"AND YOUR FATHER, JOR-EL, WAS EAGER AS ALWAYS TO PLAY HIS PART. JUDGE. JURY. AND EXECUTIONER.
"NO, I WASN'T KILLED FOR MY CRIMES.
"MY PUNISHMENT WAS WORSE THAN DEATH."

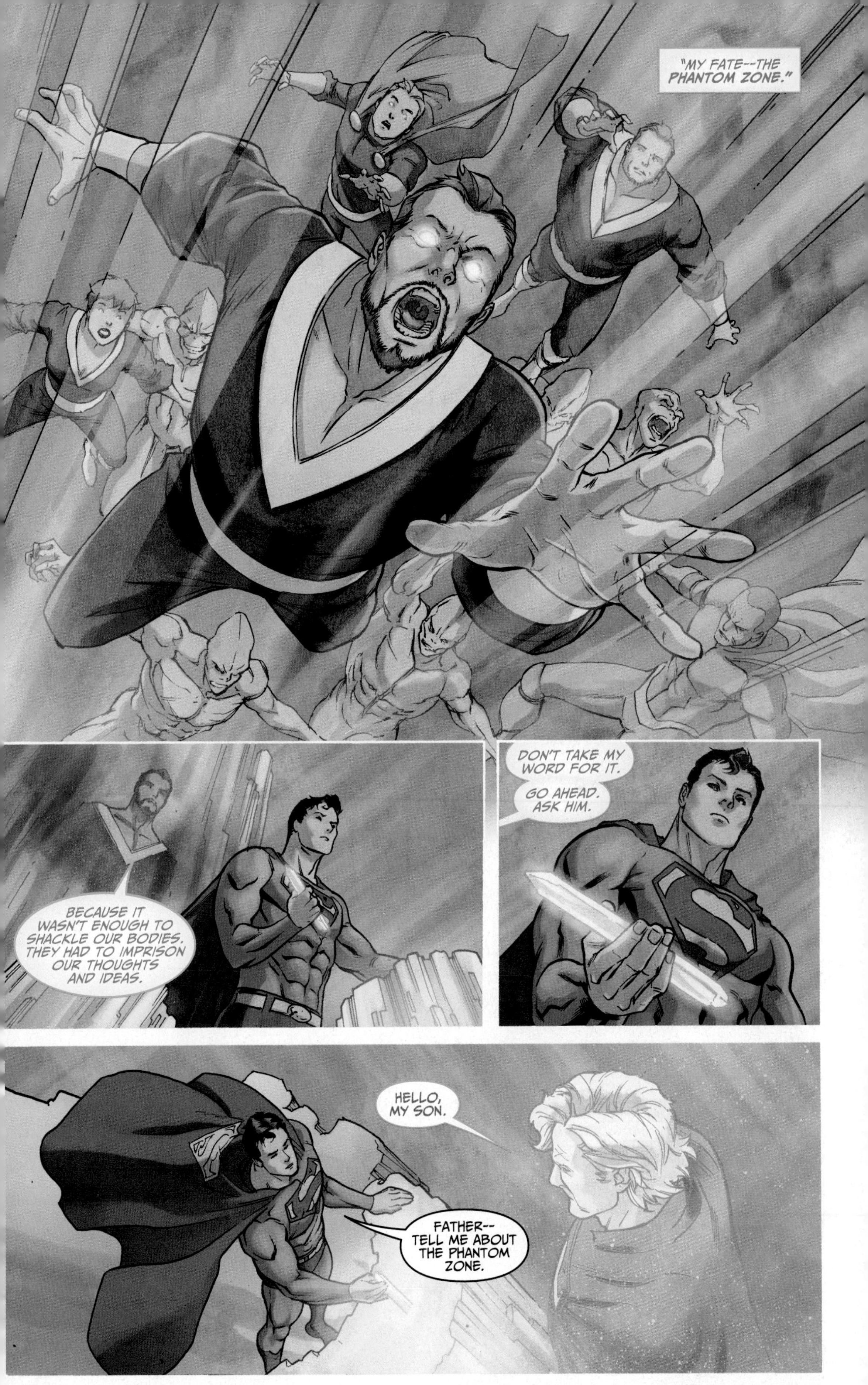
"MY FATE--THE PHANTOM ZONE."
BECAUSE IT WASN'T ENOUGH TO SHACKLE OUR BODIES. THEY HAD TO IMPRISON OUR THOUGHTS AND IDEAS.
DON'T TAKE MY WORD FOR IT.
GO AHEAD. ASK HIM.
HELLO, MY SON.
FATHER-- TELL ME ABOUT THE PHANTOM ZONE.

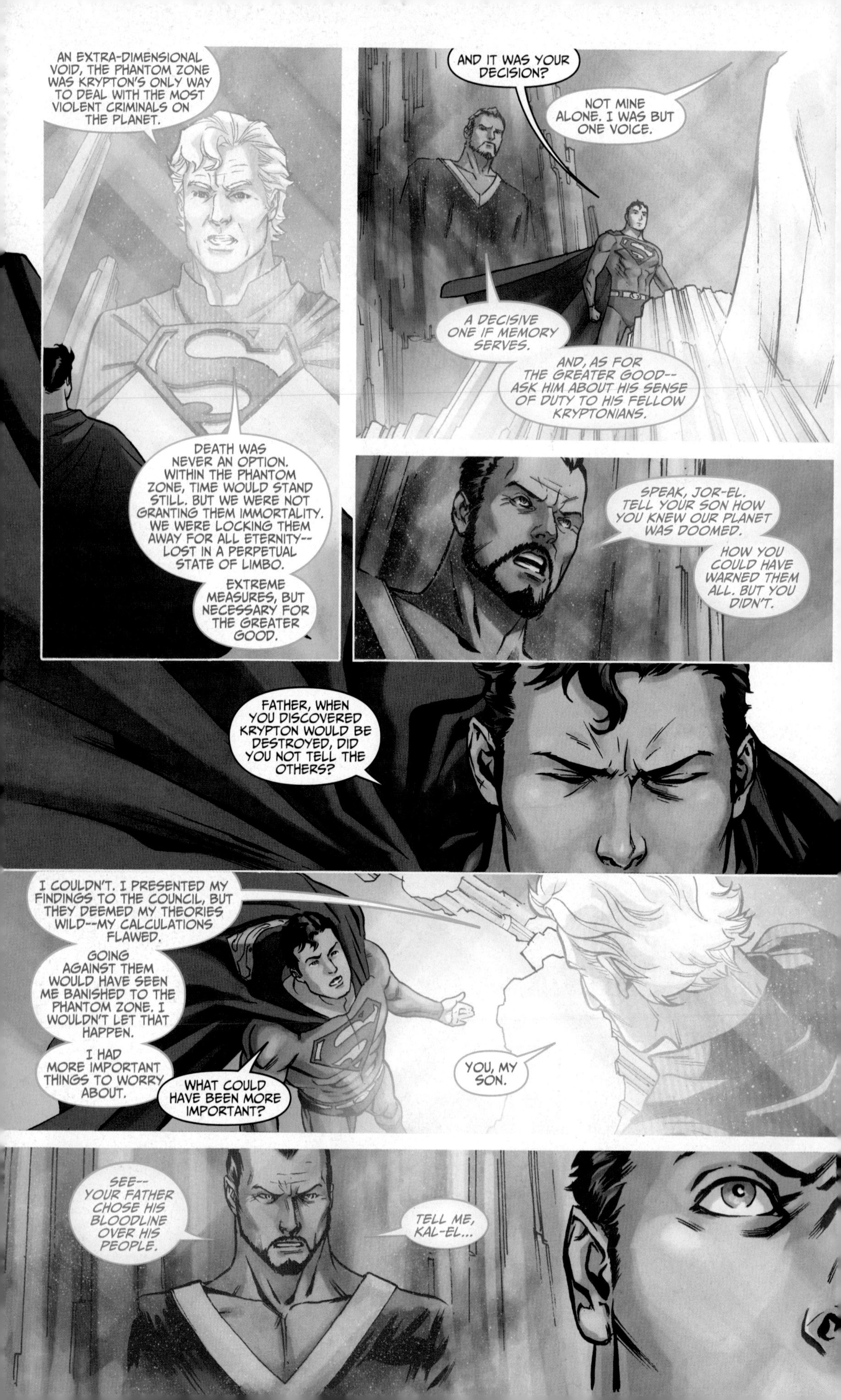

AN EXTRA-DIMENSIONAL VOID, THE PHANTOM ZONE WAS KRYPTON'S ONLY WAY TO DEAL WITH THE MOST VIOLENT CRIMINALS ON THE PLANET.
DEATH WAS NEVER AN OPTION. WITHIN THE PHANTOM ZONE, TIME WOULD STAND STILL. BUT WE WERE NOT GRANTING THEM IMMORTALITY. WE WERE LOCKING THEM AWAY FOR ALL ETERNITY--LOST IN A PERPETUAL STATE OF LIMBO.
EXTREME MEASURES, BUT NECESSARY FOR THE GREATER GOOD.
AND IT WAS YOUR DECISION?
NOT MINE ALONE. I WAS BUT ONE VOICE.
A DECISIVE ONE IF MEMORY SERVES.
AND, AS FOR THE GREATER GOOD-- ASK HIM ABOUT HIS SENSE OF DUTY TO HIS FELLOW KRYPTONIANS.
SPEAK, JOR-EL. TELL YOUR SON HOW YOU KNEW OUR PLANET WAS DOOMED.
HOW YOU COULD HAVE WARNED THEM ALL. BUT YOU DIDN'T.
FATHER, WHEN YOU DISCOVERED KRYPTON WOULD BE DESTROYED, DID YOU NOT TELL THE OTHERS?
I COULDN'T. I PRESENTED MY FINDINGS TO THE COUNCIL, BUT THEY DEEMED MY THEORIES WILD--MY CALCULATIONS FLAWED.
GOING AGAINST THEM WOULD HAVE SEEN ME BANISHED TO THE PHANTOM ZONE. I WOULDN'T LET THAT HAPPEN.
I HAD MORE IMPORTANT THINGS TO WORRY ABOUT.
WHAT COULD HAVE BEEN MORE IMPORTANT?
YOU, MY SON.
SEE-- YOUR FATHER CHOSE HIS BLOODLINE OVER HIS PEOPLE.
TELL ME, KAL-EL...

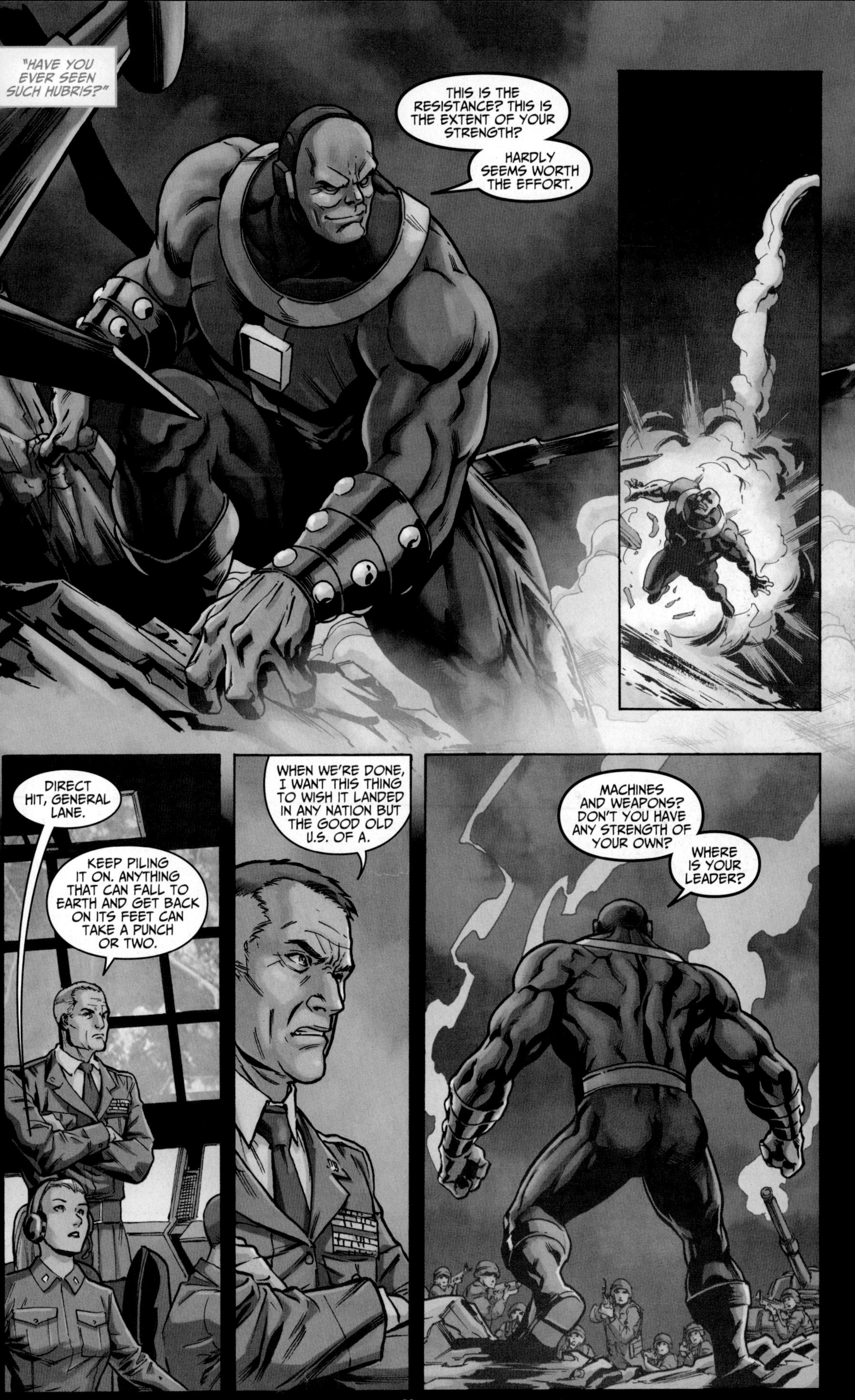
"HAVE YOU EVER SEEN SUCH HUBRIS?"
THIS IS THE RESISTANCE? THIS IS THE EXTENT OF YOUR STRENGTH?
HARDLY SEEMS WORTH THE EFFORT.
DIRECT HIT, GENERAL LANE.
KEEP PILING IT ON. ANYTHING THAT CAN FALL TO EARTH AND GET BACK ON ITS FEET CAN TAKE A PUNCH OR TWO.
WHEN WE'RE DONE, I WANT THIS THING TO WISH IT LANDED IN ANY NATION BUT THE GOOD OLD U.S. OF A.
MACHINES AND WEAPONS? DON'T YOU HAVE ANY STRENGTH OF YOUR OWN?
WHERE IS YOUR LEADER?

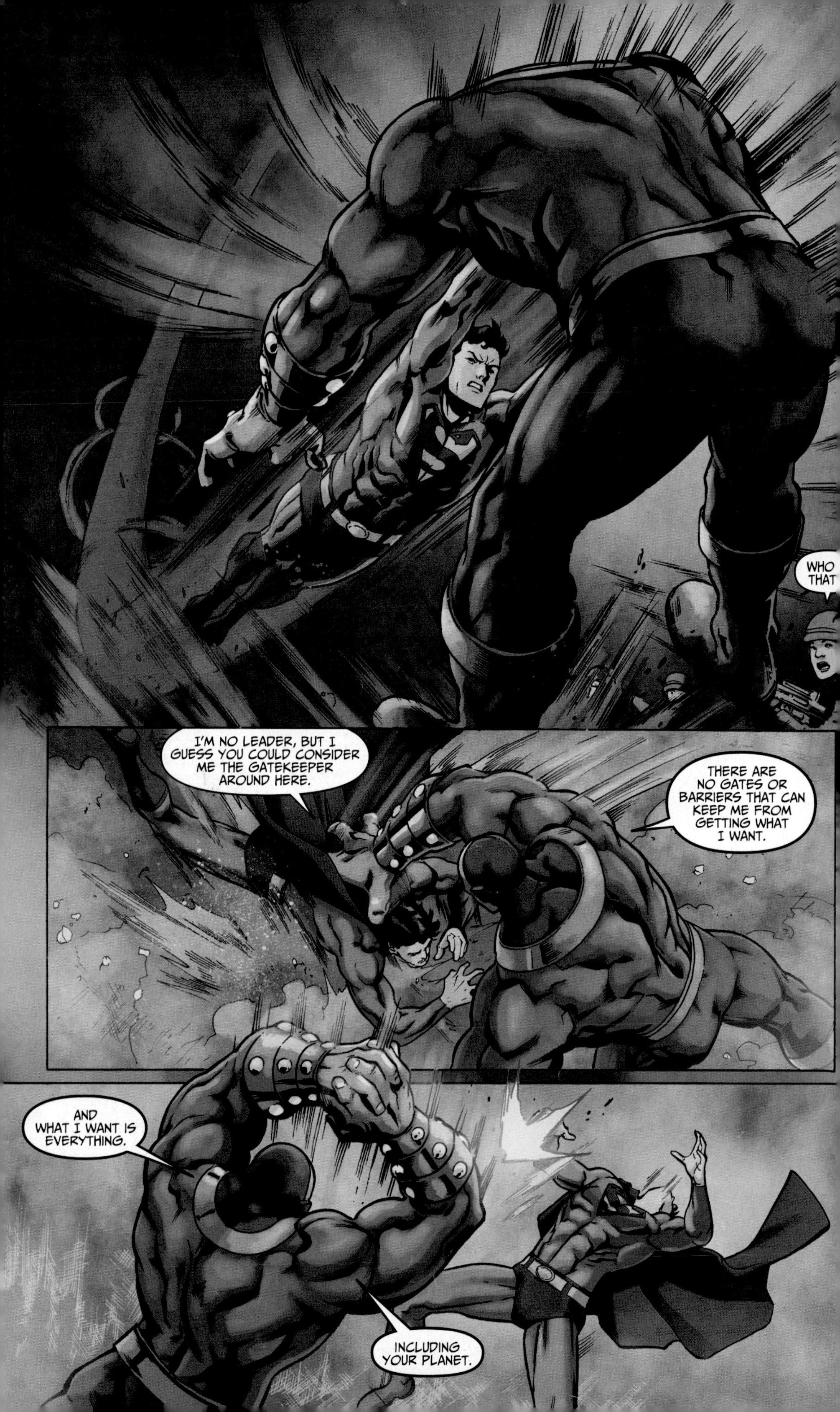

WHO
THAT
I'M NO LEADER, BUT I GUESS YOU COULD CONSIDER ME THE GATEKEEPER AROUND HERE.
THERE ARE NO GATES OR BARRIERS THAT CAN KEEP ME FROM GETTING WHAT I WANT.
AND WHAT I WANT IS EVERYTHING.
INCLUDING YOUR PLANET.

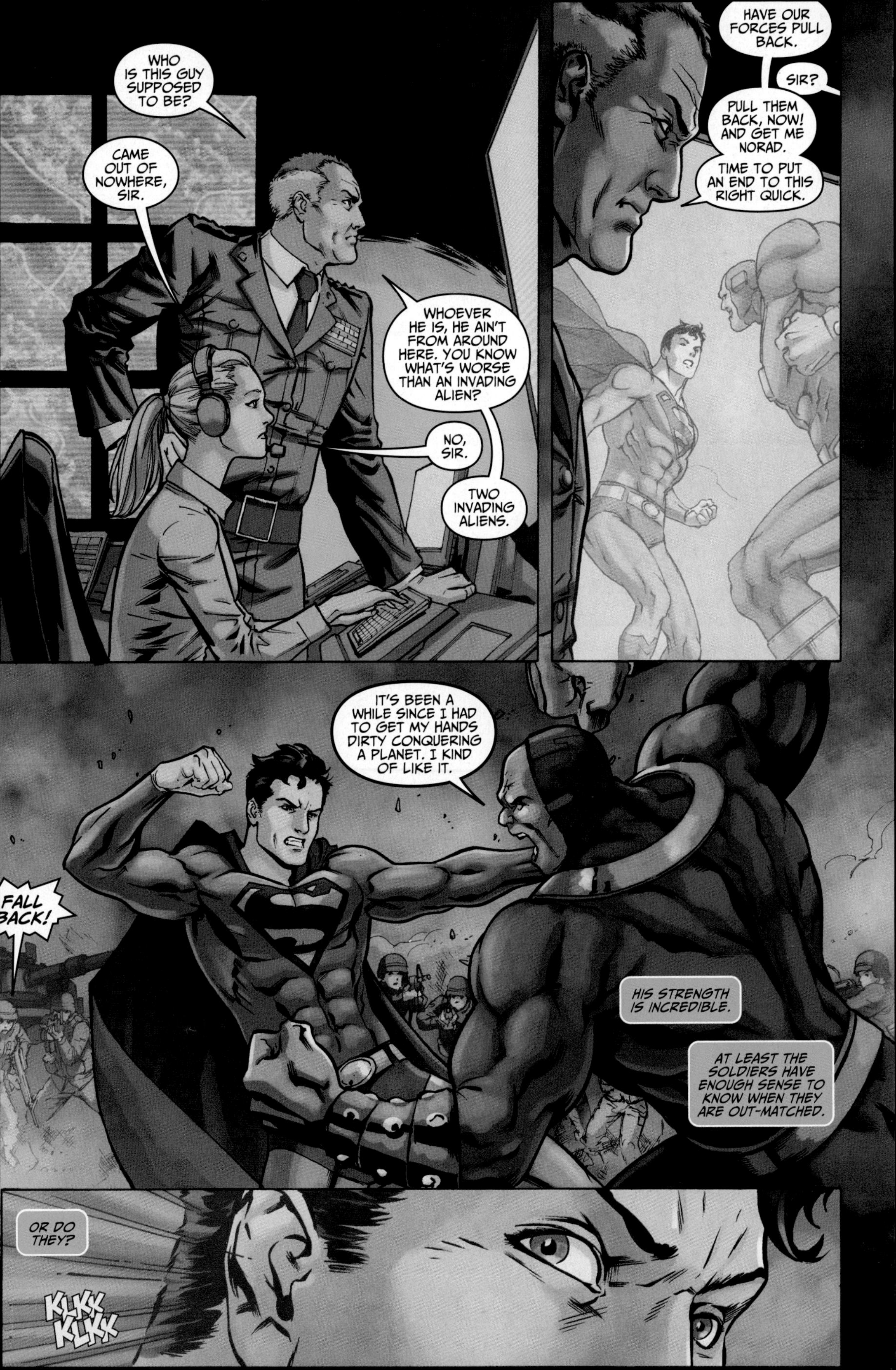
WHO IS THIS GUY SUPPOSED TO BE?
CAME OUT OF NOWHERE, SIR.
WHOEVER HE IS, HE AIN'T FROM AROUND HERE. YOU KNOW WHAT'S WORSE THAN AN INVADING ALIEN?
NO, SIR.
TWO INVADING ALIENS.
HAVE OUR FORCES PULL BACK.
SIR?
PULL THEM BACK, NOW! AND GET ME NORAD.
TIME TO PUT AN END TO THIS RIGHT QUICK.
IT'S BEEN A WHILE SINCE I HAD TO GET MY HANDS DIRTY CONQUERING A PLANET. I KIND OF LIKE IT.
FALL BACK!
HIS STRENGTH IS INCREDIBLE.
AT LEAST THE SOLDIERS HAVE ENOUGH SENSE TO KNOW WHEN THEY ARE OUT-MATCHED.
OR DO THEY?
KLKK KLKK

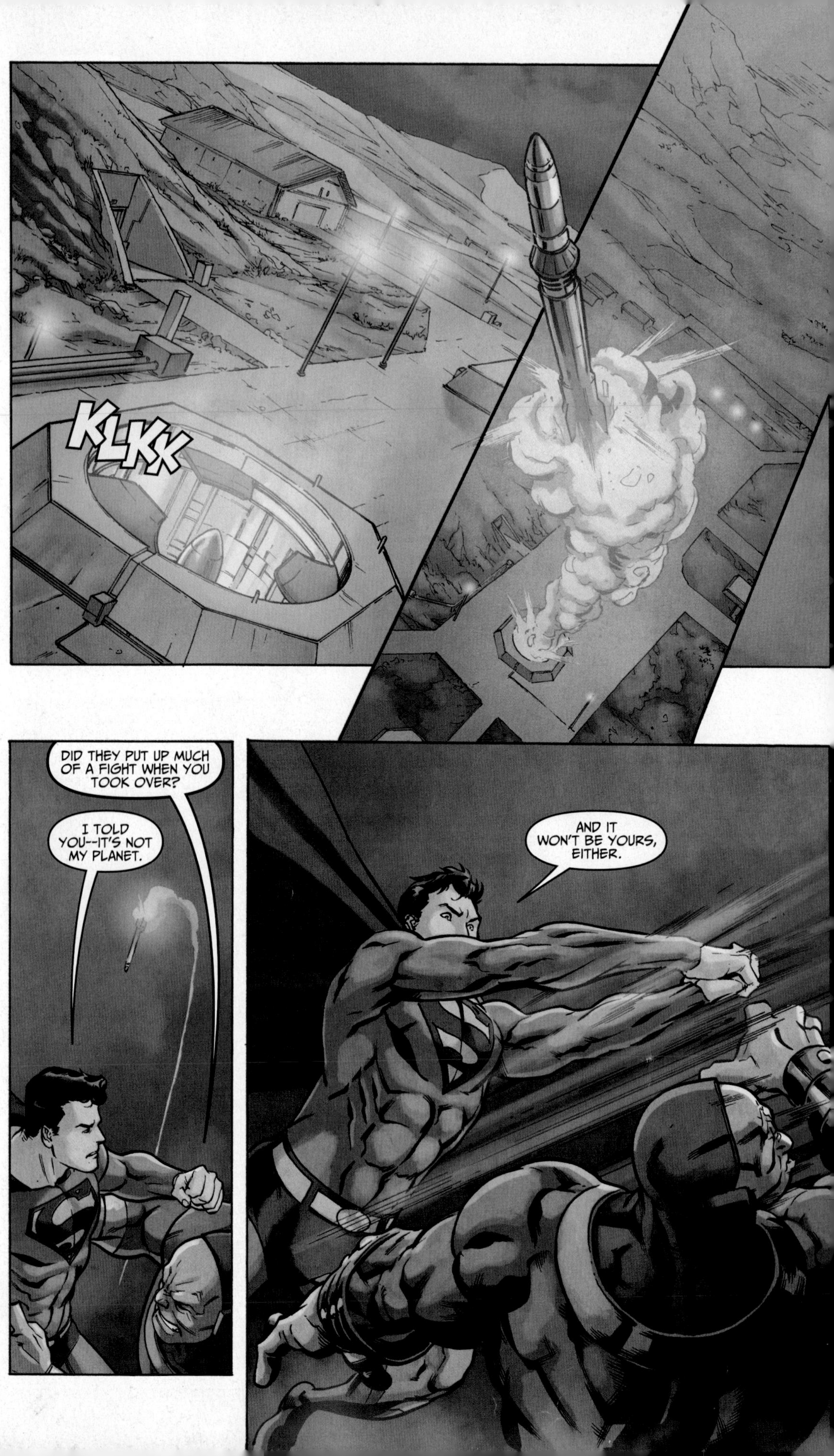
KLKK
DID THEY PUT UP MUCH OF A FIGHT WHEN YOU TOOK OVER?
I TOLD YOU--IT'S NOT MY PLANET.
AND IT WON'T BE YOURS, EITHER.

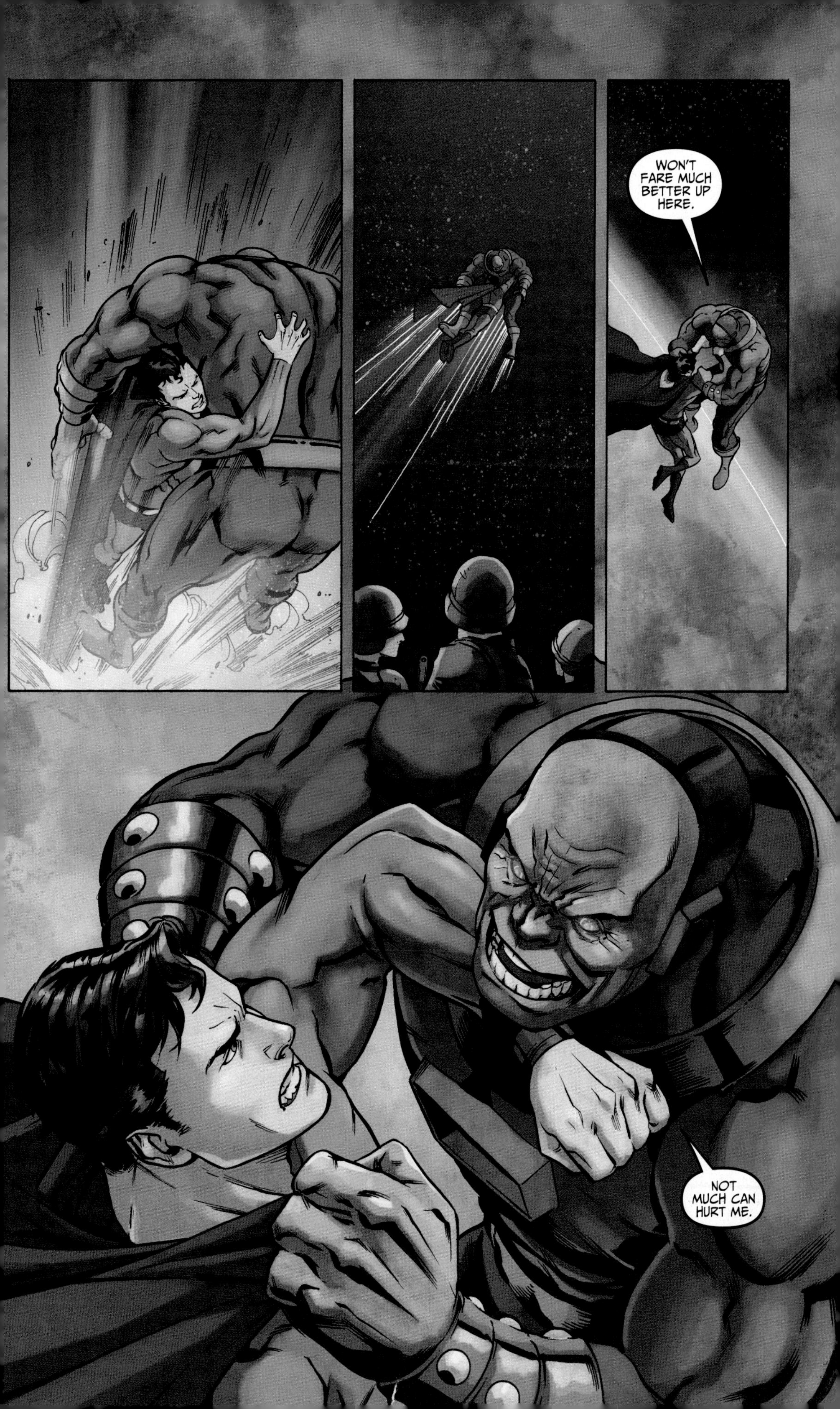
WON'T FARE MUCH BETTER UP HERE.
NOT MUCH CAN HURT ME.

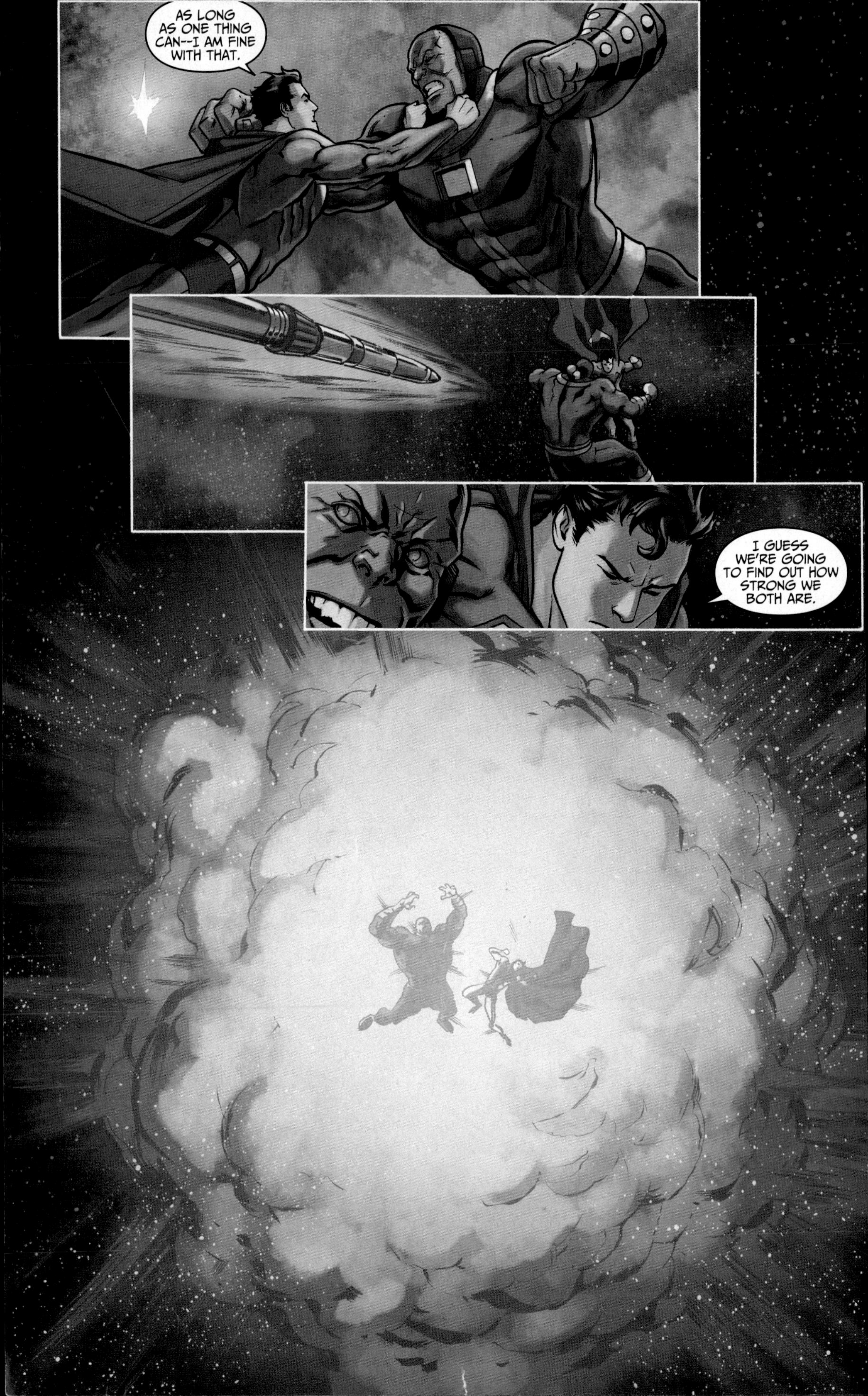
AS LONG AS ONE THING CAN--I AM FINE WITH THAT.
I GUESS WE'RE GOING TO FIND OUT HOW STRONG WE BOTH ARE.

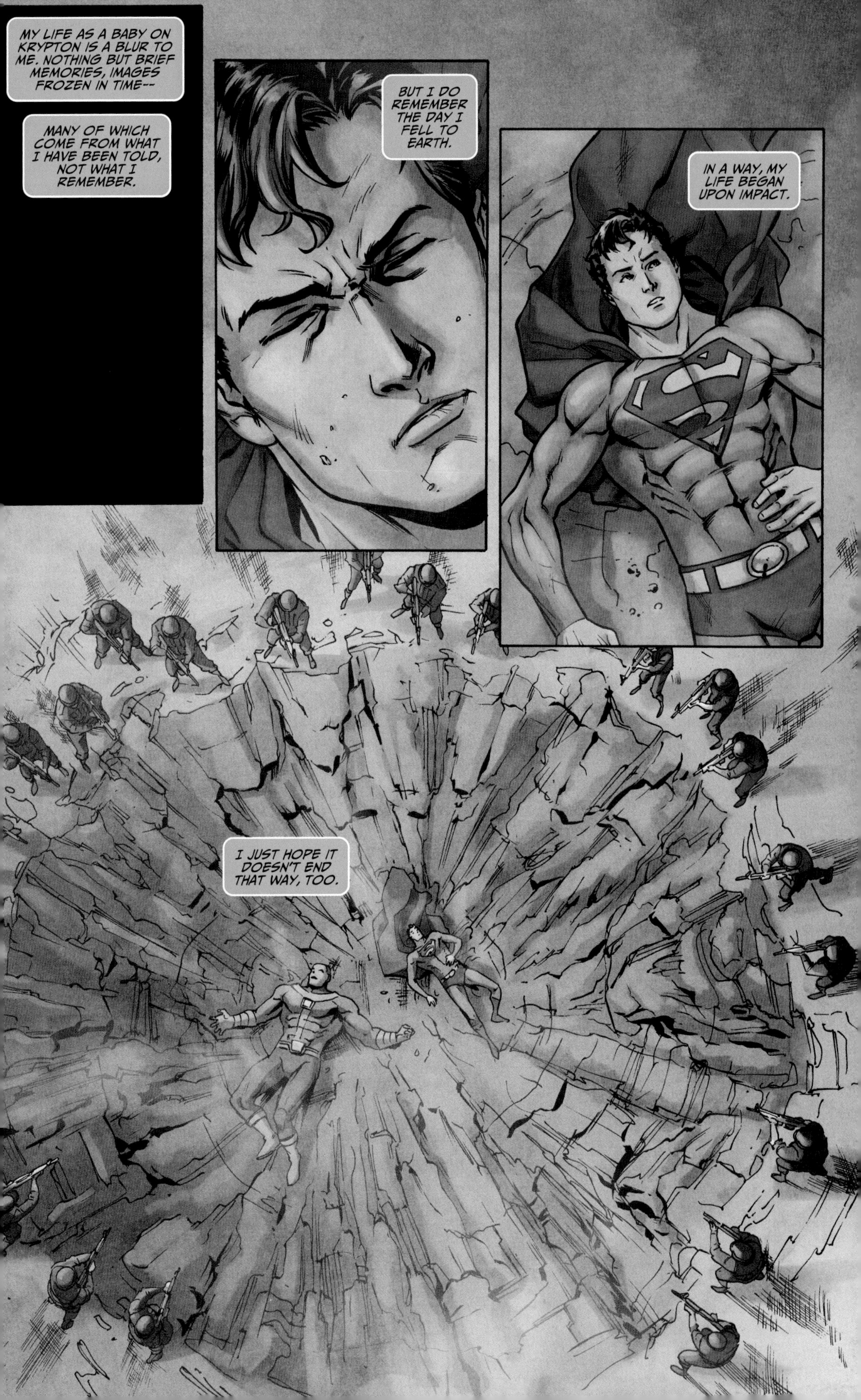
MY LIFE AS A BABY ON KRYPTON IS A BLUR TO ME. NOTHING BUT BRIEF MEMORIES, IMAGES FROZEN IN TIME--
MANY OF WHICH COME FROM WHAT I HAVE BEEN TOLD, NOT WHAT I REMEMBER.
BUT I DO REMEMBER THE DAY I FELL TO EARTH.
IN A WAY, MY LIFE BEGAN UPON IMPACT.
I JUST HOPE IT DOESN'T END THAT WAY, TOO.

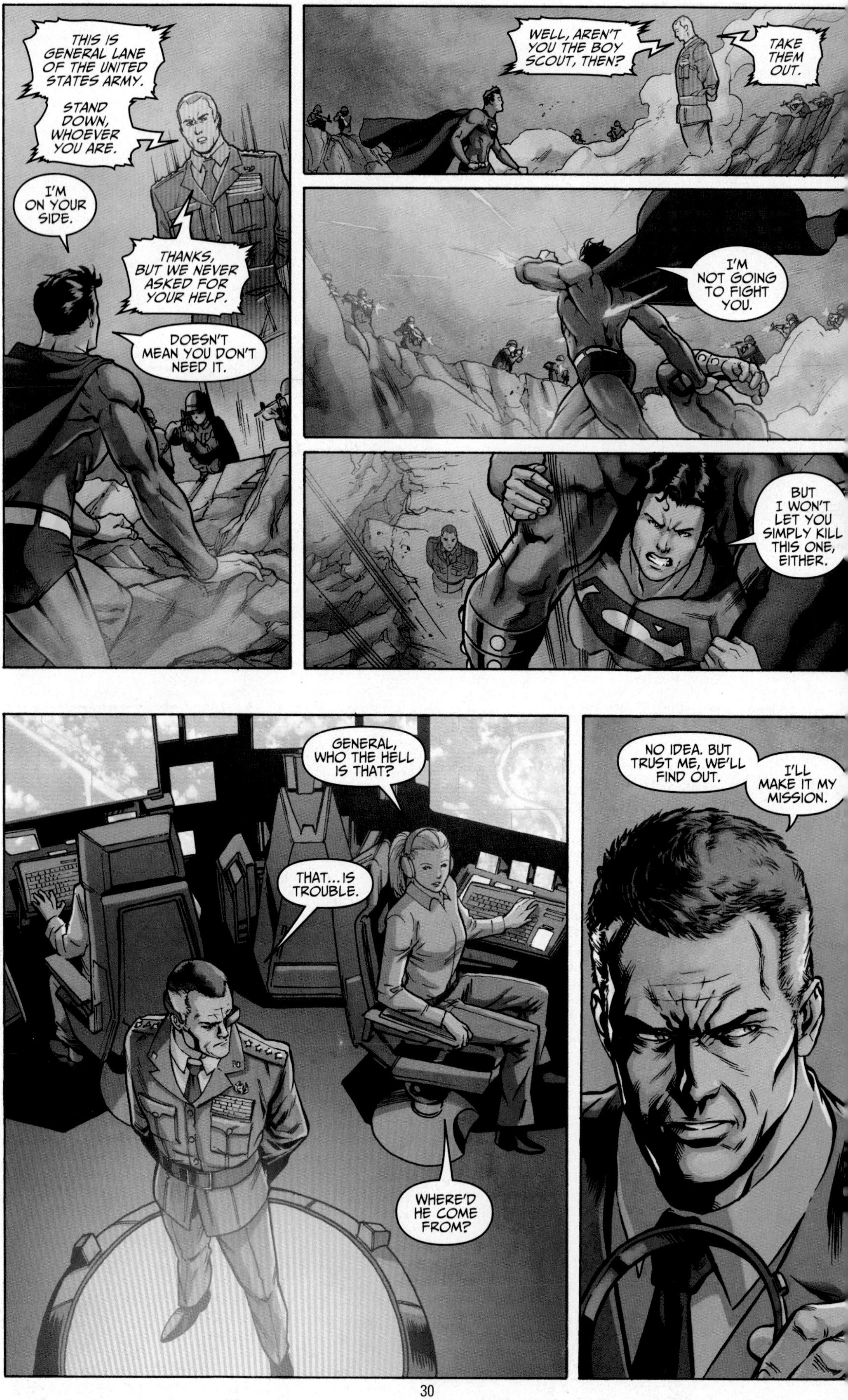

THIS IS GENERAL LANE OF THE UNITED STATES ARMY.
STAND DOWN, WHOEVER YOU ARE.
I'M ON YOUR SIDE.
THANKS, BUT WE NEVER ASKED FOR YOUR HELP.
DOESN'T MEAN YOU DON'T NEED IT.
WELL, AREN'T YOU THE BOY SCOUT, THEN?
TAKE THEM OUT.
I'M NOT GOING TO FIGHT YOU.
BUT I WON'T LET YOU SIMPLY KILL THIS ONE, EITHER.
GENERAL, WHO THE HELL IS THAT?
THAT...IS TROUBLE.
WHERE'D HE COME FROM?
NO IDEA. BUT TRUST ME, WE'LL FIND OUT.
I'LL MAKE IT MY MISSION.

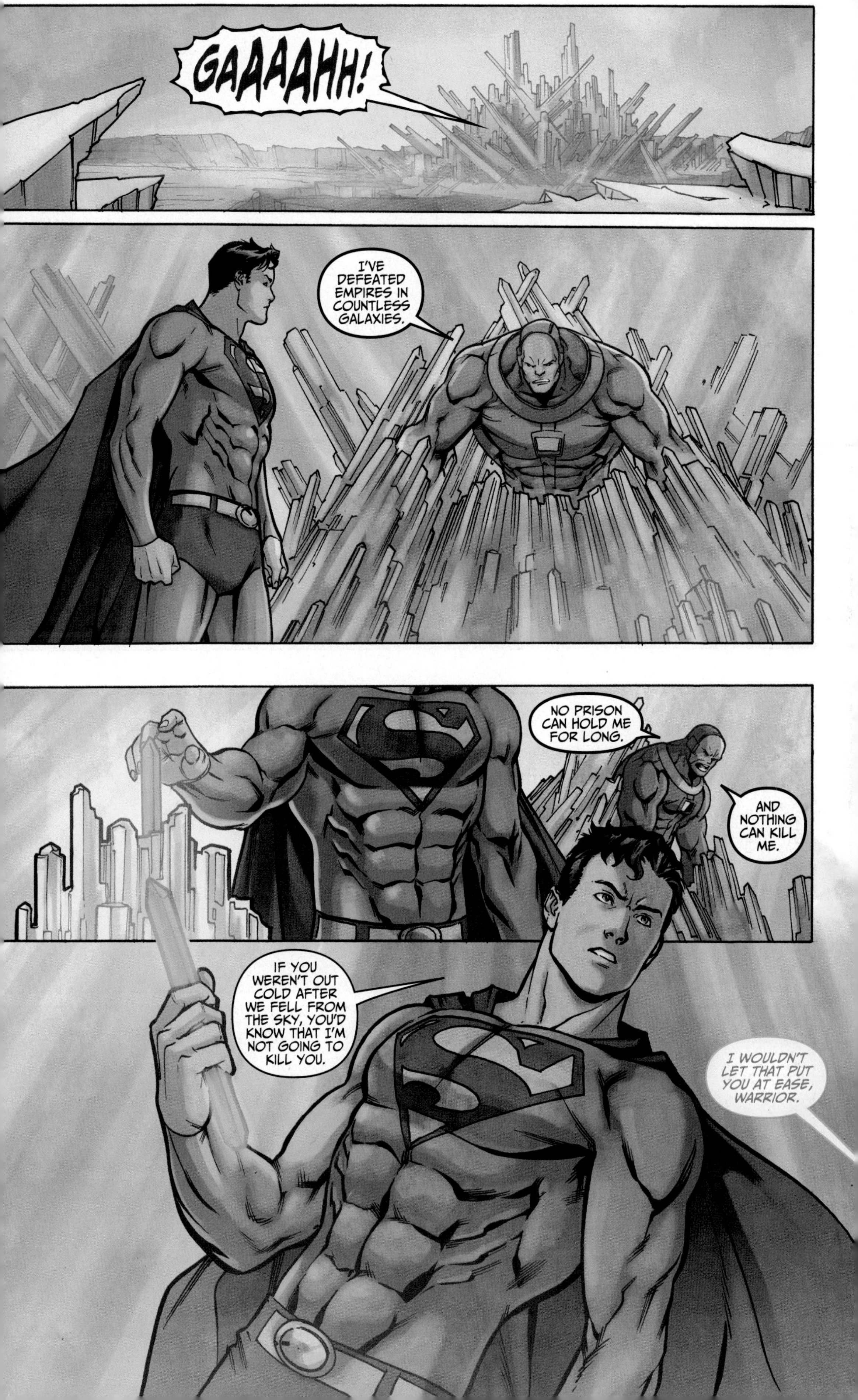
GAAAAHH!
I'VE DEFEATED EMPIRES IN COUNTLESS GALAXIES.
NO PRISON CAN HOLD ME FOR LONG.
AND NOTHING CAN KILL ME.
IF YOU WEREN'T OUT COLD AFTER WE FELL FROM THE SKY, YOU'D KNOW THAT I'M NOT GOING TO KILL YOU.
I WOULDN'T LET THAT PUT YOU AT EASE, WARRIOR.

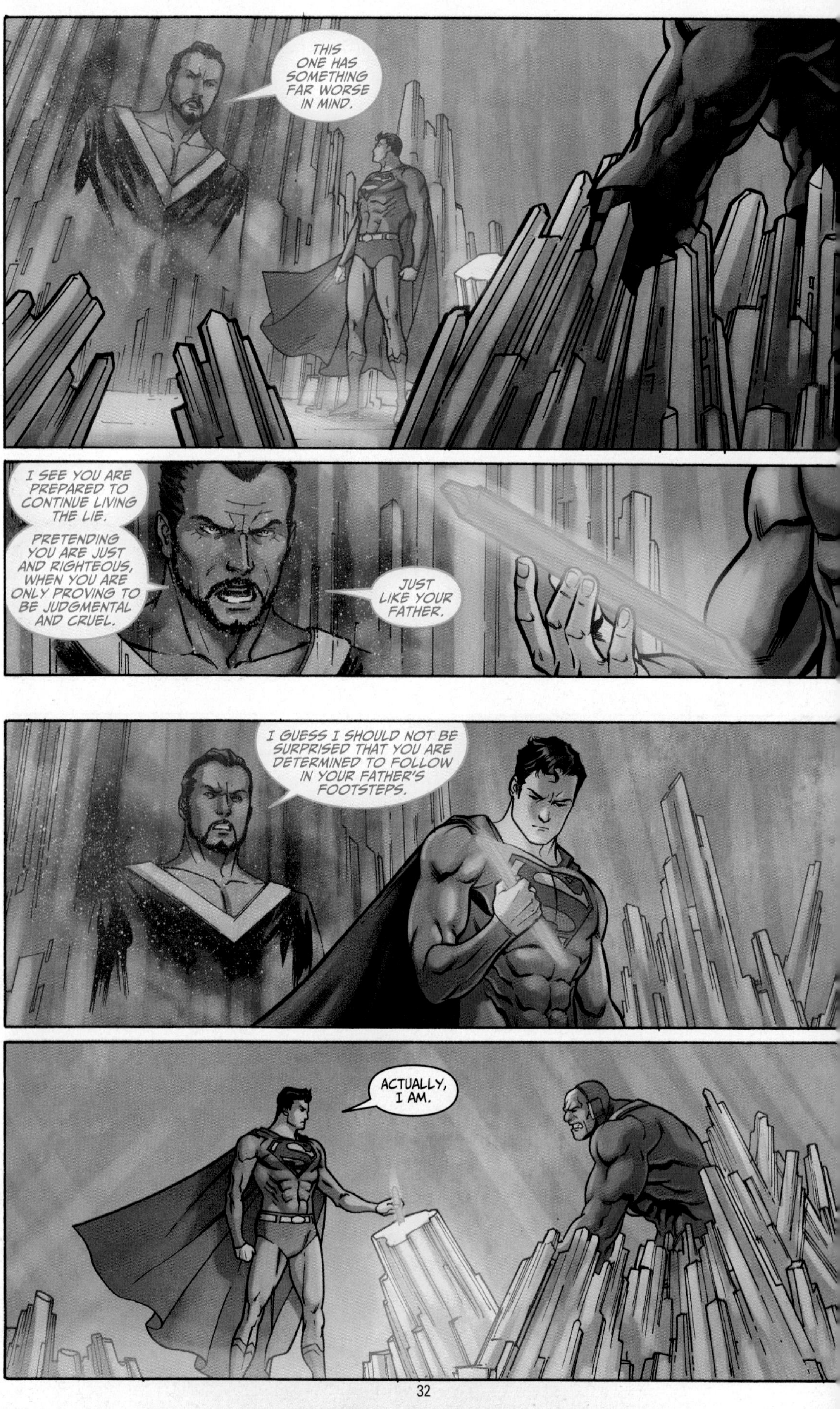

THIS ONE HAS SOMETHING FAR WORSE IN MIND.
I SEE YOU ARE PREPARED TO CONTINUE LIVING THE LIE.
PRETENDING YOU ARE JUST AND RIGHTEOUS, WHEN YOU ARE ONLY PROVING TO BE JUDGMENTAL AND CRUEL.
JUST LIKE YOUR FATHER.
I GUESS I SHOULD NOT BE SURPRISED THAT YOU ARE DETERMINED TO FOLLOW IN YOUR FATHER'S FOOTSTEPS.
ACTUALLY, I AM.

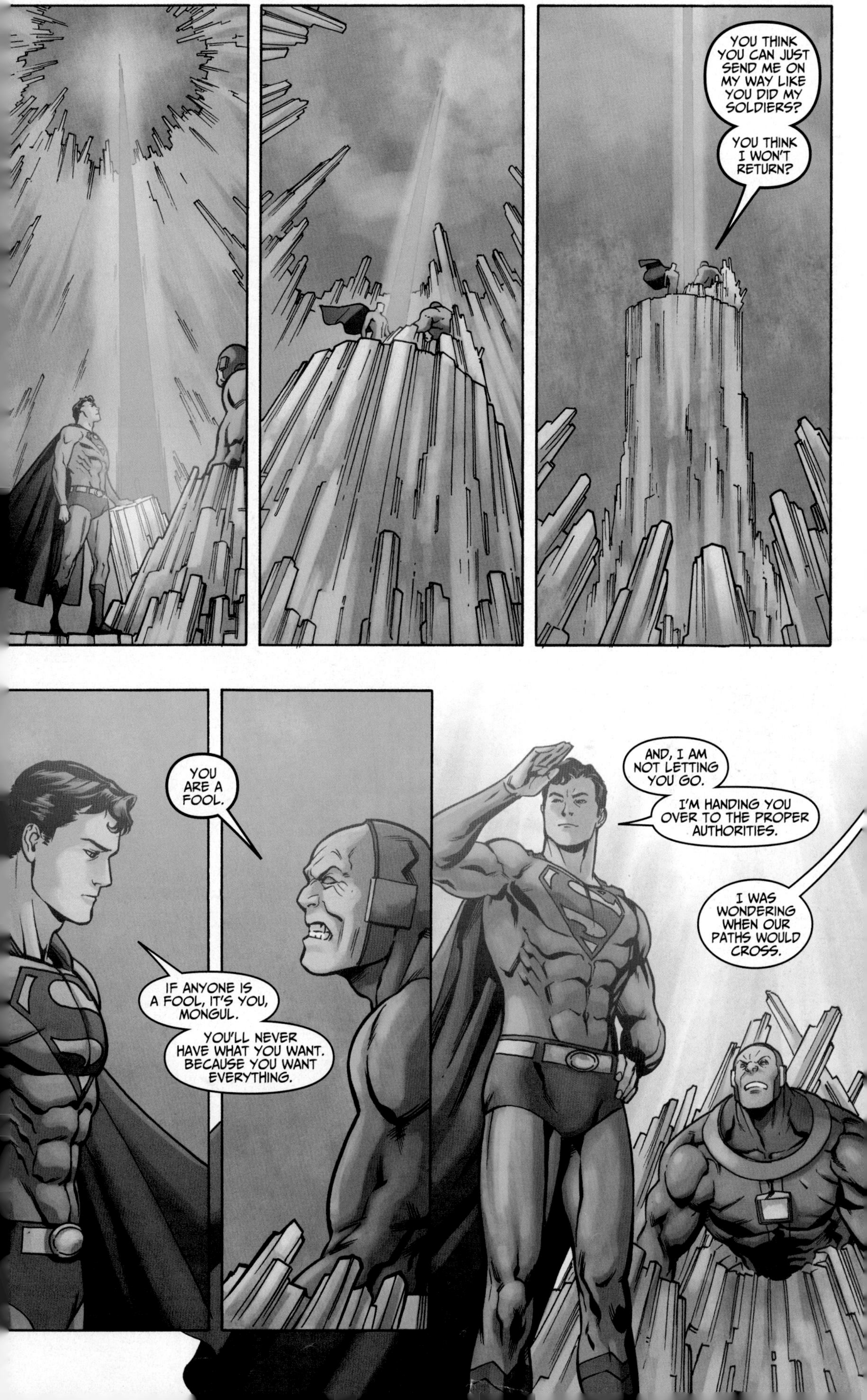
YOU THINK YOU CAN JUST SEND ME ON MY WAY LIKE YOU DID MY SOLDIERS?
YOU THINK I WON'T RETURN?
YOU ARE A FOOL.
IF ANYONE IS A FOOL, IT'S YOU, MONGUL.
YOU'LL NEVER HAVE WHAT YOU WANT. BECAUSE YOU WANT EVERYTHING.
AND, I AM NOT LETTING YOU GO.
I'M HANDING YOU OVER TO THE PROPER AUTHORITIES.
I WAS WONDERING WHEN OUR PATHS WOULD CROSS.

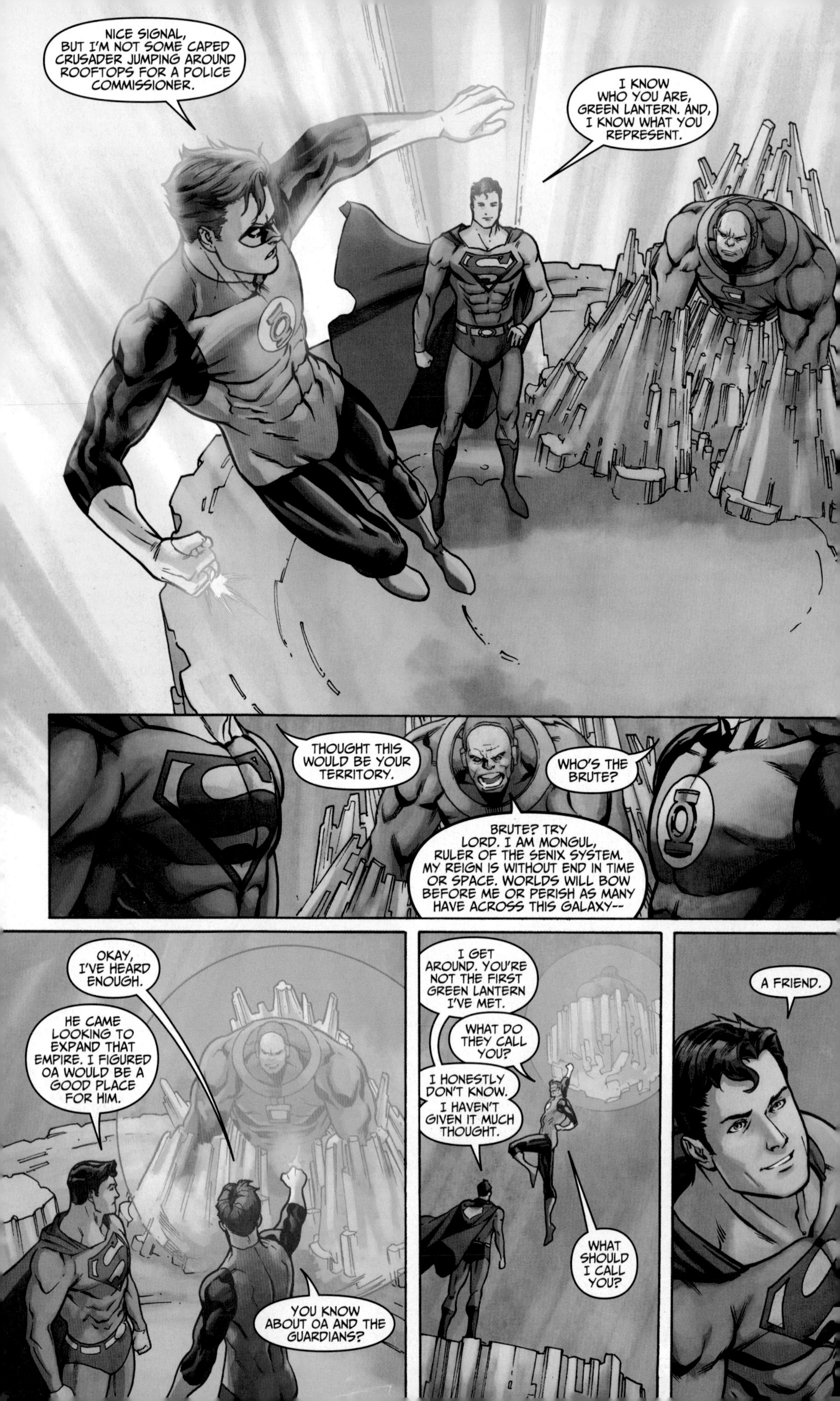
NICE SIGNAL, BUT I'M NOT SOME CAPED CRUSADER JUMPING AROUND ROOFTOPS FOR A POLICE COMMISSIONER.
I KNOW WHO YOU ARE, GREEN LANTERN. AND, I KNOW WHAT YOU REPRESENT.
THOUGHT THIS WOULD BE YOUR TERRITORY.
WHO'S THE BRUTE?
BRUTE? TRY LORD. I AM MONGUL, RULER OF THE SENIX SYSTEM. MY REIGN IS WITHOUT END IN TIME OR SPACE. WORLDS WILL BOW BEFORE ME OR PERISH AS MANY HAVE ACROSS THIS GALAXY--
OKAY, I'VE HEARD ENOUGH.
HE CAME LOOKING TO EXPAND THAT EMPIRE. I FIGURED OA WOULD BE A GOOD PLACE FOR HIM.
YOU KNOW ABOUT OA AND THE GUARDIANS?
I GET AROUND. YOU'RE NOT THE FIRST GREEN LANTERN I'VE MET.
WHAT DO THEY CALL YOU?
I HONESTLY DON'T KNOW.
I HAVEN'T GIVEN IT MUCH THOUGHT.
WHAT SHOULD I CALL YOU?
A FRIEND.

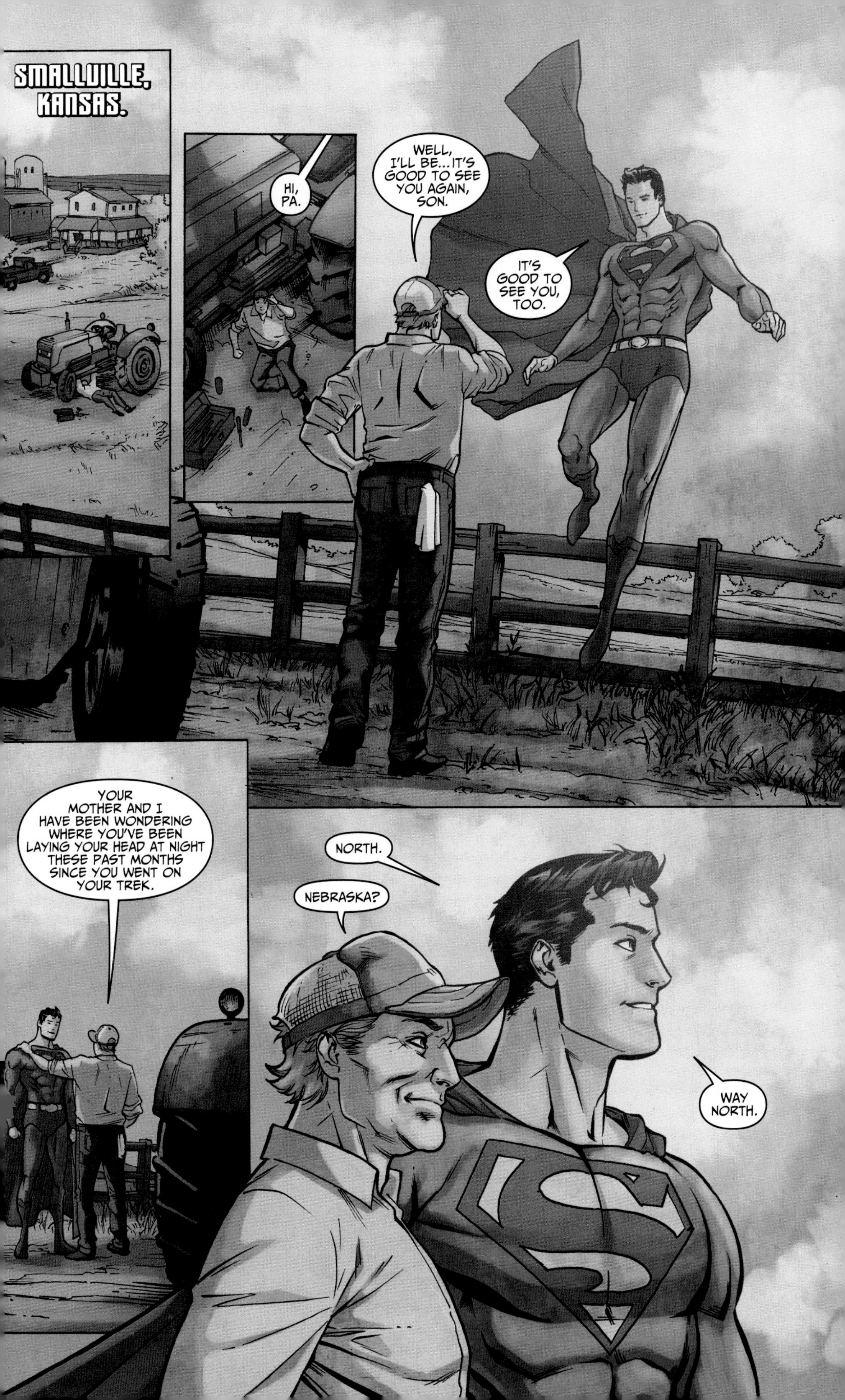
SMALLVILLE, KANSAS.
HI, PA.
WELL, I'LL BE...IT'S GOOD TO SEE YOU AGAIN, SON.
IT'S GOOD TO SEE YOU, TOO.
YOUR MOTHER AND I HAVE BEEN WONDERING WHERE YOU'VE BEEN LAYING YOUR HEAD AT NIGHT THESE PAST MONTHS SINCE YOU WENT ON YOUR TREK.
NORTH.
NEBRASKA?
WAY NORTH.

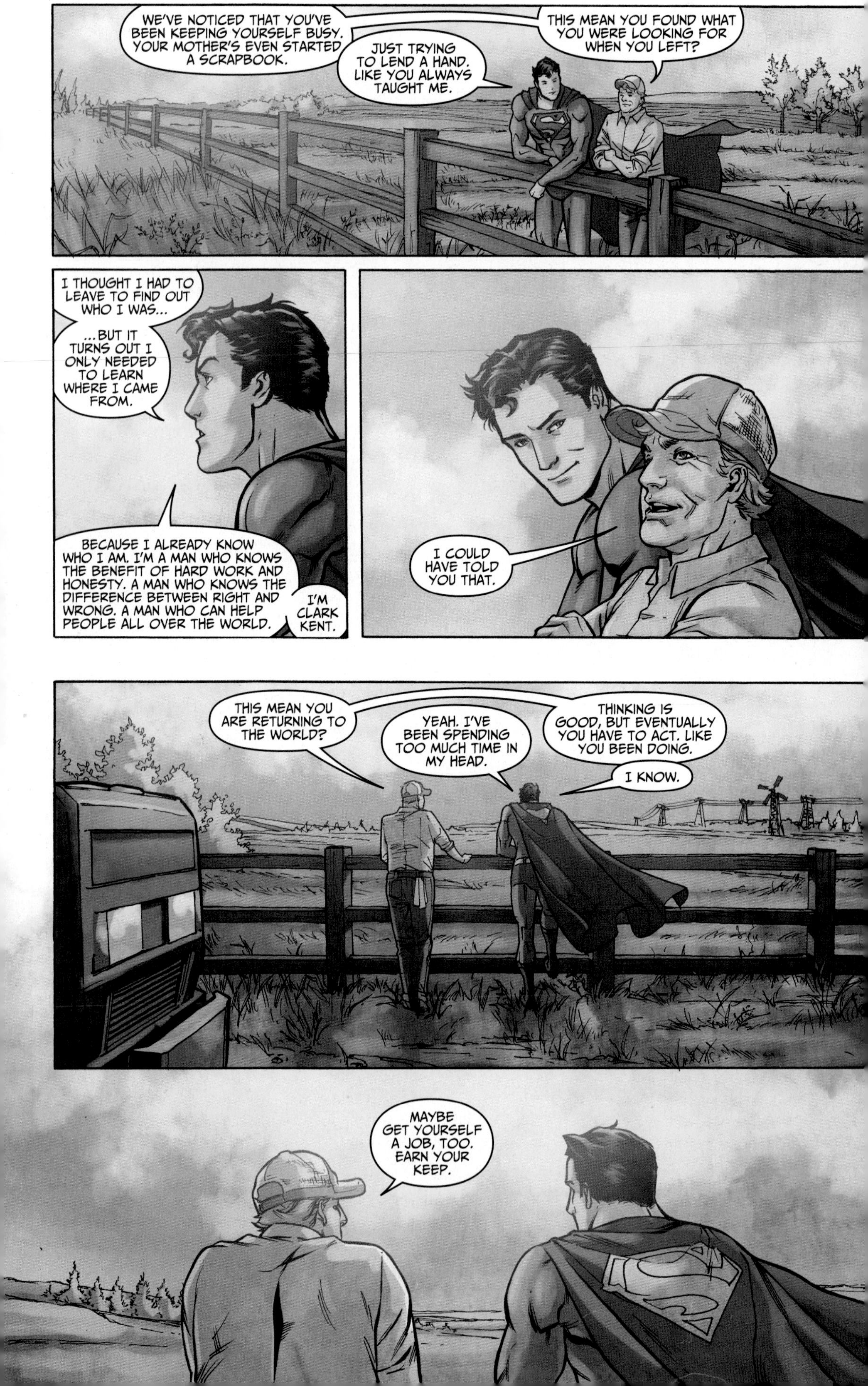
WE'VE NOTICED THAT YOU'VE BEEN KEEPING YOURSELF BUSY. YOUR MOTHER'S EVEN STARTED A SCRAPBOOK.
JUST TRYING TO LEND A HAND. LIKE YOU ALWAYS TAUGHT ME.
THIS MEAN YOU FOUND WHAT YOU WERE LOOKING FOR WHEN YOU LEFT?
I THOUGHT I HAD TO LEAVE TO FIND OUT WHO I WAS...
...BUT IT TURNS OUT I ONLY NEEDED TO LEARN WHERE I CAME FROM.
BECAUSE I ALREADY KNOW WHO I AM. I'M A MAN WHO KNOWS THE BENEFIT OF HARD WORK AND HONESTY. A MAN WHO KNOWS THE DIFFERENCE BETWEEN RIGHT AND WRONG. A MAN WHO CAN HELP PEOPLE ALL OVER THE WORLD.
I'M CLARK KENT.
I COULD HAVE TOLD YOU THAT.
THIS MEAN YOU ARE RETURNING TO THE WORLD?
YEAH. I'VE BEEN SPENDING TOO MUCH TIME IN MY HEAD.
THINKING IS GOOD, BUT EVENTUALLY YOU HAVE TO ACT. LIKE YOU BEEN DOING.
I KNOW.
MAYBE GET YOURSELF A JOB, TOO. EARN YOUR KEEP.

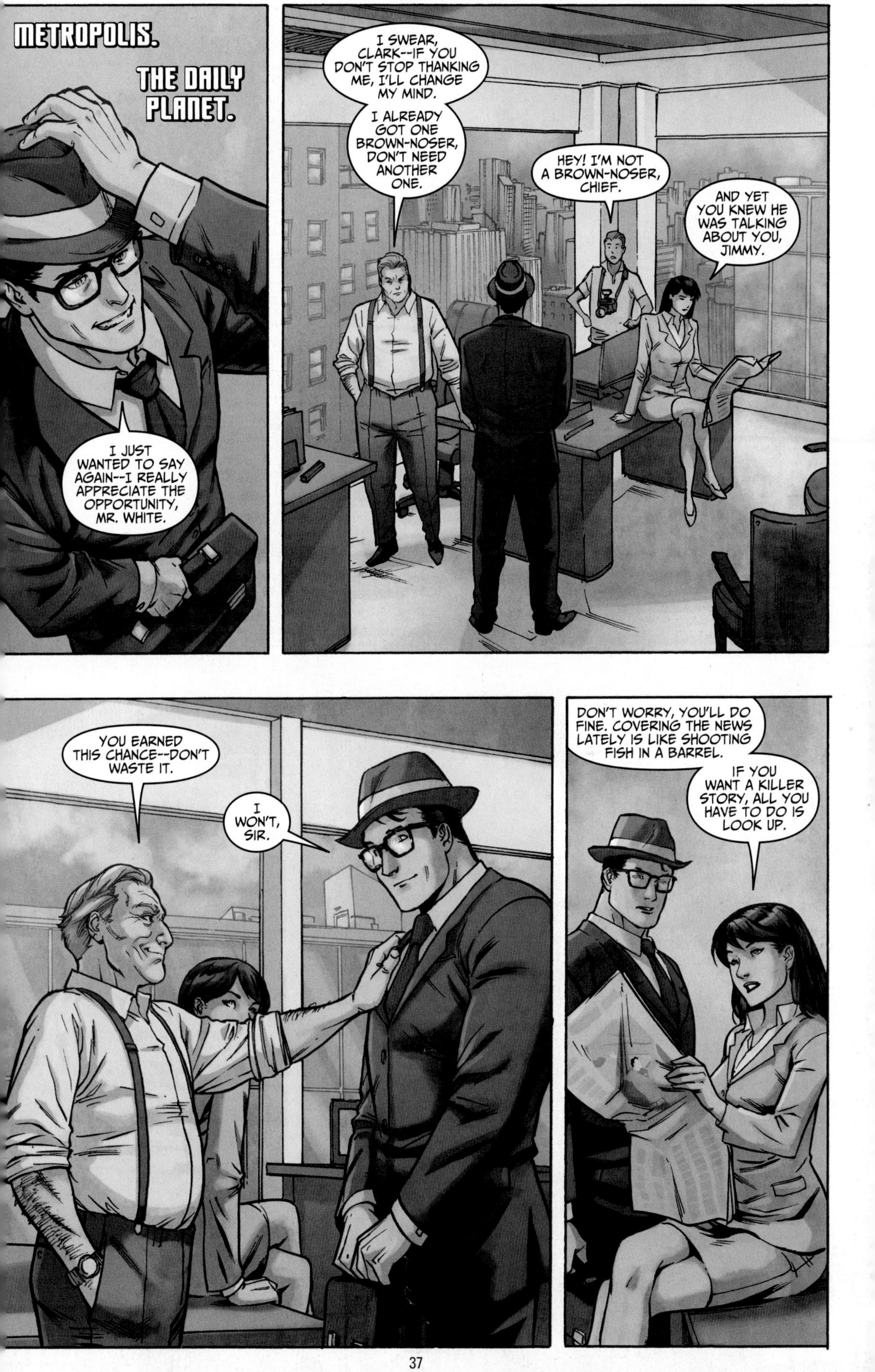
METROPOLIS.
THE DAILY PLANET.
I JUST WANTED TO SAY AGAIN--I REALLY APPRECIATE THE OPPORTUNITY, MR. WHITE.
I SWEAR, CLARK--IF YOU DON'T STOP THANKING ME, I'LL CHANGE MY MIND.
I ALREADY GOT ONE BROWN-NOSER, DON'T NEED ANOTHER ONE.
HEY! I'M NOT A BROWN-NOSER, CHIEF.
AND YET YOU KNEW HE WAS TALKING ABOUT YOU, JIMMY.
YOU EARNED THIS CHANCE--DON'T WASTE IT.
I WON'T, SIR.
DON'T WORRY, YOU'LL DO FINE. COVERING THE NEWS LATELY IS LIKE SHOOTING FISH IN A BARREL.
IF YOU WANT A KILLER STORY, ALL YOU HAVE TO DO IS LOOK UP.

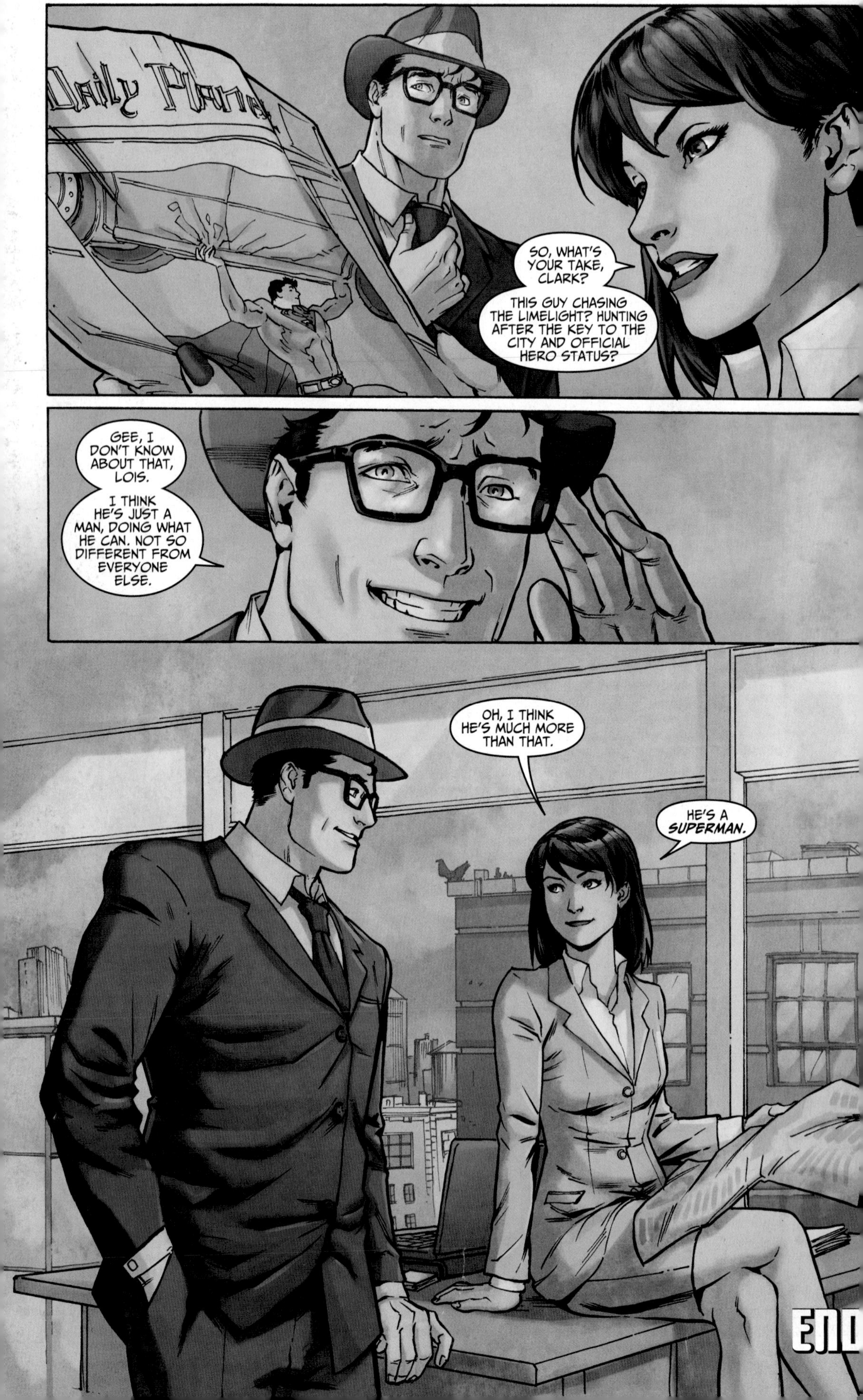
Daily Planet
SO, WHAT'S YOUR TAKE, CLARK?
THIS GUY CHASING THE LIMELIGHT? HUNTING AFTER THE KEY TO THE CITY AND OFFICIAL HERO STATUS?
GEE, I DON'T KNOW ABOUT THAT, LOIS.
I THINK HE'S JUST A MAN, DOING WHAT HE CAN. NOT SO DIFFERENT FROM EVERYONE ELSE.
OH, I THINK HE'S MUCH MORE THAN THAT.
HE'S A *SUPERMAN.*
END

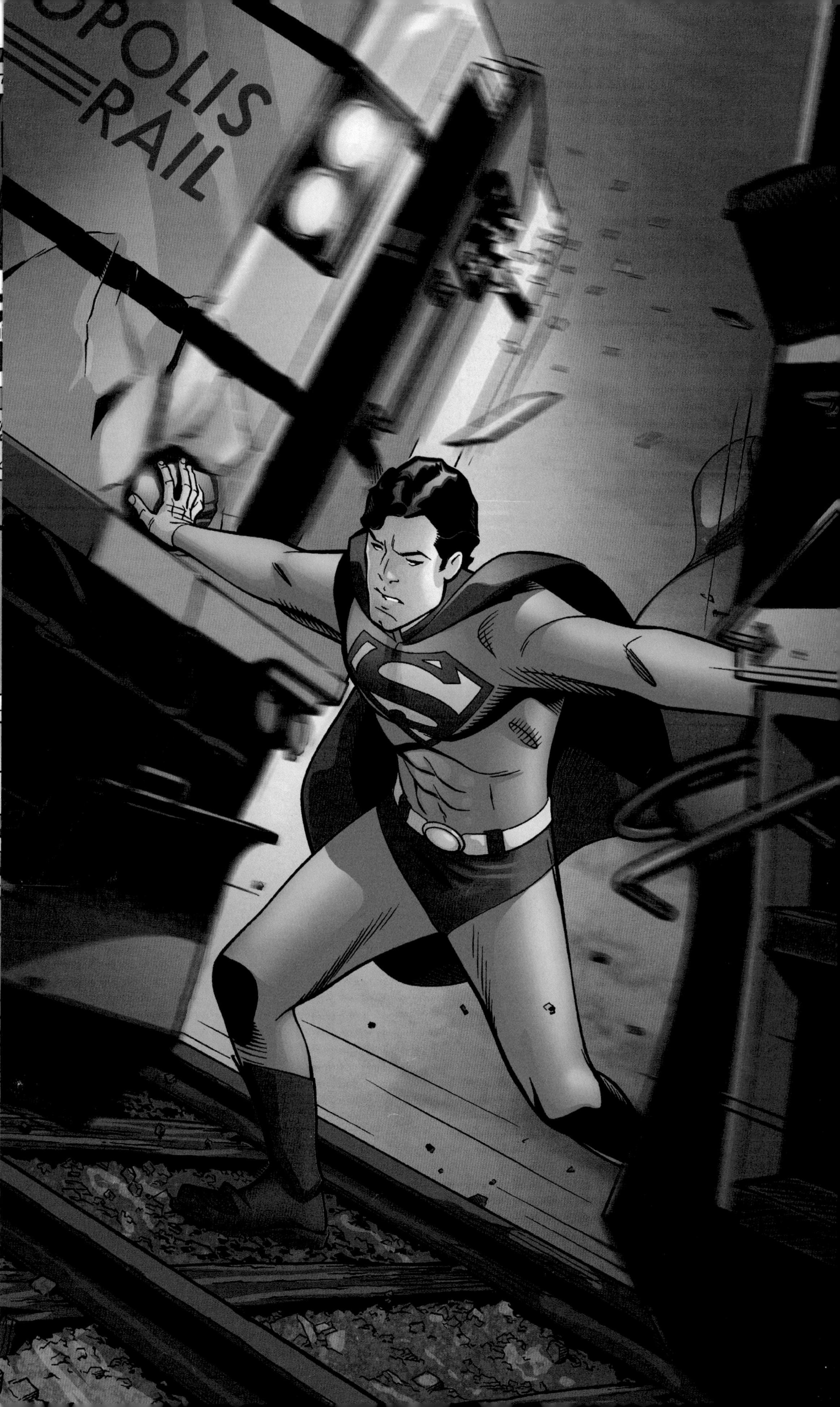
OPOLIS
RAIL

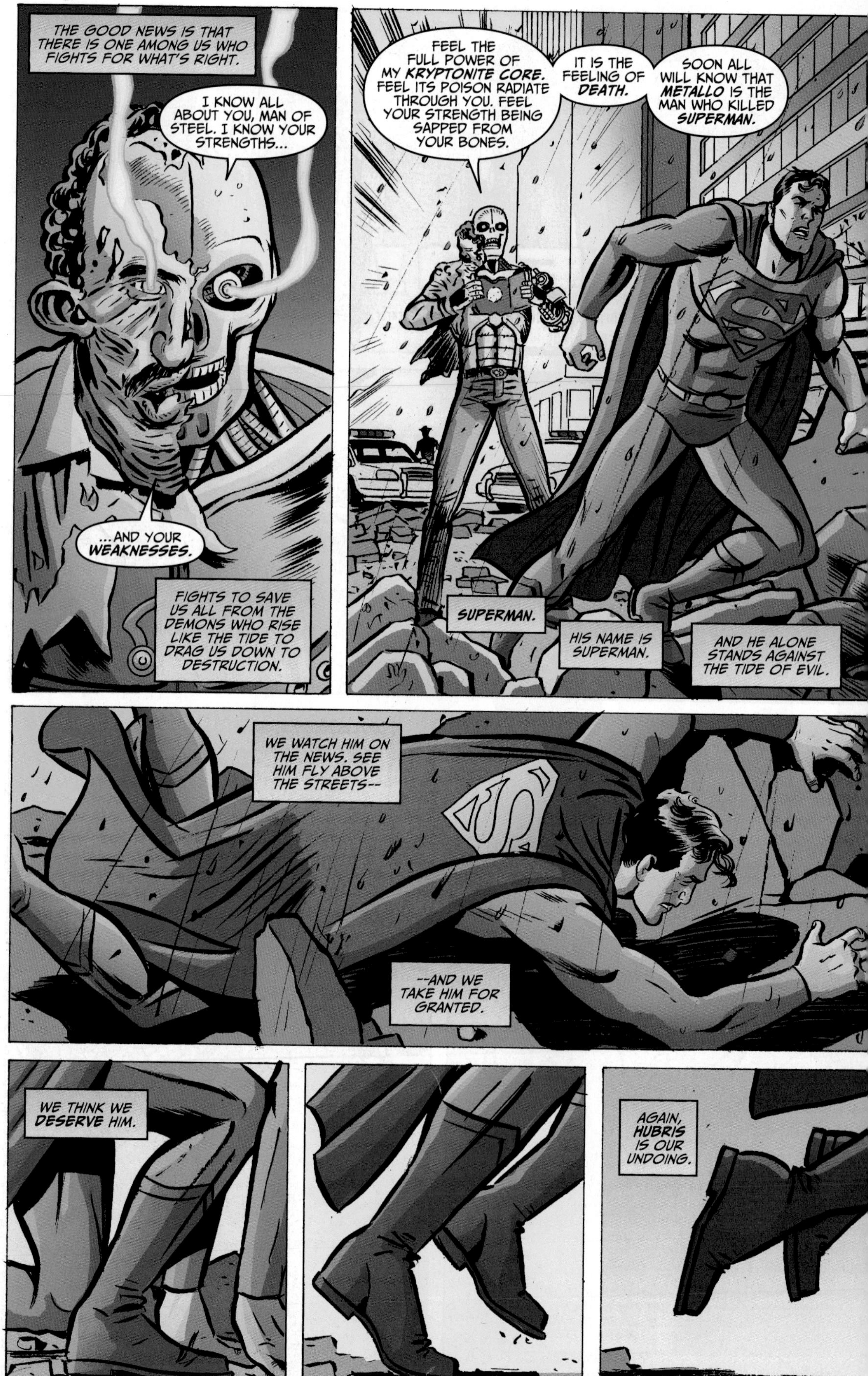
THE GOOD NEWS IS THAT THERE IS ONE AMONG US WHO FIGHTS FOR WHAT'S RIGHT.
I KNOW ALL ABOUT YOU, MAN OF STEEL. I KNOW YOUR STRENGTHS...
...AND YOUR WEAKNESSES.
FIGHTS TO SAVE US ALL FROM THE DEMONS WHO RISE LIKE THE TIDE TO DRAG US DOWN TO DESTRUCTION.
FEEL THE FULL POWER OF MY KRYPTONITE CORE. FEEL ITS POISON RADIATE THROUGH YOU. FEEL YOUR STRENGTH BEING SAPPED FROM YOUR BONES.
IT IS THE FEELING OF DEATH.
SOON ALL WILL KNOW THAT METALLO IS THE MAN WHO KILLED SUPERMAN.
SUPERMAN.
HIS NAME IS SUPERMAN.
AND HE ALONE STANDS AGAINST THE TIDE OF EVIL.
WE WATCH HIM ON THE NEWS. SEE HIM FLY ABOVE THE STREETS--
--AND WE TAKE HIM FOR GRANTED.
WE THINK WE DESERVE HIM.
AGAIN, HUBRIS IS OUR UNDOING.

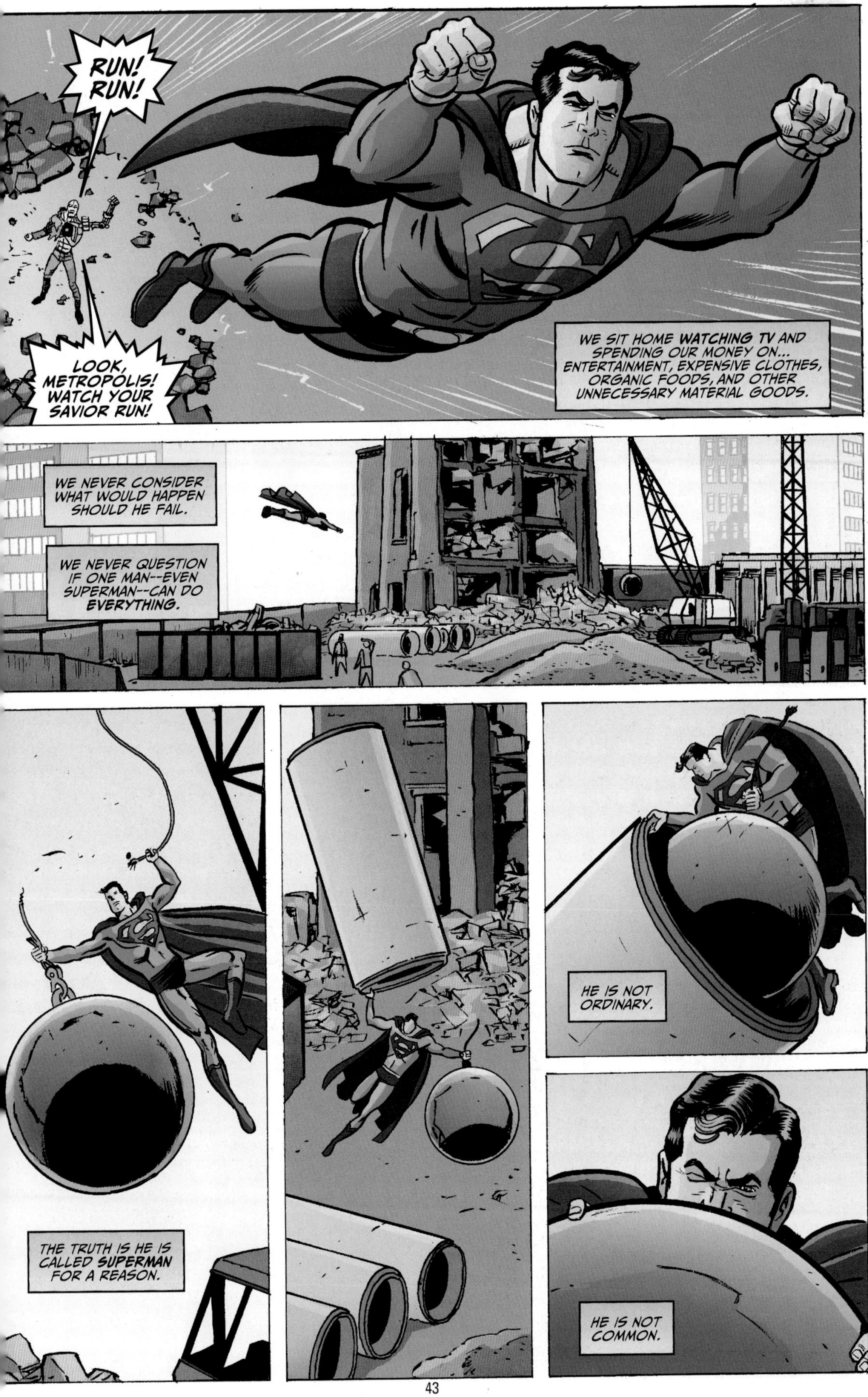
RUN! RUN!
LOOK, METROPOLIS! WATCH YOUR SAVIOR RUN!
WE SIT HOME WATCHING TV AND SPENDING OUR MONEY ON... ENTERTAINMENT, EXPENSIVE CLOTHES, ORGANIC FOODS, AND OTHER UNNECESSARY MATERIAL GOODS.
WE NEVER CONSIDER WHAT WOULD HAPPEN SHOULD HE FAIL.
WE NEVER QUESTION IF ONE MAN--EVEN SUPERMAN--CAN DO EVERYTHING.
THE TRUTH IS HE IS CALLED SUPERMAN FOR A REASON.
HE IS NOT ORDINARY.
HE IS NOT COMMON.

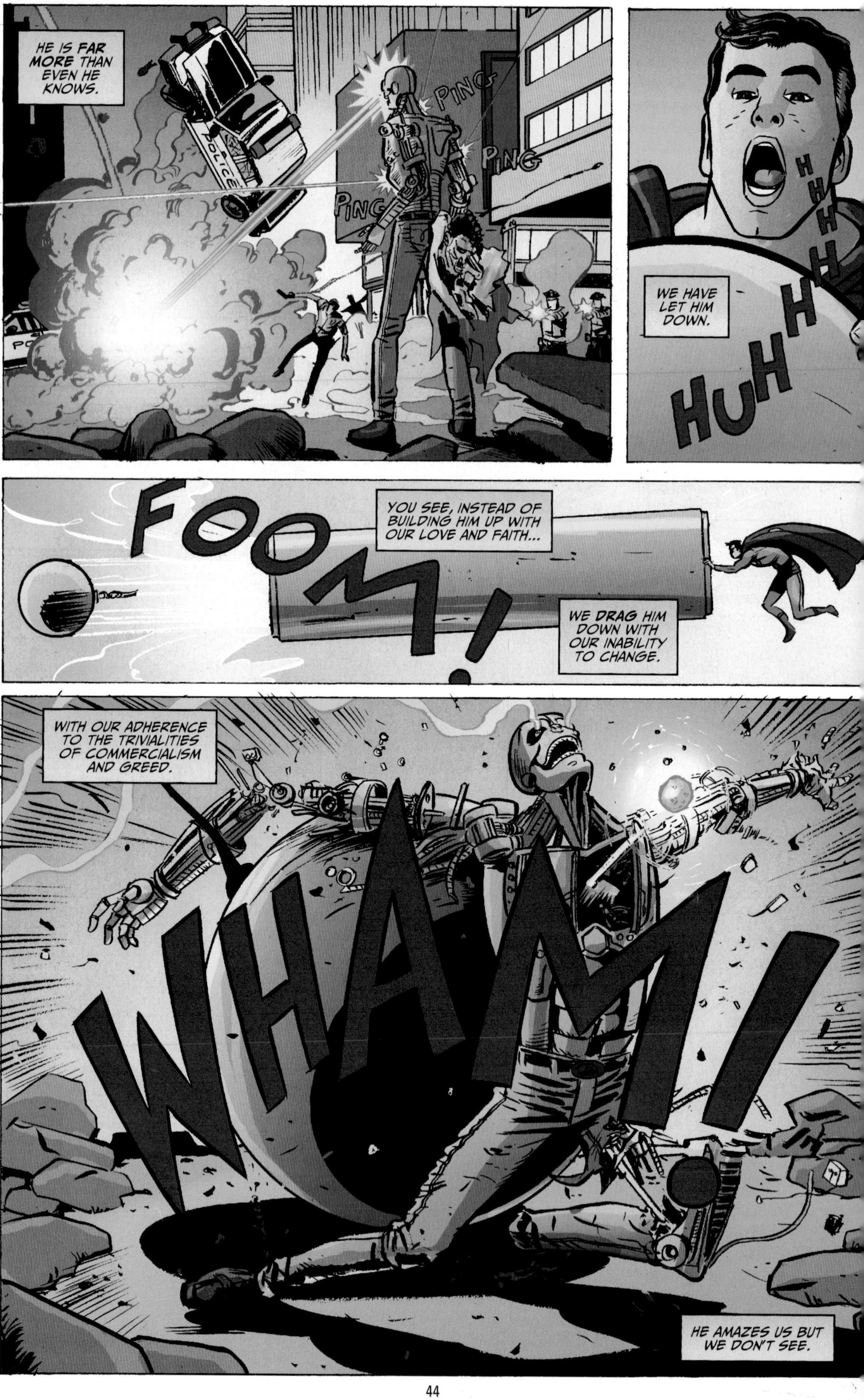
HE IS FAR MORE THAN EVEN HE KNOWS.
PING
PING
PING
POLICE
WE HAVE LET HIM DOWN.
HUHHHHHHH
FOOM!
YOU SEE, INSTEAD OF BUILDING HIM UP WITH OUR LOVE AND FAITH...
WE DRAG HIM DOWN WITH OUR INABILITY TO CHANGE.
WITH OUR ADHERENCE TO THE TRIVIALITIES OF COMMERCIALISM AND GREED.
WHAM!
HE AMAZES US BUT WE DON'T SEE.

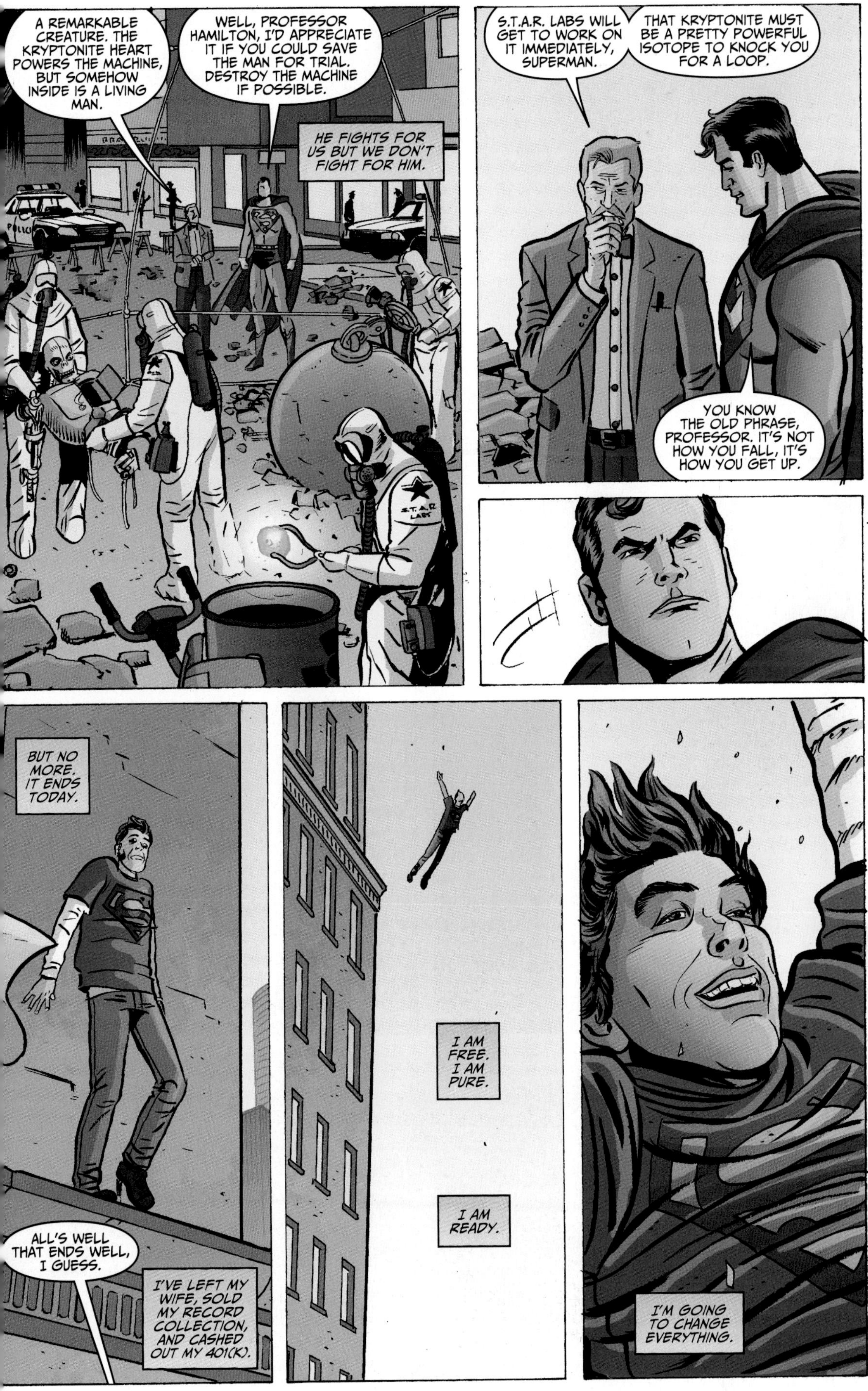
A REMARKABLE CREATURE. THE KRYPTONITE HEART POWERS THE MACHINE, BUT SOMEHOW INSIDE IS A LIVING MAN.
WELL, PROFESSOR HAMILTON, I'D APPRECIATE IT IF YOU COULD SAVE THE MAN FOR TRIAL. DESTROY THE MACHINE IF POSSIBLE.
HE FIGHTS FOR US BUT WE DON'T FIGHT FOR HIM.
S.T.A.R. LABS WILL GET TO WORK ON IT IMMEDIATELY, SUPERMAN.
THAT KRYPTONITE MUST BE A PRETTY POWERFUL ISOTOPE TO KNOCK YOU FOR A LOOP.
YOU KNOW THE OLD PHRASE, PROFESSOR. IT'S NOT HOW YOU FALL, IT'S HOW YOU GET UP.
BUT NO MORE. IT ENDS TODAY.
ALL'S WELL THAT ENDS WELL, I GUESS.
I'VE LEFT MY WIFE, SOLD MY RECORD COLLECTION, AND CASHED OUT MY 401(K).
I AM FREE. I AM PURE.
I AM READY.
I'M GOING TO CHANGE EVERYTHING.

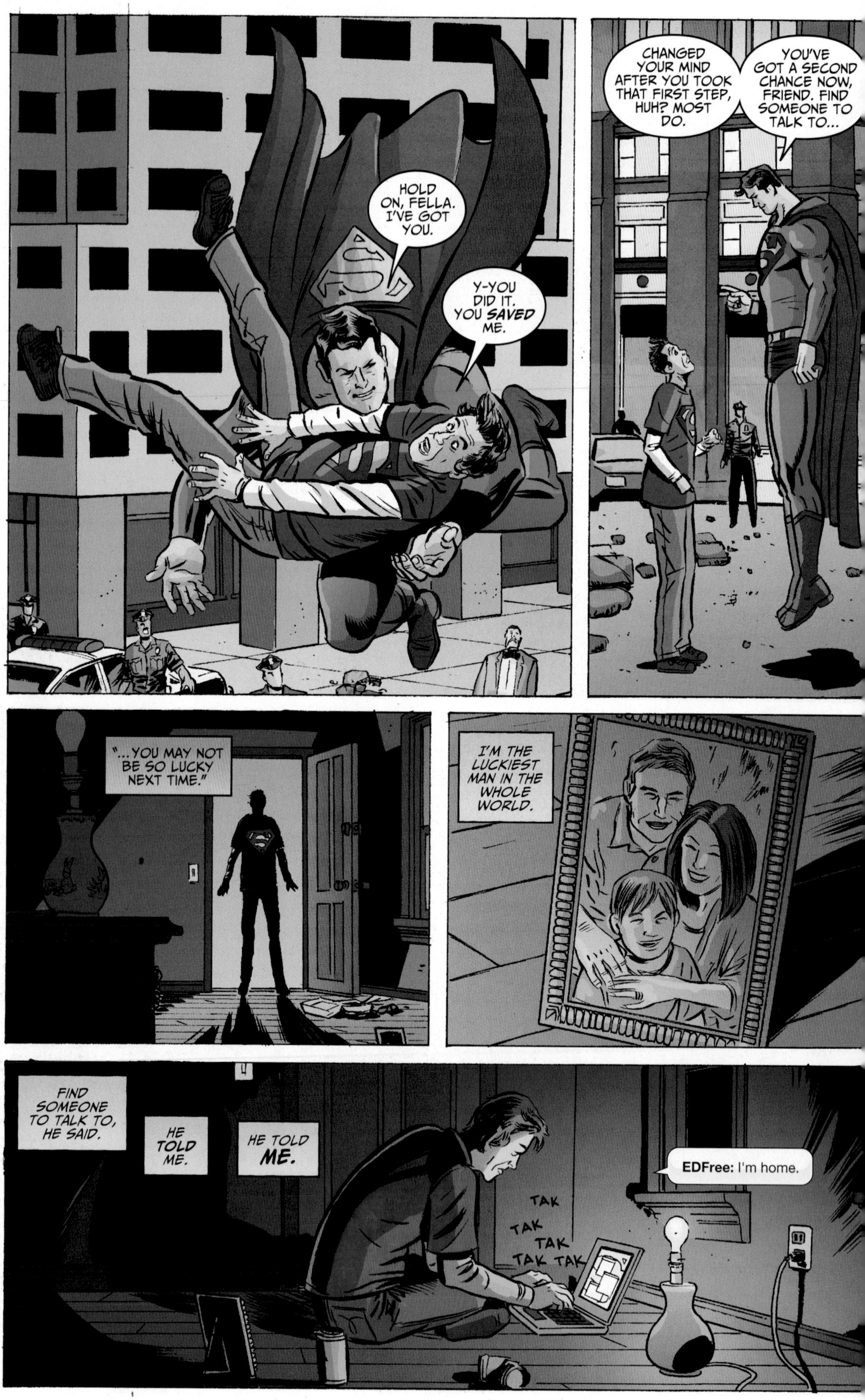
HOLD ON, FELLA. I'VE GOT YOU.
Y-YOU DID IT. YOU *SAVED* ME.
CHANGED YOUR MIND AFTER YOU TOOK THAT FIRST STEP, HUH? MOST DO.
YOU'VE GOT A SECOND CHANCE NOW, FRIEND. FIND SOMEONE TO TALK TO...
"...YOU MAY NOT BE SO LUCKY NEXT TIME."
I'M THE LUCKIEST MAN IN THE WHOLE WORLD.
FIND SOMEONE TO TALK TO, HE SAID.
HE TOLD ME.
HE TOLD **ME.**
TAK TAK TAK TAK TAK
EDFree: I'm home.

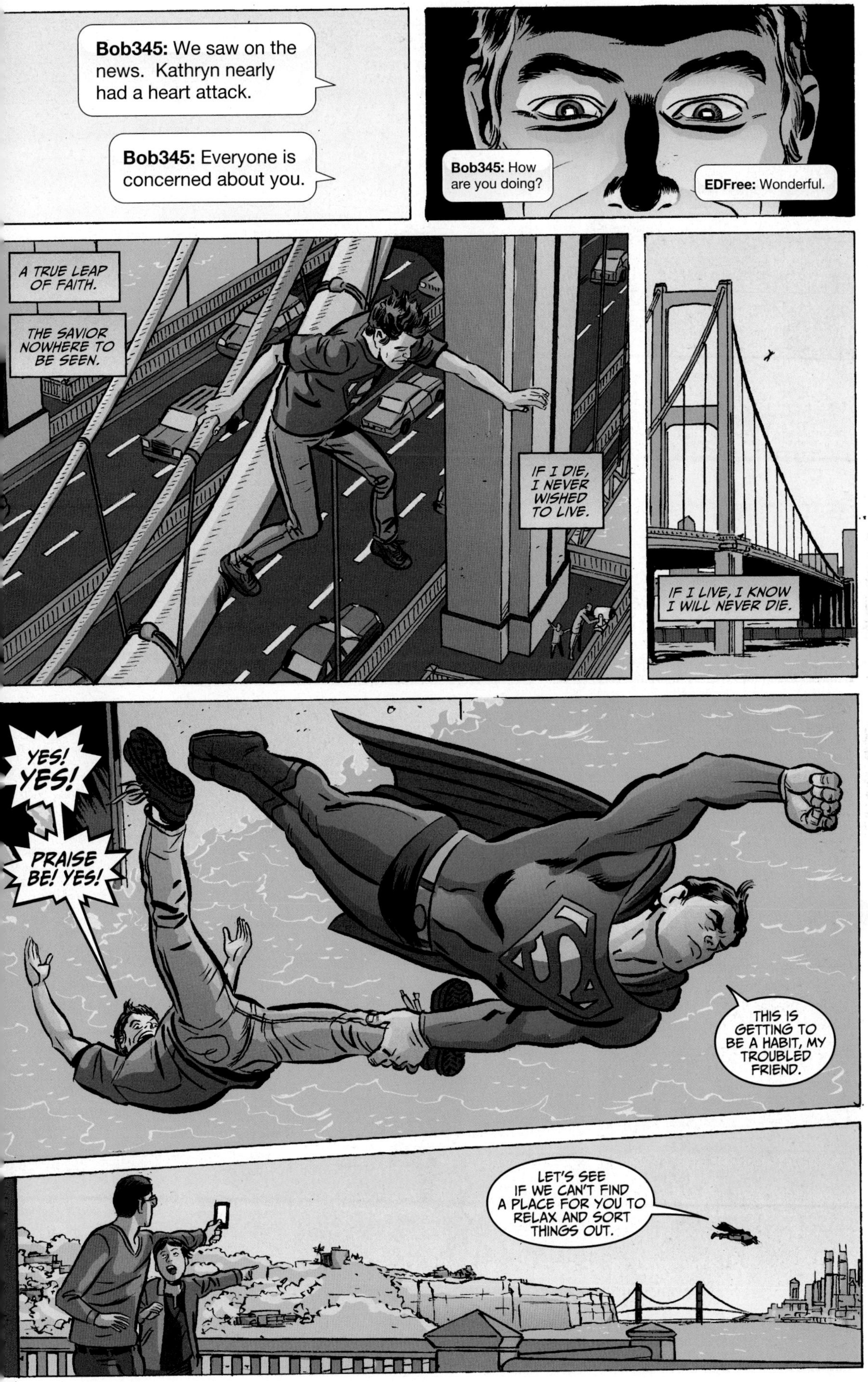
Bob345: We saw on the news. Kathryn nearly had a heart attack.
Bob345: Everyone is concerned about you.
Bob345: How are you doing?
EDFree: Wonderful.
A TRUE LEAP OF FAITH.
THE SAVIOR NOWHERE TO BE SEEN.
IF I DIE, I NEVER WISHED TO LIVE.
IF I LIVE, I KNOW I WILL NEVER DIE.
YES! YES!
PRAISE BE! YES!
THIS IS GETTING TO BE A HABIT, MY TROUBLED FRIEND.
LET'S SEE IF WE CAN'T FIND A PLACE FOR YOU TO RELAX AND SORT THINGS OUT.

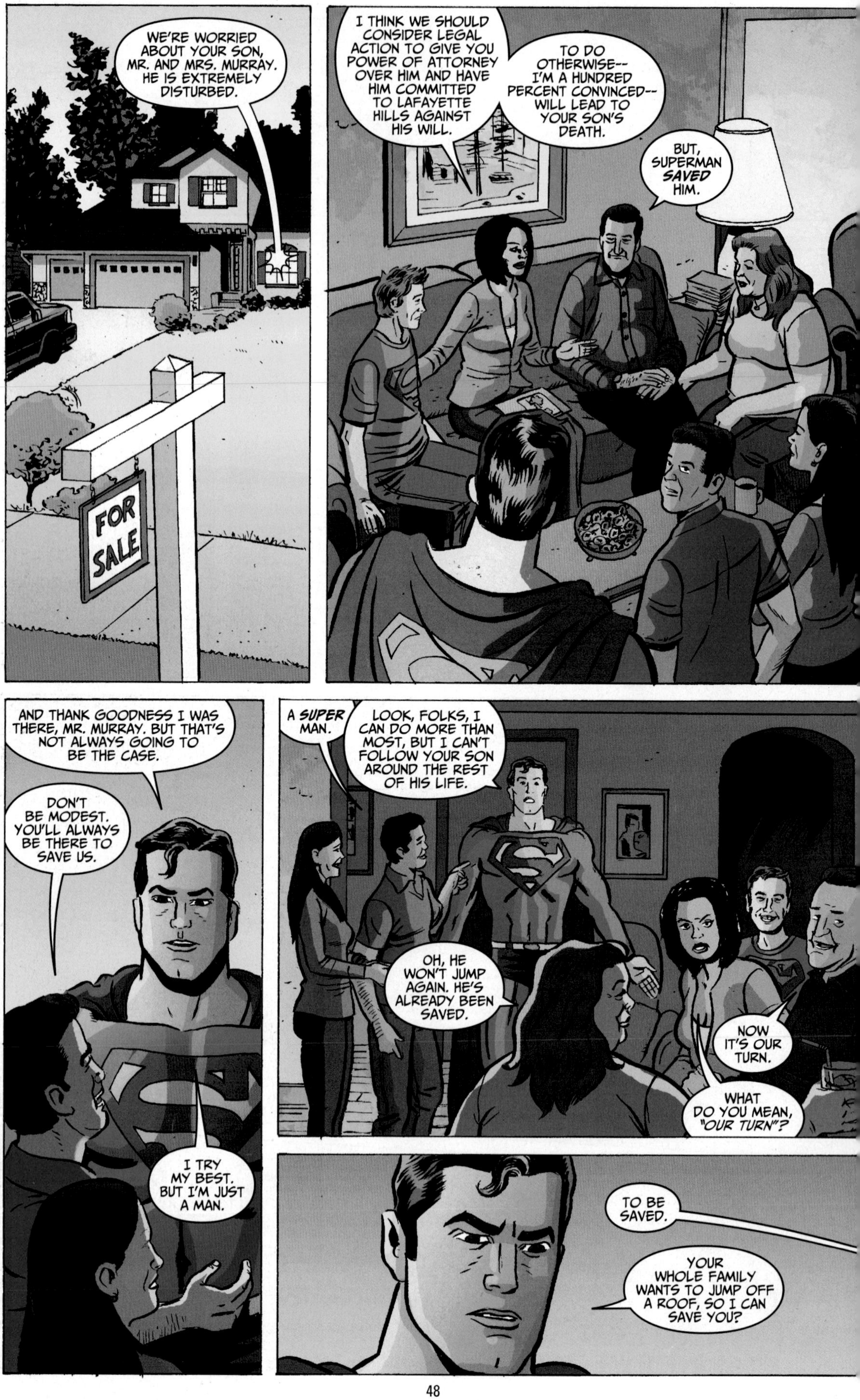
WE'RE WORRIED ABOUT YOUR SON, MR. AND MRS. MURRAY. HE IS EXTREMELY DISTURBED.
FOR SALE
I THINK WE SHOULD CONSIDER LEGAL ACTION TO GIVE YOU POWER OF ATTORNEY OVER HIM AND HAVE HIM COMMITTED TO LAFAYETTE HILLS AGAINST HIS WILL.
TO DO OTHERWISE-- I'M A HUNDRED PERCENT CONVINCED-- WILL LEAD TO YOUR SON'S DEATH.
BUT, SUPERMAN *SAVED* HIM.
AND THANK GOODNESS I WAS THERE, MR. MURRAY. BUT THAT'S NOT ALWAYS GOING TO BE THE CASE.
DON'T BE MODEST. YOU'LL ALWAYS BE THERE TO SAVE US.
I TRY MY BEST. BUT I'M JUST A MAN.
A *SUPER* MAN.
LOOK, FOLKS, I CAN DO MORE THAN MOST, BUT I CAN'T FOLLOW YOUR SON AROUND THE REST OF HIS LIFE.
OH, HE WON'T JUMP AGAIN. HE'S ALREADY BEEN SAVED.
NOW IT'S OUR TURN.
WHAT DO YOU MEAN, *"OUR TURN"*?
TO BE SAVED.
YOUR WHOLE FAMILY WANTS TO JUMP OFF A ROOF, SO I CAN SAVE YOU?

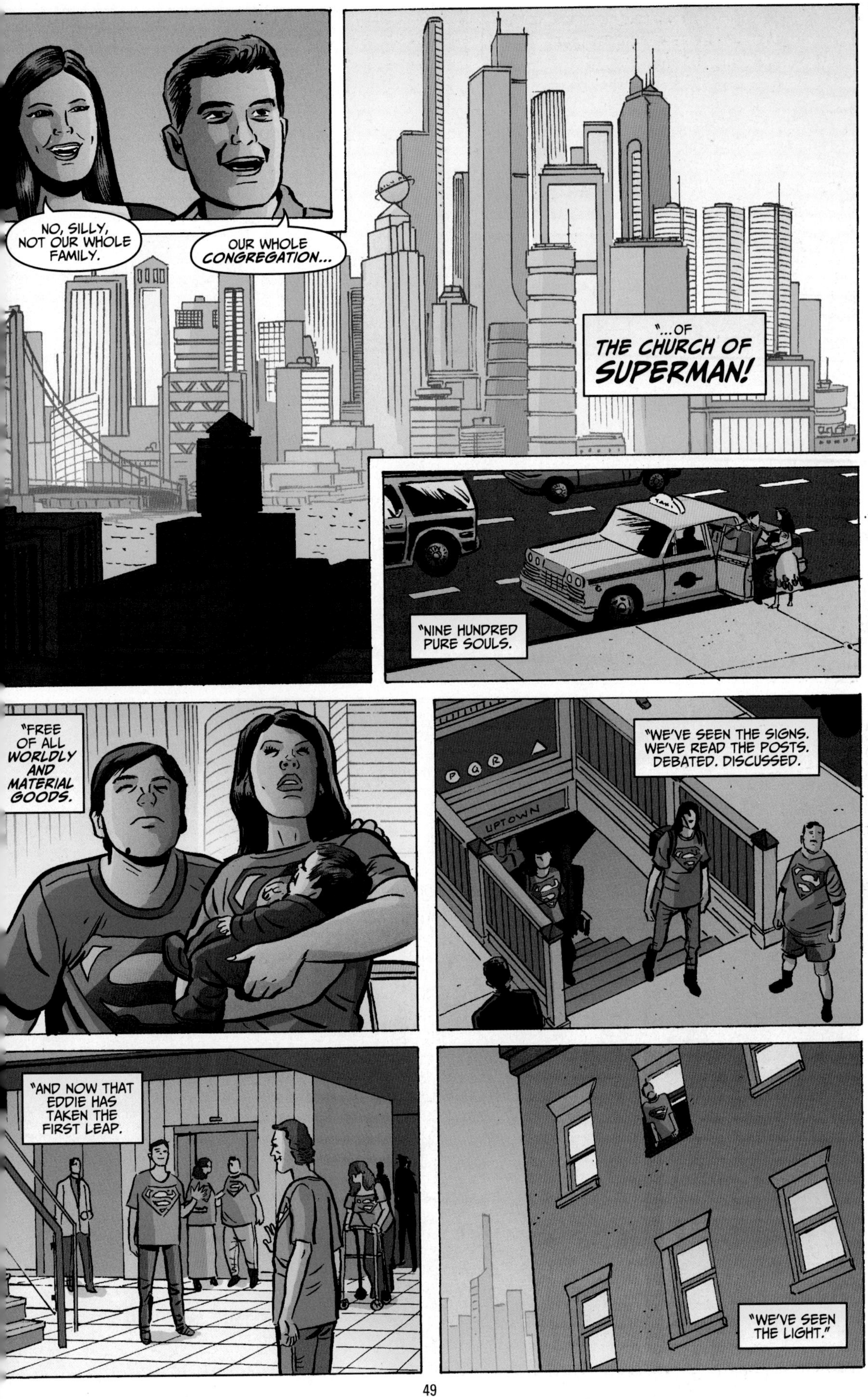
NO, SILLY, NOT OUR WHOLE FAMILY.
OUR WHOLE CONGREGATION...
"...OF THE CHURCH OF SUPERMAN!
"NINE HUNDRED PURE SOULS.
"FREE OF ALL WORLDLY AND MATERIAL GOODS.
"WE'VE SEEN THE SIGNS. WE'VE READ THE POSTS. DEBATED. DISCUSSED.
UPTOWN
"AND NOW THAT EDDIE HAS TAKEN THE FIRST LEAP.
"WE'VE SEEN THE LIGHT."

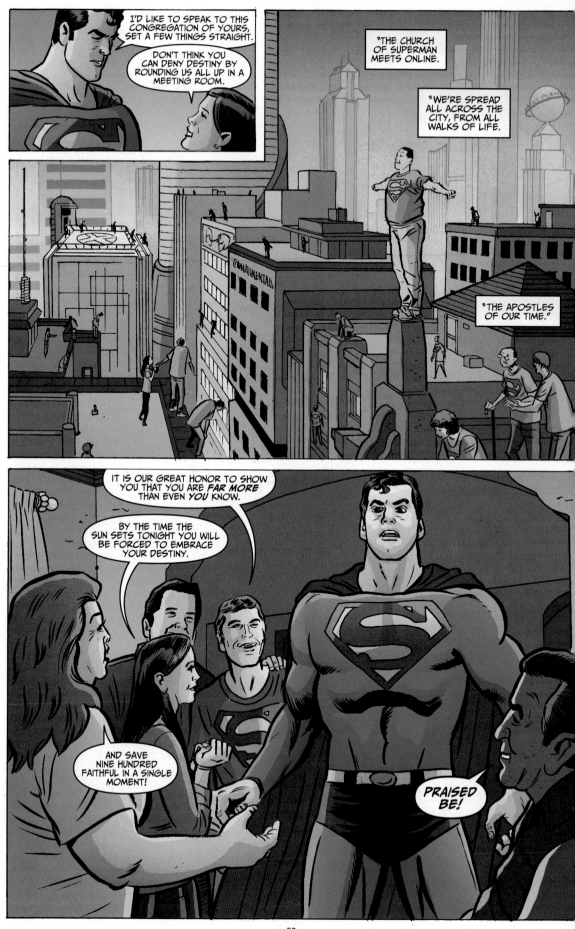

I'D LIKE TO SPEAK TO THIS CONGREGATION OF YOURS, SET A FEW THINGS STRAIGHT.

DON'T THINK YOU CAN DENY DESTINY BY ROUNDING US ALL UP IN A MEETING ROOM.

"THE CHURCH OF SUPERMAN MEETS ONLINE.

"WE'RE SPREAD ALL ACROSS THE CITY, FROM ALL WALKS OF LIFE.

"THE APOSTLES OF OUR TIME."

IT IS OUR GREAT HONOR TO SHOW YOU THAT YOU ARE FAR MORE THAN EVEN YOU KNOW.

BY THE TIME THE SUN SETS TONIGHT YOU WILL BE FORCED TO EMBRACE YOUR DESTINY.

AND SAVE NINE HUNDRED FAITHFUL IN A SINGLE MOMENT!

PRAISED BE!

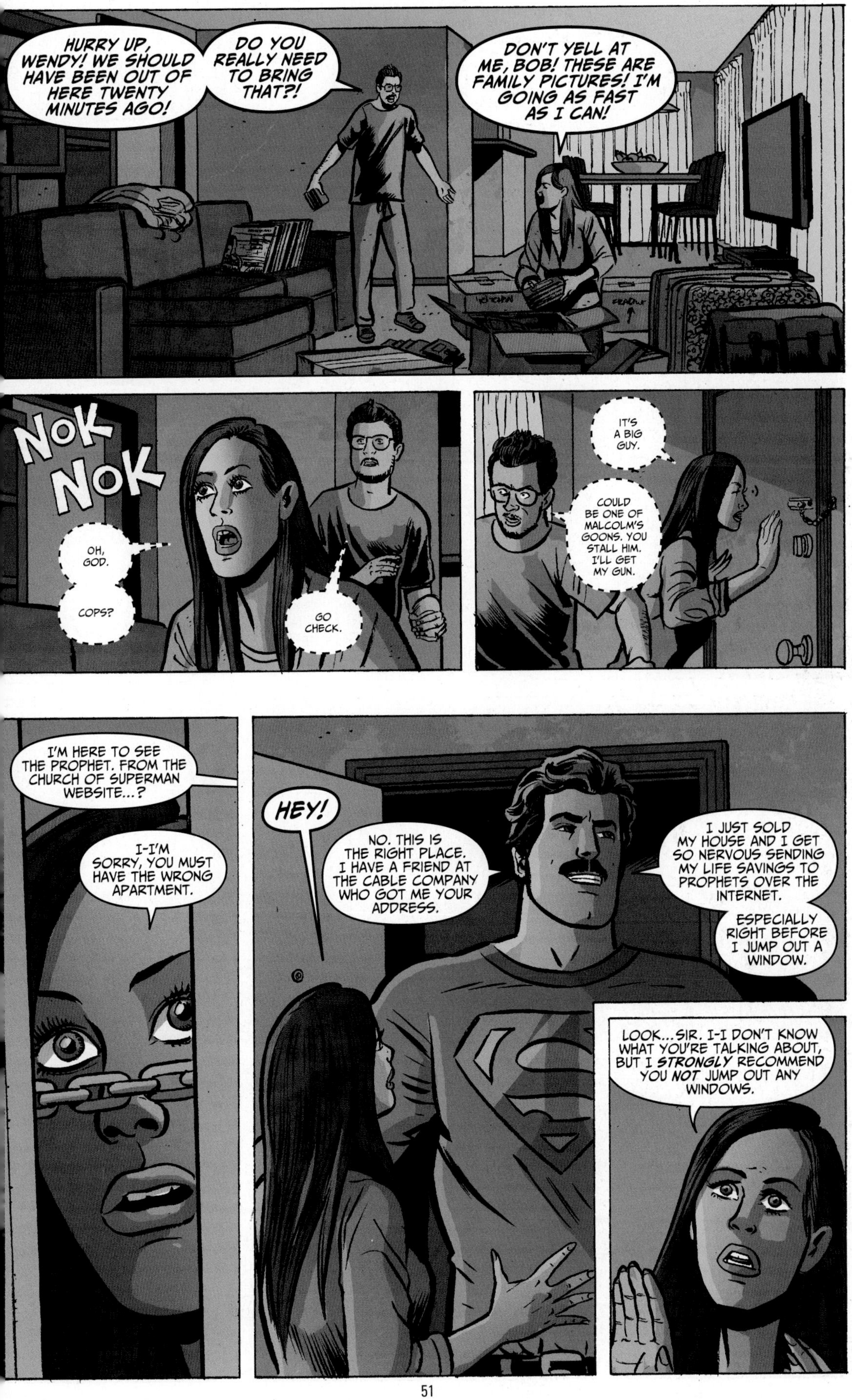
HURRY UP, WENDY! WE SHOULD HAVE BEEN OUT OF HERE TWENTY MINUTES AGO!
DO YOU REALLY NEED TO BRING THAT?!
DON'T YELL AT ME, BOB! THESE ARE FAMILY PICTURES! I'M GOING AS FAST AS I CAN!
NOK NOK
OH, GOD.
COPS?
GO CHECK.
IT'S A BIG GUY.
COULD BE ONE OF MALCOLM'S GOONS. YOU STALL HIM. I'LL GET MY GUN.
I'M HERE TO SEE THE PROPHET. FROM THE CHURCH OF SUPERMAN WEBSITE...?
I-I'M SORRY, YOU MUST HAVE THE WRONG APARTMENT.
HEY!
NO. THIS IS THE RIGHT PLACE. I HAVE A FRIEND AT THE CABLE COMPANY WHO GOT ME YOUR ADDRESS.
I JUST SOLD MY HOUSE AND I GET SO NERVOUS SENDING MY LIFE SAVINGS TO PROPHETS OVER THE INTERNET.
ESPECIALLY RIGHT BEFORE I JUMP OUT A WINDOW.
LOOK...SIR. I-I DON'T KNOW WHAT YOU'RE TALKING ABOUT, BUT I STRONGLY RECOMMEND YOU NOT JUMP OUT ANY WINDOWS.

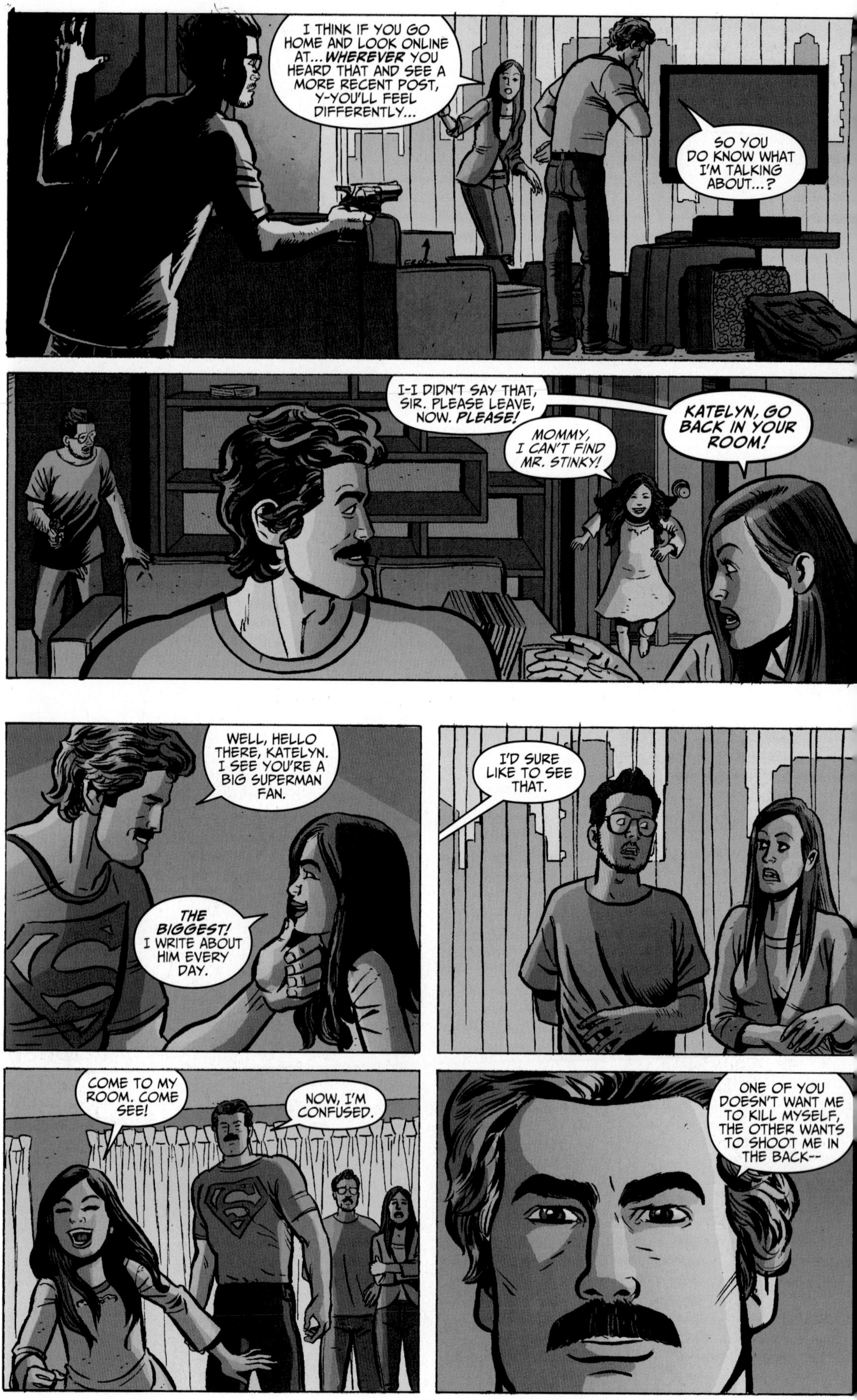
I THINK IF YOU GO HOME AND LOOK ONLINE AT... WHEREVER YOU HEARD THAT AND SEE A MORE RECENT POST, Y-YOU'LL FEEL DIFFERENTLY...
SO YOU DO KNOW WHAT I'M TALKING ABOUT...?
I-I DIDN'T SAY THAT, SIR. PLEASE LEAVE, NOW. PLEASE!
MOMMY, I CAN'T FIND MR. STINKY!
KATELYN, GO BACK IN YOUR ROOM!
WELL, HELLO THERE, KATELYN. I SEE YOU'RE A BIG SUPERMAN FAN.
THE BIGGEST! I WRITE ABOUT HIM EVERY DAY.
I'D SURE LIKE TO SEE THAT.
COME TO MY ROOM. COME SEE!
NOW, I'M CONFUSED.
ONE OF YOU DOESN'T WANT ME TO KILL MYSELF, THE OTHER WANTS TO SHOOT ME IN THE BACK--

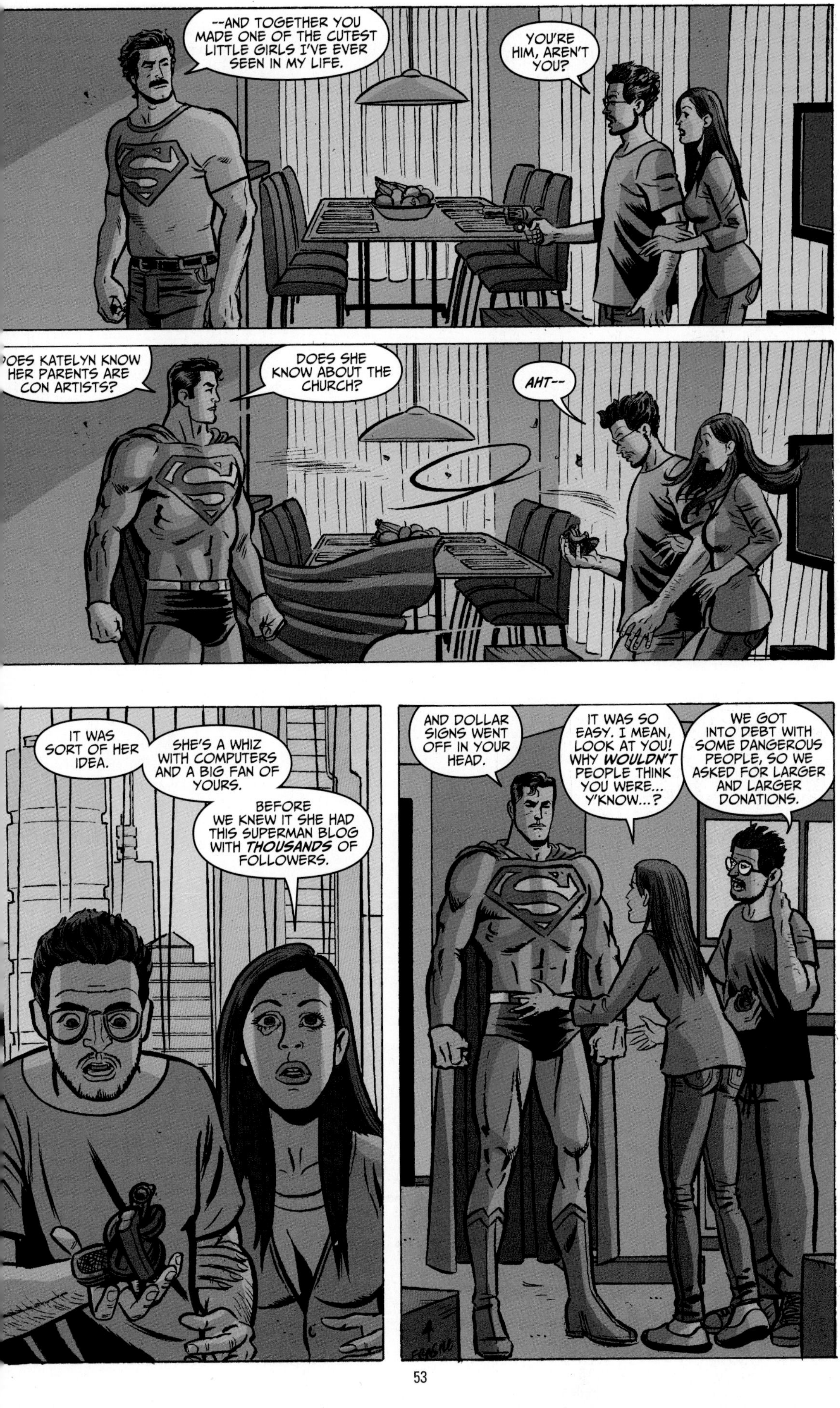

--AND TOGETHER YOU MADE ONE OF THE CUTEST LITTLE GIRLS I'VE EVER SEEN IN MY LIFE.
YOU'RE HIM, AREN'T YOU?
DOES KATELYN KNOW HER PARENTS ARE CON ARTISTS?
DOES SHE KNOW ABOUT THE CHURCH?
AHT--
IT WAS SORT OF HER IDEA.
SHE'S A WHIZ WITH COMPUTERS AND A BIG FAN OF YOURS.
BEFORE WE KNEW IT SHE HAD THIS SUPERMAN BLOG WITH THOUSANDS OF FOLLOWERS.
AND DOLLAR SIGNS WENT OFF IN YOUR HEAD.
IT WAS SO EASY. I MEAN, LOOK AT YOU! WHY WOULDN'T PEOPLE THINK YOU WERE... Y'KNOW...?
WE GOT INTO DEBT WITH SOME DANGEROUS PEOPLE, SO WE ASKED FOR LARGER AND LARGER DONATIONS.

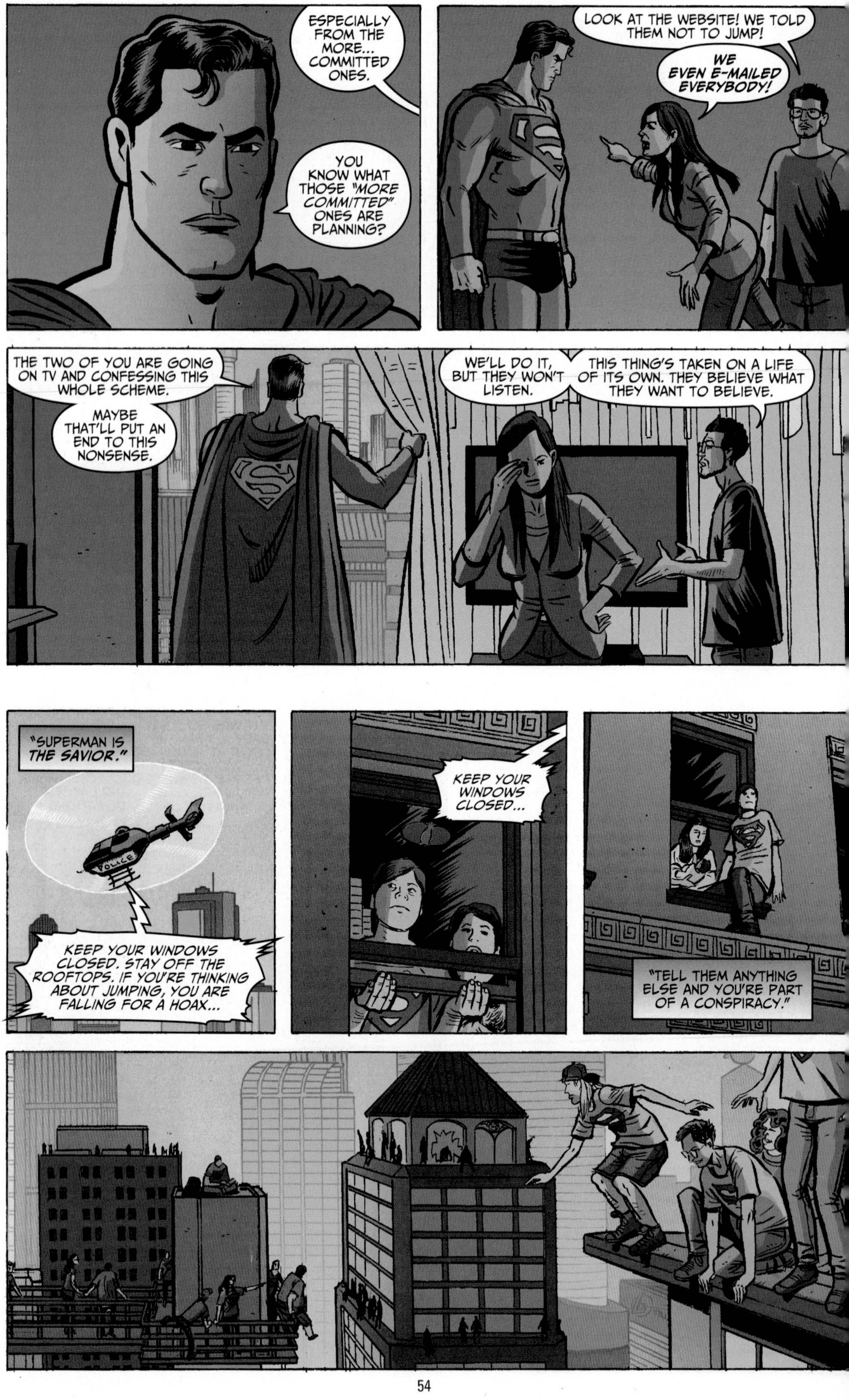

ESPECIALLY FROM THE MORE... COMMITTED ONES.
YOU KNOW WHAT THOSE "MORE COMMITTED" ONES ARE PLANNING?
LOOK AT THE WEBSITE! WE TOLD THEM NOT TO JUMP!
WE EVEN E-MAILED EVERYBODY!
THE TWO OF YOU ARE GOING ON TV AND CONFESSING THIS WHOLE SCHEME.
MAYBE THAT'LL PUT AN END TO THIS NONSENSE.
WE'LL DO IT, BUT THEY WON'T LISTEN.
THIS THING'S TAKEN ON A LIFE OF ITS OWN. THEY BELIEVE WHAT THEY WANT TO BELIEVE.
"SUPERMAN IS THE SAVIOR."
POLICE
KEEP YOUR WINDOWS CLOSED. STAY OFF THE ROOFTOPS. IF YOU'RE THINKING ABOUT JUMPING, YOU ARE FALLING FOR A HOAX...
KEEP YOUR WINDOWS CLOSED...
"TELL THEM ANYTHING ELSE AND YOU'RE PART OF A CONSPIRACY."

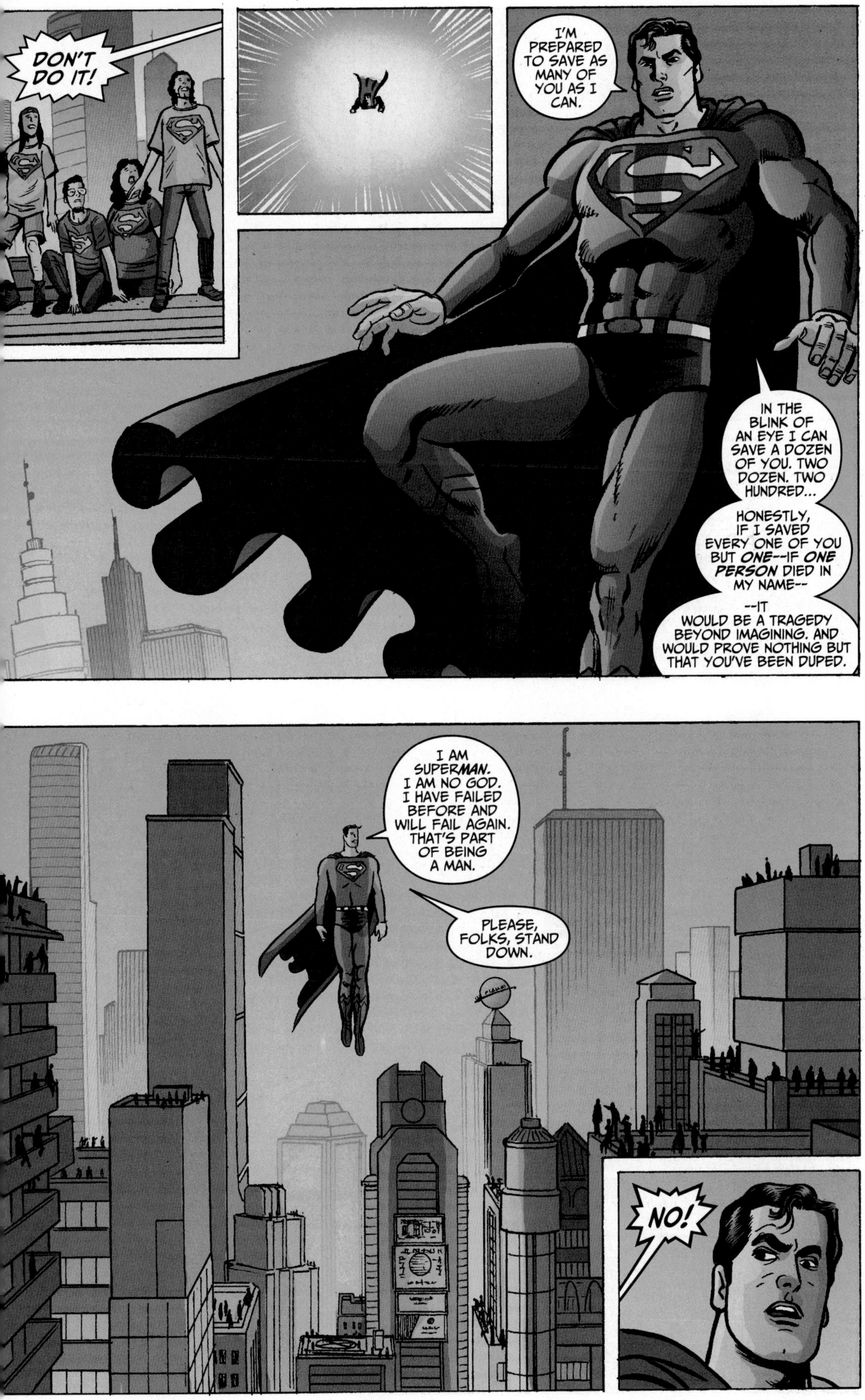
DON'T DO IT!
I'M PREPARED TO SAVE AS MANY OF YOU AS I CAN.
IN THE BLINK OF AN EYE I CAN SAVE A DOZEN OF YOU. TWO DOZEN. TWO HUNDRED...
HONESTLY, IF I SAVED EVERY ONE OF YOU BUT *ONE*--IF *ONE PERSON* DIED IN MY NAME--
--IT WOULD BE A TRAGEDY BEYOND IMAGINING. AND WOULD PROVE NOTHING BUT THAT YOU'VE BEEN DUPED.
I AM SUPER*MAN*. I AM NO GOD. I HAVE FAILED BEFORE AND WILL FAIL AGAIN. THAT'S PART OF BEING A MAN.
PLEASE, FOLKS, STAND DOWN.
NO!

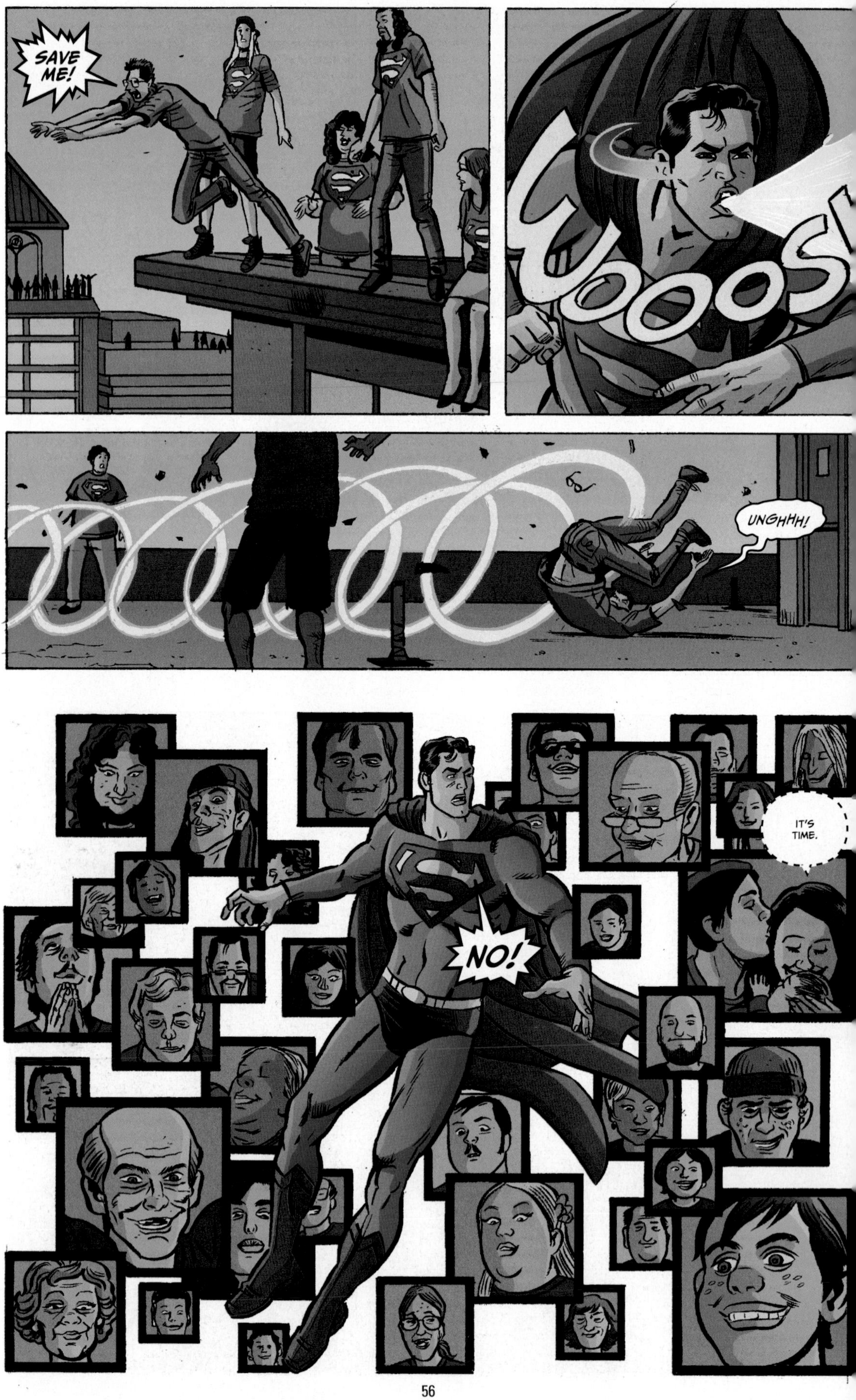
SAVE ME!
WOOOSH
UNGHHH!
IT'S TIME.
NO!

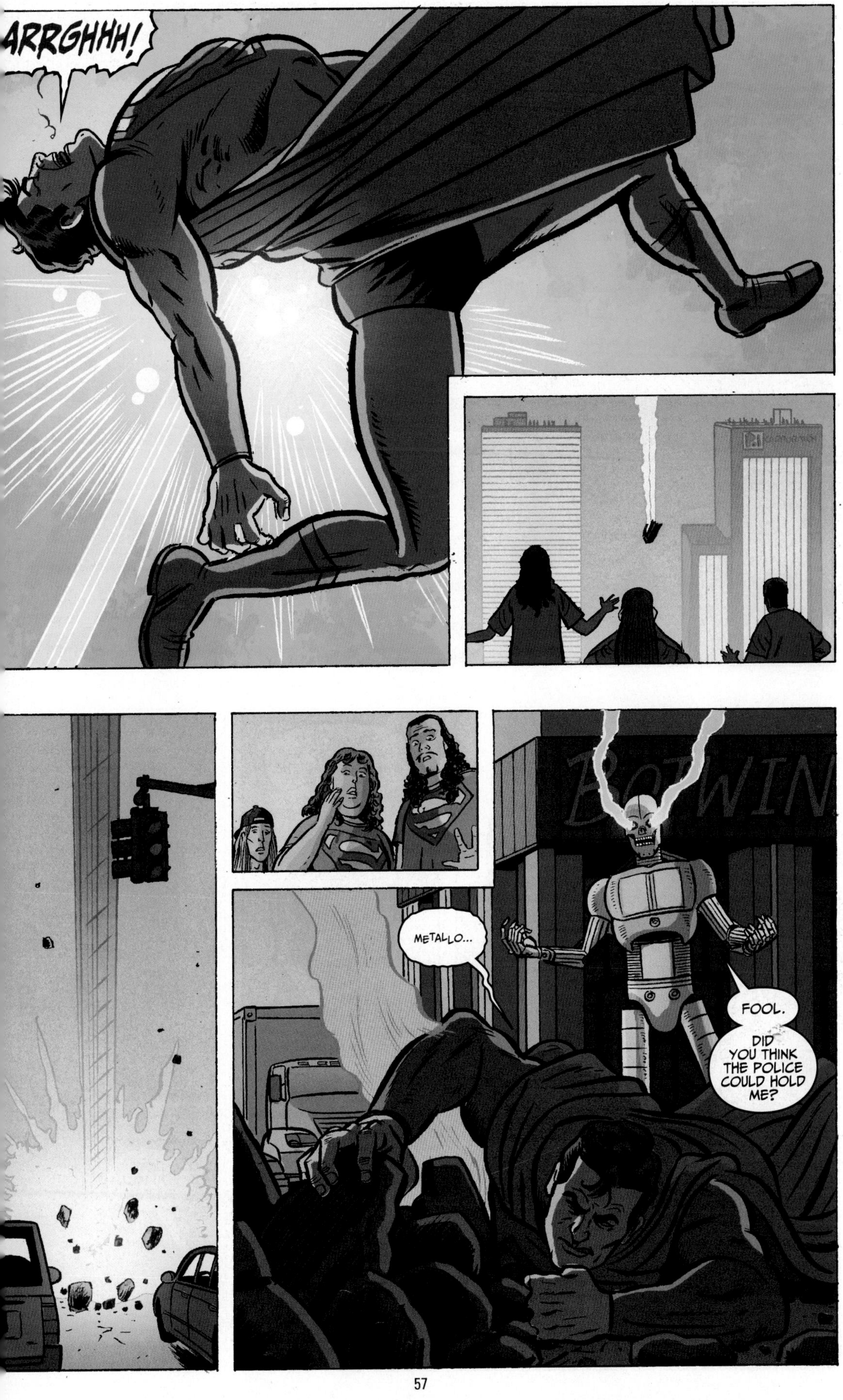
ARRGHHH!
METALLO...
FOOL.
DID YOU THINK THE POLICE COULD HOLD ME?

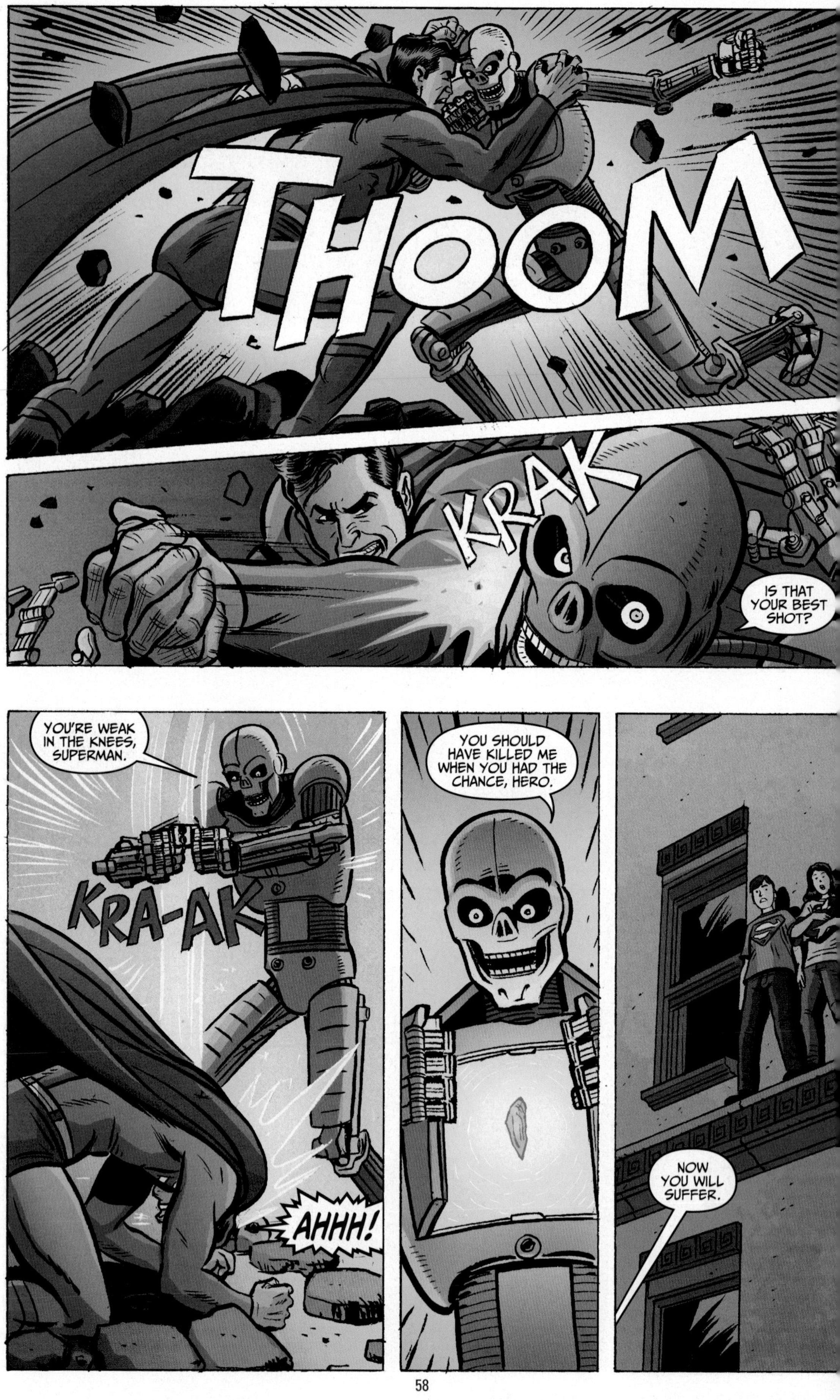
THOOM
KRAK
IS THAT YOUR BEST SHOT?
YOU'RE WEAK IN THE KNEES, SUPERMAN.
KRA-AK
AHHH!
YOU SHOULD HAVE KILLED ME WHEN YOU HAD THE CHANCE, HERO.
NOW YOU WILL SUFFER.

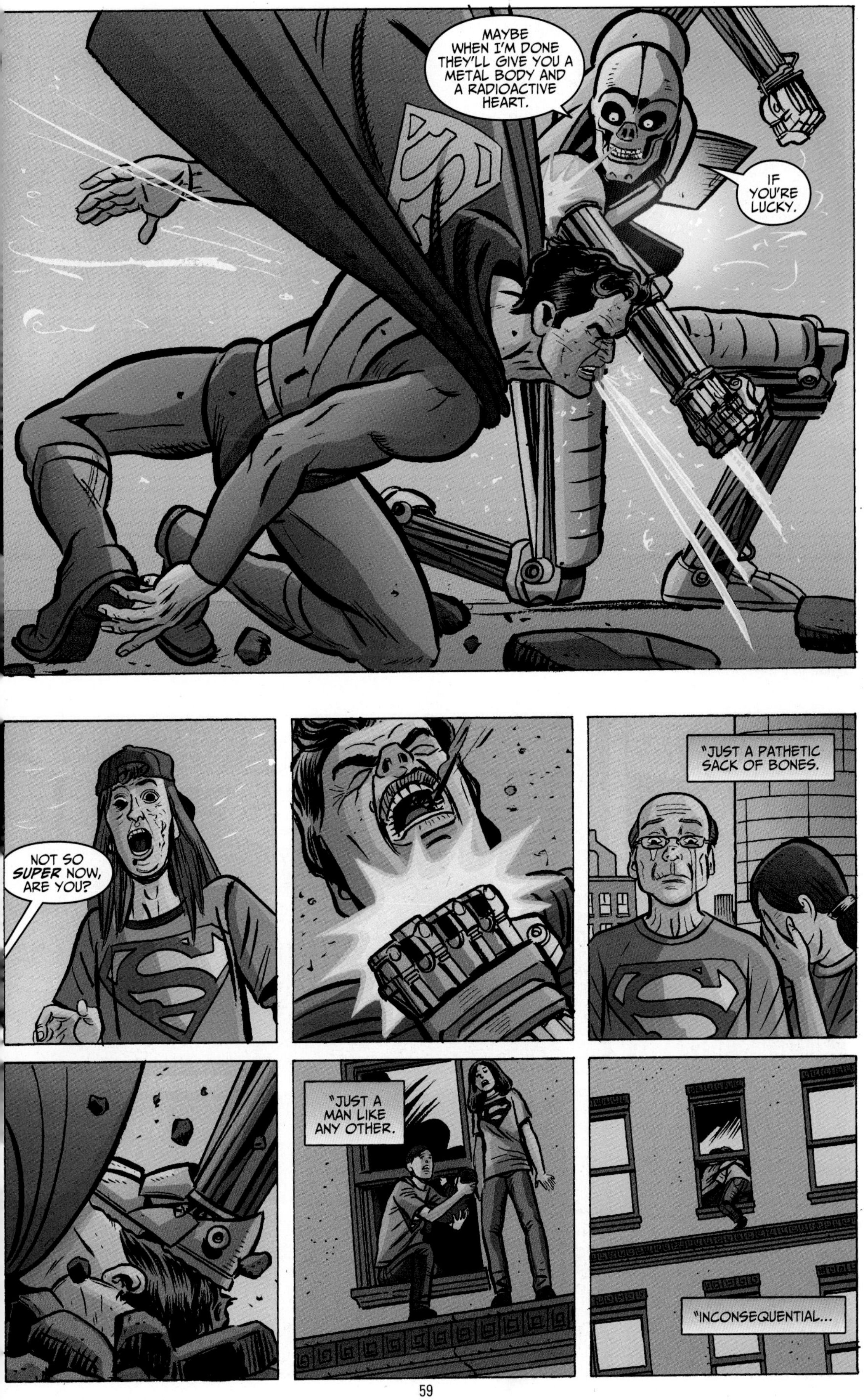
MAYBE WHEN I'M DONE THEY'LL GIVE YOU A METAL BODY AND A RADIOACTIVE HEART.
IF YOU'RE LUCKY.
NOT SO SUPER NOW, ARE YOU?
"JUST A PATHETIC SACK OF BONES.
"JUST A MAN LIKE ANY OTHER.
"INCONSEQUENTIAL...

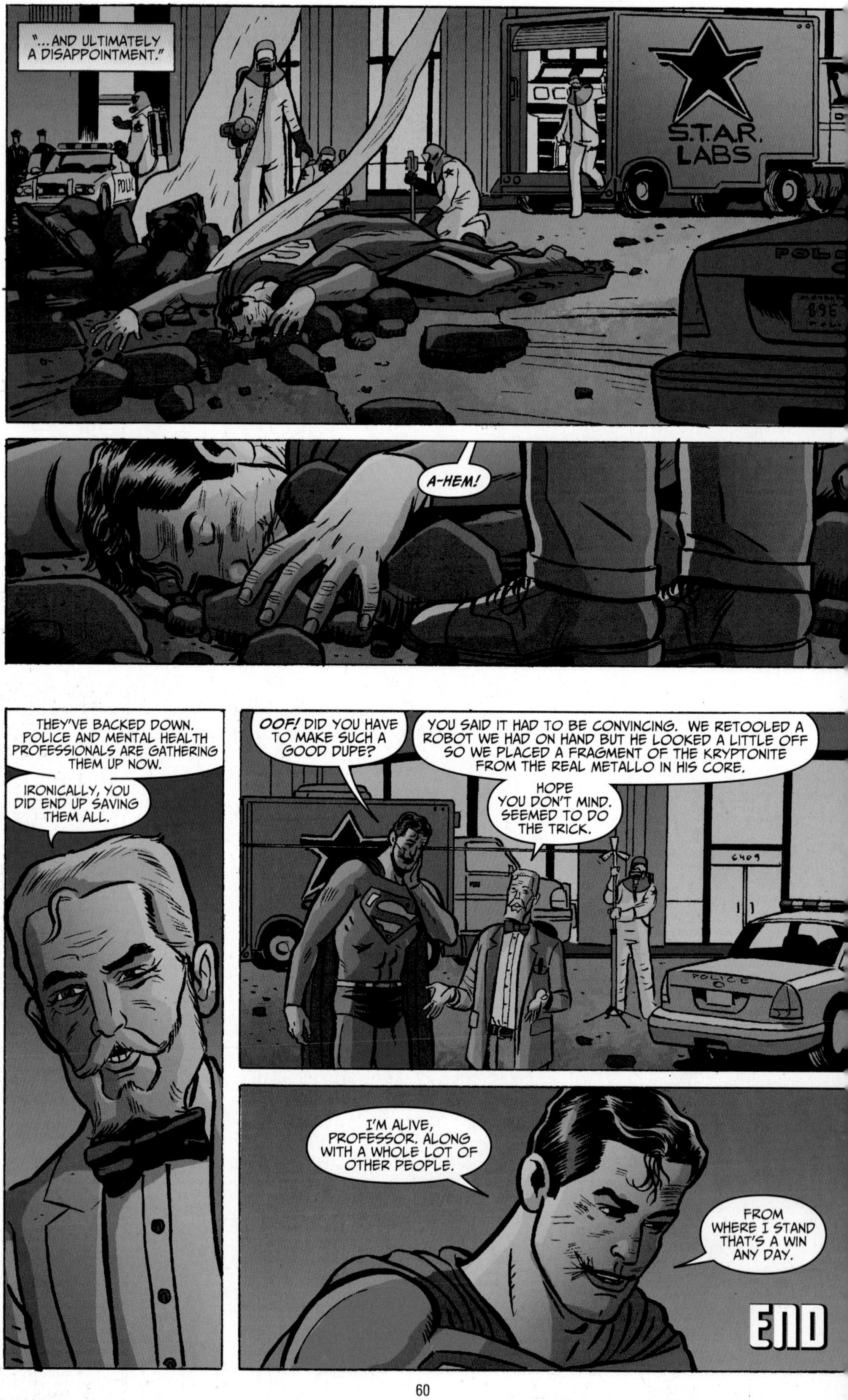
"...AND ULTIMATELY A DISAPPOINTMENT."
S.T.A.R. LABS
A-HEM!
THEY'VE BACKED DOWN. POLICE AND MENTAL HEALTH PROFESSIONALS ARE GATHERING THEM UP NOW.
IRONICALLY, YOU DID END UP SAVING THEM ALL.
OOF! DID YOU HAVE TO MAKE SUCH A GOOD DUPE?
YOU SAID IT HAD TO BE CONVINCING. WE RETOOLED A ROBOT WE HAD ON HAND BUT HE LOOKED A LITTLE OFF SO WE PLACED A FRAGMENT OF THE KRYPTONITE FROM THE REAL METALLO IN HIS CORE.
HOPE YOU DON'T MIND. SEEMED TO DO THE TRICK.
I'M ALIVE, PROFESSOR. ALONG WITH A WHOLE LOT OF OTHER PEOPLE.
FROM WHERE I STAND THAT'S A WIN ANY DAY.
END

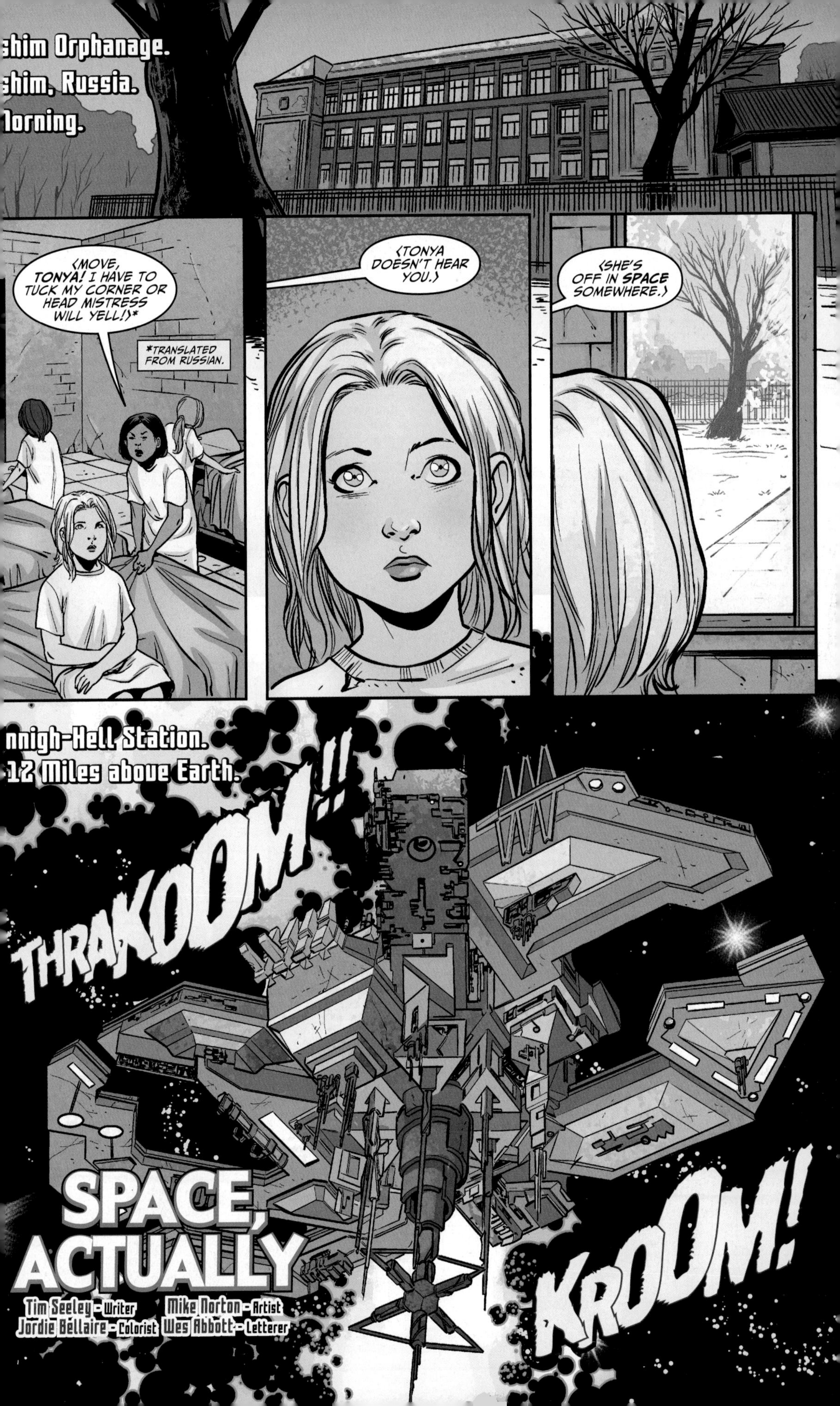

shim Orphanage.
shim, Russia.
lorning.
‹MOVE, TONYA! I HAVE TO TUCK MY CORNER OR HEAD MISTRESS WILL YELL!›*
*TRANSLATED FROM RUSSIAN.
‹TONYA DOESN'T HEAR YOU.›
‹SHE'S OFF IN SPACE SOMEWHERE.›
nnigh-Hell Station.
12 Miles above Earth.
THRAKOOM!!
KROOM!
SPACE, ACTUALLY
Tim Seeley - Writer
Mike Norton - Artist
Jordie Bellaire - Colorist
Wes Abbott - Letterer

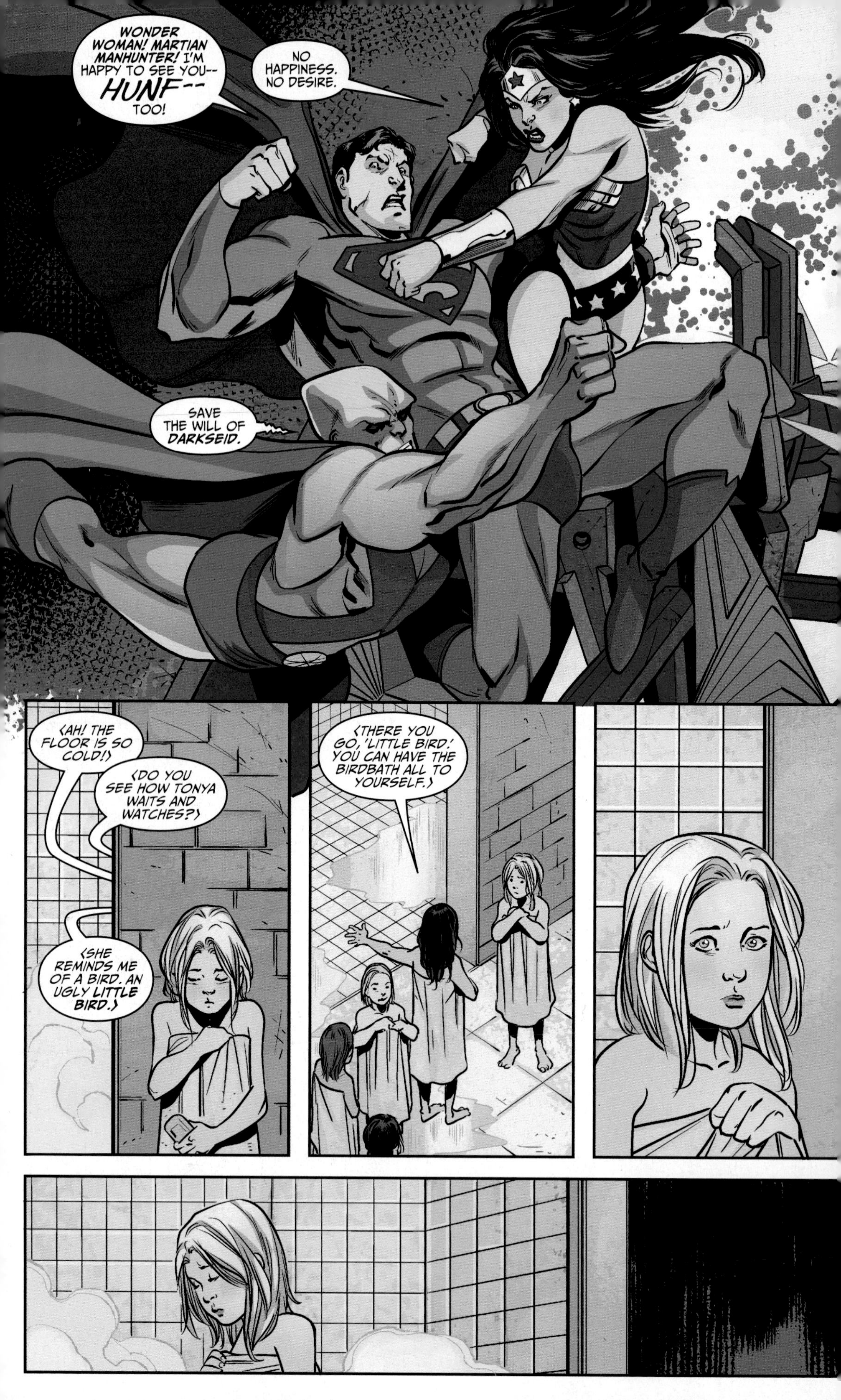
WONDER WOMAN! MARTIAN MANHUNTER! I'M HAPPY TO SEE YOU-- HUNF-- TOO!
NO HAPPINESS. NO DESIRE.
SAVE THE WILL OF DARKSEID.
‹AH! THE FLOOR IS SO COLD!›
‹DO YOU SEE HOW TONYA WAITS AND WATCHES?›
‹SHE REMINDS ME OF A BIRD. AN UGLY LITTLE BIRD.›
‹THERE YOU GO, 'LITTLE BIRD.' YOU CAN HAVE THE BIRDBATH ALL TO YOURSELF.›

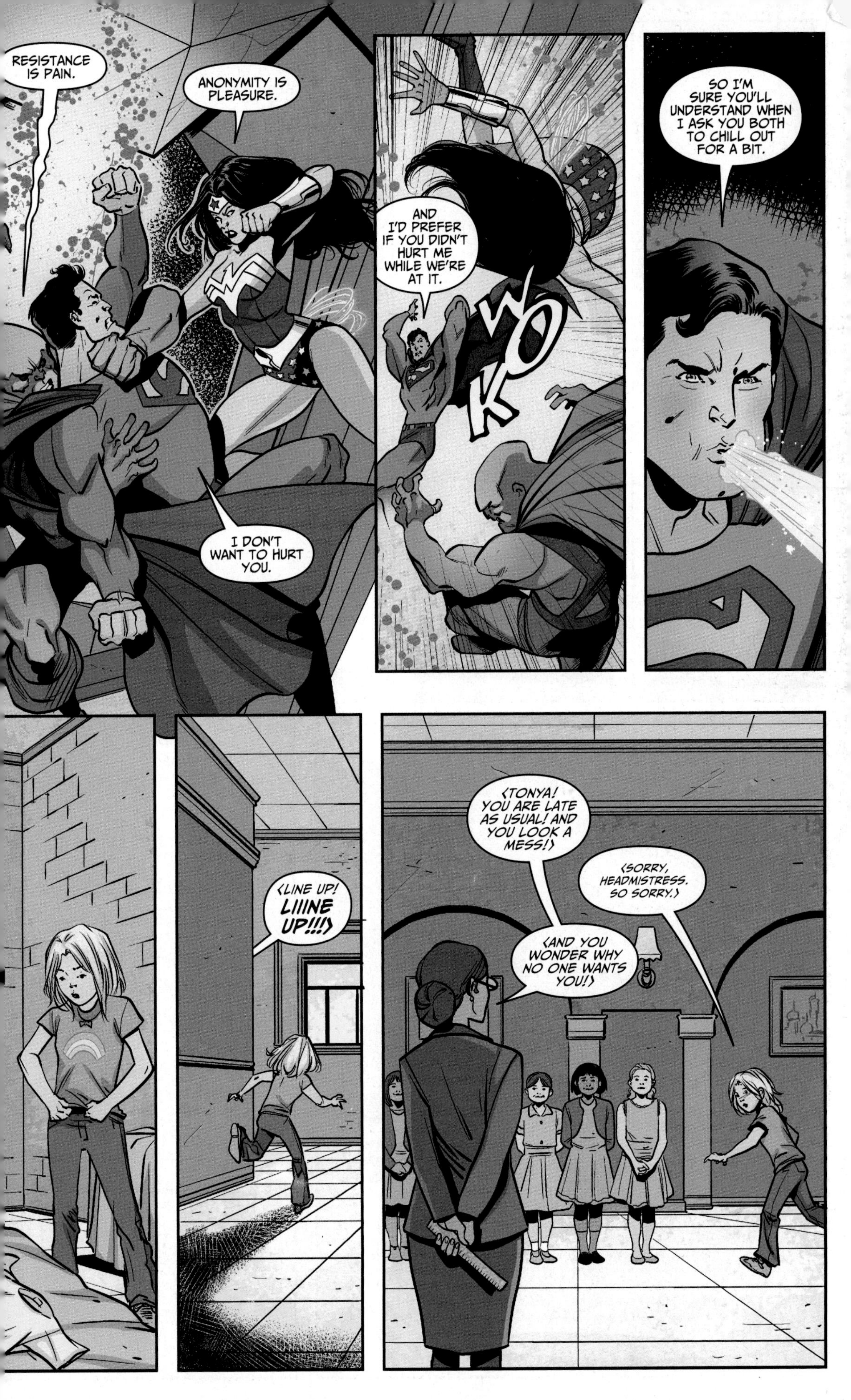

RESISTANCE IS PAIN.
ANONYMITY IS PLEASURE.
I DON'T WANT TO HURT YOU.
AND I'D PREFER IF YOU DIDN'T HURT ME WHILE WE'RE AT IT.
WOOK
SO I'M SURE YOU'LL UNDERSTAND WHEN I ASK YOU BOTH TO CHILL OUT FOR A BIT.
<LINE UP! LIIINE UP!!!>
<TONYA! YOU ARE LATE AS USUAL! AND YOU LOOK A MESS!>
<SORRY, HEADMISTRESS. SO SORRY.>
<AND YOU WONDER WHY NO ONE WANTS YOU!>

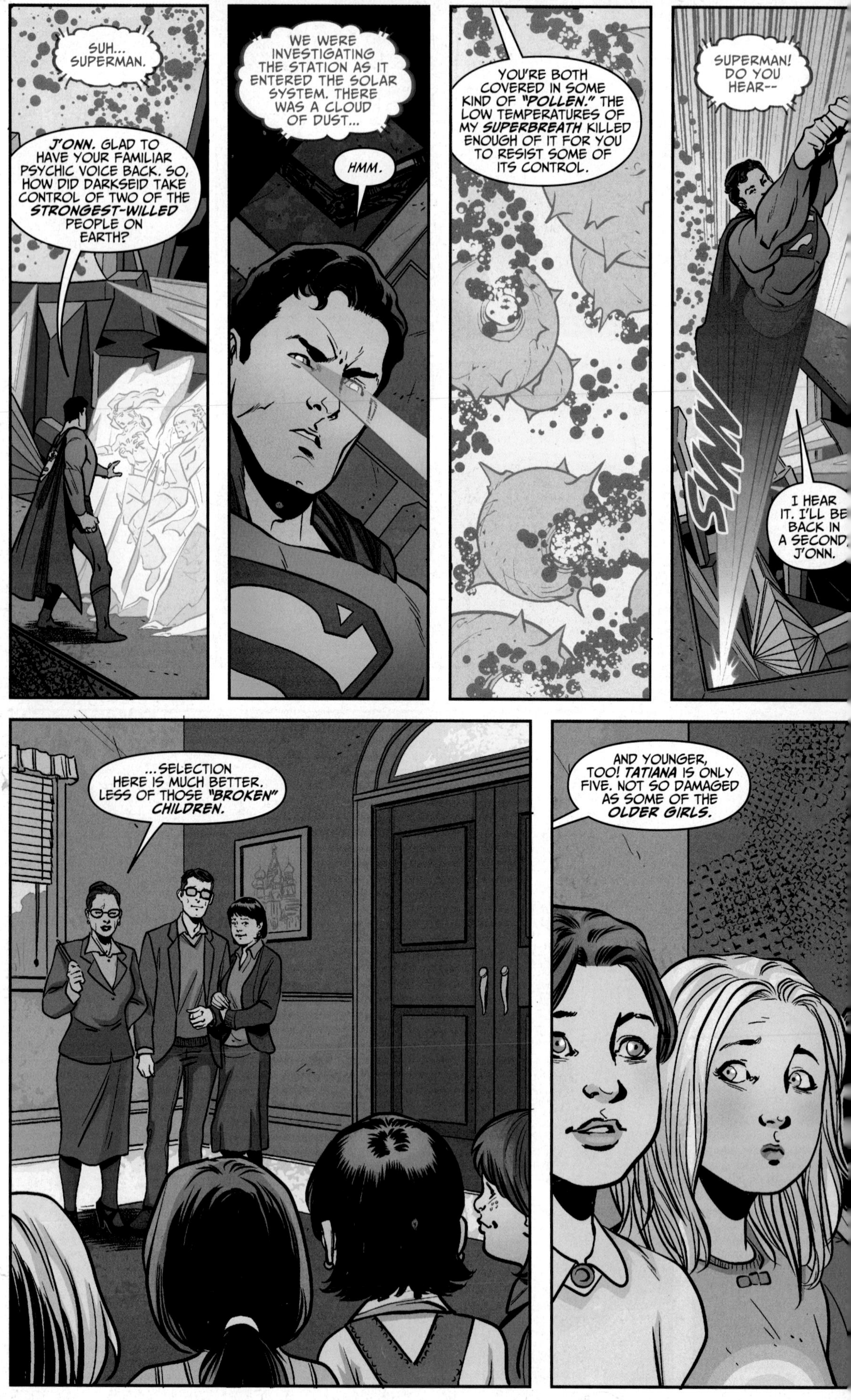
SUH... SUPERMAN.
J'ONN. GLAD TO HAVE YOUR FAMILIAR PSYCHIC VOICE BACK. SO, HOW DID DARKSEID TAKE CONTROL OF TWO OF THE STRONGEST-WILLED PEOPLE ON EARTH?
WE WERE INVESTIGATING THE STATION AS IT ENTERED THE SOLAR SYSTEM. THERE WAS A CLOUD OF DUST...
HMM.
YOU'RE BOTH COVERED IN SOME KIND OF "POLLEN." THE LOW TEMPERATURES OF MY SUPERBREATH KILLED ENOUGH OF IT FOR YOU TO RESIST SOME OF ITS CONTROL.
SUPERMAN! DO YOU HEAR--
SWM
I HEAR IT. I'LL BE BACK IN A SECOND, J'ONN.
...SELECTION HERE IS MUCH BETTER. LESS OF THOSE "BROKEN" CHILDREN.
AND YOUNGER, TOO! TATIANA IS ONLY FIVE. NOT SO DAMAGED AS SOME OF THE OLDER GIRLS.

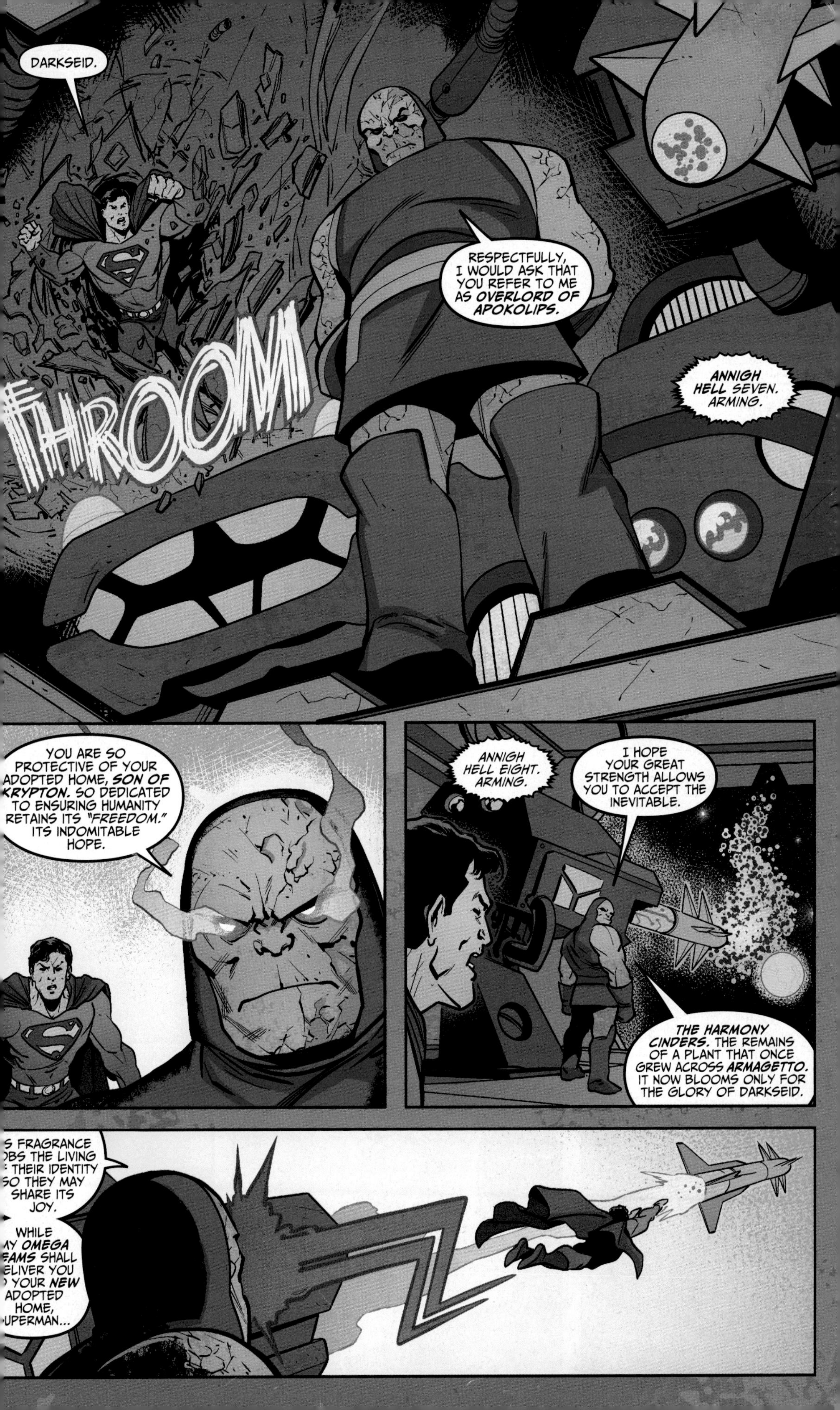
DARKSEID.
RESPECTFULLY, I WOULD ASK THAT YOU REFER TO ME AS OVERLORD OF APOKOLIPS.
THROOM
ANNIGH HELL SEVEN. ARMING.
YOU ARE SO PROTECTIVE OF YOUR ADOPTED HOME, SON OF KRYPTON. SO DEDICATED TO ENSURING HUMANITY RETAINS ITS "FREEDOM." ITS INDOMITABLE HOPE.
ANNIGH HELL EIGHT. ARMING.
I HOPE YOUR GREAT STRENGTH ALLOWS YOU TO ACCEPT THE INEVITABLE.
THE HARMONY CINDERS. THE REMAINS OF A PLANT THAT ONCE GREW ACROSS ARMAGETTO. IT NOW BLOOMS ONLY FOR THE GLORY OF DARKSEID.
S FRAGRANCE OBS THE LIVING THEIR IDENTITY SO THEY MAY SHARE ITS JOY.
WHILE MY OMEGA EAMS SHALL ELIVER YOU YOUR NEW ADOPTED HOME, UPERMAN...

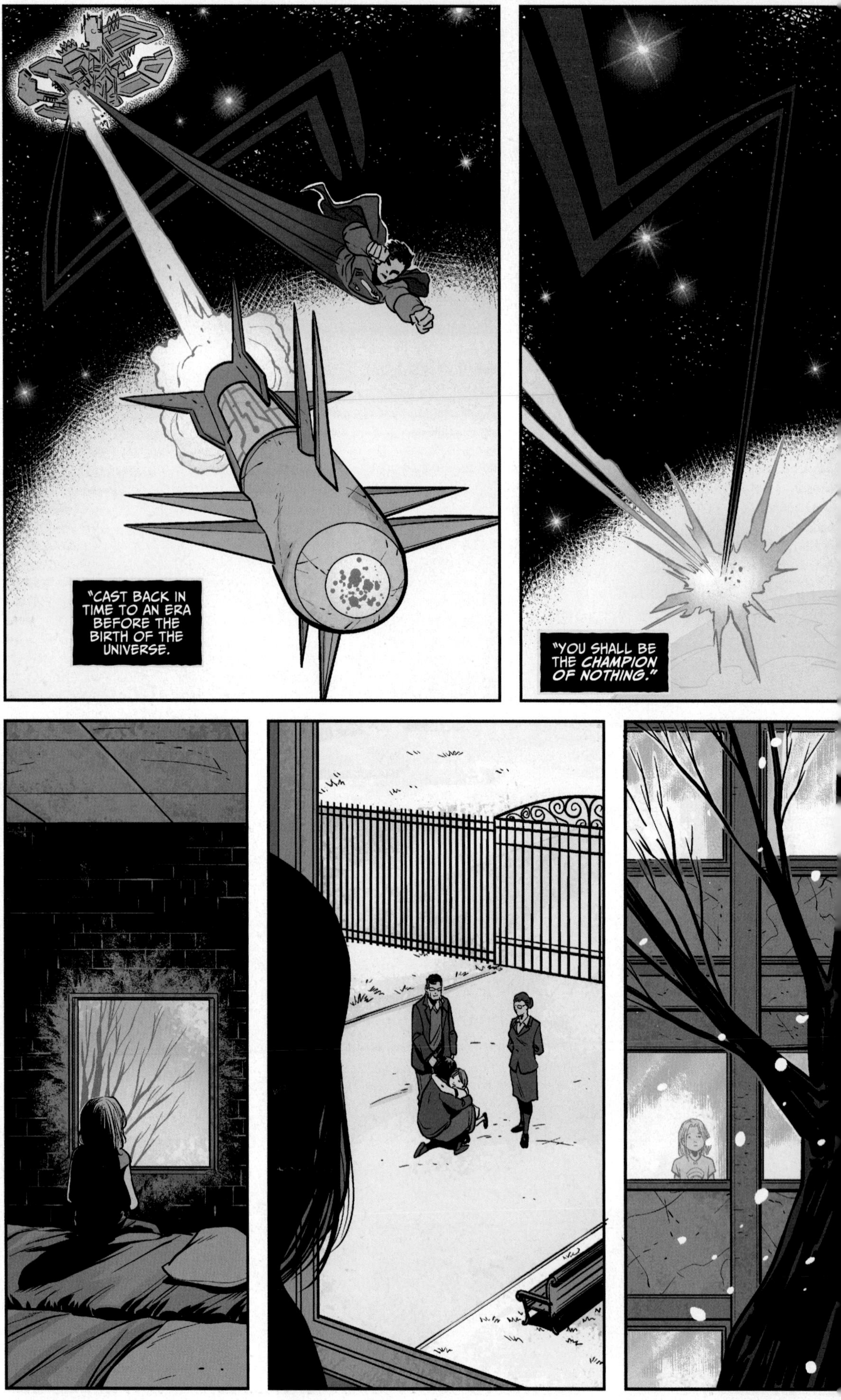
"CAST BACK IN TIME TO AN ERA BEFORE THE BIRTH OF THE UNIVERSE.
"YOU SHALL BE THE CHAMPION OF NOTHING."

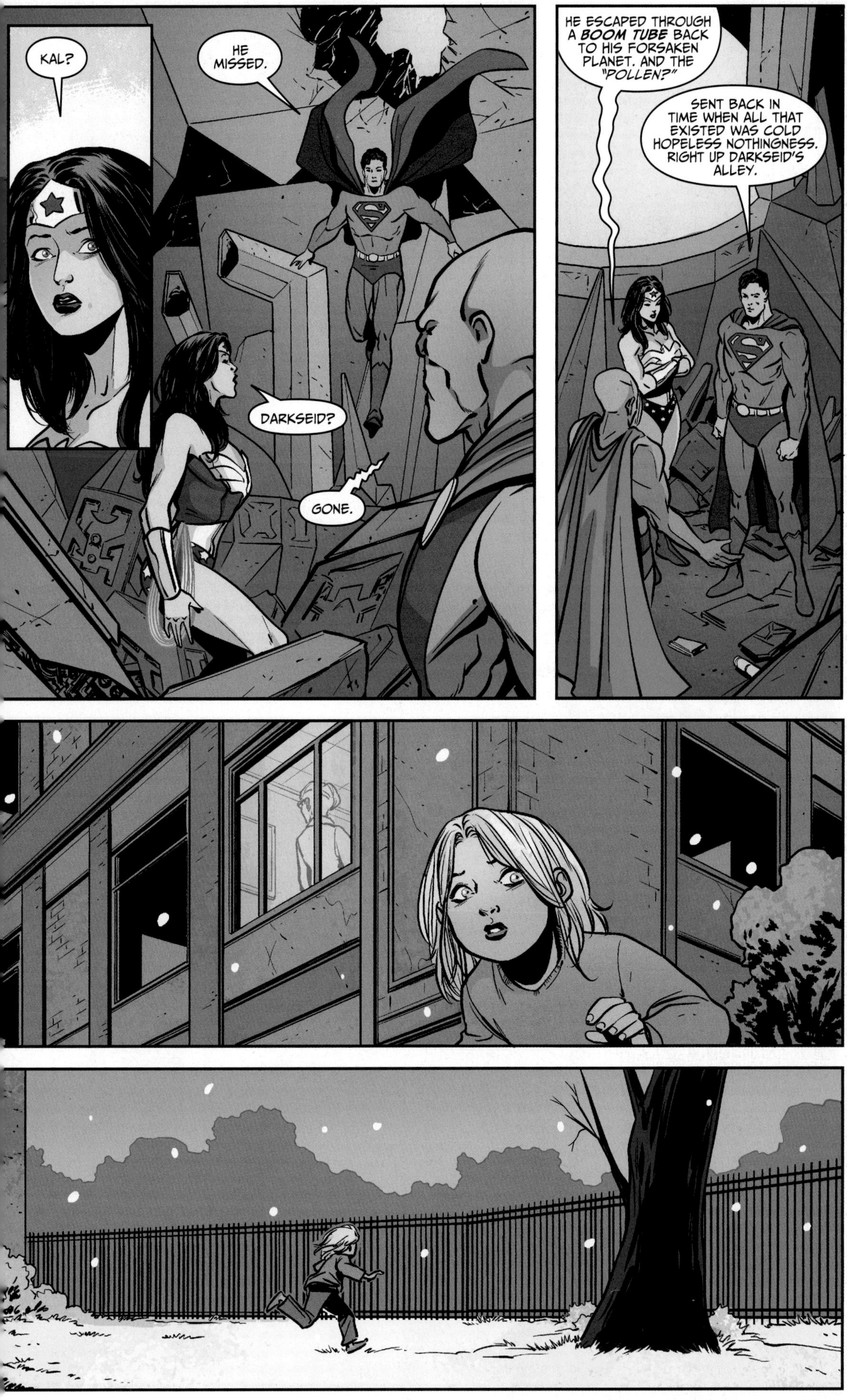
KAL?
HE MISSED.
DARKSEID?
GONE.
HE ESCAPED THROUGH A BOOM TUBE BACK TO HIS FORSAKEN PLANET. AND THE "POLLEN?"
SENT BACK IN TIME WHEN ALL THAT EXISTED WAS COLD HOPELESS NOTHINGNESS. RIGHT UP DARKSEID'S ALLEY.

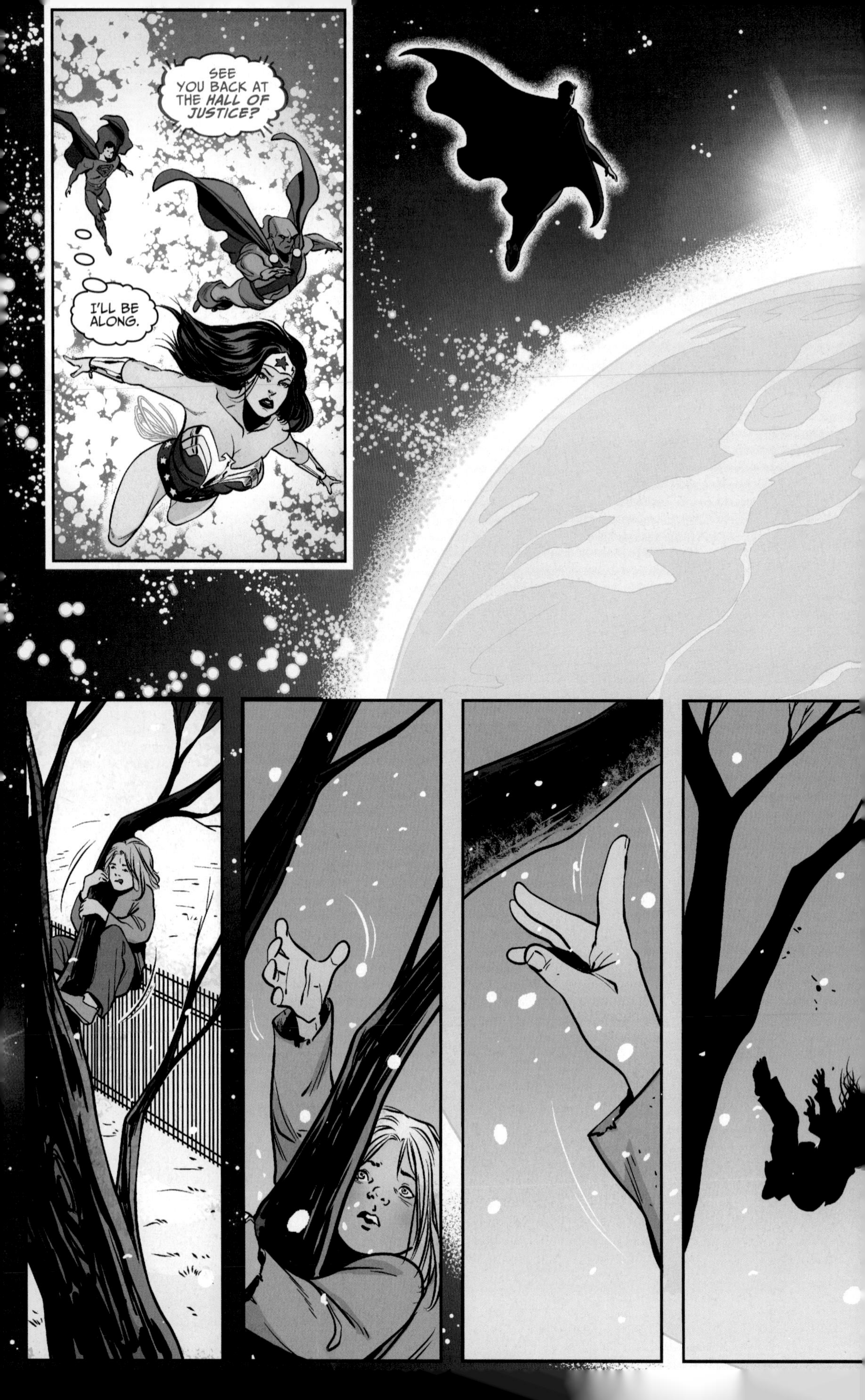
SEE YOU BACK AT THE HALL OF JUSTICE?
I'LL BE ALONG.

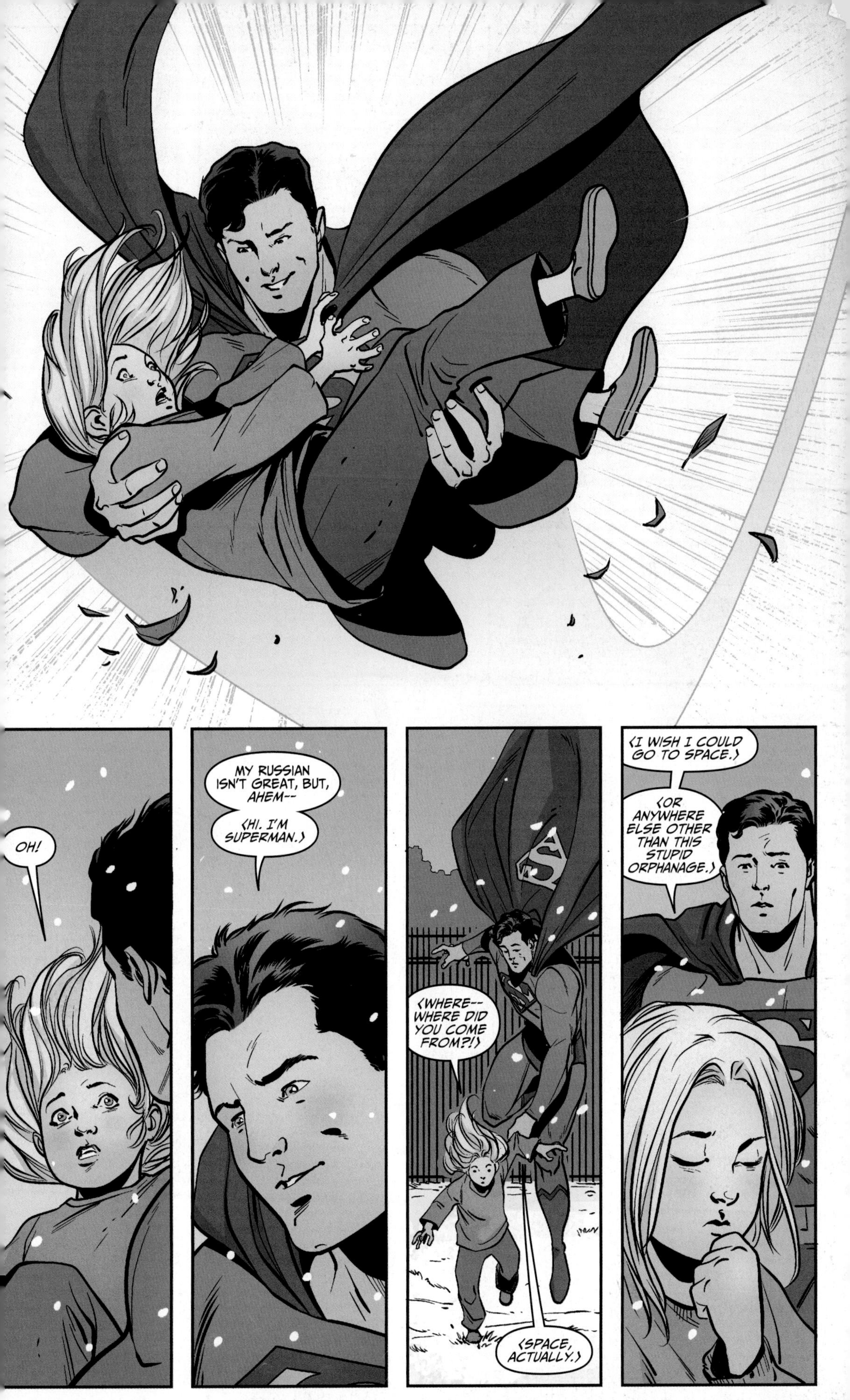
OH!
MY RUSSIAN ISN'T GREAT, BUT, AHEM--
‹HI. I'M SUPERMAN.›
‹WHERE-- WHERE DID YOU COME FROM?!›
‹SPACE, ACTUALLY.›
‹I WISH I COULD GO TO SPACE.›
‹OR ANYWHERE ELSE OTHER THAN THIS STUPID ORPHANAGE.›

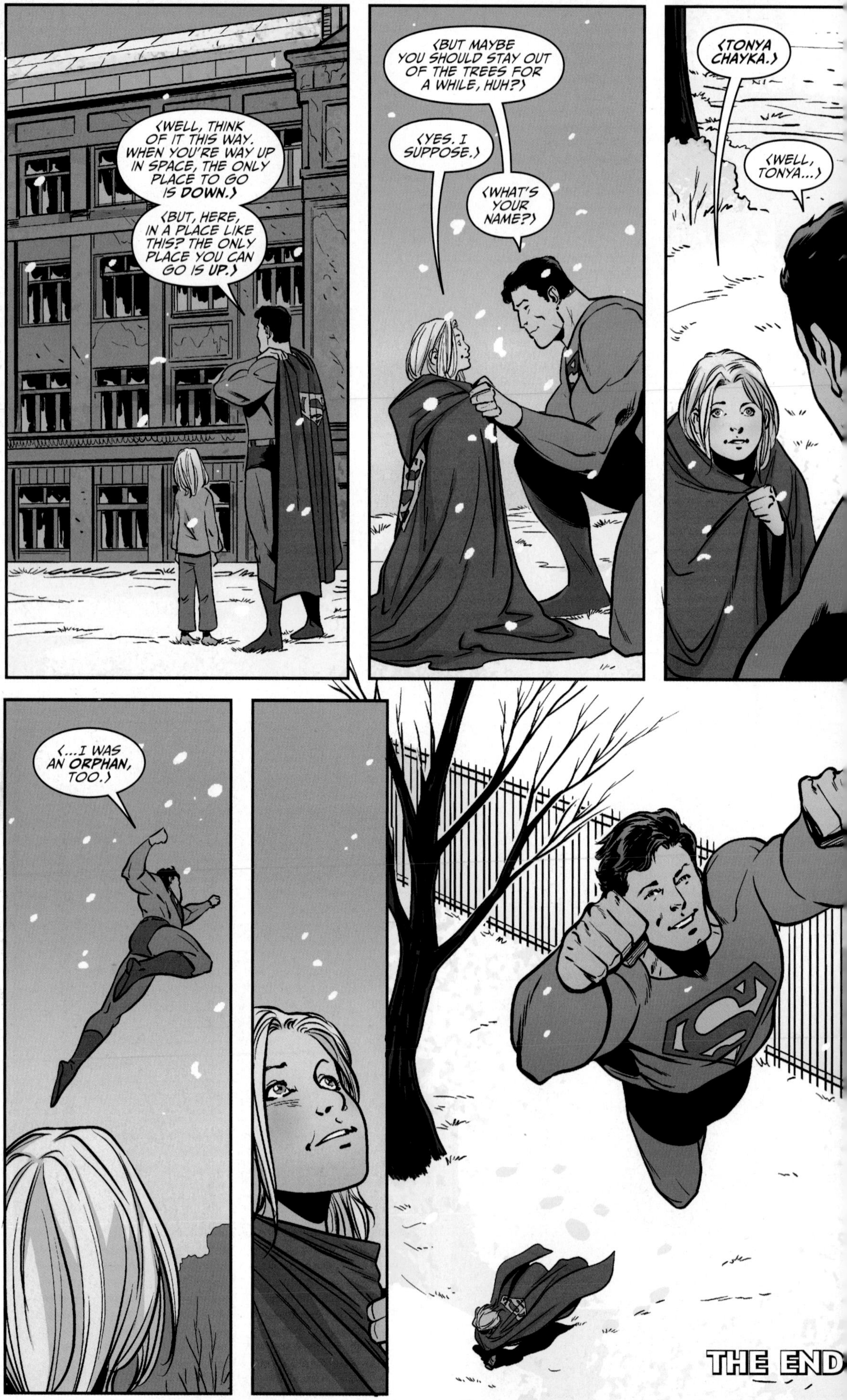
‹WELL, THINK OF IT THIS WAY. WHEN YOU'RE WAY UP IN SPACE, THE ONLY PLACE TO GO IS **DOWN**.›
‹BUT, HERE, IN A PLACE LIKE THIS? THE ONLY PLACE YOU CAN GO IS **UP**.›
‹BUT MAYBE YOU SHOULD STAY OUT OF THE TREES FOR A WHILE, HUH?›
‹YES. I SUPPOSE.›
‹WHAT'S YOUR NAME?›
‹TONYA CHAYKA.›
‹WELL, TONYA...›
‹...I WAS AN **ORPHAN**, TOO.›
THE END

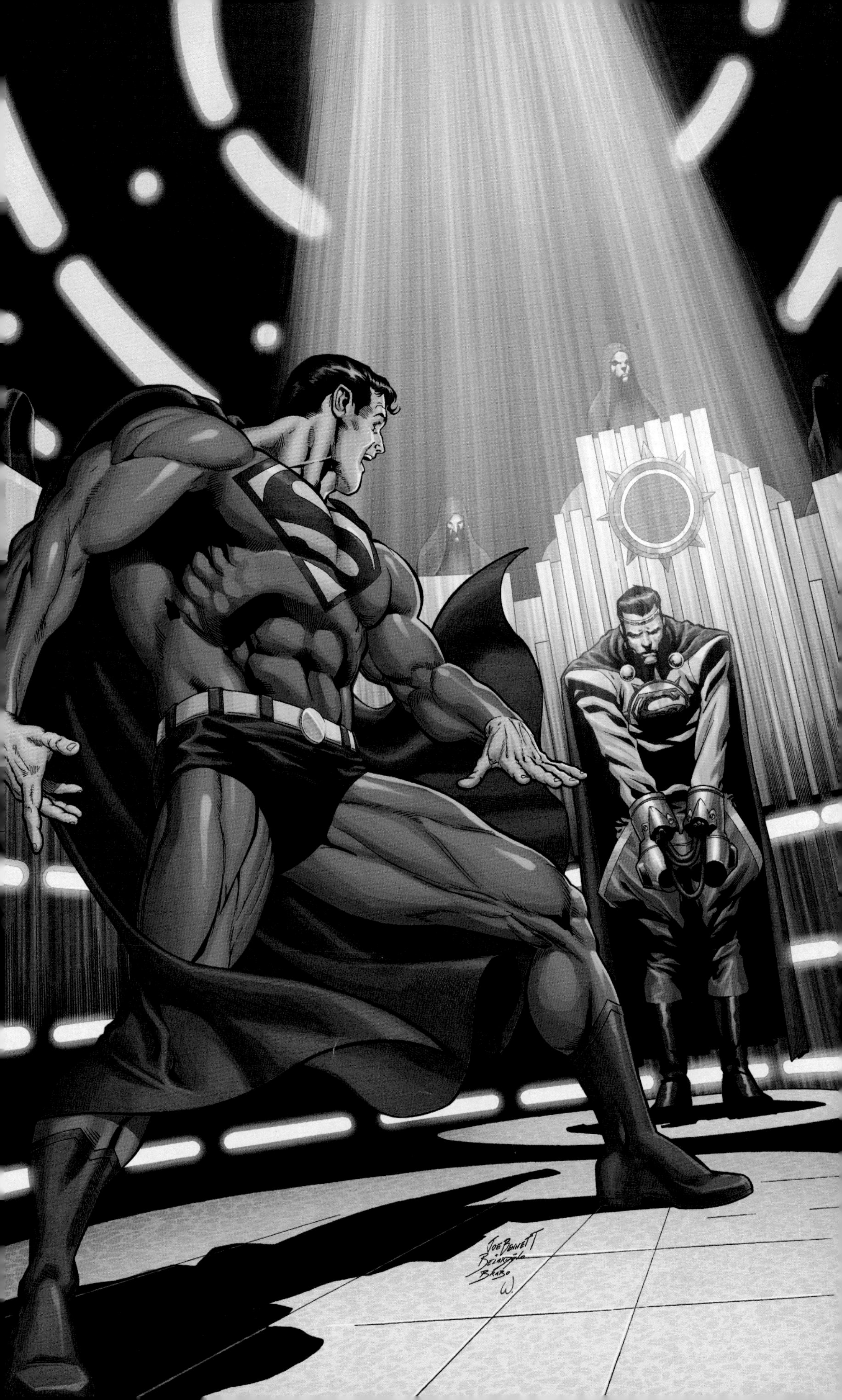

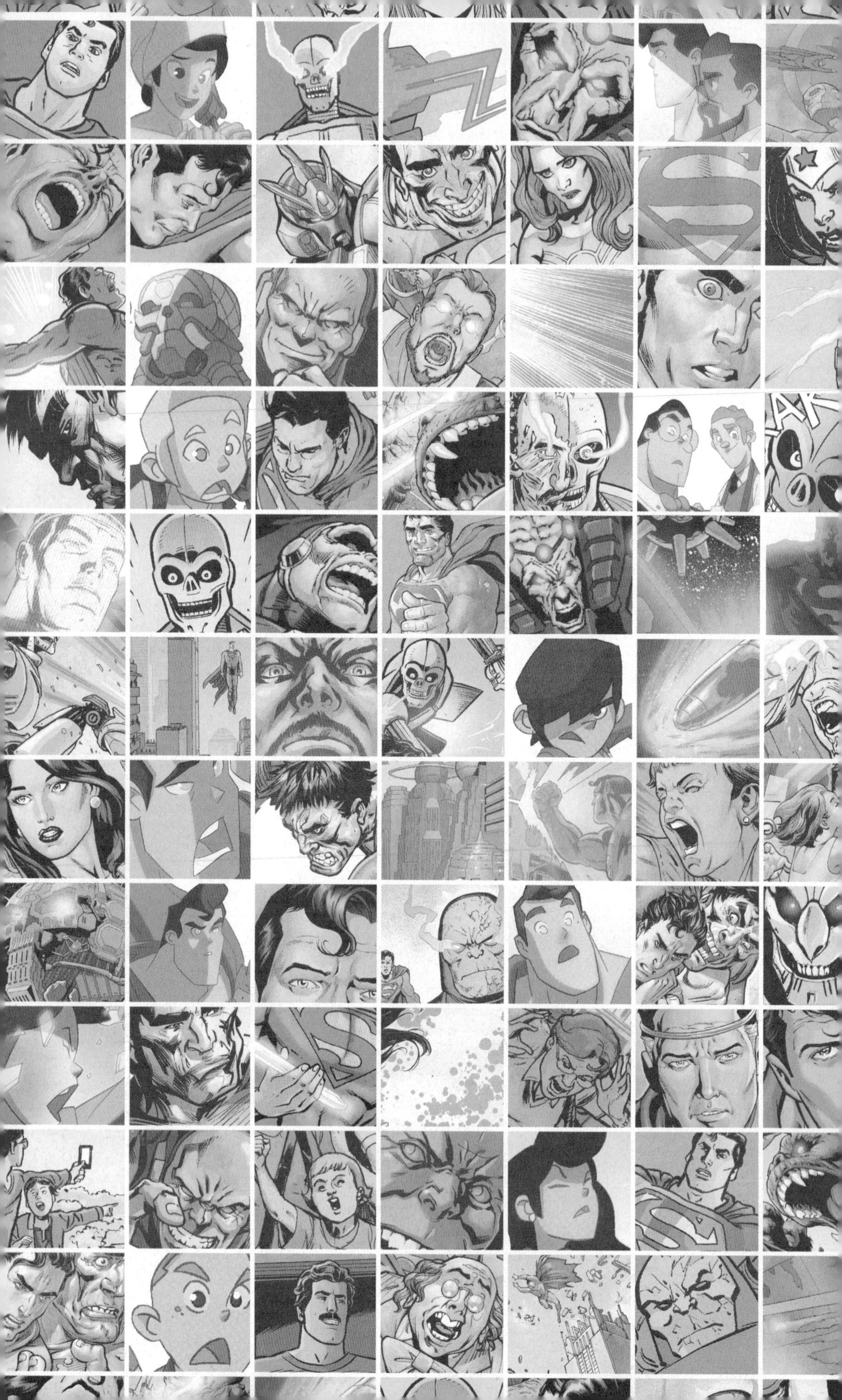

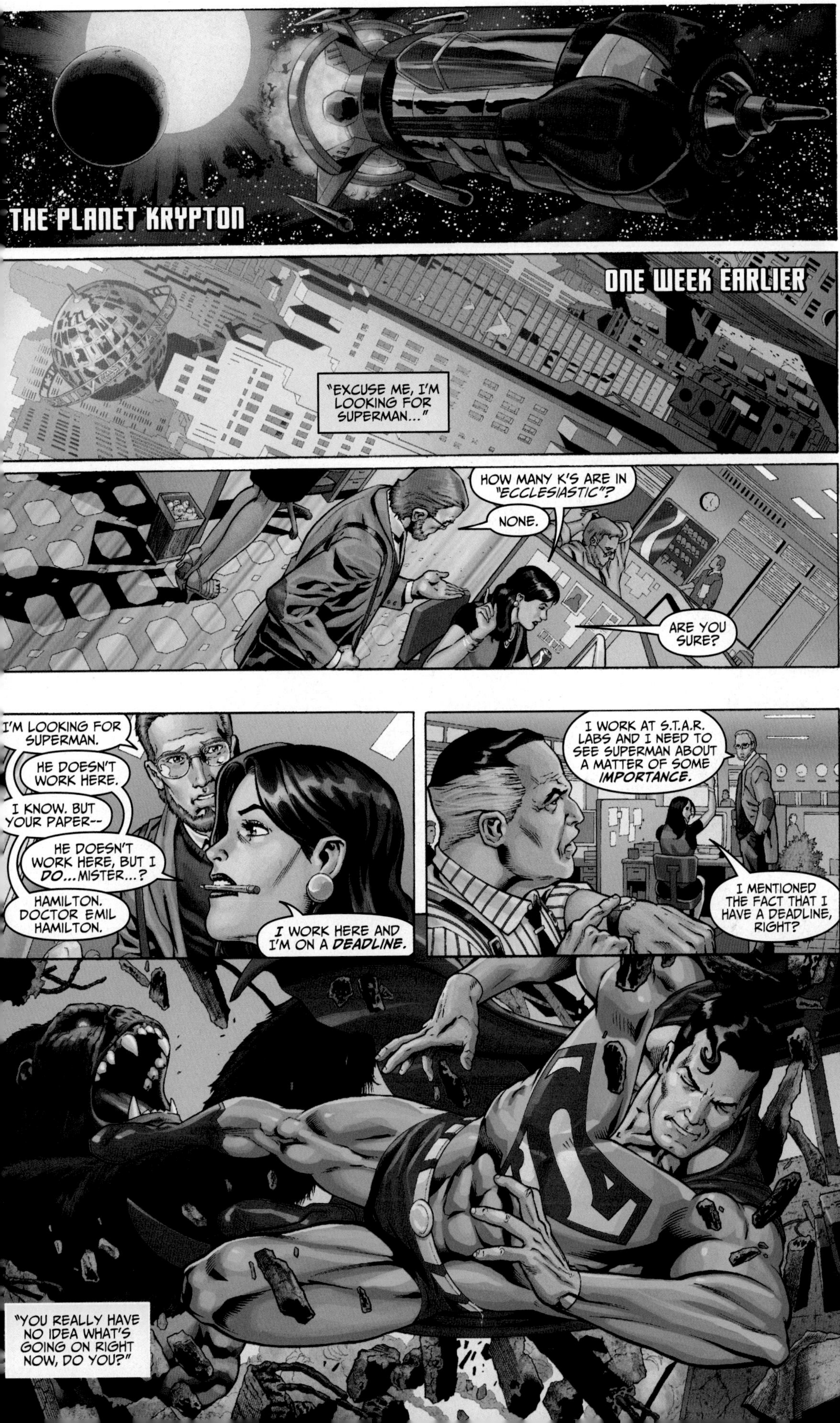

THE PLANET KRYPTON
ONE WEEK EARLIER
"EXCUSE ME, I'M LOOKING FOR SUPERMAN..."
HOW MANY K'S ARE IN "ECCLESIASTIC"?
NONE.
ARE YOU SURE?
I'M LOOKING FOR SUPERMAN.
HE DOESN'T WORK HERE.
I KNOW. BUT YOUR PAPER--
HE DOESN'T WORK HERE, BUT I DO... MISTER...?
HAMILTON. DOCTOR EMIL HAMILTON.
I WORK HERE AND I'M ON A DEADLINE.
I WORK AT S.T.A.R. LABS AND I NEED TO SEE SUPERMAN ABOUT A MATTER OF SOME IMPORTANCE.
I MENTIONED THE FACT THAT I HAVE A DEADLINE, RIGHT?
"YOU REALLY HAVE NO IDEA WHAT'S GOING ON RIGHT NOW, DO YOU?"

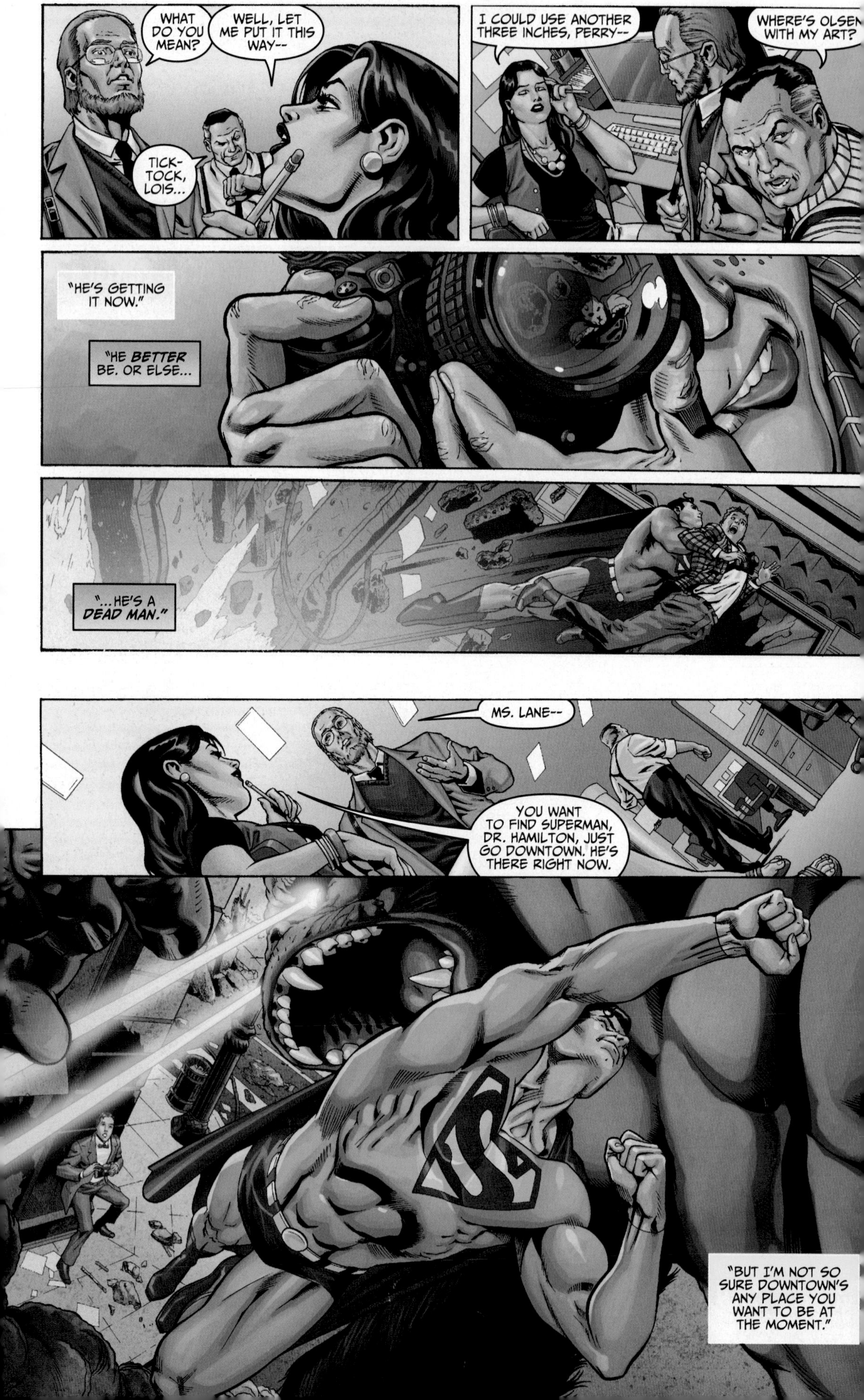
WHAT DO YOU MEAN?
WELL, LET ME PUT IT THIS WAY--
TICK-TOCK, LOIS...
I COULD USE ANOTHER THREE INCHES, PERRY--
WHERE'S OLSEN WITH MY ART?
"HE'S GETTING IT NOW."
"HE BETTER BE. OR ELSE...
"...HE'S A DEAD MAN."
MS. LANE--
YOU WANT TO FIND SUPERMAN, DR. HAMILTON, JUST GO DOWNTOWN. HE'S THERE RIGHT NOW.
"BUT I'M NOT SO SURE DOWNTOWN'S ANY PLACE YOU WANT TO BE AT THE MOMENT."

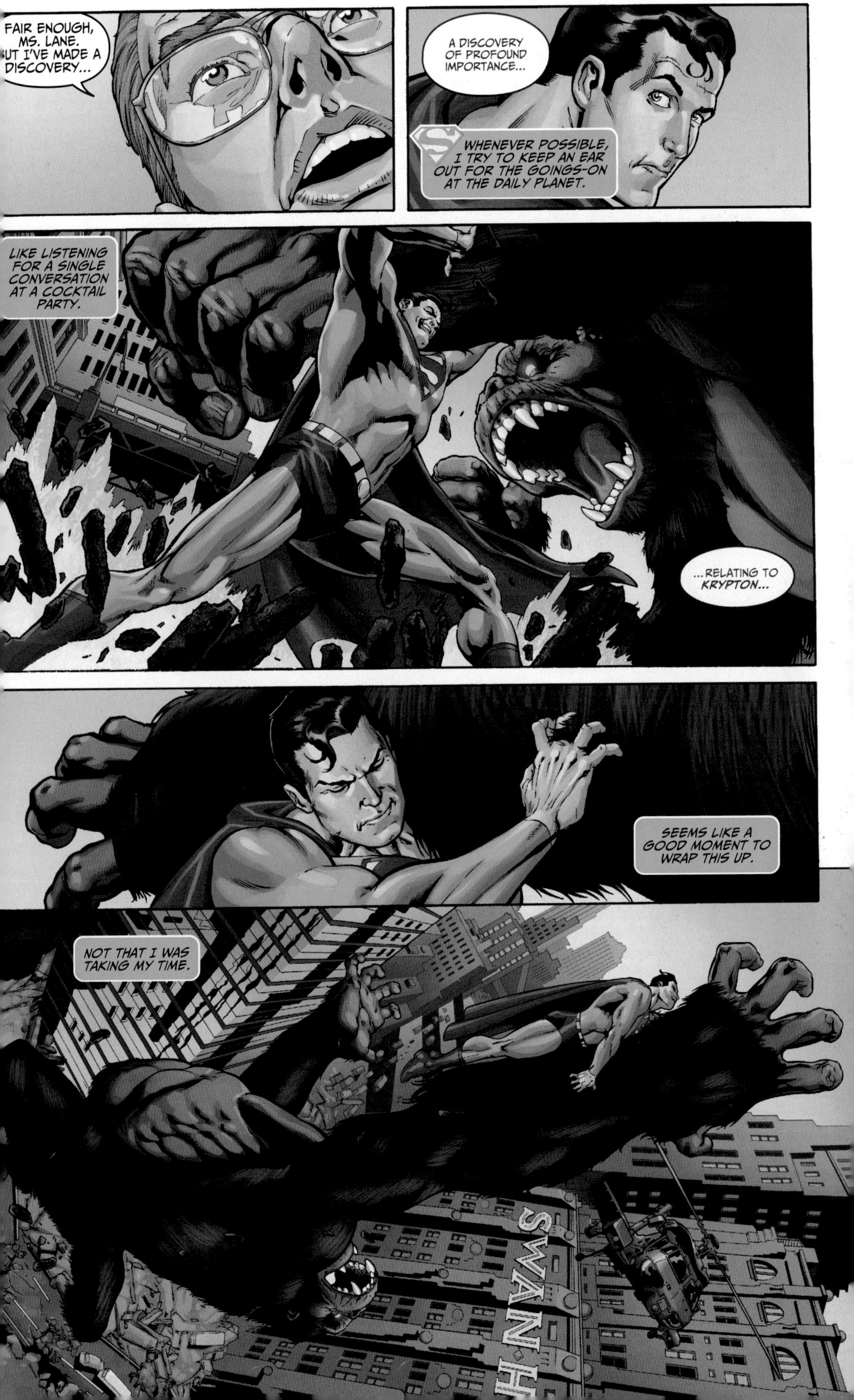
FAIR ENOUGH, MS. LANE. BUT I'VE MADE A DISCOVERY...
A DISCOVERY OF PROFOUND IMPORTANCE...
WHENEVER POSSIBLE, I TRY TO KEEP AN EAR OUT FOR THE GOINGS-ON AT THE DAILY PLANET.
LIKE LISTENING FOR A SINGLE CONVERSATION AT A COCKTAIL PARTY.
...RELATING TO KRYPTON...
SEEMS LIKE A GOOD MOMENT TO WRAP THIS UP.
NOT THAT I WAS TAKING MY TIME.
SWAN

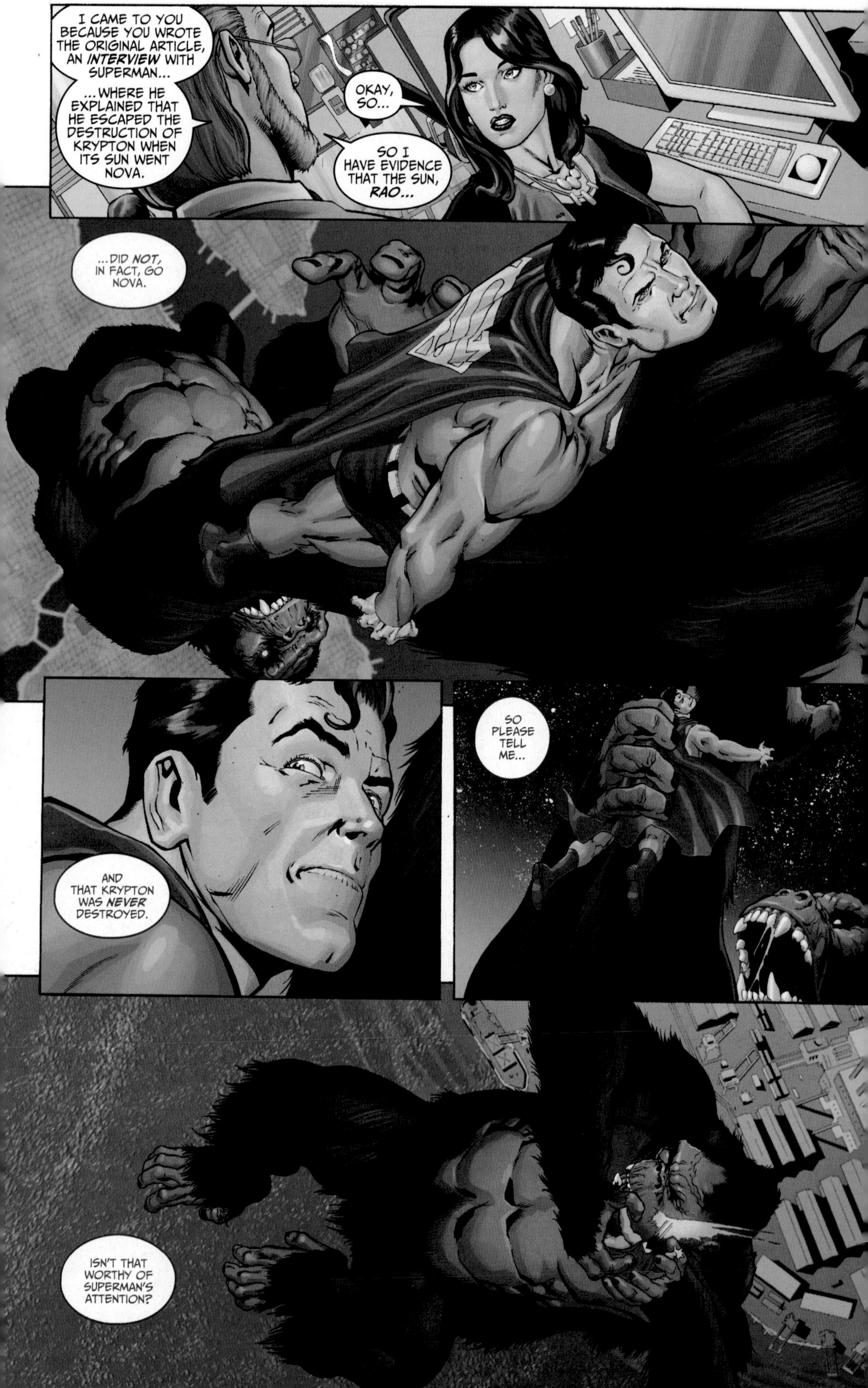

I CAME TO YOU BECAUSE YOU WROTE THE ORIGINAL ARTICLE, AN *INTERVIEW* WITH SUPERMAN...
...WHERE HE EXPLAINED THAT HE ESCAPED THE DESTRUCTION OF KRYPTON WHEN ITS SUN WENT NOVA.
OKAY, SO...
SO I HAVE EVIDENCE THAT THE SUN, *RAO*...
...DID *NOT*, IN FACT, GO NOVA.
AND THAT KRYPTON WAS *NEVER* DESTROYED.
SO PLEASE TELL ME...
ISN'T THAT WORTHY OF SUPERMAN'S ATTENTION?

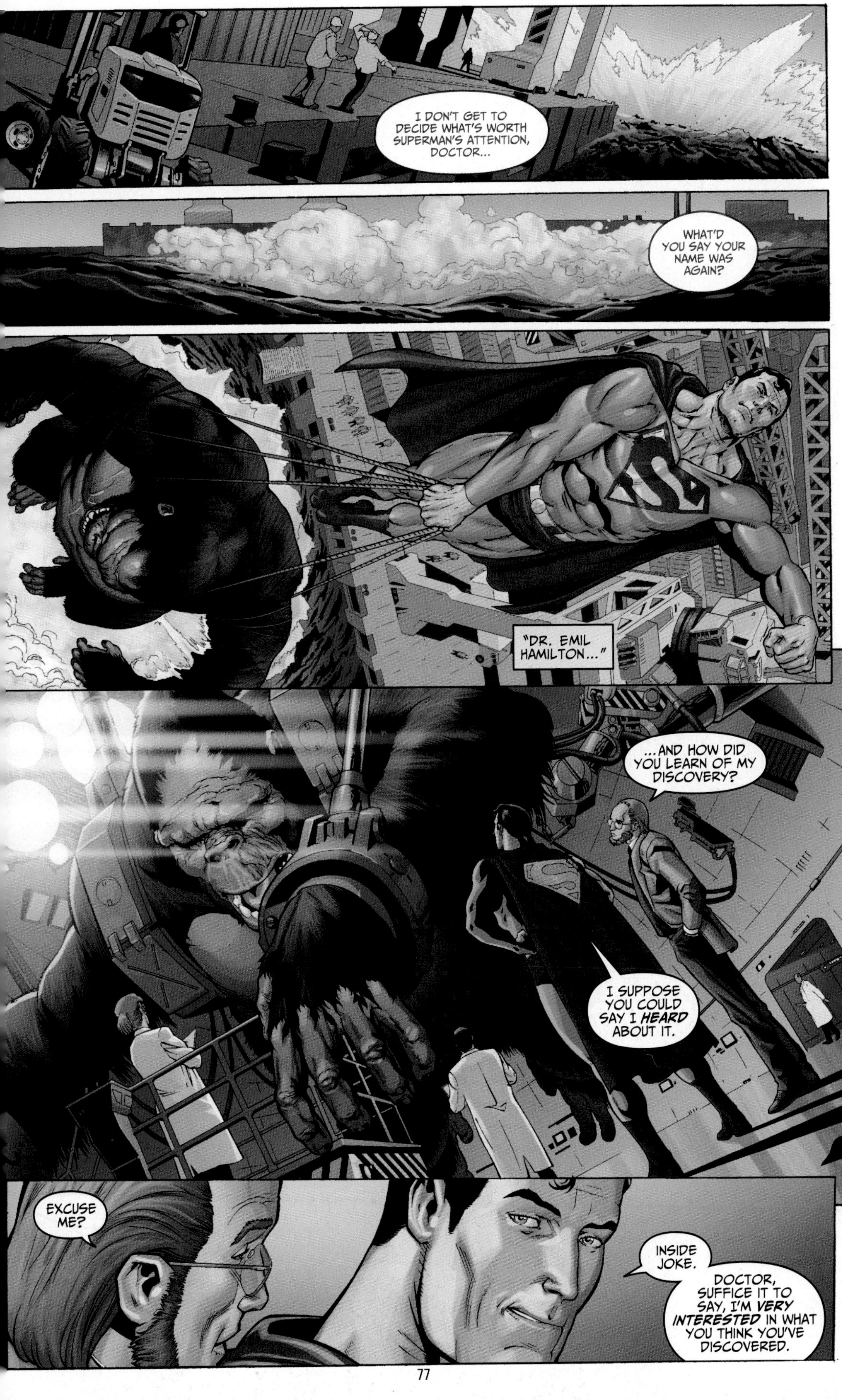
I DON'T GET TO DECIDE WHAT'S WORTH SUPERMAN'S ATTENTION, DOCTOR...
WHAT'D YOU SAY YOUR NAME WAS AGAIN?
"DR. EMIL HAMILTON..."
...AND HOW DID YOU LEARN OF MY DISCOVERY?
I SUPPOSE YOU COULD SAY I HEARD ABOUT IT.
EXCUSE ME?
INSIDE JOKE.
DOCTOR, SUFFICE IT TO SAY, I'M VERY INTERESTED IN WHAT YOU THINK YOU'VE DISCOVERED.

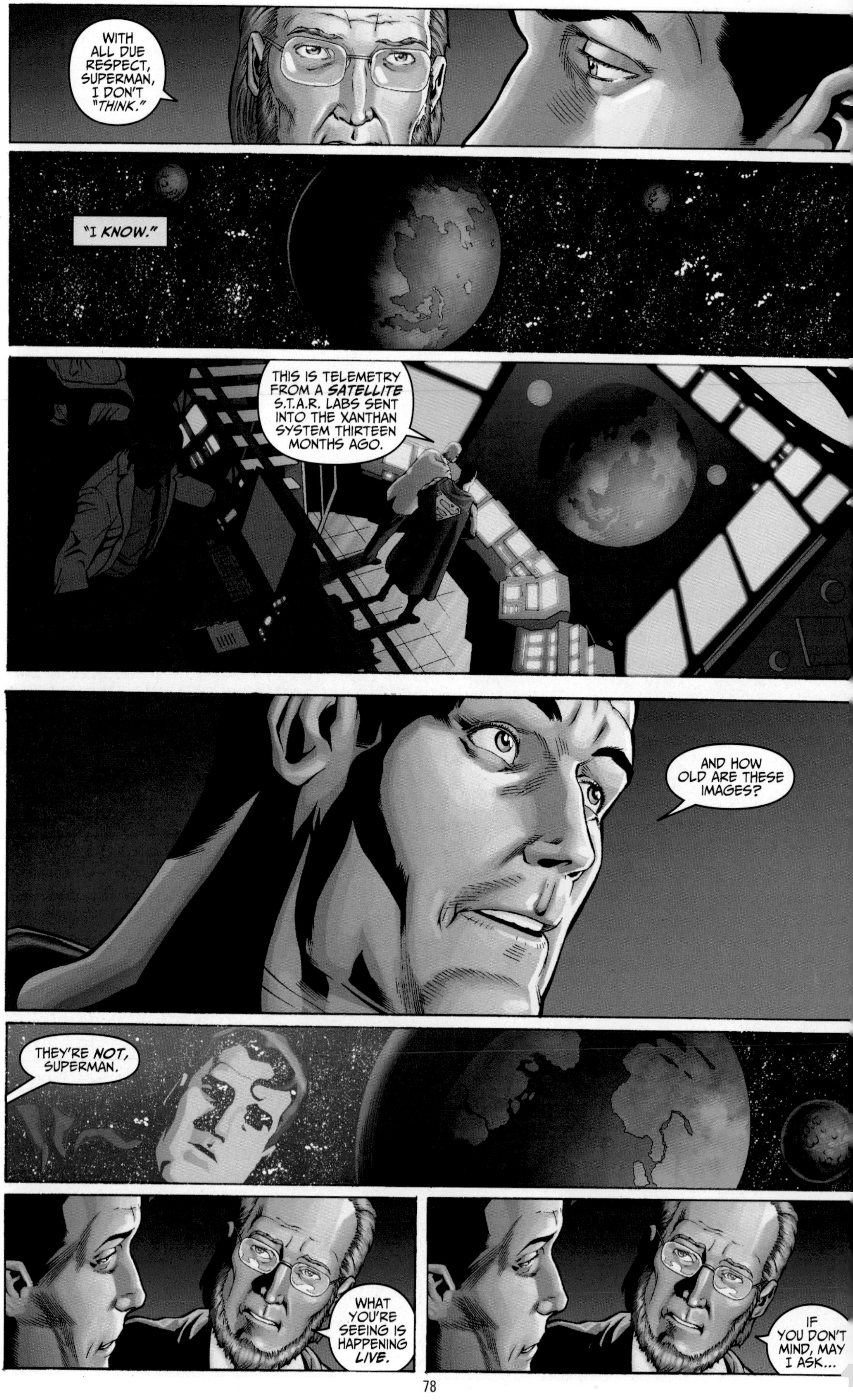
WITH ALL DUE RESPECT, SUPERMAN, I DON'T "THINK."
"I KNOW."
THIS IS TELEMETRY FROM A SATELLITE S.T.A.R. LABS SENT INTO THE XANTHAN SYSTEM THIRTEEN MONTHS AGO.
AND HOW OLD ARE THESE IMAGES?
THEY'RE NOT, SUPERMAN.
WHAT YOU'RE SEEING IS HAPPENING LIVE.
IF YOU DON'T MIND, MAY I ASK...

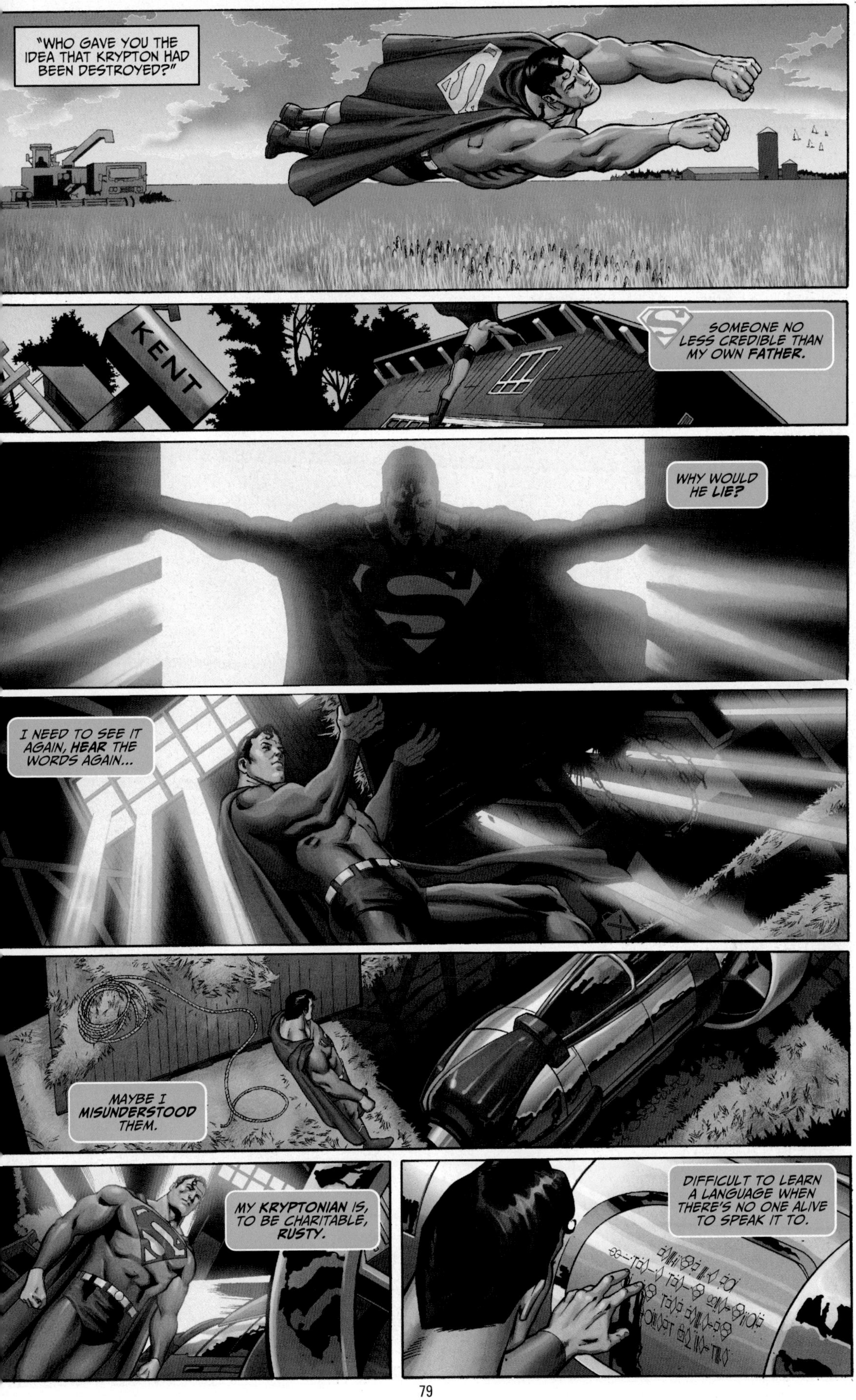
"WHO GAVE YOU THE IDEA THAT KRYPTON HAD BEEN DESTROYED?"
KENT
SOMEONE NO LESS CREDIBLE THAN MY OWN FATHER.
WHY WOULD HE LIE?
I NEED TO SEE IT AGAIN, HEAR THE WORDS AGAIN...
MAYBE I MISUNDERSTOOD THEM.
MY KRYPTONIAN IS, TO BE CHARITABLE, RUSTY.
DIFFICULT TO LEARN A LANGUAGE WHEN THERE'S NO ONE ALIVE TO SPEAK IT TO.

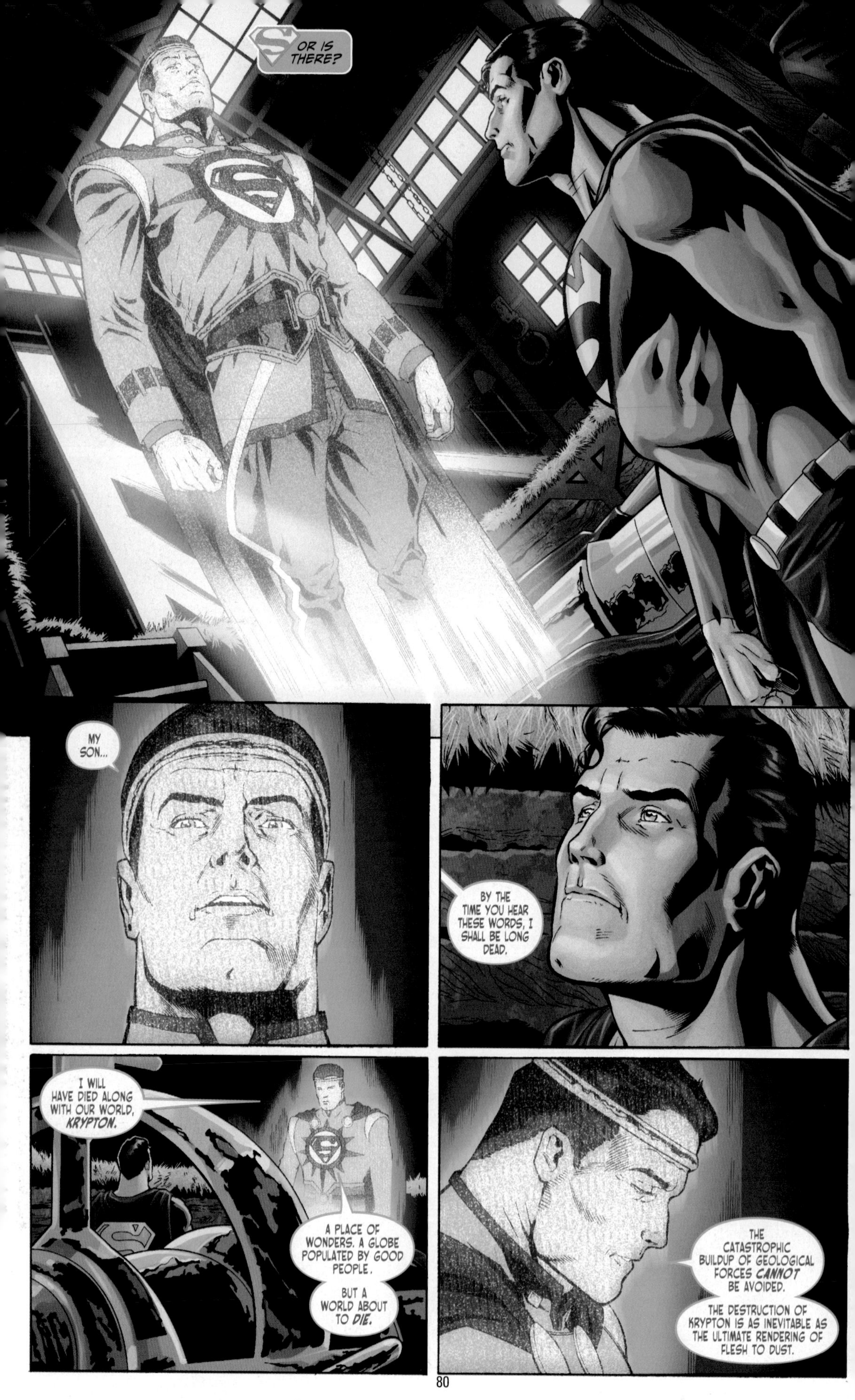
OR IS THERE?
MY SON...
BY THE TIME YOU HEAR THESE WORDS, I SHALL BE LONG DEAD.
I WILL HAVE DIED ALONG WITH OUR WORLD, KRYPTON.
A PLACE OF WONDERS. A GLOBE POPULATED BY GOOD PEOPLE.
BUT A WORLD ABOUT TO DIE.
THE CATASTROPHIC BUILDUP OF GEOLOGICAL FORCES CANNOT BE AVOIDED.
THE DESTRUCTION OF KRYPTON IS AS INEVITABLE AS THE ULTIMATE RENDERING OF FLESH TO DUST.

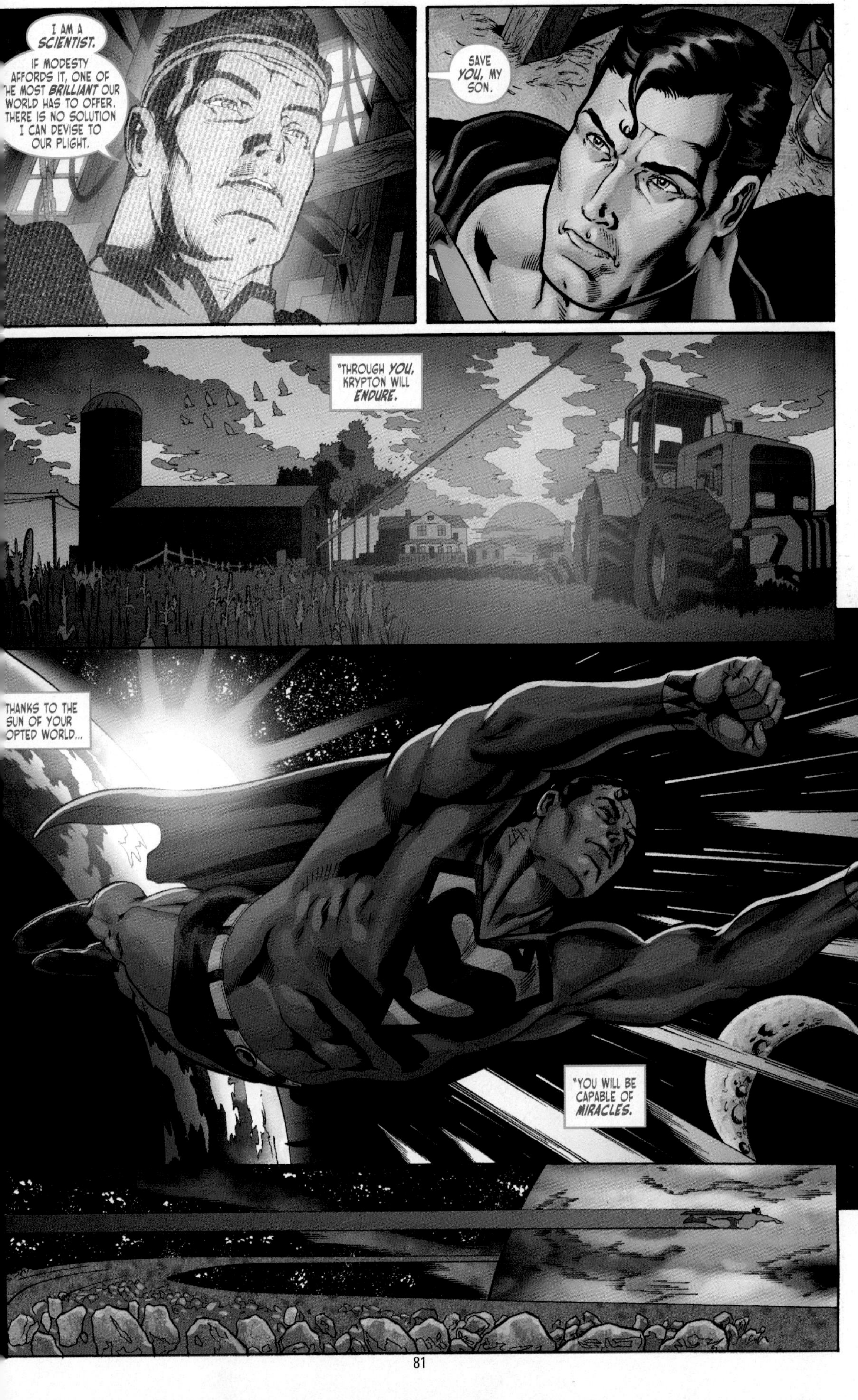
I AM A SCIENTIST.
IF MODESTY AFFORDS IT, ONE OF HE MOST BRILLIANT OUR WORLD HAS TO OFFER. THERE IS NO SOLUTION I CAN DEVISE TO OUR PLIGHT.
SAVE YOU, MY SON.
"THROUGH YOU, KRYPTON WILL ENDURE.
THANKS TO THE SUN OF YOUR OPTED WORLD...
"YOU WILL BE CAPABLE OF MIRACLES.

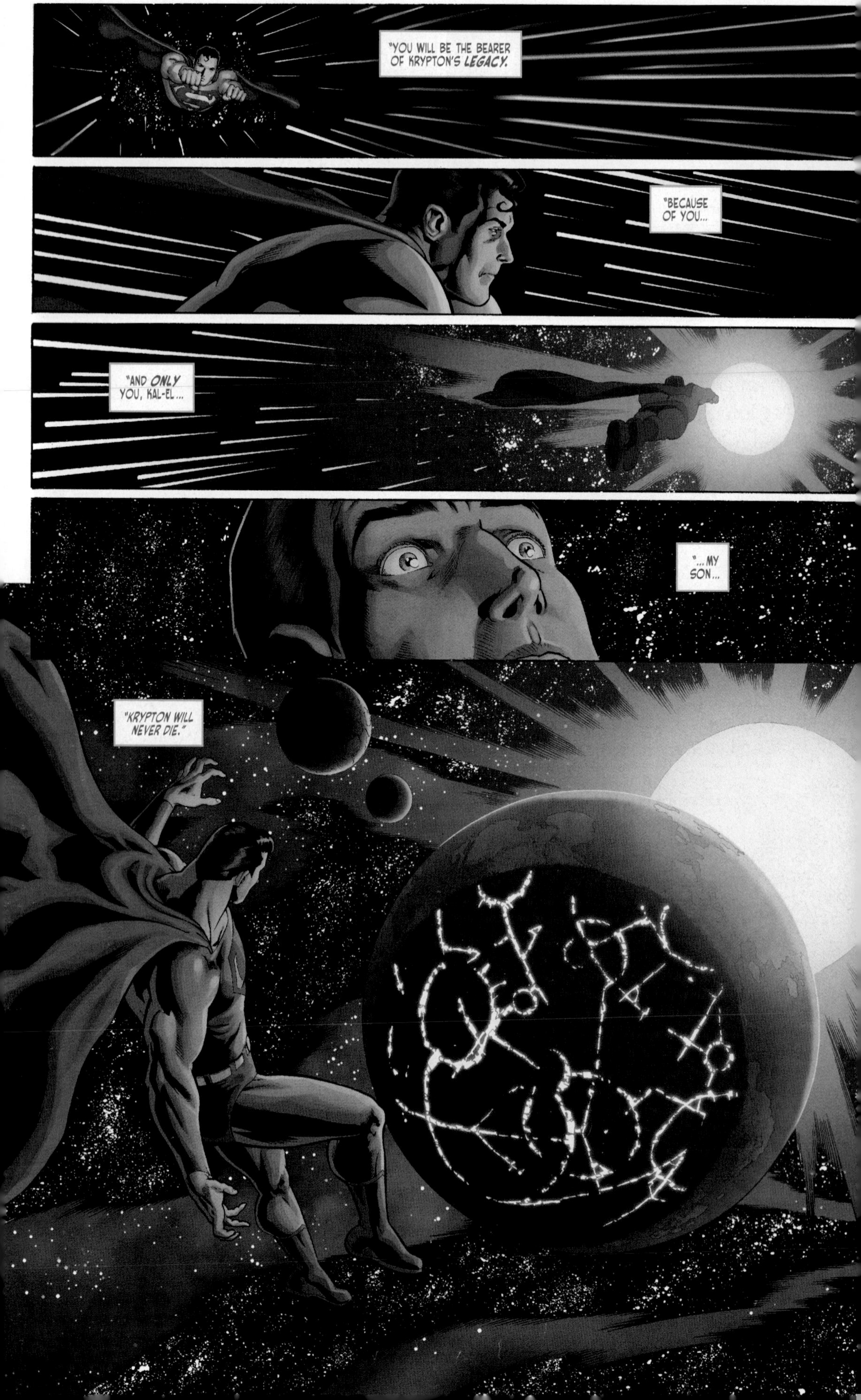
"YOU WILL BE THE BEARER OF KRYPTON'S LEGACY.
"BECAUSE OF YOU...
"AND ONLY YOU, KAL-EL...
"...MY SON...
"KRYPTON WILL NEVER DIE."

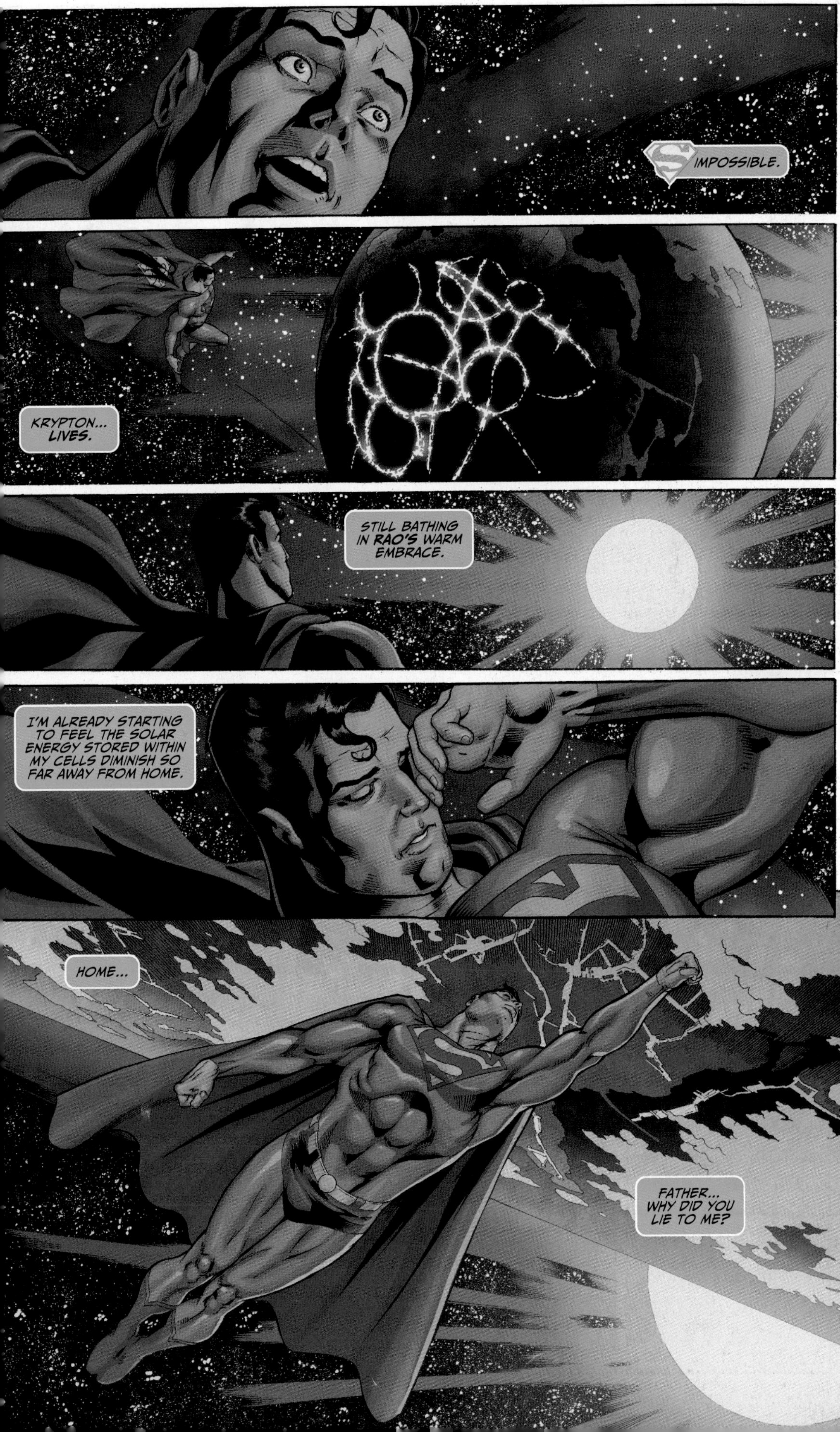

IMPOSSIBLE.
KRYPTON... LIVES.
STILL BATHING IN RAO'S WARM EMBRACE.
I'M ALREADY STARTING TO FEEL THE SOLAR ENERGY STORED WITHIN MY CELLS DIMINISH SO FAR AWAY FROM HOME.
HOME...
FATHER... WHY DID YOU LIE TO ME?

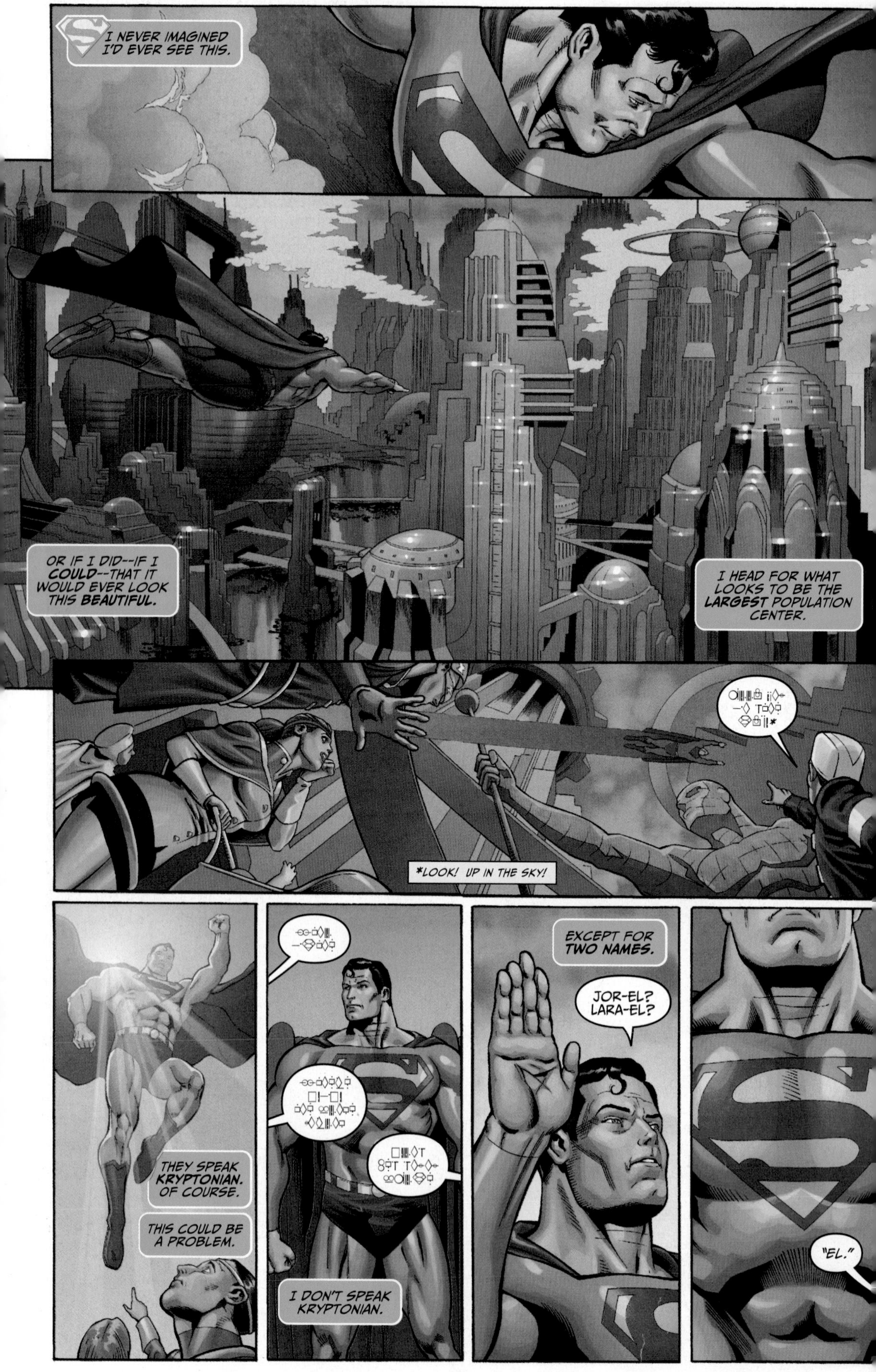
I NEVER IMAGINED I'D EVER SEE THIS.
OR IF I DID--IF I COULD--THAT IT WOULD EVER LOOK THIS BEAUTIFUL.
I HEAD FOR WHAT LOOKS TO BE THE LARGEST POPULATION CENTER.
*LOOK! UP IN THE SKY!
THEY SPEAK KRYPTONIAN. OF COURSE.
THIS COULD BE A PROBLEM.
I DON'T SPEAK KRYPTONIAN.
EXCEPT FOR TWO NAMES.
JOR-EL? LARA-EL?
"EL."

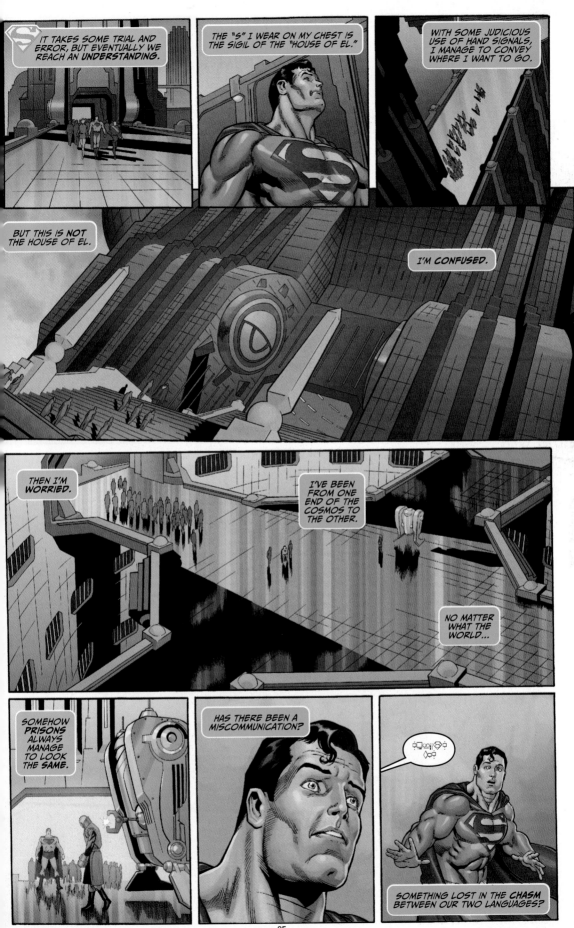

IT TAKES SOME TRIAL AND ERROR, BUT EVENTUALLY WE REACH AN UNDERSTANDING.

THE "S" I WEAR ON MY CHEST IS THE SIGIL OF THE "HOUSE OF EL."

WITH SOME JUDICIOUS USE OF HAND SIGNALS, I MANAGE TO CONVEY WHERE I WANT TO GO.

BUT THIS IS NOT THE HOUSE OF EL.

I'M CONFUSED.

THEN I'M WORRIED.

I'VE BEEN FROM ONE END OF THE COSMOS TO THE OTHER.

NO MATTER WHAT THE WORLD...

SOMEHOW PRISONS ALWAYS MANAGE TO LOOK THE SAME.

HAS THERE BEEN A MISCOMMUNICATION?

SOMETHING LOST IN THE CHASM BETWEEN OUR TWO LANGUAGES?

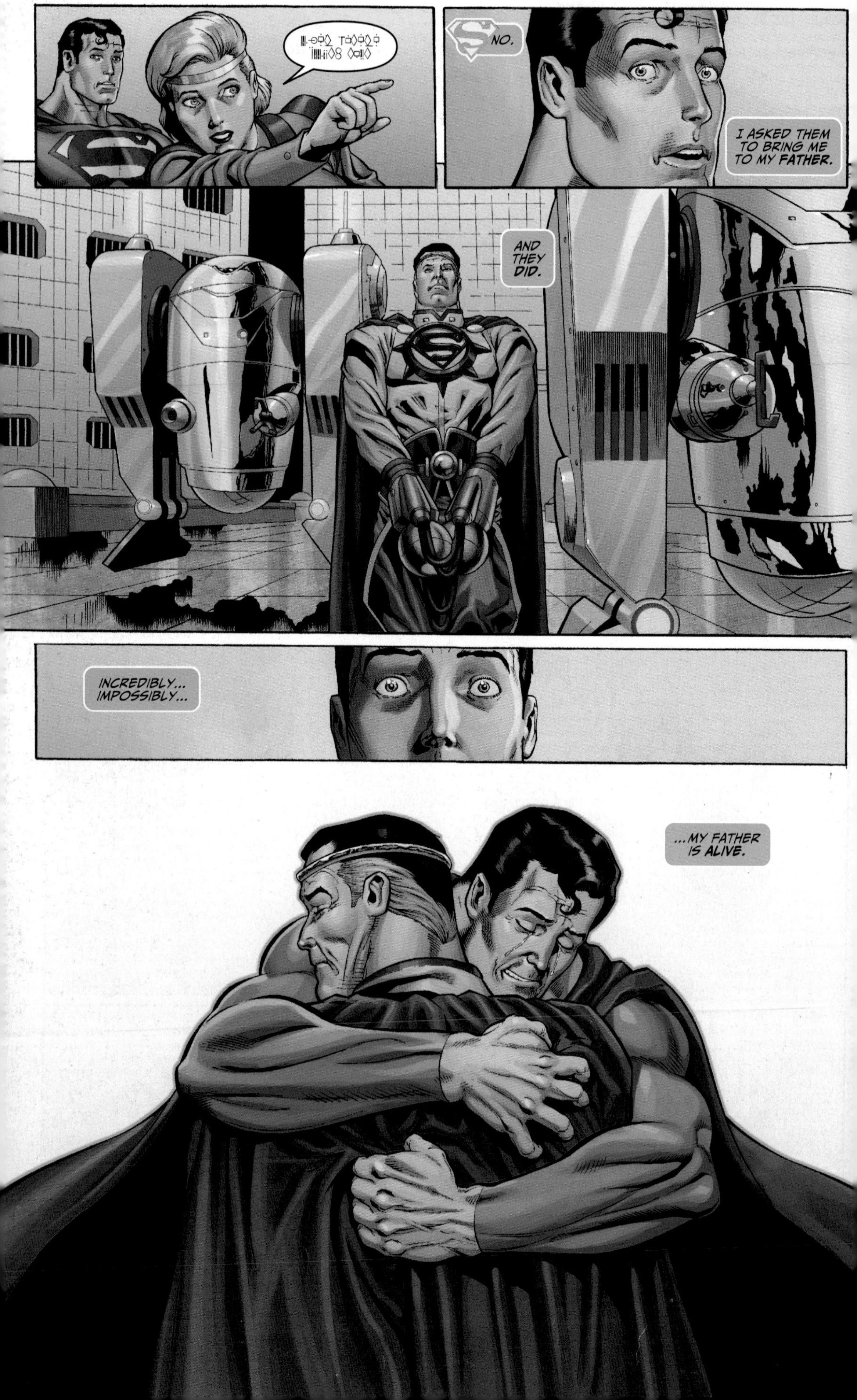
NO.
I ASKED THEM TO BRING ME TO MY FATHER.
AND THEY DID.
INCREDIBLY... IMPOSSIBLY...
...MY FATHER IS ALIVE.

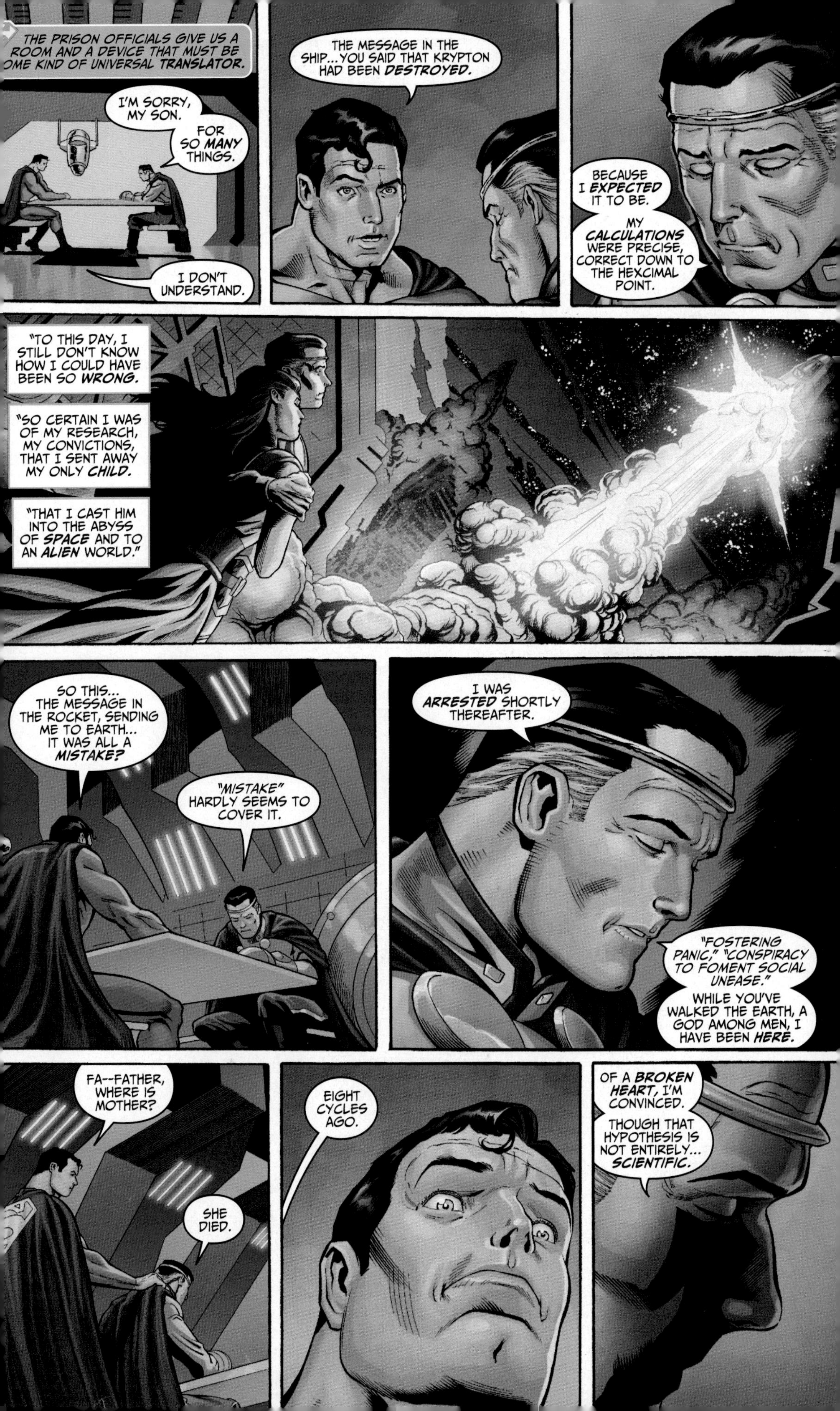

THE PRISON OFFICIALS GIVE US A ROOM AND A DEVICE THAT MUST BE OME KIND OF UNIVERSAL TRANSLATOR.
I'M SORRY, MY SON.
FOR SO MANY THINGS.
I DON'T UNDERSTAND.
THE MESSAGE IN THE SHIP...YOU SAID THAT KRYPTON HAD BEEN DESTROYED.
BECAUSE I EXPECTED IT TO BE.
MY CALCULATIONS WERE PRECISE, CORRECT DOWN TO THE HEXCIMAL POINT.
"TO THIS DAY, I STILL DON'T KNOW HOW I COULD HAVE BEEN SO WRONG.
"SO CERTAIN I WAS OF MY RESEARCH, MY CONVICTIONS, THAT I SENT AWAY MY ONLY CHILD.
"THAT I CAST HIM INTO THE ABYSS OF SPACE AND TO AN ALIEN WORLD."
SO THIS... THE MESSAGE IN THE ROCKET, SENDING ME TO EARTH... IT WAS ALL A MISTAKE?
"MISTAKE" HARDLY SEEMS TO COVER IT.
I WAS ARRESTED SHORTLY THEREAFTER.
"FOSTERING PANIC," "CONSPIRACY TO FOMENT SOCIAL UNEASE."
WHILE YOU'VE WALKED THE EARTH, A GOD AMONG MEN, I HAVE BEEN HERE.
FA--FATHER, WHERE IS MOTHER?
SHE DIED.
EIGHT CYCLES AGO.
OF A BROKEN HEART, I'M CONVINCED.
THOUGH THAT HYPOTHESIS IS NOT ENTIRELY... SCIENTIFIC.

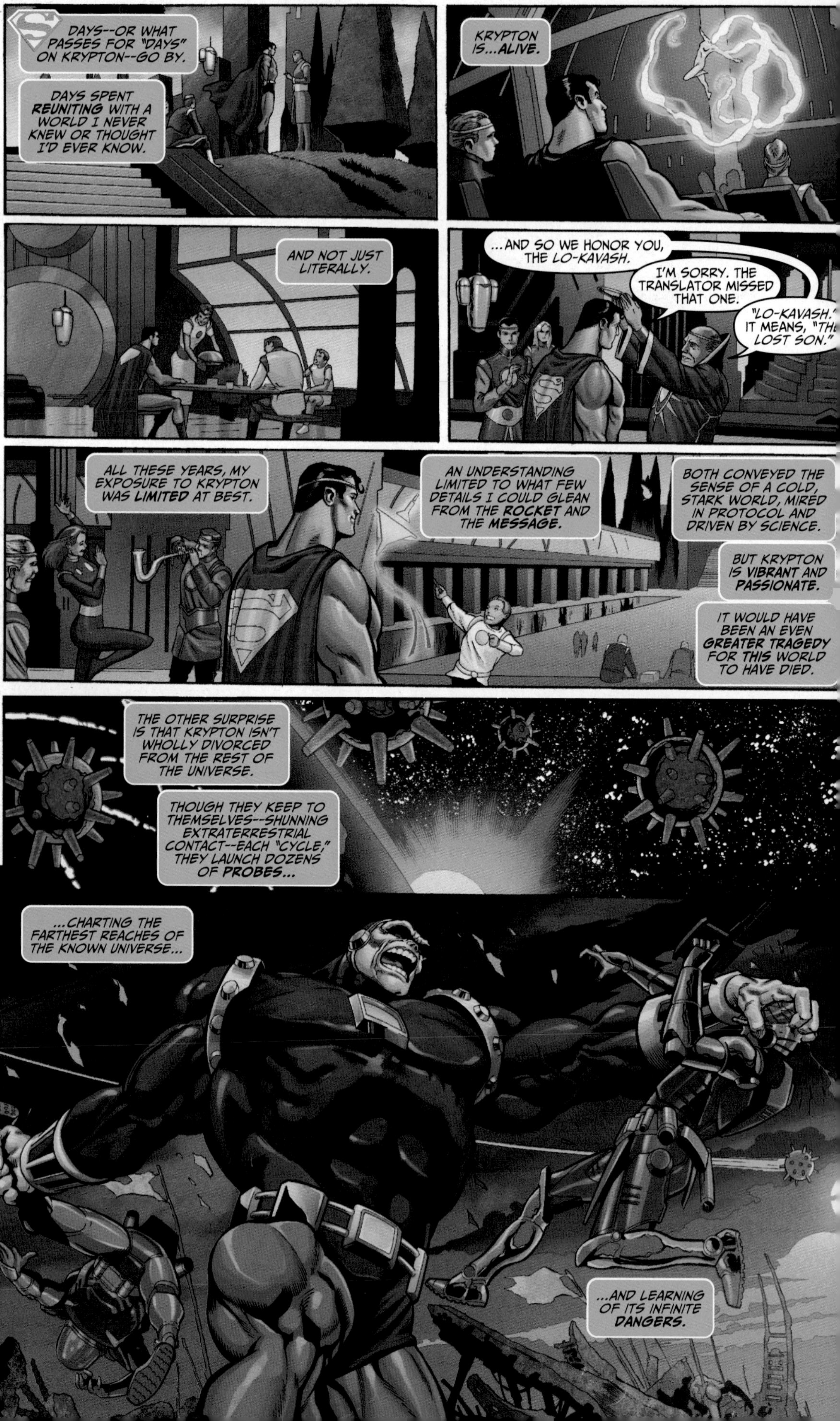
DAYS--OR WHAT PASSES FOR "DAYS" ON KRYPTON--GO BY.
DAYS SPENT REUNITING WITH A WORLD I NEVER KNEW OR THOUGHT I'D EVER KNOW.
KRYPTON IS...ALIVE.
AND NOT JUST LITERALLY.
...AND SO WE HONOR YOU, THE LO-KAVASH.
I'M SORRY. THE TRANSLATOR MISSED THAT ONE.
"LO-KAVASH." IT MEANS, "TH LOST SON."
ALL THESE YEARS, MY EXPOSURE TO KRYPTON WAS LIMITED AT BEST.
AN UNDERSTANDING LIMITED TO WHAT FEW DETAILS I COULD GLEAN FROM THE ROCKET AND THE MESSAGE.
BOTH CONVEYED THE SENSE OF A COLD, STARK WORLD, MIRED IN PROTOCOL AND DRIVEN BY SCIENCE.
BUT KRYPTON IS VIBRANT AND PASSIONATE.
IT WOULD HAVE BEEN AN EVEN GREATER TRAGEDY FOR THIS WORLD TO HAVE DIED.
THE OTHER SURPRISE IS THAT KRYPTON ISN'T WHOLLY DIVORCED FROM THE REST OF THE UNIVERSE.
THOUGH THEY KEEP TO THEMSELVES--SHUNNING EXTRATERRESTRIAL CONTACT--EACH "CYCLE," THEY LAUNCH DOZENS OF PROBES...
...CHARTING THE FARTHEST REACHES OF THE KNOWN UNIVERSE...
...AND LEARNING OF ITS INFINITE DANGERS.

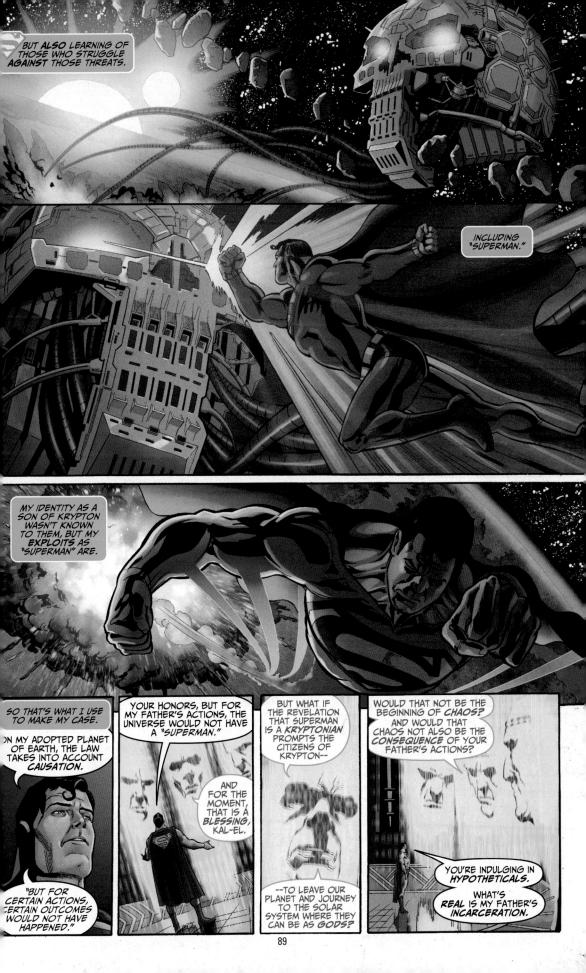

BUT **ALSO LEARNING OF** THOSE WHO STRUGGLE **AGAINST** THOSE THREATS.

INCLUDING "SUPERMAN."

MY IDENTITY AS A SON OF KRYPTON WASN'T KNOWN TO THEM, BUT MY **EXPLOITS** AS "SUPERMAN" ARE.

SO THAT'S WHAT I USE TO MAKE MY CASE.

ON MY ADOPTED PLANET OF EARTH, THE LAW TAKES INTO ACCOUNT **CAUSATION.**

"BUT FOR **CERTAIN ACTIONS, CERTAIN OUTCOMES** WOULD NOT HAVE HAPPENED."

YOUR HONORS, BUT FOR MY FATHER'S ACTIONS, THE UNIVERSE WOULD NOT HAVE A "SUPERMAN."

AND FOR THE MOMENT, THAT IS A **BLESSING,** KAL-EL.

BUT WHAT IF THE REVELATION THAT SUPERMAN IS A **KRYPTONIAN** PROMPTS THE CITIZENS OF KRYPTON--

--TO LEAVE OUR PLANET AND JOURNEY TO THE SOLAR SYSTEM WHERE THEY CAN BE AS **GODS?**

WOULD THAT NOT BE THE BEGINNING OF **CHAOS?** AND WOULD THAT CHAOS NOT ALSO BE THE **CONSEQUENCE OF YOUR** FATHER'S ACTIONS?

YOU'RE INDULGING IN **HYPOTHETICALS.**

WHAT'S **REAL** IS MY FATHER'S **INCARCERATION.**

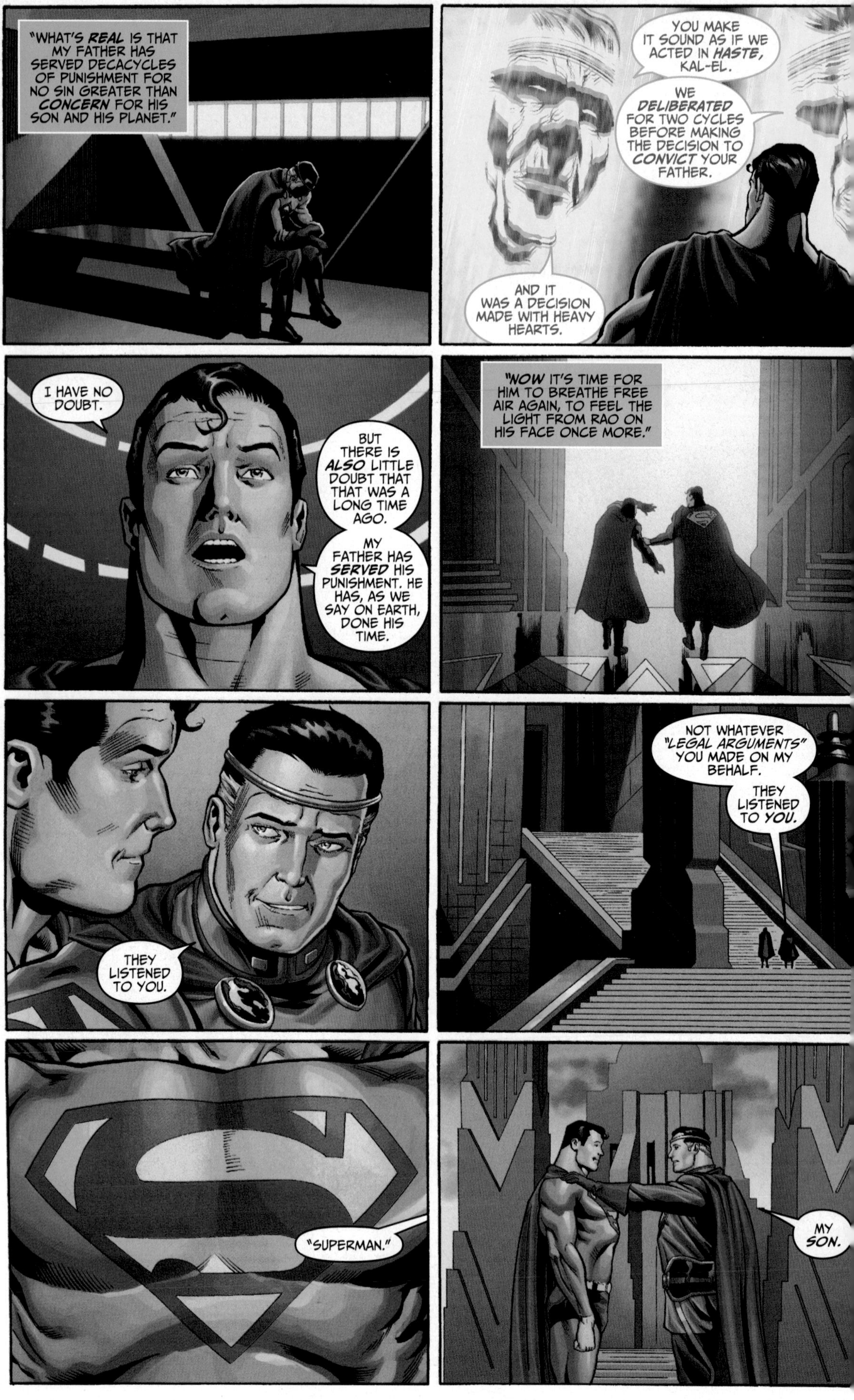
"WHAT'S REAL IS THAT MY FATHER HAS SERVED DECACYCLES OF PUNISHMENT FOR NO SIN GREATER THAN CONCERN FOR HIS SON AND HIS PLANET."
YOU MAKE IT SOUND AS IF WE ACTED IN HASTE, KAL-EL.
WE DELIBERATED FOR TWO CYCLES BEFORE MAKING THE DECISION TO CONVICT YOUR FATHER.
AND IT WAS A DECISION MADE WITH HEAVY HEARTS.
I HAVE NO DOUBT.
BUT THERE IS ALSO LITTLE DOUBT THAT THAT WAS A LONG TIME AGO.
MY FATHER HAS SERVED HIS PUNISHMENT. HE HAS, AS WE SAY ON EARTH, DONE HIS TIME.
"NOW IT'S TIME FOR HIM TO BREATHE FREE AIR AGAIN, TO FEEL THE LIGHT FROM RAO ON HIS FACE ONCE MORE."
THEY LISTENED TO YOU.
NOT WHATEVER "LEGAL ARGUMENTS" YOU MADE ON MY BEHALF.
THEY LISTENED TO YOU.
"SUPERMAN."
MY SON.

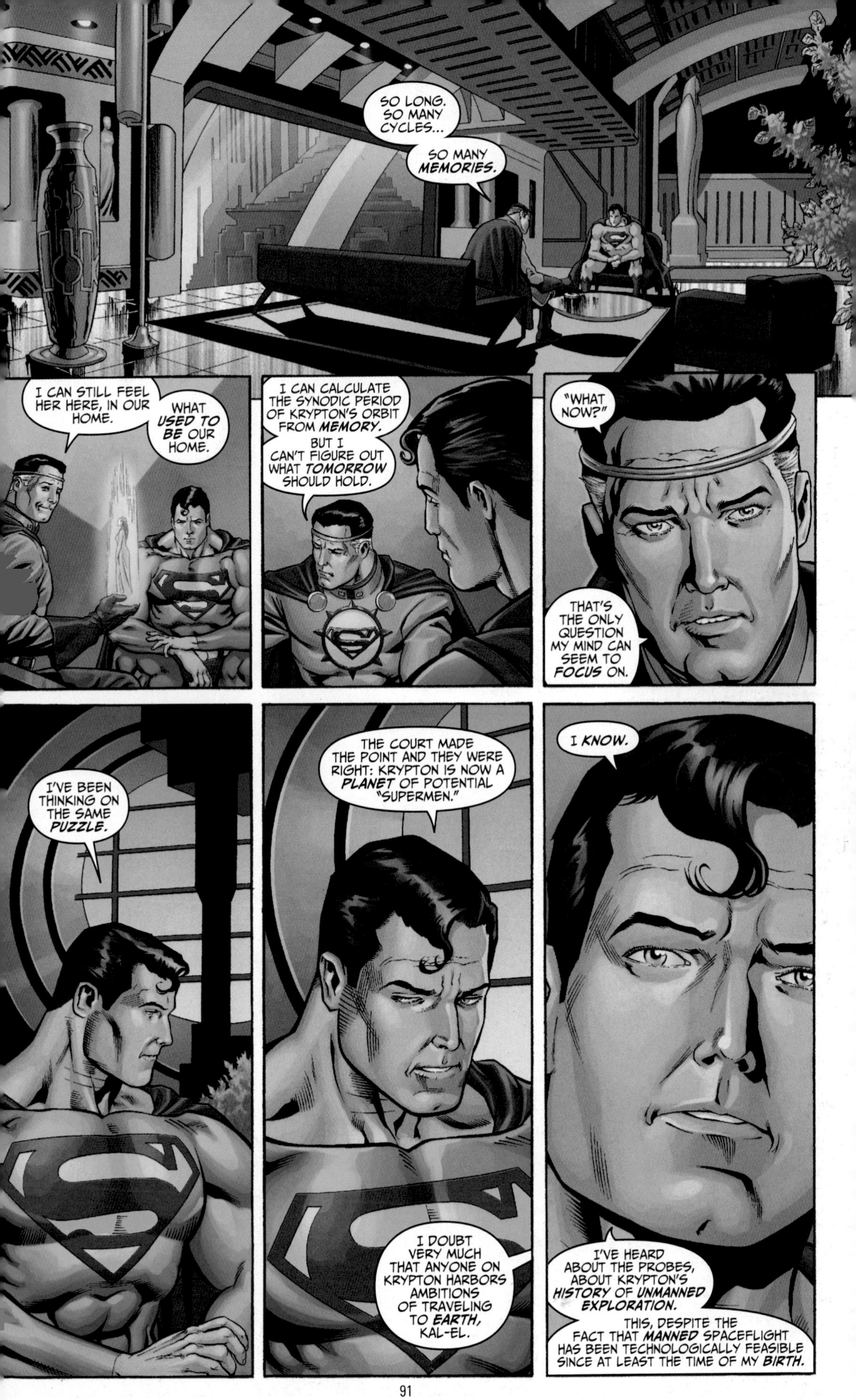
SO LONG. SO MANY CYCLES...
SO MANY MEMORIES.
I CAN STILL FEEL HER HERE, IN OUR HOME.
WHAT USED TO BE OUR HOME.
I CAN CALCULATE THE SYNODIC PERIOD OF KRYPTON'S ORBIT FROM MEMORY.
BUT I CAN'T FIGURE OUT WHAT TOMORROW SHOULD HOLD.
"WHAT NOW?"
THAT'S THE ONLY QUESTION MY MIND CAN SEEM TO FOCUS ON.
I'VE BEEN THINKING ON THE SAME PUZZLE.
THE COURT MADE THE POINT AND THEY WERE RIGHT: KRYPTON IS NOW A PLANET OF POTENTIAL "SUPERMEN."
I DOUBT VERY MUCH THAT ANYONE ON KRYPTON HARBORS AMBITIONS OF TRAVELING TO EARTH, KAL-EL.
I KNOW.
I'VE HEARD ABOUT THE PROBES, ABOUT KRYPTON'S HISTORY OF UNMANNED EXPLORATION.
THIS, DESPITE THE FACT THAT MANNED SPACEFLIGHT HAS BEEN TECHNOLOGICALLY FEASIBLE SINCE AT LEAST THE TIME OF MY BIRTH.

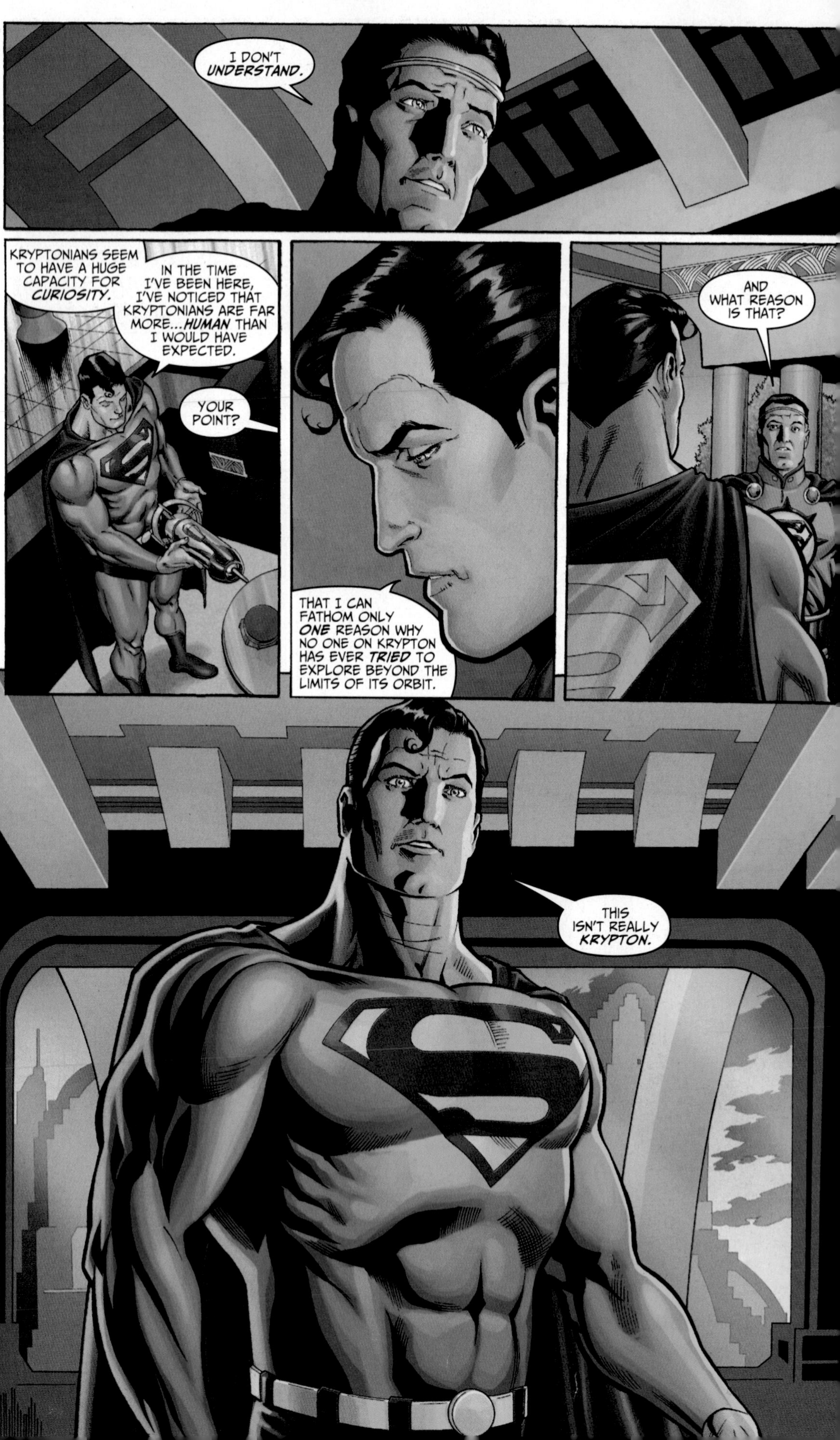
I DON'T UNDERSTAND.
KRYPTONIANS SEEM TO HAVE A HUGE CAPACITY FOR CURIOSITY.
IN THE TIME I'VE BEEN HERE, I'VE NOTICED THAT KRYPTONIANS ARE FAR MORE... HUMAN THAN I WOULD HAVE EXPECTED.
YOUR POINT?
THAT I CAN FATHOM ONLY ONE REASON WHY NO ONE ON KRYPTON HAS EVER TRIED TO EXPLORE BEYOND THE LIMITS OF ITS ORBIT.
AND WHAT REASON IS THAT?
THIS ISN'T REALLY KRYPTON.

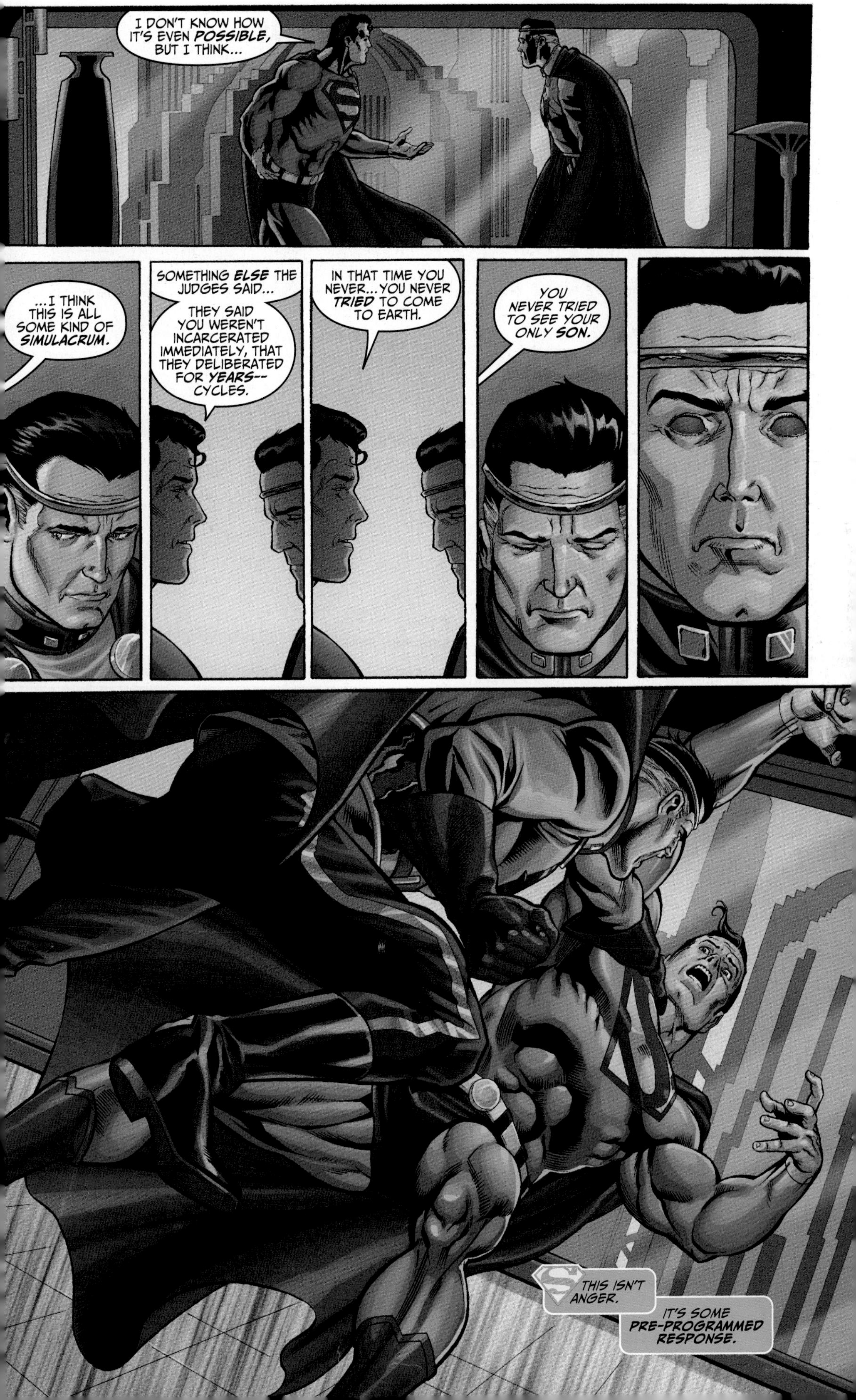
I DON'T KNOW HOW IT'S EVEN POSSIBLE, BUT I THINK...
...I THINK THIS IS ALL SOME KIND OF SIMULACRUM.
SOMETHING ELSE THE JUDGES SAID...
THEY SAID YOU WEREN'T INCARCERATED IMMEDIATELY, THAT THEY DELIBERATED FOR YEARS-- CYCLES.
IN THAT TIME YOU NEVER...YOU NEVER TRIED TO COME TO EARTH.
YOU NEVER TRIED TO SEE YOUR ONLY SON.
THIS ISN'T ANGER.
IT'S SOME PRE-PROGRAMMED RESPONSE.

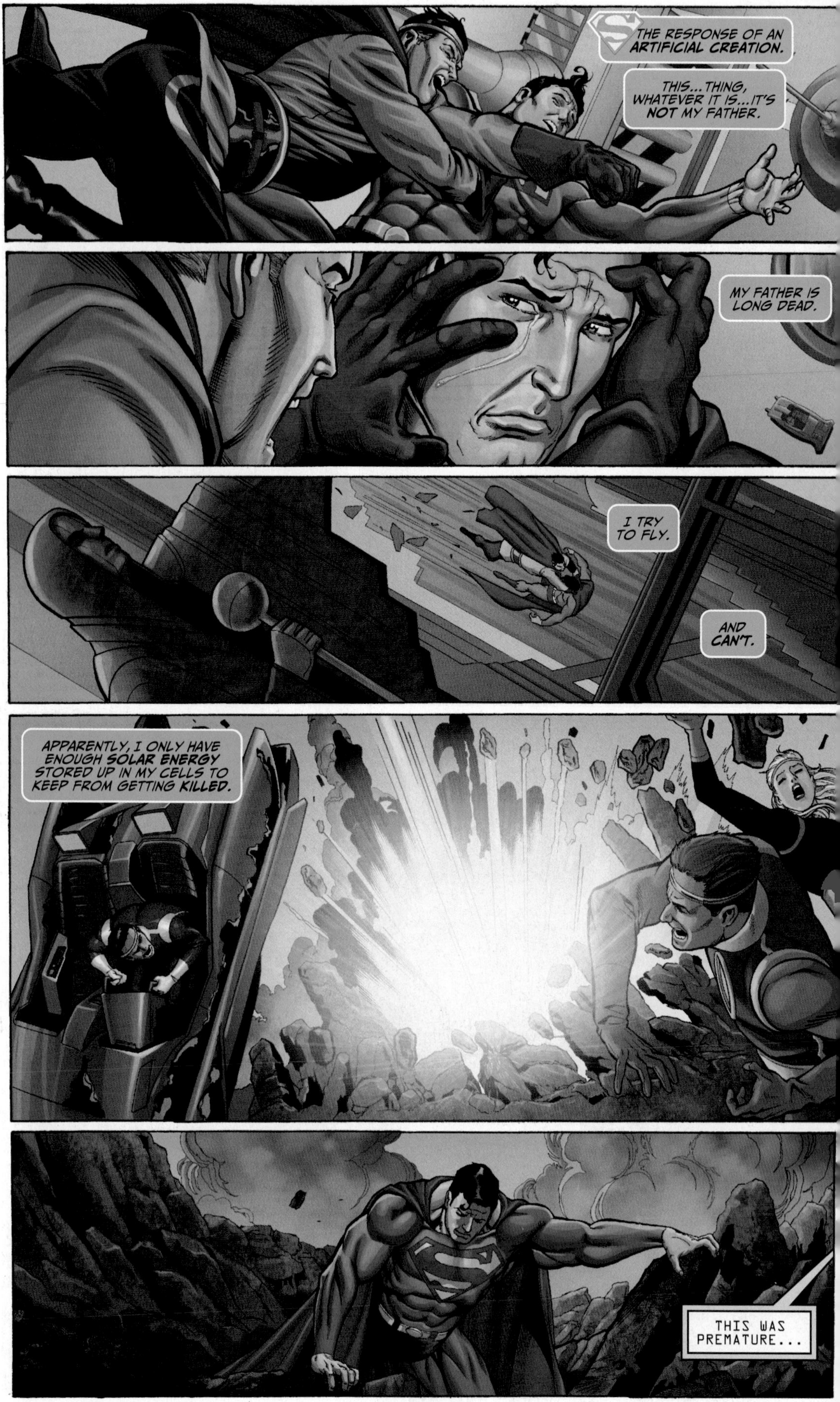
THE RESPONSE OF AN ARTIFICIAL CREATION.
THIS...THING, WHATEVER IT IS...IT'S NOT MY FATHER.
MY FATHER IS LONG DEAD.
I TRY TO FLY.
AND CAN'T.
APPARENTLY, I ONLY HAVE ENOUGH SOLAR ENERGY STORED UP IN MY CELLS TO KEEP FROM GETTING KILLED.
THIS WAS PREMATURE...

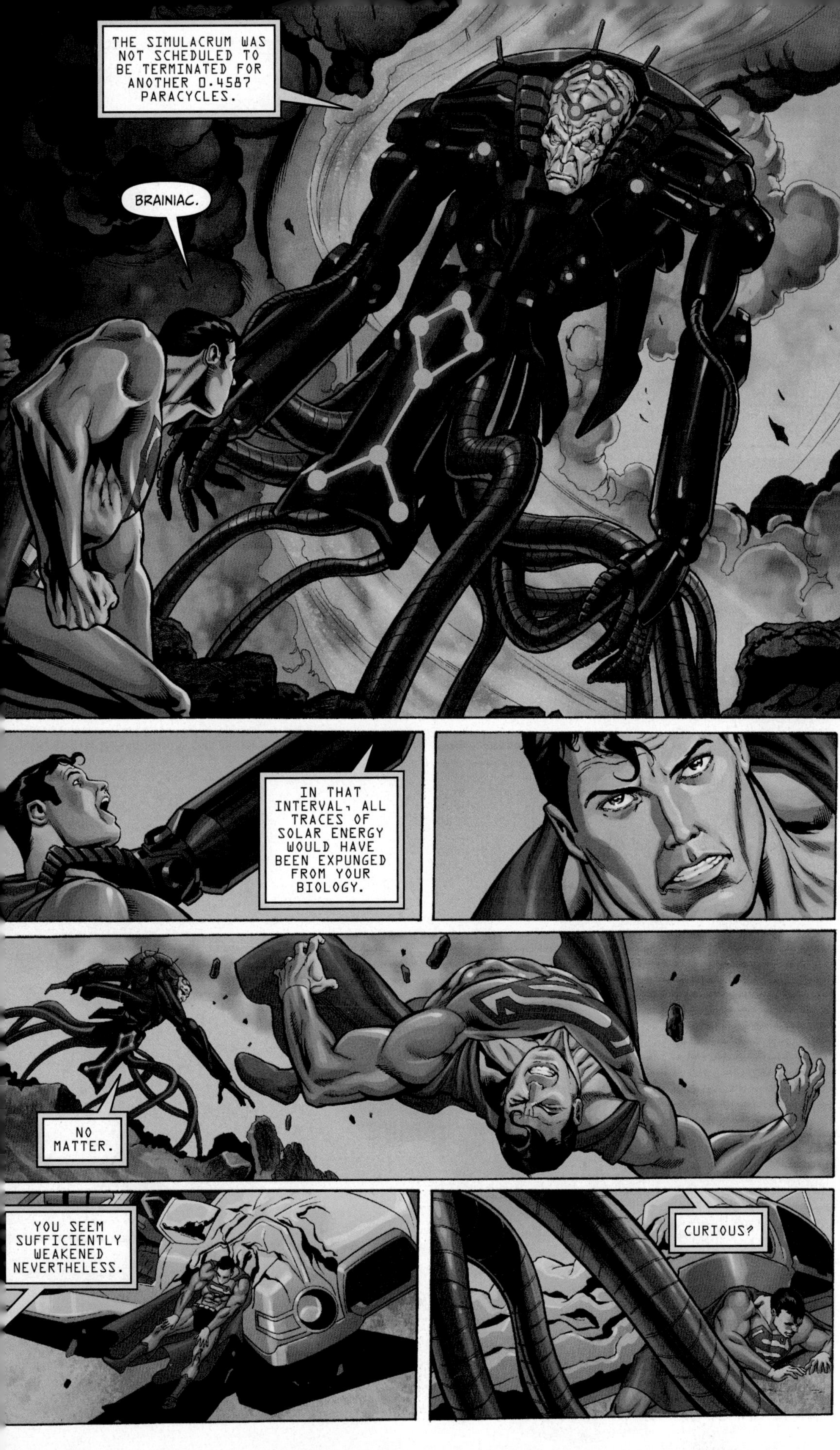
THE SIMULACRUM WAS NOT SCHEDULED TO BE TERMINATED FOR ANOTHER 0.4587 PARACYCLES.
BRAINIAC.
IN THAT INTERVAL, ALL TRACES OF SOLAR ENERGY WOULD HAVE BEEN EXPUNGED FROM YOUR BIOLOGY.
NO MATTER.
YOU SEEM SUFFICIENTLY WEAKENED NEVERTHELESS.
CURIOUS?

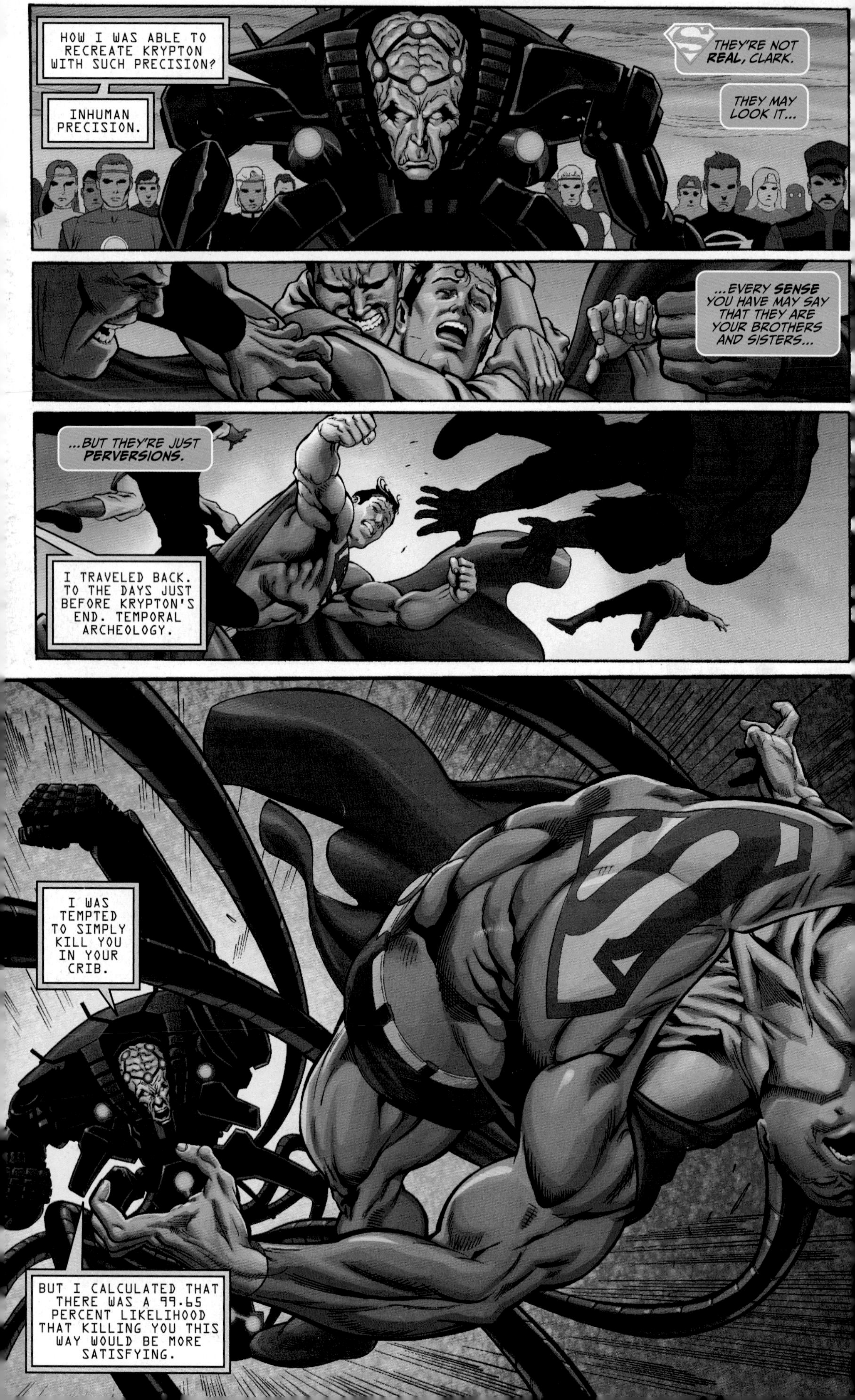

HOW I WAS ABLE TO RECREATE KRYPTON WITH SUCH PRECISION?
INHUMAN PRECISION.
THEY'RE NOT REAL, CLARK.
THEY MAY LOOK IT...
...EVERY SENSE YOU HAVE MAY SAY THAT THEY ARE YOUR BROTHERS AND SISTERS...
...BUT THEY'RE JUST PERVERSIONS.
I TRAVELED BACK. TO THE DAYS JUST BEFORE KRYPTON'S END. TEMPORAL ARCHEOLOGY.
I WAS TEMPTED TO SIMPLY KILL YOU IN YOUR CRIB.
BUT I CALCULATED THAT THERE WAS A 99.65 PERCENT LIKELIHOOD THAT KILLING YOU THIS WAY WOULD BE MORE SATISFYING.

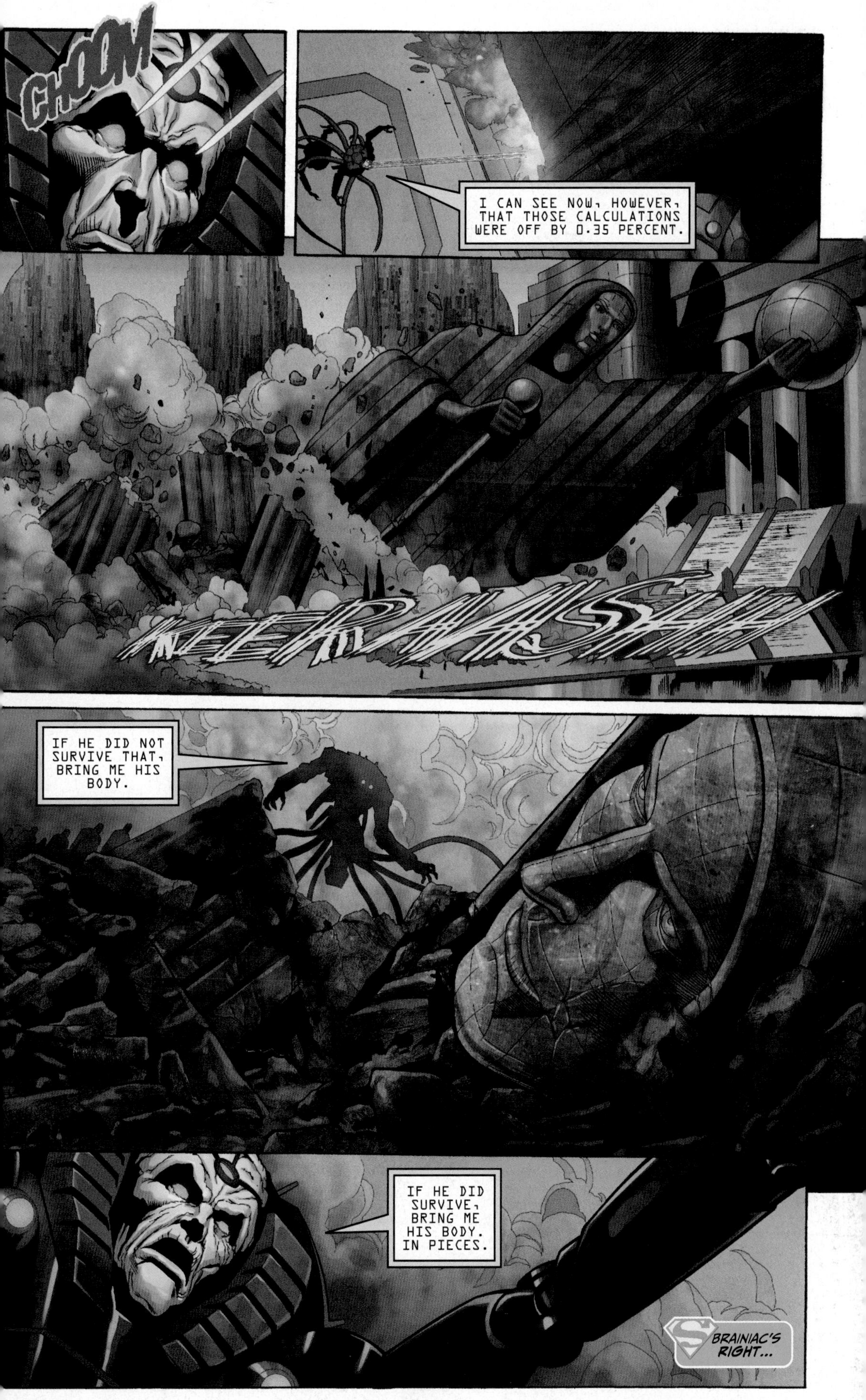
CHOOM
I CAN SEE NOW, HOWEVER, THAT THOSE CALCULATIONS WERE OFF BY 0.35 PERCENT.
KERRASHH
IF HE DID NOT SURVIVE THAT, BRING ME HIS BODY.
IF HE DID SURVIVE, BRING ME HIS BODY. IN PIECES.
BRAINIAC'S RIGHT...

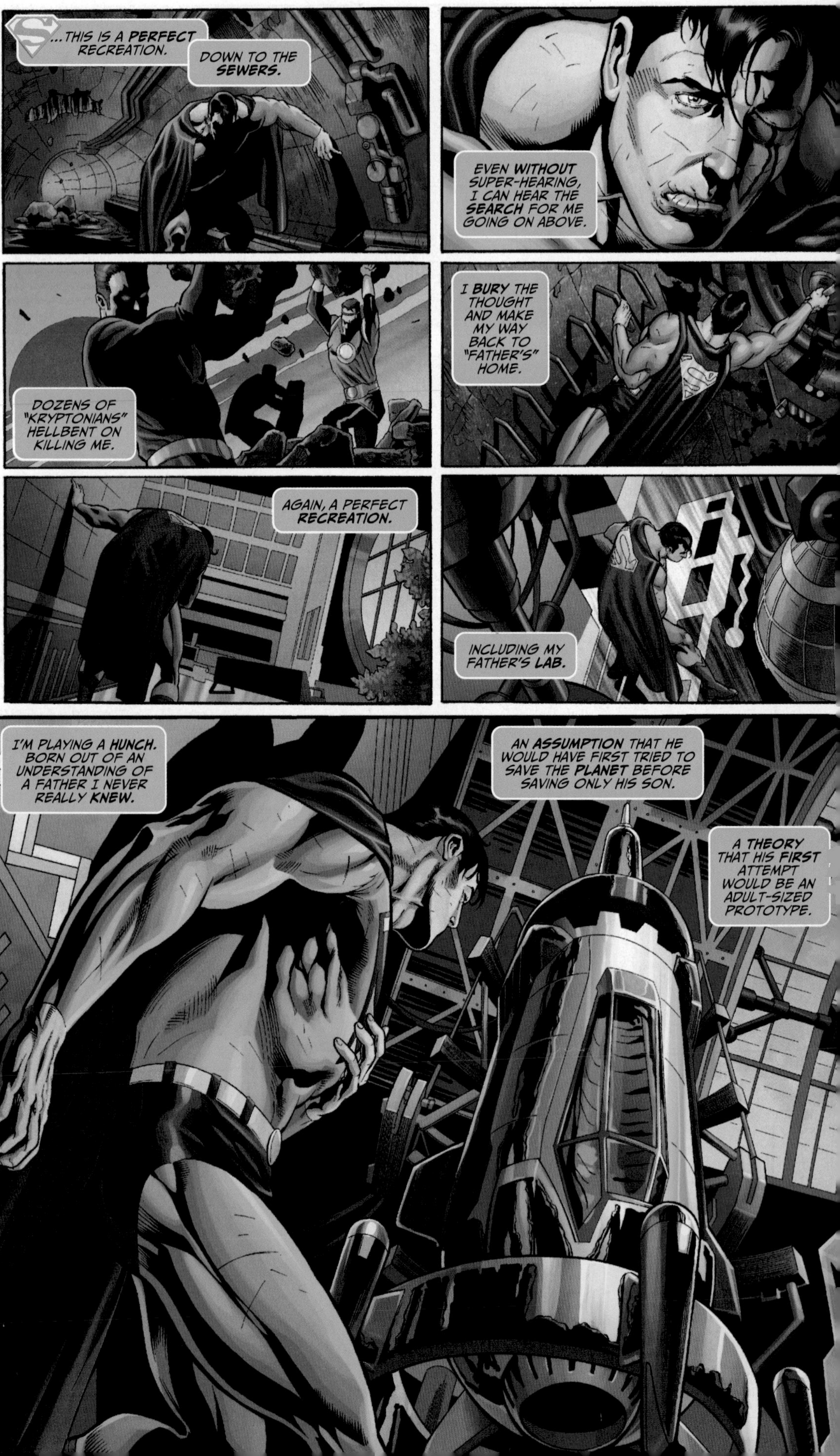
...THIS IS A PERFECT RECREATION.
DOWN TO THE SEWERS.
EVEN WITHOUT SUPER-HEARING, I CAN HEAR THE SEARCH FOR ME GOING ON ABOVE.
DOZENS OF "KRYPTONIANS" HELLBENT ON KILLING ME.
I BURY THE THOUGHT AND MAKE MY WAY BACK TO "FATHER'S" HOME.
AGAIN, A PERFECT RECREATION.
INCLUDING MY FATHER'S LAB.
I'M PLAYING A HUNCH. BORN OUT OF AN UNDERSTANDING OF A FATHER I NEVER REALLY KNEW.
AN ASSUMPTION THAT HE WOULD HAVE FIRST TRIED TO SAVE THE PLANET BEFORE SAVING ONLY HIS SON.
A THEORY THAT HIS FIRST ATTEMPT WOULD BE AN ADULT-SIZED PROTOTYPE.

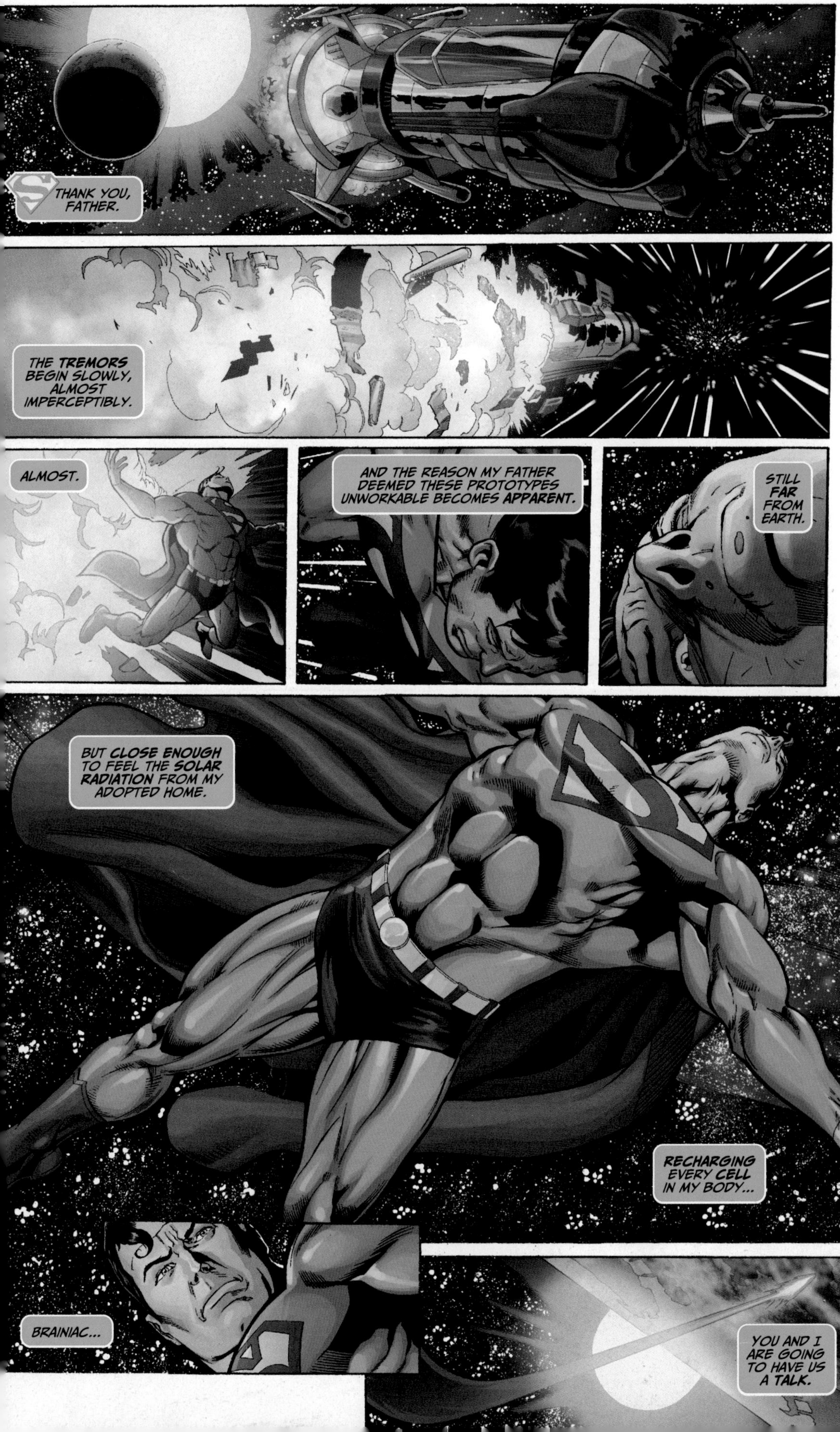
THANK YOU, FATHER.
THE TREMORS BEGIN SLOWLY, ALMOST IMPERCEPTIBLY.
ALMOST.
AND THE REASON MY FATHER DEEMED THESE PROTOTYPES UNWORKABLE BECOMES APPARENT.
STILL FAR FROM EARTH.
BUT CLOSE ENOUGH TO FEEL THE SOLAR RADIATION FROM MY ADOPTED HOME.
RECHARGING EVERY CELL IN MY BODY...
BRAINIAC...
YOU AND I ARE GOING TO HAVE US A TALK.

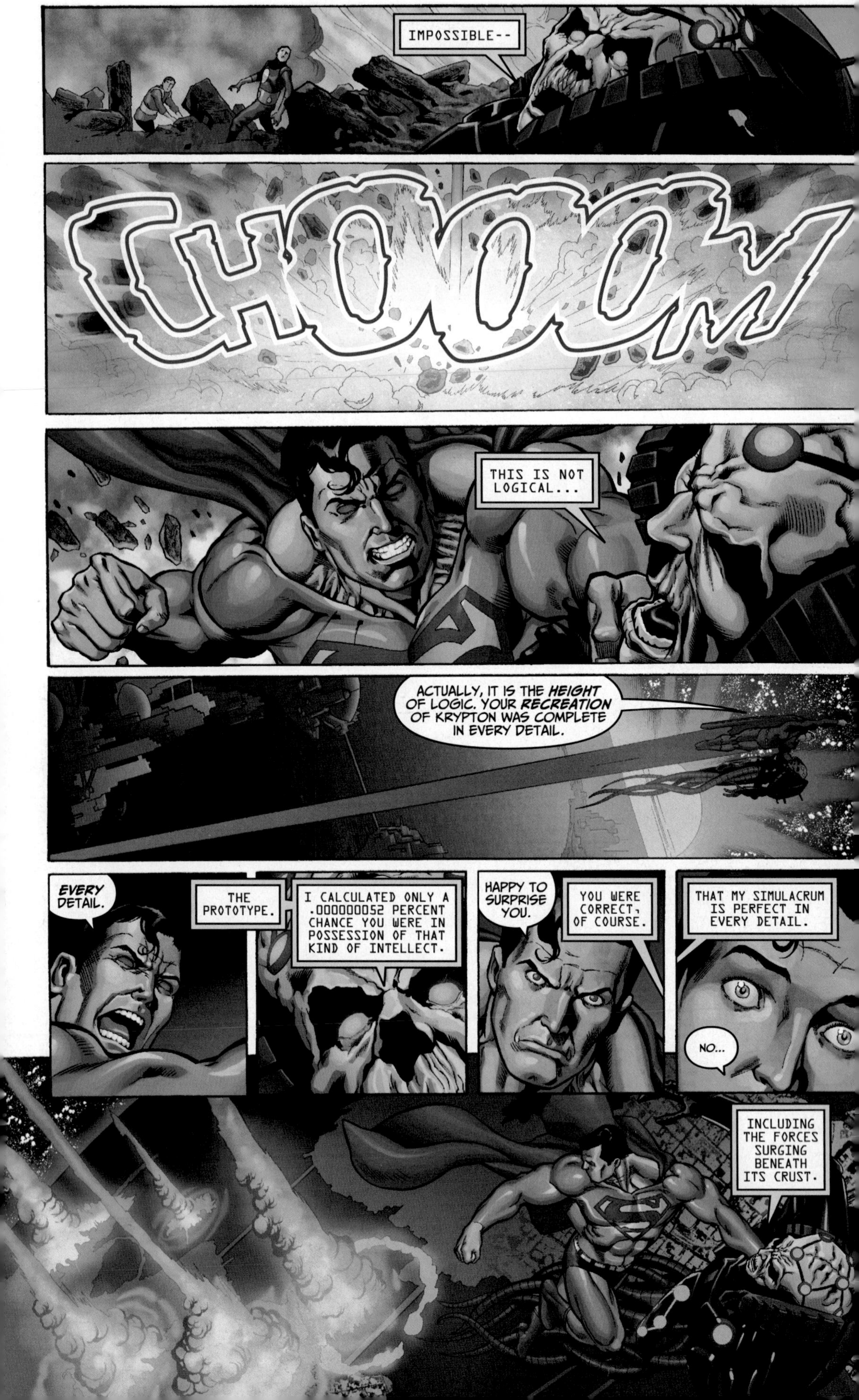
IMPOSSIBLE--
CHOOOOM
THIS IS NOT LOGICAL...
ACTUALLY, IT IS THE HEIGHT OF LOGIC. YOUR RECREATION OF KRYPTON WAS COMPLETE IN EVERY DETAIL.
EVERY DETAIL.
THE PROTOTYPE.
I CALCULATED ONLY A .00000052 PERCENT CHANCE YOU WERE IN POSSESSION OF THAT KIND OF INTELLECT.
HAPPY TO SURPRISE YOU.
YOU WERE CORRECT, OF COURSE.
THAT MY SIMULACRUM IS PERFECT IN EVERY DETAIL.
NO...
INCLUDING THE FORCES SURGING BENEATH ITS CRUST.

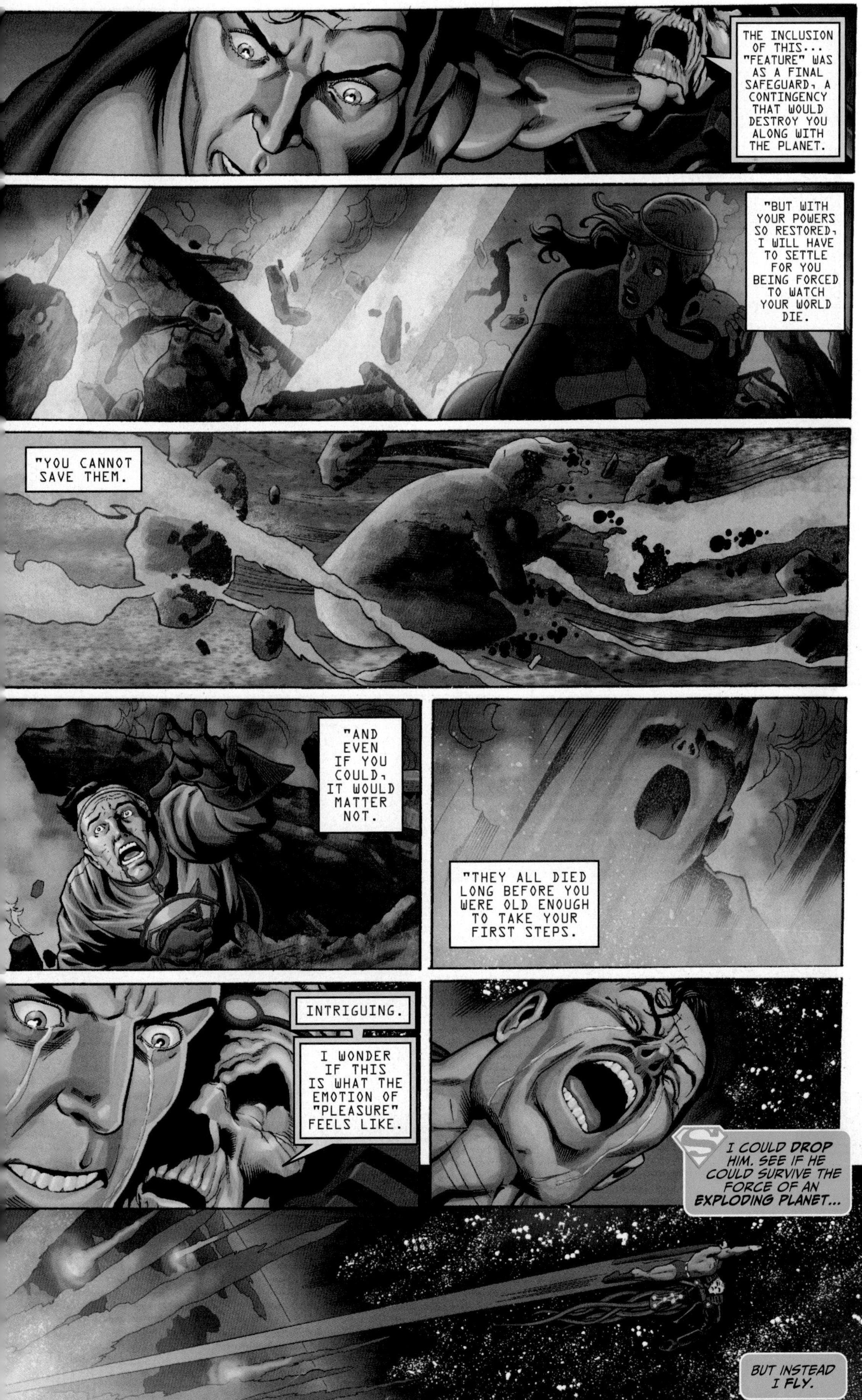
THE INCLUSION OF THIS... "FEATURE" WAS AS A FINAL SAFEGUARD, A CONTINGENCY THAT WOULD DESTROY YOU ALONG WITH THE PLANET.
"BUT WITH YOUR POWERS SO RESTORED, I WILL HAVE TO SETTLE FOR YOU BEING FORCED TO WATCH YOUR WORLD DIE.
"YOU CANNOT SAVE THEM.
"AND EVEN IF YOU COULD, IT WOULD MATTER NOT.
"THEY ALL DIED LONG BEFORE YOU WERE OLD ENOUGH TO TAKE YOUR FIRST STEPS.
INTRIGUING.
I WONDER IF THIS IS WHAT THE EMOTION OF "PLEASURE" FEELS LIKE.
I COULD DROP HIM. SEE IF HE COULD SURVIVE THE FORCE OF AN EXPLODING PLANET...
BUT INSTEAD I FLY.

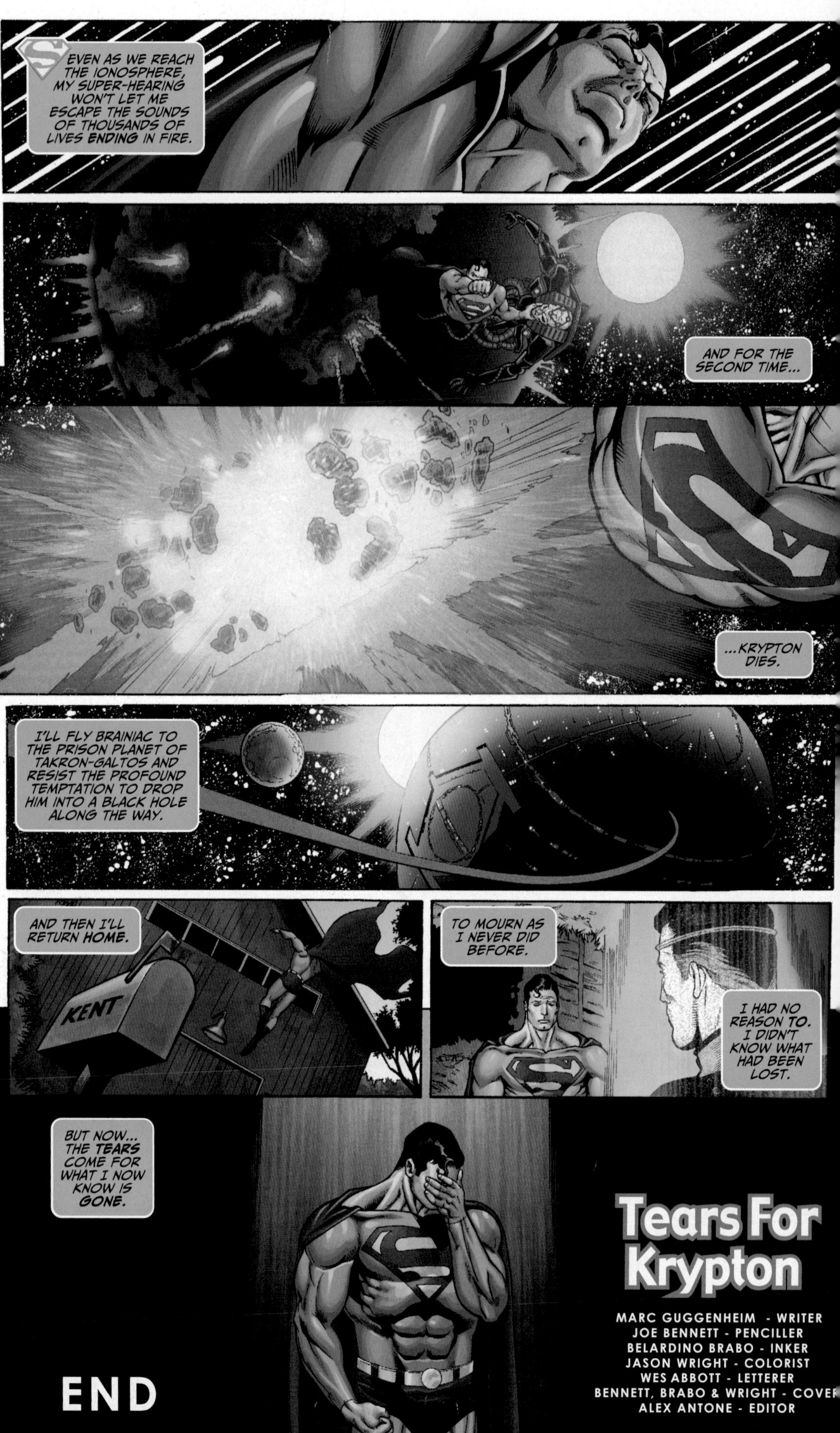

EVEN AS WE REACH THE IONOSPHERE, MY SUPER-HEARING WON'T LET ME ESCAPE THE SOUNDS OF THOUSANDS OF LIVES ENDING IN FIRE.
AND FOR THE SECOND TIME...
...KRYPTON DIES.
I'LL FLY BRAINIAC TO THE PRISON PLANET OF TAKRON-GALTOS AND RESIST THE PROFOUND TEMPTATION TO DROP HIM INTO A BLACK HOLE ALONG THE WAY.
AND THEN I'LL RETURN HOME.
KENT
TO MOURN AS I NEVER DID BEFORE.
I HAD NO REASON TO. I DIDN'T KNOW WHAT HAD BEEN LOST.
BUT NOW... THE TEARS COME FOR WHAT I NOW KNOW IS GONE.
END
Tears For Krypton
MARC GUGGENHEIM - WRITER
JOE BENNETT - PENCILLER
BELARDINO BRABO - INKER
JASON WRIGHT - COLORIST
WES ABBOTT - LETTERER
BENNETT, BRABO & WRIGHT - COVER
ALEX ANTONE - EDITOR

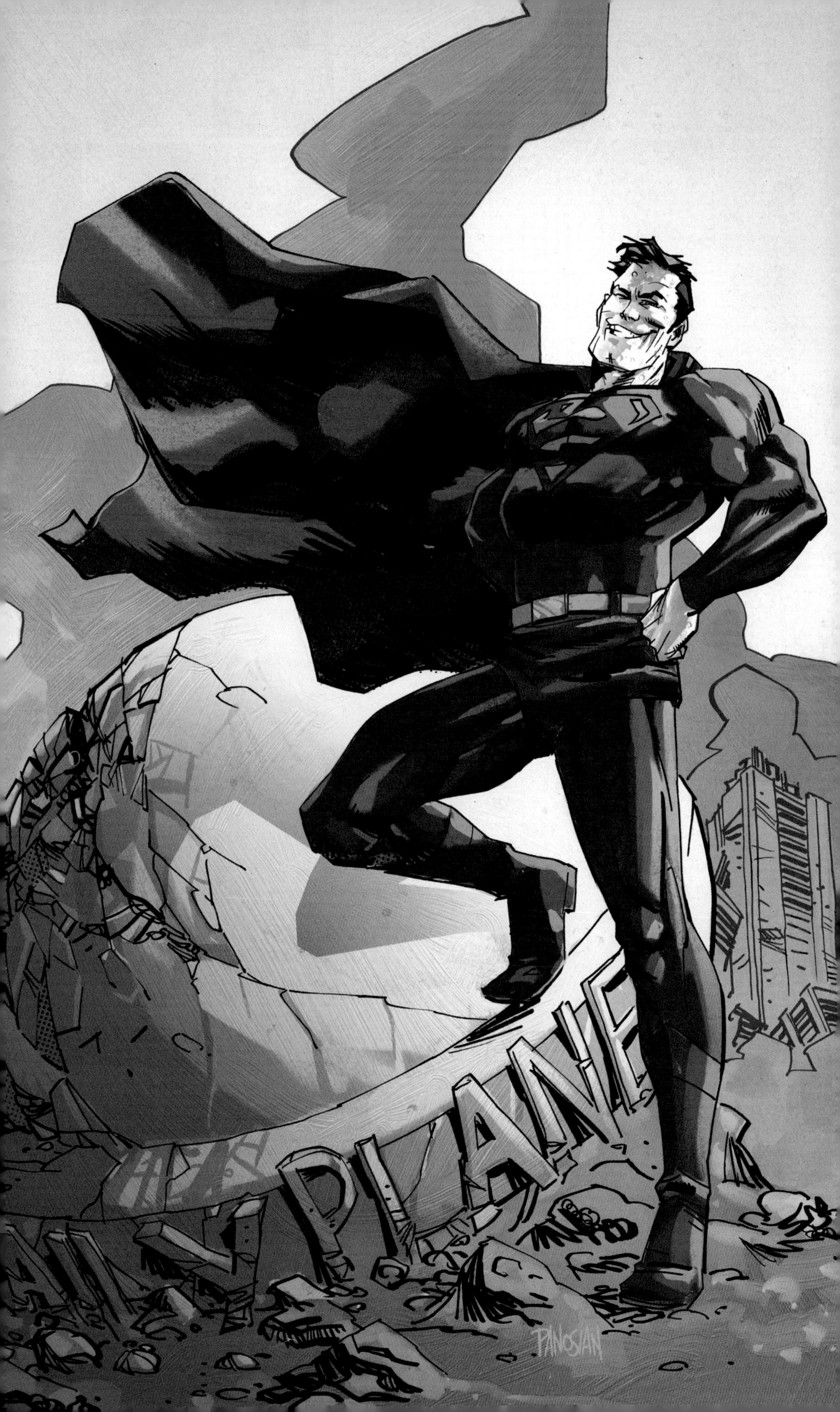
PANOSIAN

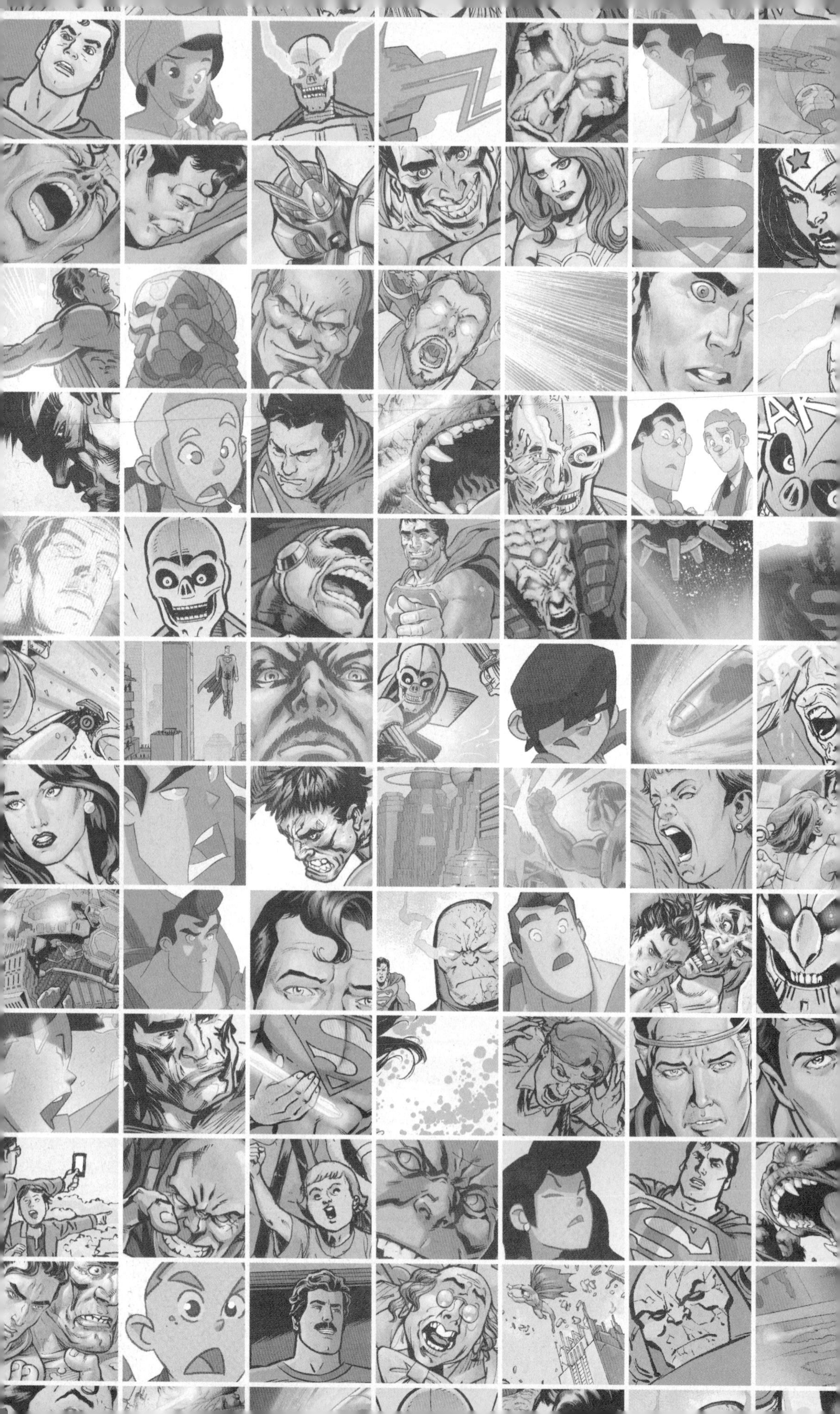

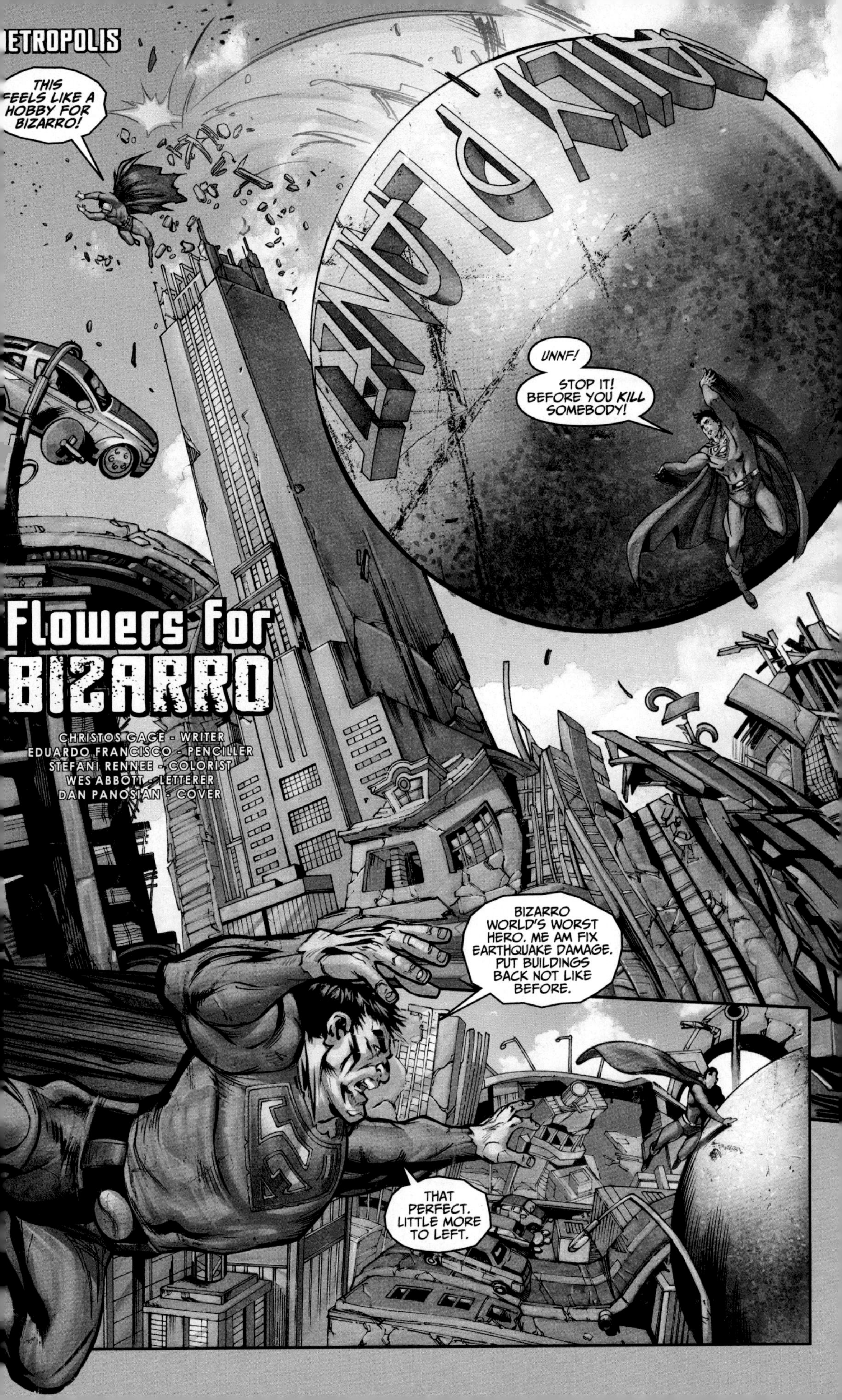

ETROPOLIS
THIS FEELS LIKE A HOBBY FOR BIZARRO!
UNNF!
STOP IT! BEFORE YOU KILL SOMEBODY!
Flowers for BIZARRO
CHRISTOS GAGE - WRITER
EDUARDO FRANCISCO - PENCILLER
STEFANI RENNEE - COLORIST
WES ABBOTT - LETTERER
DAN PANOSIAN - COVER
BIZARRO WORLD'S WORST HERO. ME AM FIX EARTHQUAKE DAMAGE. PUT BUILDINGS BACK NOT LIKE BEFORE.
THAT PERFECT. LITTLE MORE TO LEFT.

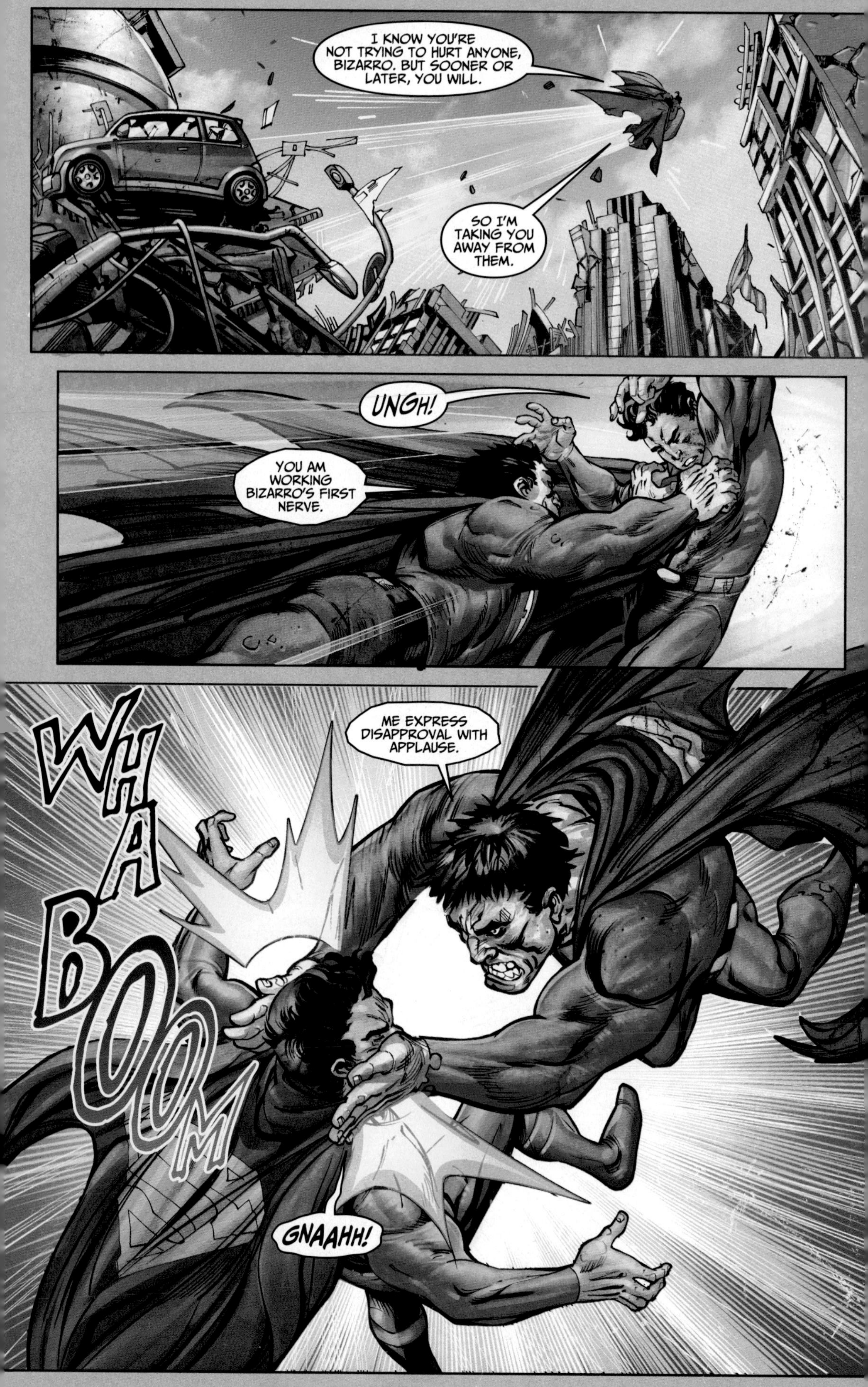
I KNOW YOU'RE NOT TRYING TO HURT ANYONE, BIZARRO. BUT SOONER OR LATER, YOU WILL.
SO I'M TAKING YOU AWAY FROM THEM.
UNGH!
YOU AM WORKING BIZARRO'S FIRST NERVE.
WHABOOOM
ME EXPRESS DISAPPROVAL WITH APPLAUSE.
GNAAHH!

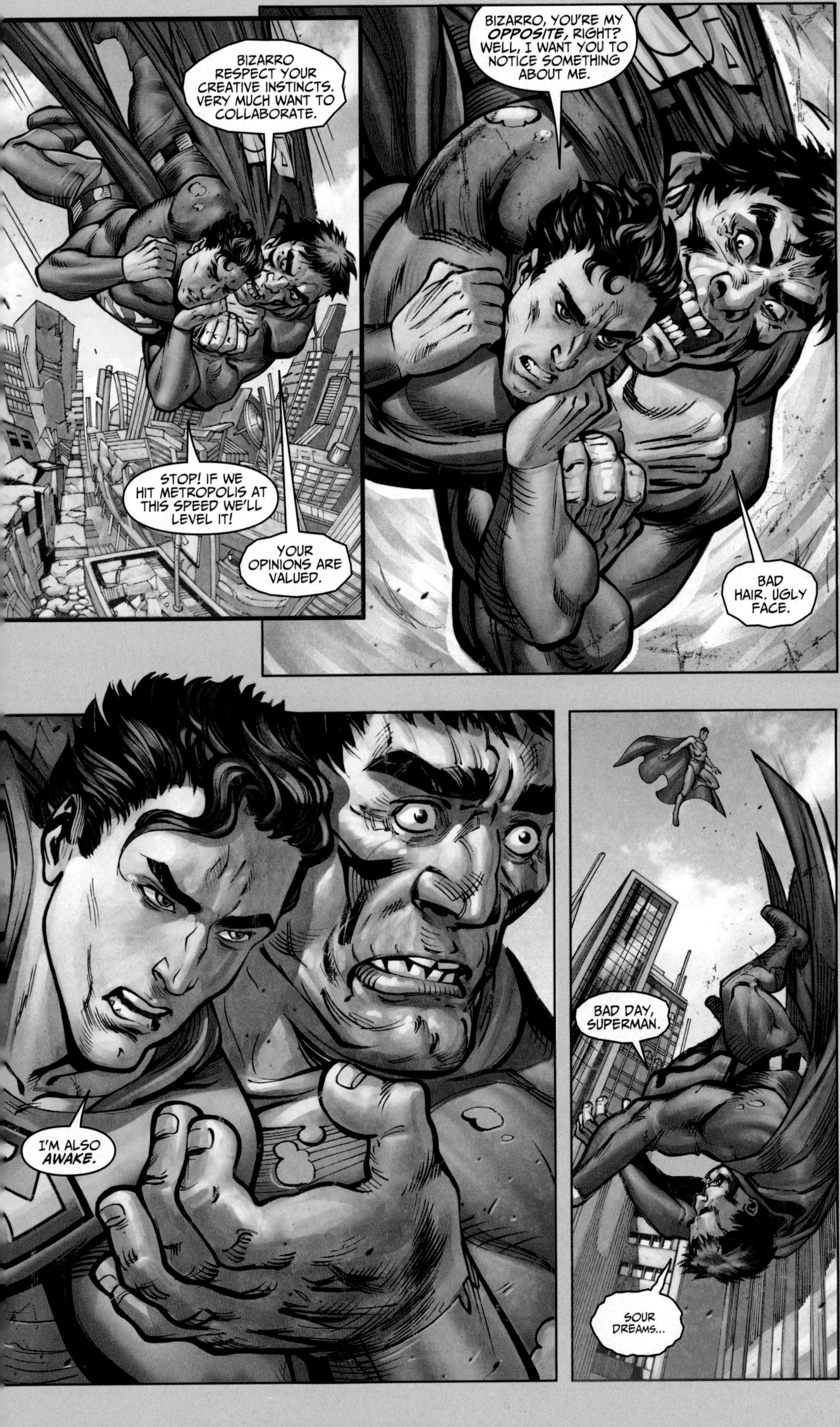
BIZARRO RESPECT YOUR CREATIVE INSTINCTS. VERY MUCH WANT TO COLLABORATE.
STOP! IF WE HIT METROPOLIS AT THIS SPEED WE'LL LEVEL IT!
YOUR OPINIONS ARE VALUED.
BIZARRO, YOU'RE MY *OPPOSITE*, RIGHT? WELL, I WANT YOU TO NOTICE SOMETHING ABOUT ME.
BAD HAIR. UGLY FACE.
I'M ALSO *AWAKE.*
BAD DAY, SUPERMAN.
SOUR DREAMS...

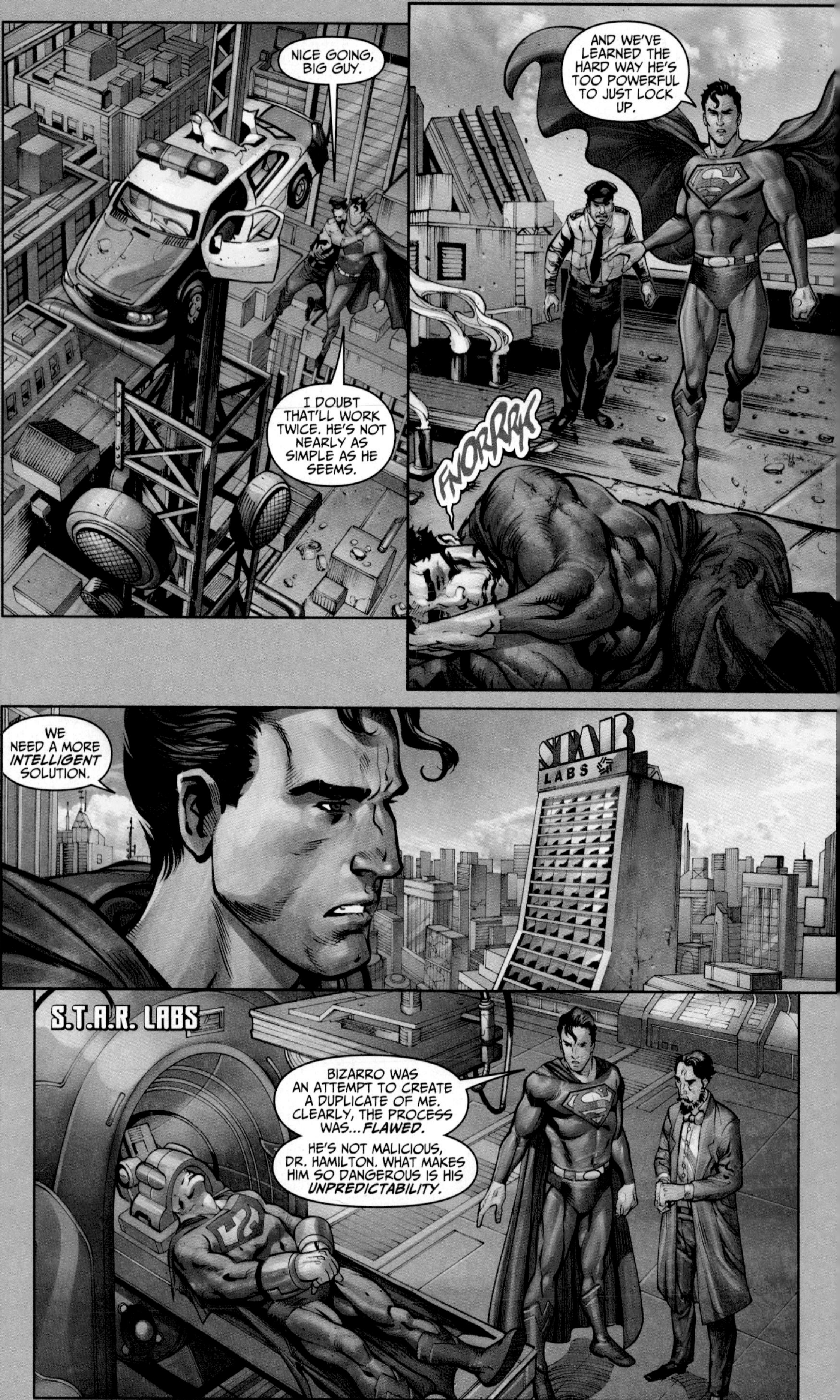
NICE GOING, BIG GUY.
I DOUBT THAT'LL WORK TWICE. HE'S NOT NEARLY AS SIMPLE AS HE SEEMS.
AND WE'VE LEARNED THE HARD WAY HE'S TOO POWERFUL TO JUST LOCK UP.
FNORRRK
WE NEED A MORE *INTELLIGENT* SOLUTION.
STAR LABS
S.T.A.R. LABS
BIZARRO WAS AN ATTEMPT TO CREATE A DUPLICATE OF ME. CLEARLY, THE PROCESS WAS... ***FLAWED.***
HE'S NOT MALICIOUS, DR. HAMILTON. WHAT MAKES HIM SO DANGEROUS IS HIS ***UNPREDICTABILITY.***

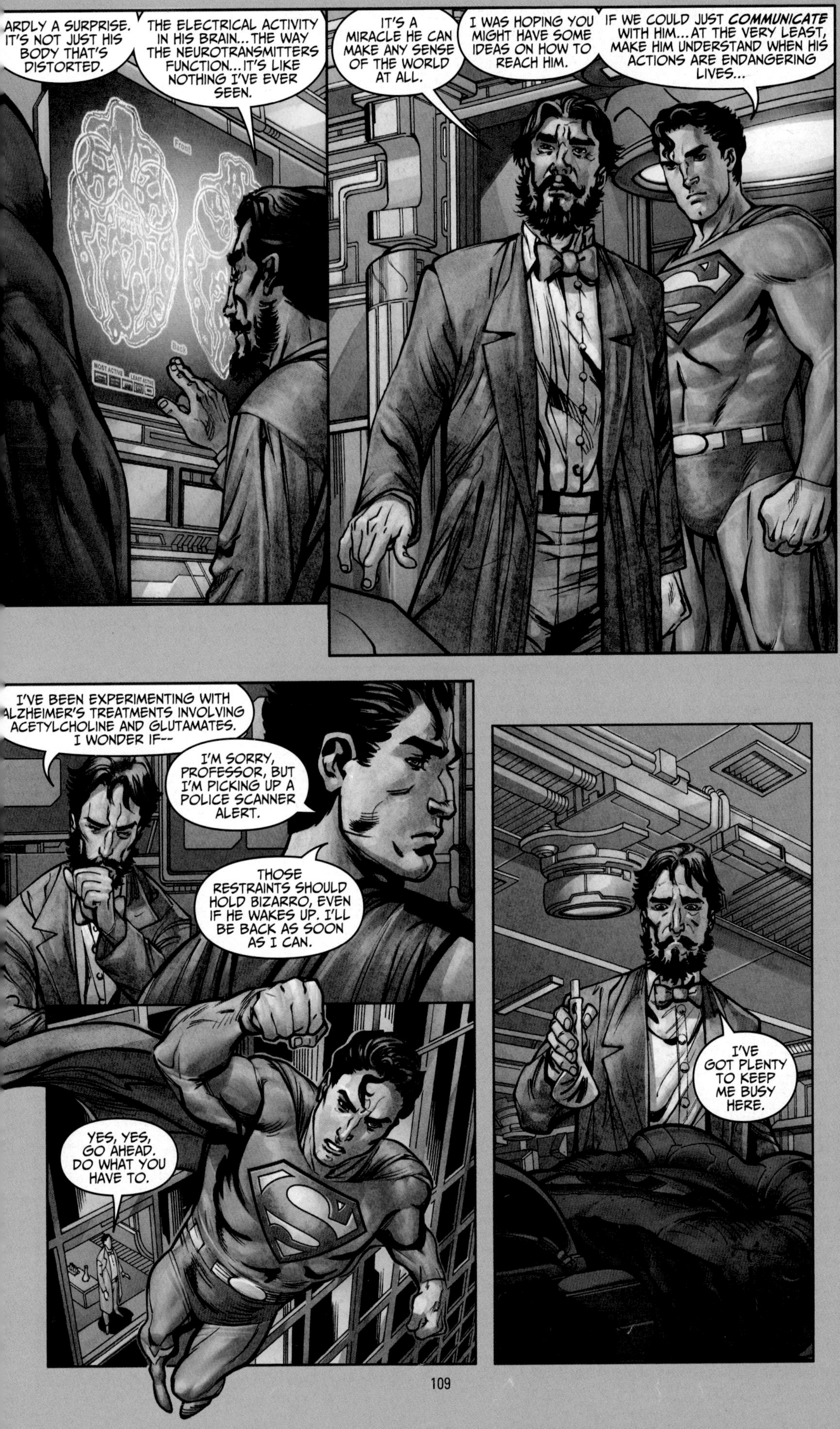
ARDLY A SURPRISE. IT'S NOT JUST HIS BODY THAT'S DISTORTED.
THE ELECTRICAL ACTIVITY IN HIS BRAIN...THE WAY THE NEUROTRANSMITTERS FUNCTION...IT'S LIKE NOTHING I'VE EVER SEEN.
Front
Back
MOST ACTIVE
LEAST ACTIVE
IT'S A MIRACLE HE CAN MAKE ANY SENSE OF THE WORLD AT ALL.
I WAS HOPING YOU MIGHT HAVE SOME IDEAS ON HOW TO REACH HIM.
IF WE COULD JUST COMMUNICATE WITH HIM...AT THE VERY LEAST, MAKE HIM UNDERSTAND WHEN HIS ACTIONS ARE ENDANGERING LIVES...
I'VE BEEN EXPERIMENTING WITH ALZHEIMER'S TREATMENTS INVOLVING ACETYLCHOLINE AND GLUTAMATES. I WONDER IF--
I'M SORRY, PROFESSOR, BUT I'M PICKING UP A POLICE SCANNER ALERT.
THOSE RESTRAINTS SHOULD HOLD BIZARRO, EVEN IF HE WAKES UP. I'LL BE BACK AS SOON AS I CAN.
YES, YES, GO AHEAD. DO WHAT YOU HAVE TO.
I'VE GOT PLENTY TO KEEP ME BUSY HERE.

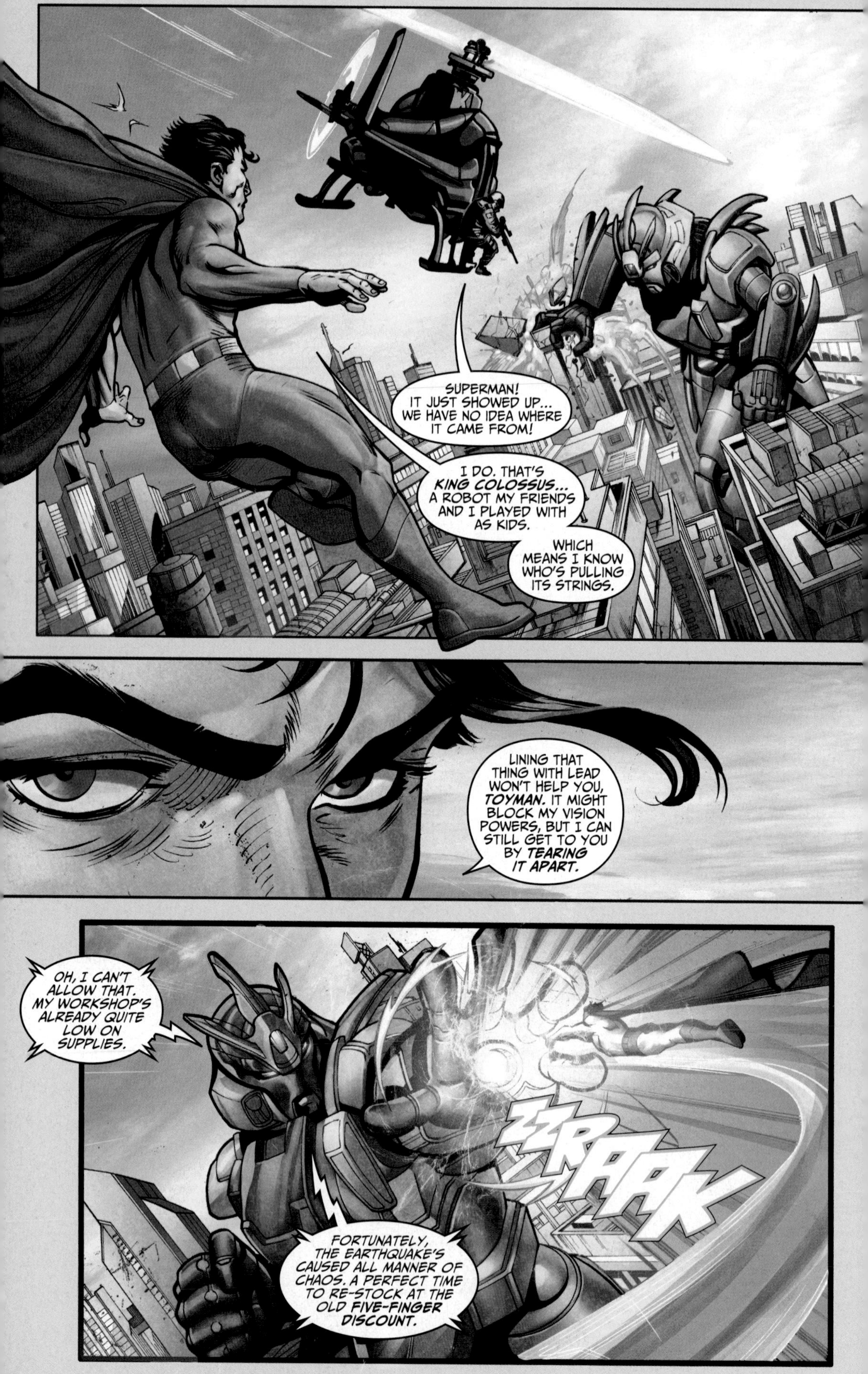

SUPERMAN! IT JUST SHOWED UP... WE HAVE NO IDEA WHERE IT CAME FROM!
I DO. THAT'S KING COLOSSUS... A ROBOT MY FRIENDS AND I PLAYED WITH AS KIDS.
WHICH MEANS I KNOW WHO'S PULLING ITS STRINGS.
LINING THAT THING WITH LEAD WON'T HELP YOU, TOYMAN. IT MIGHT BLOCK MY VISION POWERS, BUT I CAN STILL GET TO YOU BY TEARING IT APART.
OH, I CAN'T ALLOW THAT. MY WORKSHOP'S ALREADY QUITE LOW ON SUPPLIES.
ZZRAAK
FORTUNATELY, THE EARTHQUAKE'S CAUSED ALL MANNER OF CHAOS. A PERFECT TIME TO RE-STOCK AT THE OLD FIVE-FINGER DISCOUNT.

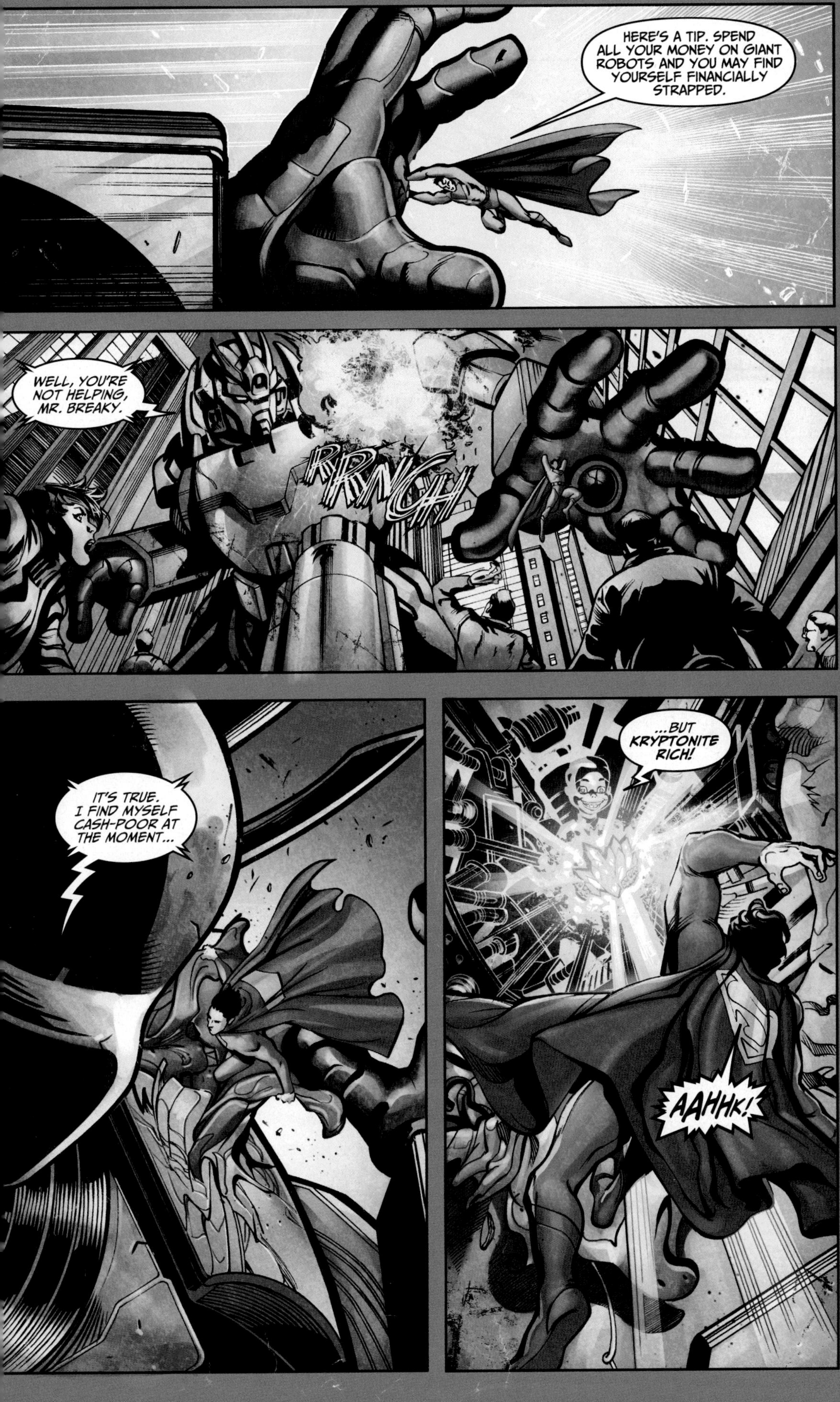
HERE'S A TIP. SPEND ALL YOUR MONEY ON GIANT ROBOTS AND YOU MAY FIND YOURSELF FINANCIALLY STRAPPED.
WELL, YOU'RE NOT HELPING, MR. BREAKY.
RRNCH
IT'S TRUE. I FIND MYSELF CASH-POOR AT THE MOMENT...
...BUT KRYPTONITE RICH!
AAHHK!

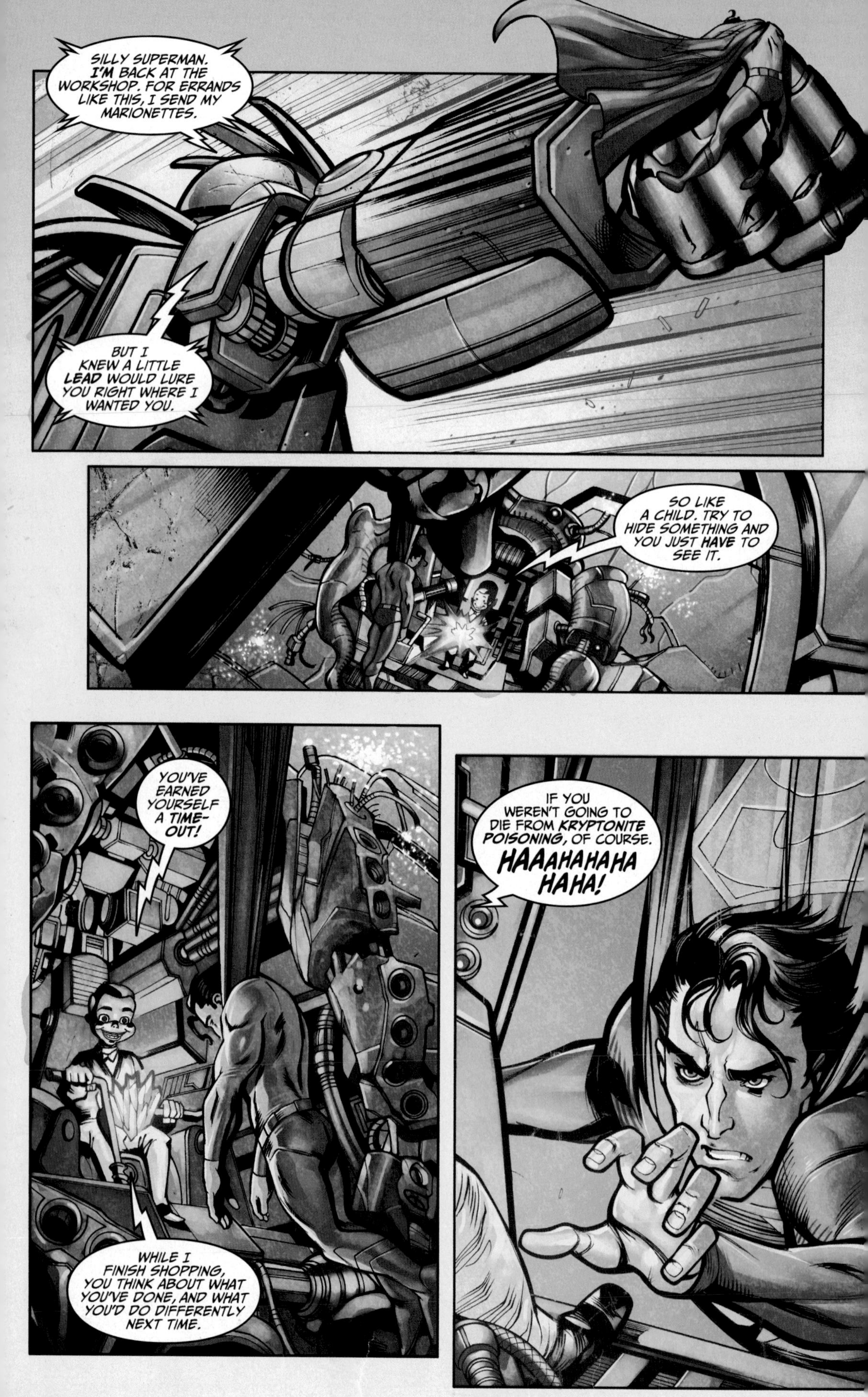
SILLY SUPERMAN. I'M BACK AT THE WORKSHOP. FOR ERRANDS LIKE THIS, I SEND MY MARIONETTES.
BUT I KNEW A LITTLE LEAD WOULD LURE YOU RIGHT WHERE I WANTED YOU.
SO LIKE A CHILD. TRY TO HIDE SOMETHING AND YOU JUST HAVE TO SEE IT.
YOU'VE EARNED YOURSELF A TIME-OUT!
WHILE I FINISH SHOPPING, YOU THINK ABOUT WHAT YOU'VE DONE, AND WHAT YOU'D DO DIFFERENTLY NEXT TIME.
IF YOU WEREN'T GOING TO DIE FROM KRYPTONITE POISONING, OF COURSE.
HAAAHAHAHA HAHA!

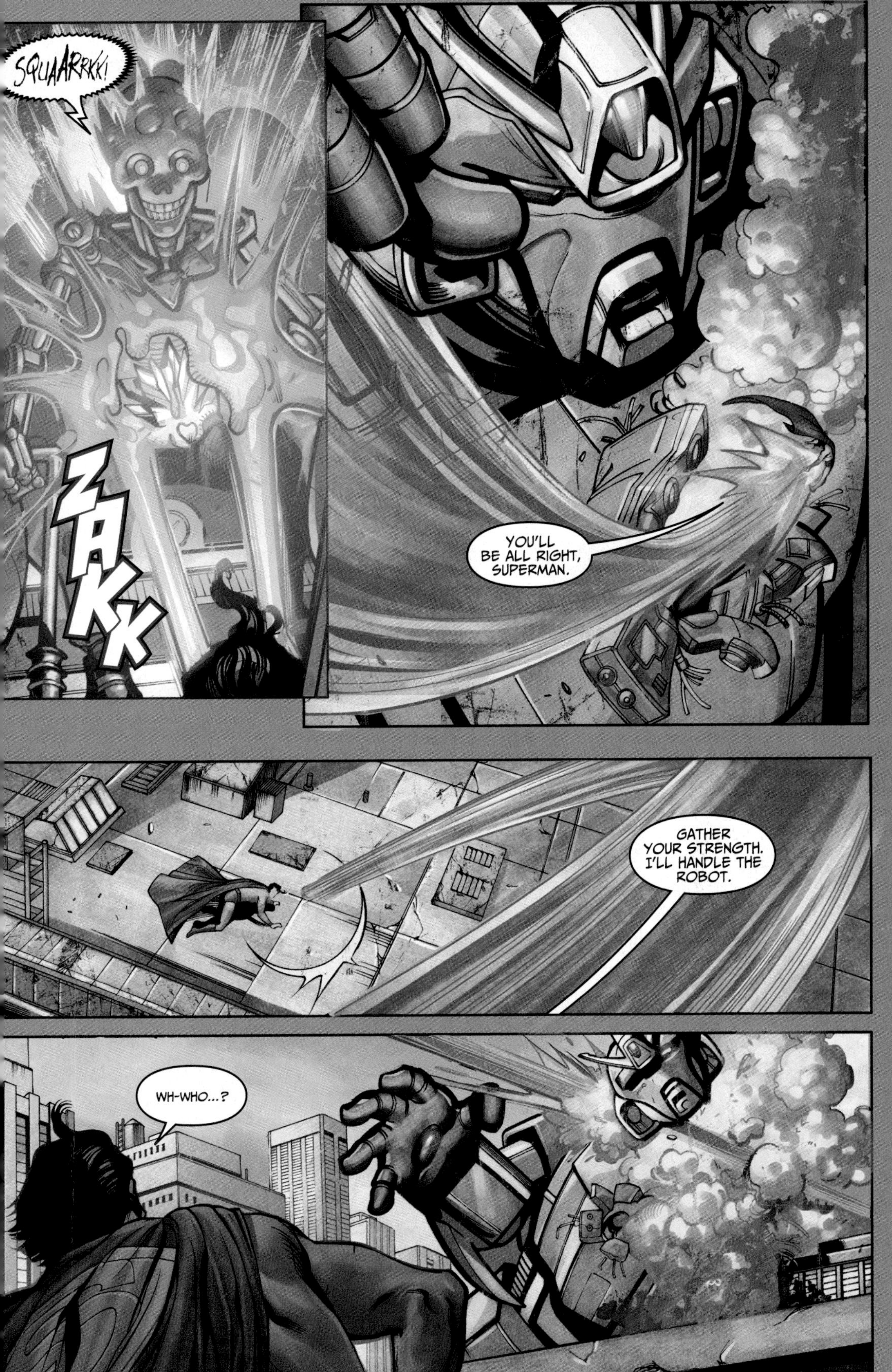
SQUAARRKK!
ZAKK
YOU'LL BE ALL RIGHT, SUPERMAN.
GATHER YOUR STRENGTH. I'LL HANDLE THE ROBOT.
WH-WHO...?

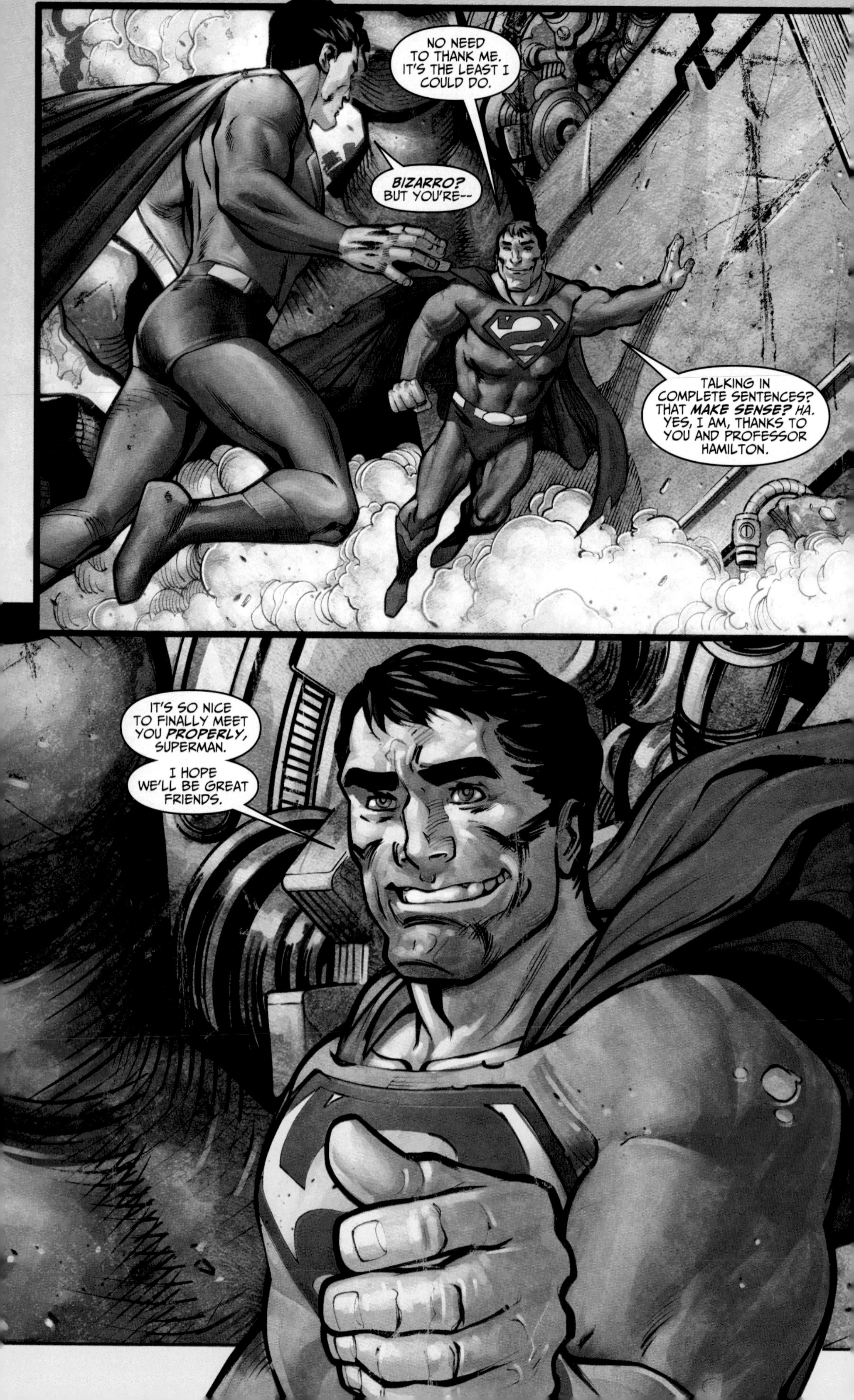
NO NEED TO THANK ME. IT'S THE LEAST I COULD DO.
BIZARRO? BUT YOU'RE--
TALKING IN COMPLETE SENTENCES? THAT *MAKE SENSE?* HA. YES, I AM, THANKS TO YOU AND PROFESSOR HAMILTON.
IT'S SO NICE TO FINALLY MEET YOU *PROPERLY,* SUPERMAN.
I HOPE WE'LL BE GREAT FRIENDS.

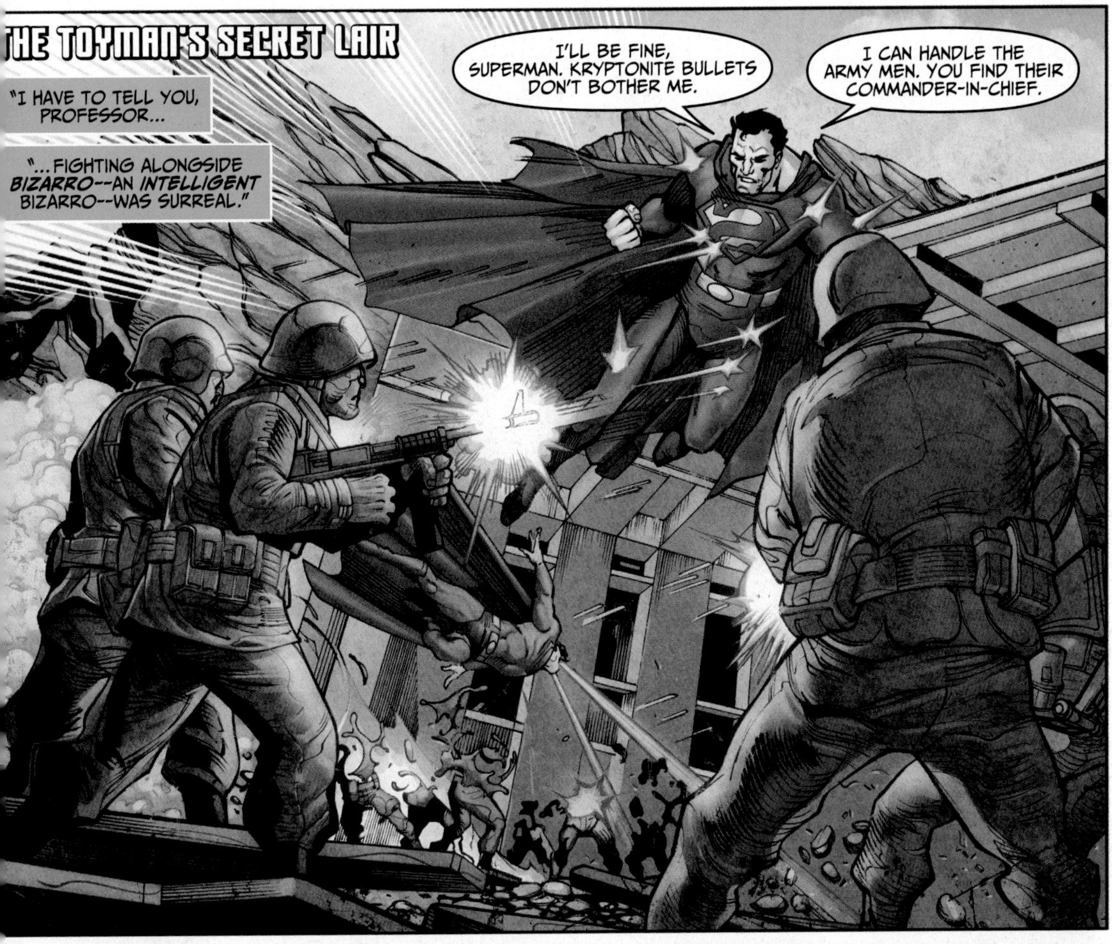
THE TOYMAN'S SECRET LAIR
"I HAVE TO TELL YOU, PROFESSOR...
"...FIGHTING ALONGSIDE BIZARRO--AN INTELLIGENT BIZARRO--WAS SURREAL."
I'LL BE FINE, SUPERMAN. KRYPTONITE BULLETS DON'T BOTHER ME.
I CAN HANDLE THE ARMY MEN. YOU FIND THEIR COMMANDER-IN-CHIEF.

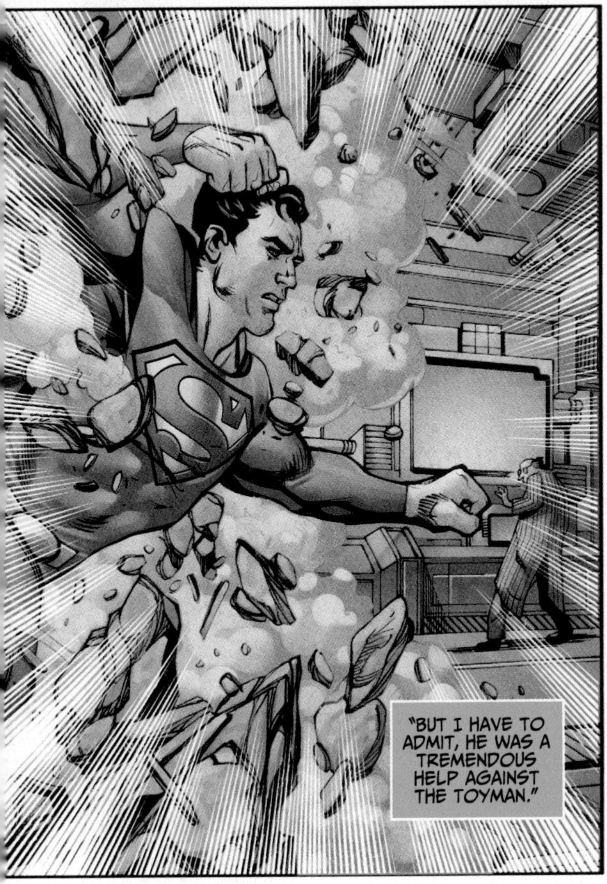
"BUT I HAVE TO ADMIT, HE WAS A TREMENDOUS HELP AGAINST THE TOYMAN."

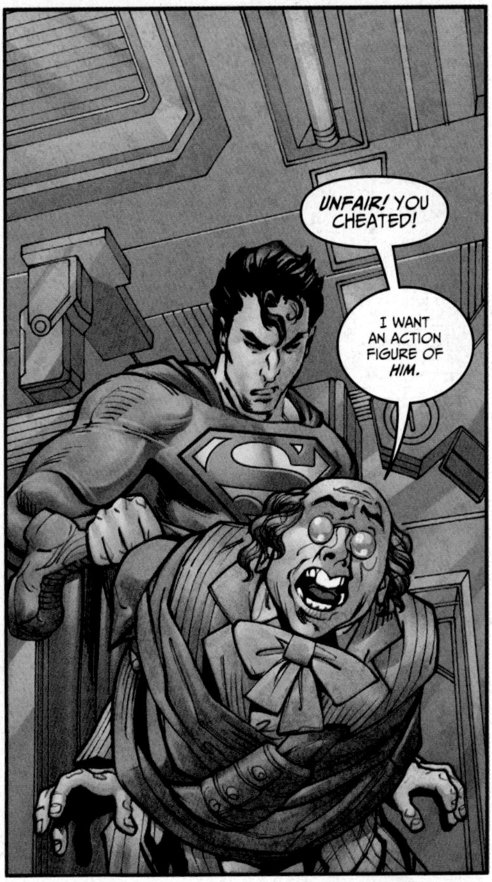
UNFAIR! YOU CHEATED!
I WANT AN ACTION FIGURE OF HIM.

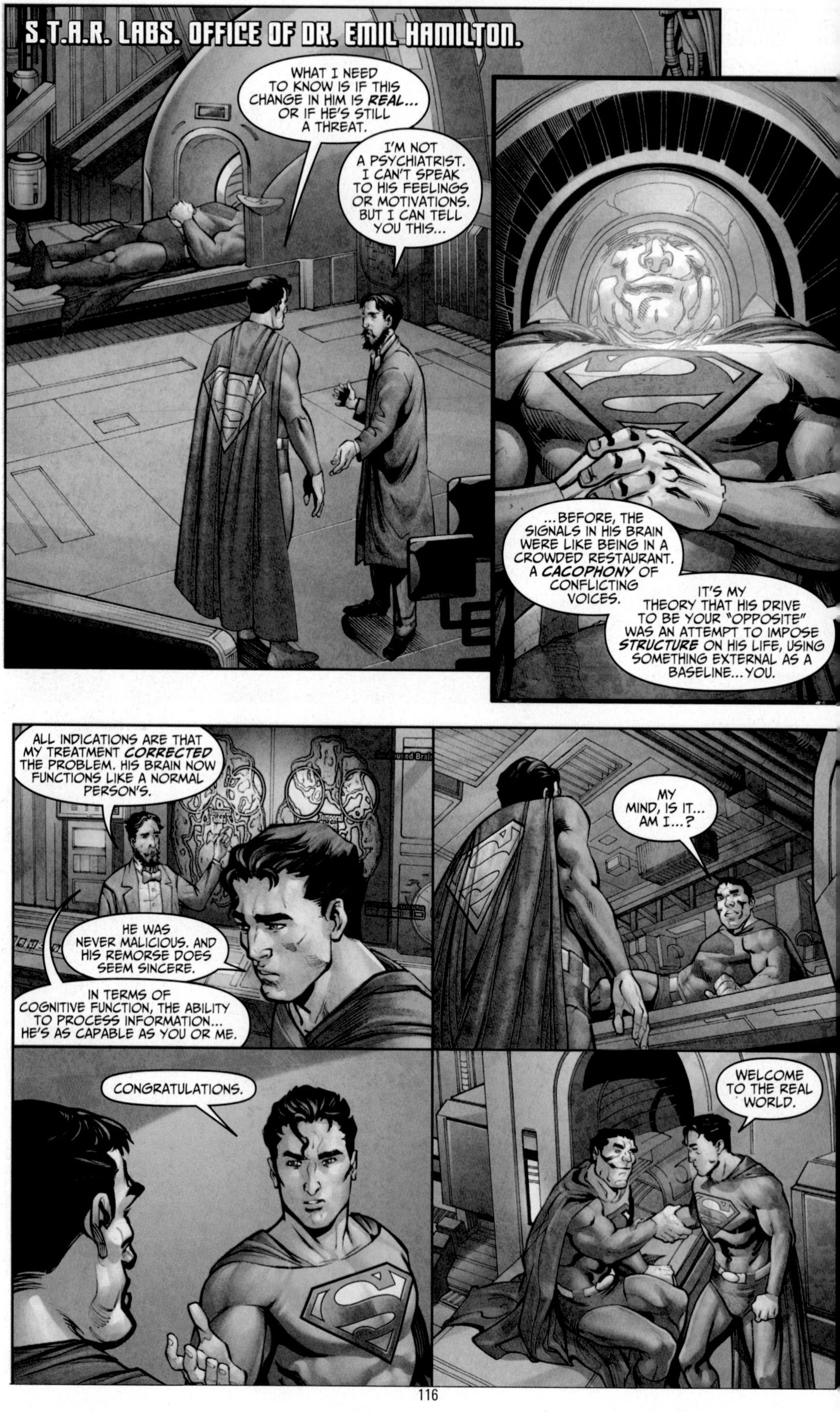
S.T.A.R. LABS. OFFICE OF DR. EMIL HAMILTON.
WHAT I NEED TO KNOW IS IF THIS CHANGE IN HIM IS REAL... OR IF HE'S STILL A THREAT.
I'M NOT A PSYCHIATRIST. I CAN'T SPEAK TO HIS FEELINGS OR MOTIVATIONS. BUT I CAN TELL YOU THIS...
...BEFORE, THE SIGNALS IN HIS BRAIN WERE LIKE BEING IN A CROWDED RESTAURANT. A CACOPHONY OF CONFLICTING VOICES.
IT'S MY THEORY THAT HIS DRIVE TO BE YOUR "OPPOSITE" WAS AN ATTEMPT TO IMPOSE STRUCTURE ON HIS LIFE, USING SOMETHING EXTERNAL AS A BASELINE... YOU.
ALL INDICATIONS ARE THAT MY TREATMENT CORRECTED THE PROBLEM. HIS BRAIN NOW FUNCTIONS LIKE A NORMAL PERSON'S.
HE WAS NEVER MALICIOUS. AND HIS REMORSE DOES SEEM SINCERE.
IN TERMS OF COGNITIVE FUNCTION, THE ABILITY TO PROCESS INFORMATION... HE'S AS CAPABLE AS YOU OR ME.
MY MIND, IS IT... AM I...?
CONGRATULATIONS.
WELCOME TO THE REAL WORLD.

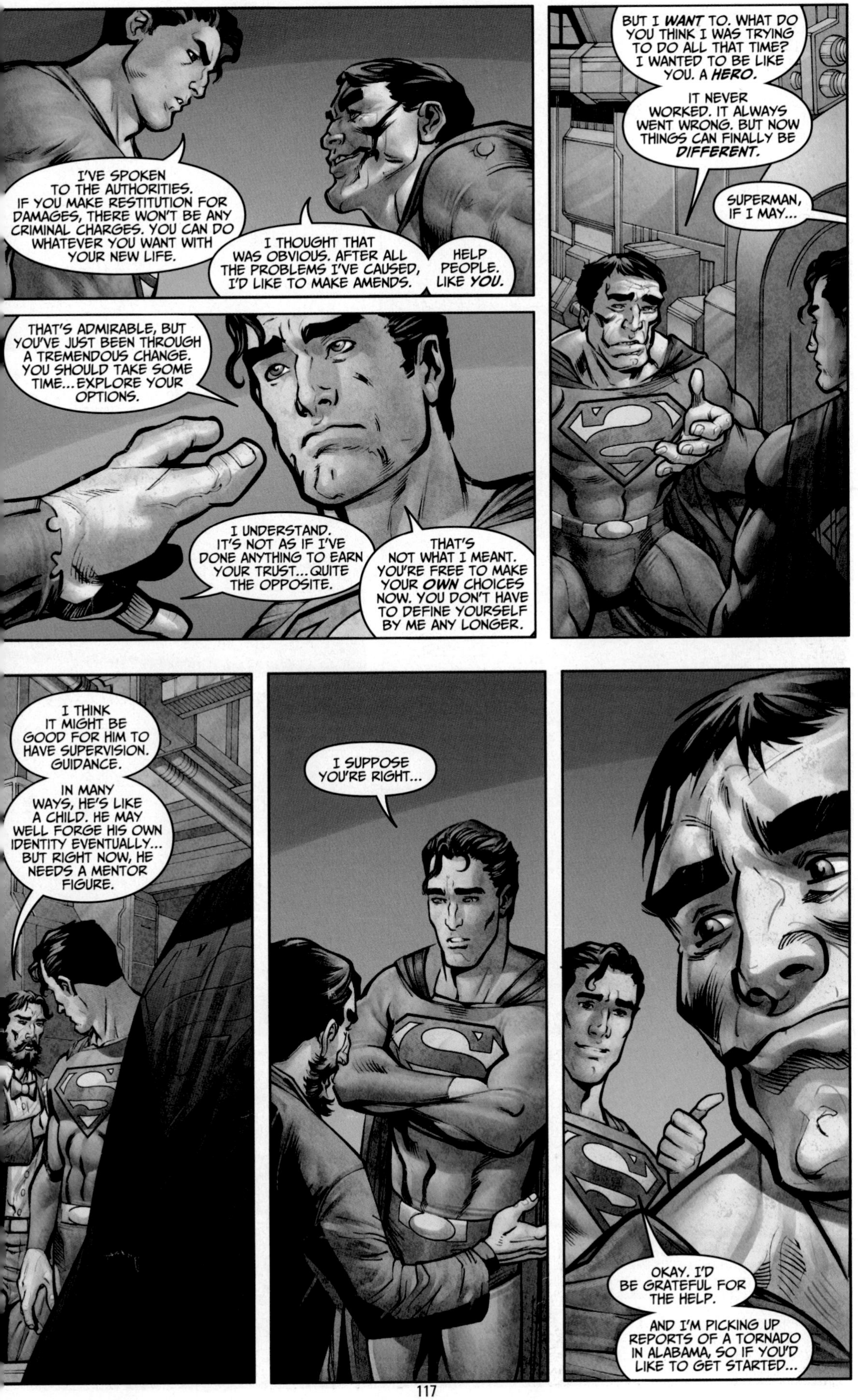
I'VE SPOKEN TO THE AUTHORITIES. IF YOU MAKE RESTITUTION FOR DAMAGES, THERE WON'T BE ANY CRIMINAL CHARGES. YOU CAN DO WHATEVER YOU WANT WITH YOUR NEW LIFE.
I THOUGHT THAT WAS OBVIOUS. AFTER ALL THE PROBLEMS I'VE CAUSED, I'D LIKE TO MAKE AMENDS.
HELP PEOPLE. LIKE *YOU.*
THAT'S ADMIRABLE, BUT YOU'VE JUST BEEN THROUGH A TREMENDOUS CHANGE. YOU SHOULD TAKE SOME TIME... EXPLORE YOUR OPTIONS.
I UNDERSTAND. IT'S NOT AS IF I'VE DONE ANYTHING TO EARN YOUR TRUST... QUITE THE OPPOSITE.
THAT'S NOT WHAT I MEANT. YOU'RE FREE TO MAKE YOUR *OWN* CHOICES NOW. YOU DON'T HAVE TO DEFINE YOURSELF BY ME ANY LONGER.
BUT I *WANT* TO. WHAT DO YOU THINK I WAS TRYING TO DO ALL THAT TIME? I WANTED TO BE LIKE YOU. A *HERO.*
IT NEVER WORKED. IT ALWAYS WENT WRONG. BUT NOW THINGS CAN FINALLY BE *DIFFERENT.*
SUPERMAN, IF I MAY...
I THINK IT MIGHT BE GOOD FOR HIM TO HAVE SUPERVISION. GUIDANCE.
IN MANY WAYS, HE'S LIKE A CHILD. HE MAY WELL FORGE HIS OWN IDENTITY EVENTUALLY... BUT RIGHT NOW, HE NEEDS A MENTOR FIGURE.
I SUPPOSE YOU'RE RIGHT...
OKAY. I'D BE GRATEFUL FOR THE HELP.
AND I'M PICKING UP REPORTS OF A TORNADO IN ALABAMA, SO IF YOU'D LIKE TO GET STARTED...

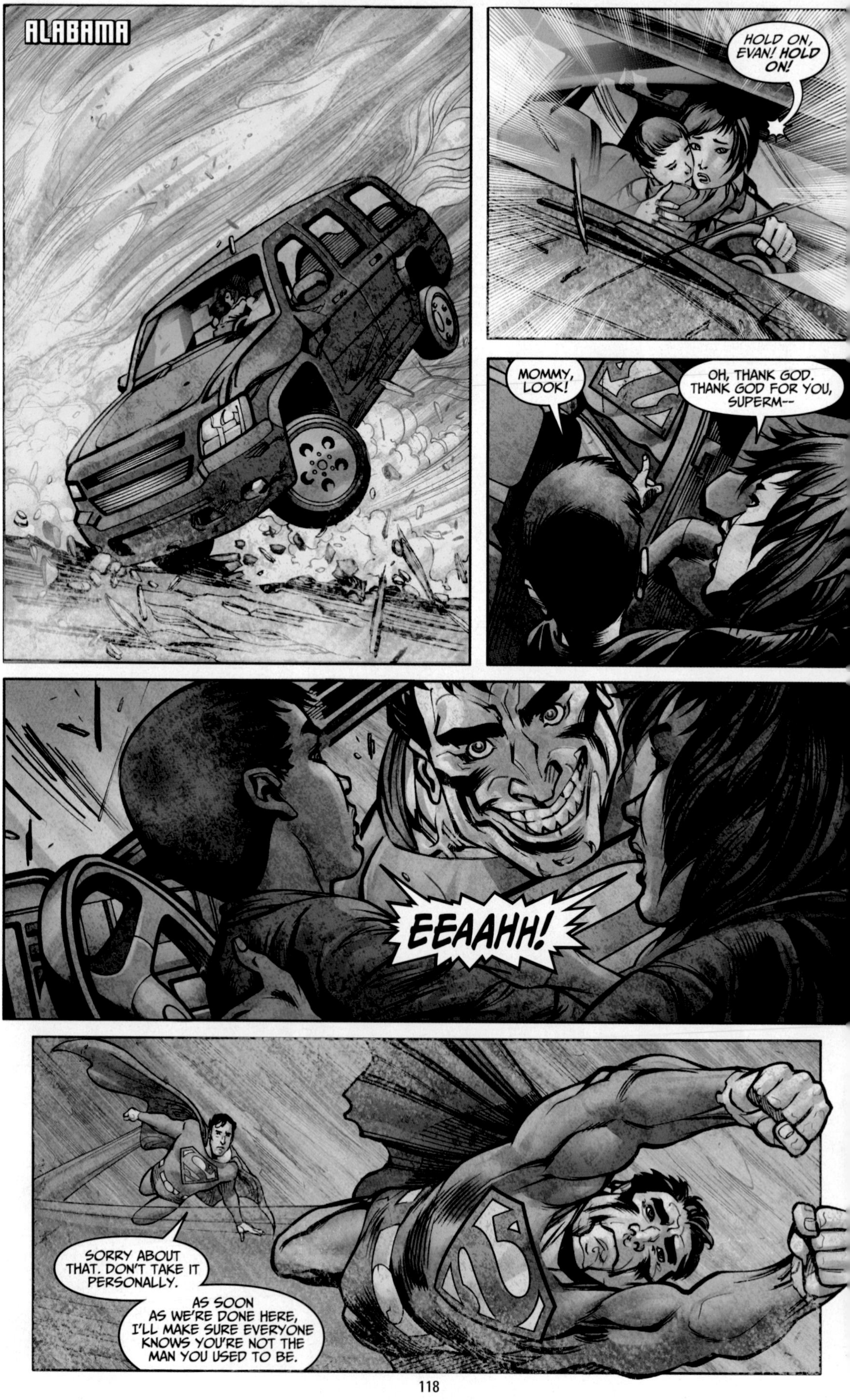
ALABAMA
HOLD ON, EVAN! HOLD ON!
MOMMY, LOOK!
OH, THANK GOD. THANK GOD FOR YOU, SUPERM--
EEAAHH!
SORRY ABOUT THAT. DON'T TAKE IT PERSONALLY.
AS SOON AS WE'RE DONE HERE, I'LL MAKE SURE EVERYONE KNOWS YOU'RE NOT THE MAN YOU USED TO BE.

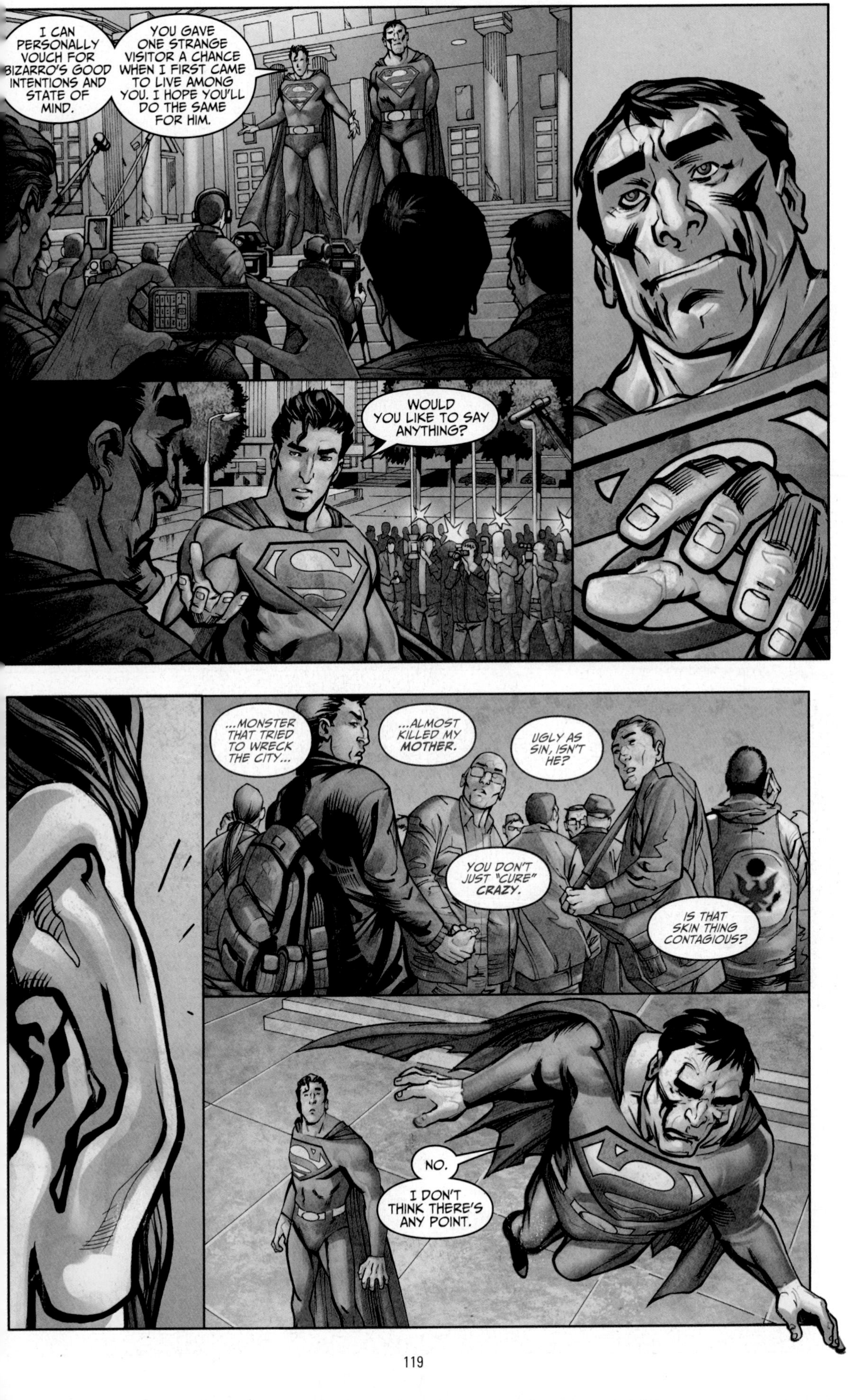

I CAN PERSONALLY VOUCH FOR BIZARRO'S GOOD INTENTIONS AND STATE OF MIND.
YOU GAVE ONE STRANGE VISITOR A CHANCE WHEN I FIRST CAME TO LIVE AMONG YOU. I HOPE YOU'LL DO THE SAME FOR HIM.
WOULD YOU LIKE TO SAY ANYTHING?
...MONSTER THAT TRIED TO WRECK THE CITY...
...ALMOST KILLED MY MOTHER.
UGLY AS SIN, ISN'T HE?
YOU DON'T JUST "CURE" CRAZY.
IS THAT SKIN THING CONTAGIOUS?
NO.
I DON'T THINK THERE'S ANY POINT.

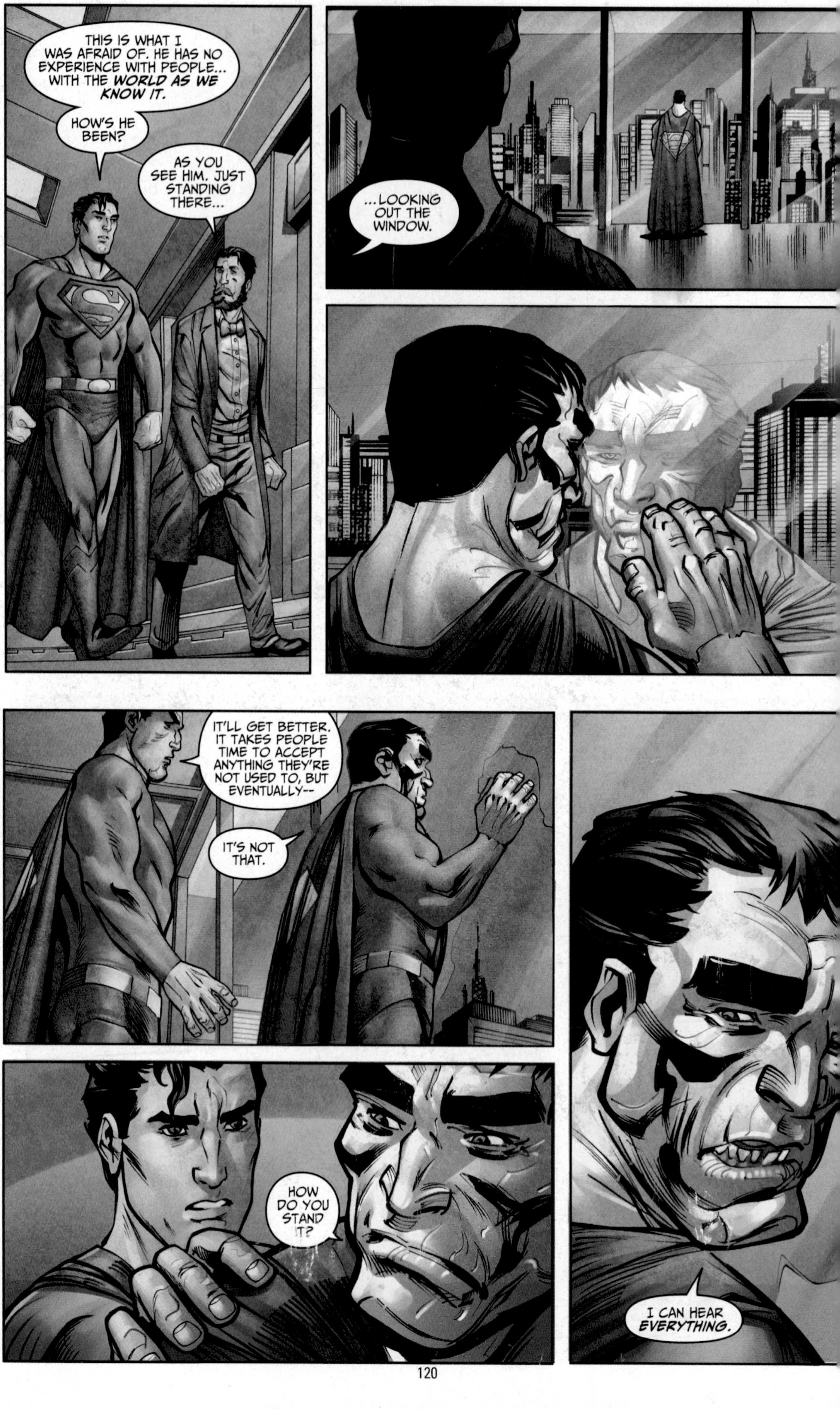
THIS IS WHAT I WAS AFRAID OF. HE HAS NO EXPERIENCE WITH PEOPLE... WITH THE *WORLD AS WE KNOW IT.*
HOW'S HE BEEN?
AS YOU SEE HIM. JUST STANDING THERE...
...LOOKING OUT THE WINDOW.
IT'LL GET BETTER. IT TAKES PEOPLE TIME TO ACCEPT ANYTHING THEY'RE NOT USED TO, BUT EVENTUALLY--
IT'S NOT THAT.
HOW DO YOU STAND IT?
I CAN HEAR *EVERYTHING.*

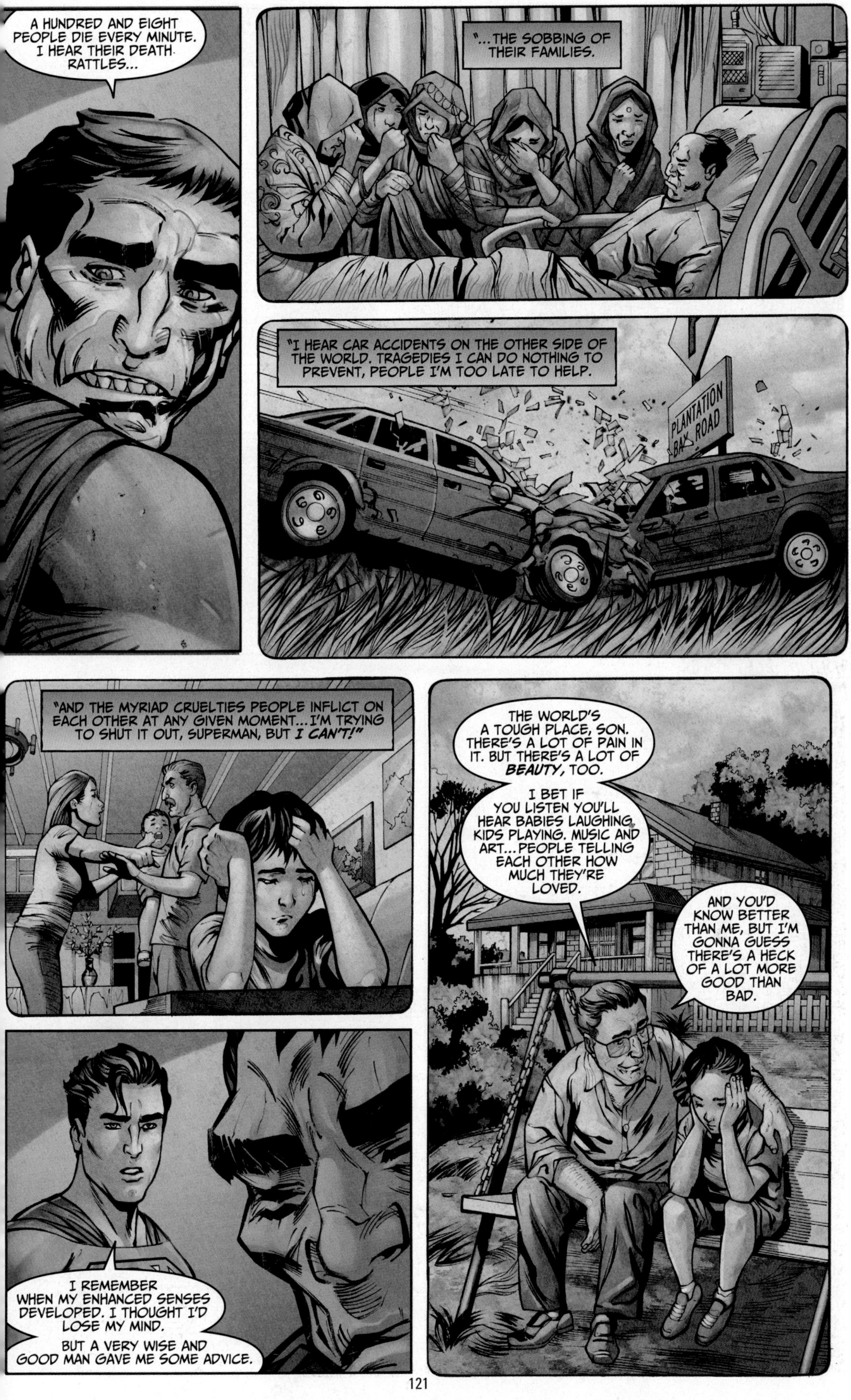
A HUNDRED AND EIGHT PEOPLE DIE EVERY MINUTE. I HEAR THEIR DEATH RATTLES...
"...THE SOBBING OF THEIR FAMILIES.
"I HEAR CAR ACCIDENTS ON THE OTHER SIDE OF THE WORLD. TRAGEDIES I CAN DO NOTHING TO PREVENT, PEOPLE I'M TOO LATE TO HELP.
PLANTATION BAY ROAD
"AND THE MYRIAD CRUELTIES PEOPLE INFLICT ON EACH OTHER AT ANY GIVEN MOMENT...I'M TRYING TO SHUT IT OUT, SUPERMAN, BUT I CAN'T!"
THE WORLD'S A TOUGH PLACE, SON. THERE'S A LOT OF PAIN IN IT. BUT THERE'S A LOT OF BEAUTY, TOO.
I BET IF YOU LISTEN YOU'LL HEAR BABIES LAUGHING, KIDS PLAYING. MUSIC AND ART...PEOPLE TELLING EACH OTHER HOW MUCH THEY'RE LOVED.
AND YOU'D KNOW BETTER THAN ME, BUT I'M GONNA GUESS THERE'S A HECK OF A LOT MORE GOOD THAN BAD.
I REMEMBER WHEN MY ENHANCED SENSES DEVELOPED. I THOUGHT I'D LOSE MY MIND.
BUT A VERY WISE AND GOOD MAN GAVE ME SOME ADVICE.

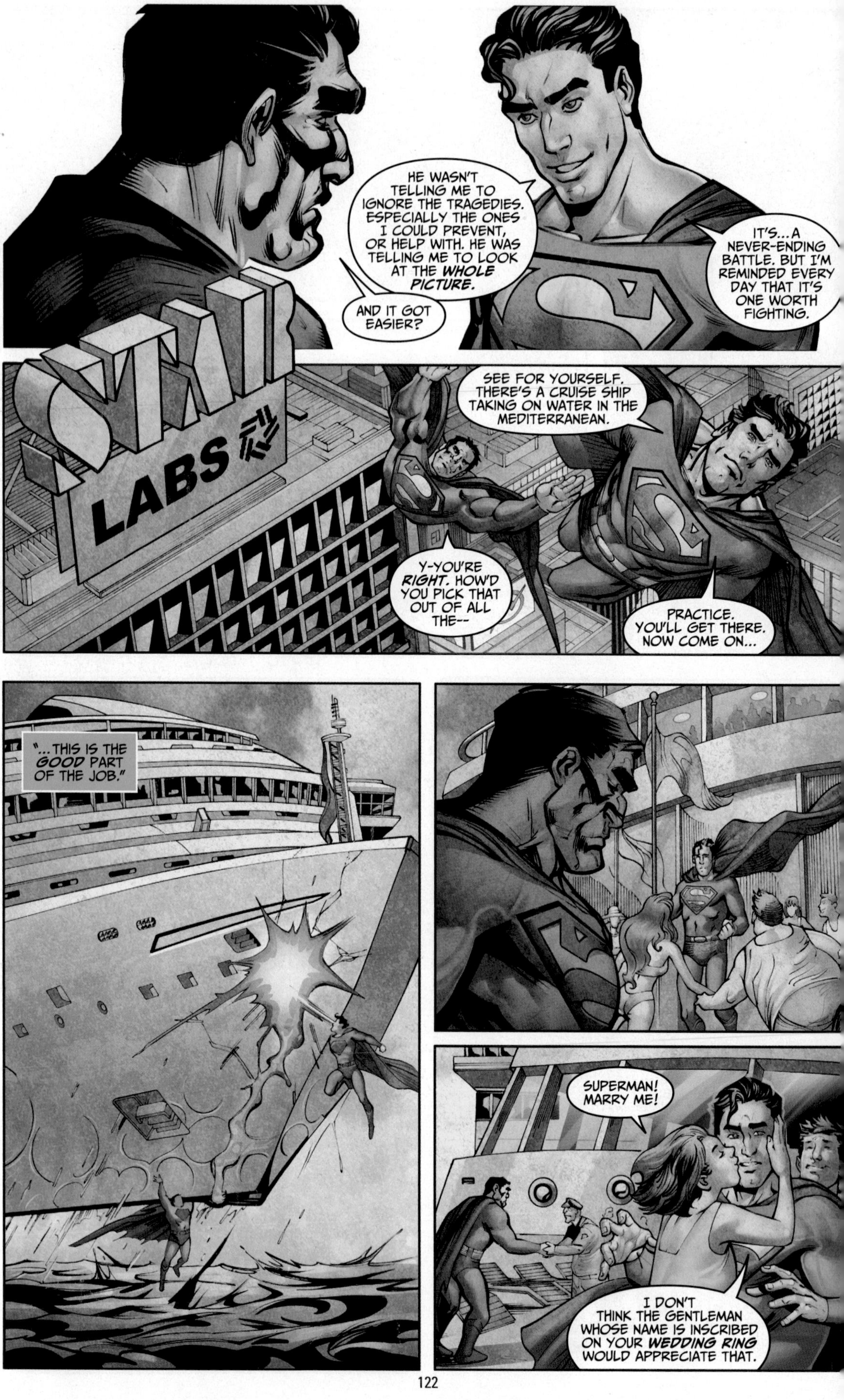

HE WASN'T TELLING ME TO IGNORE THE TRAGEDIES. ESPECIALLY THE ONES I COULD PREVENT, OR HELP WITH. HE WAS TELLING ME TO LOOK AT THE *WHOLE PICTURE.*
AND IT GOT EASIER?
IT'S...A NEVER-ENDING BATTLE. BUT I'M REMINDED EVERY DAY THAT IT'S ONE WORTH FIGHTING.
STAR LABS
SEE FOR YOURSELF. THERE'S A CRUISE SHIP TAKING ON WATER IN THE MEDITERRANEAN.
Y-YOU'RE *RIGHT.* HOW'D YOU PICK THAT OUT OF ALL THE--
PRACTICE. YOU'LL GET THERE. NOW COME ON...
"...THIS IS THE *GOOD* PART OF THE JOB."
SUPERMAN! MARRY ME!
I DON'T THINK THE GENTLEMAN WHOSE NAME IS INSCRIBED ON YOUR *WEDDING RING* WOULD APPRECIATE THAT.

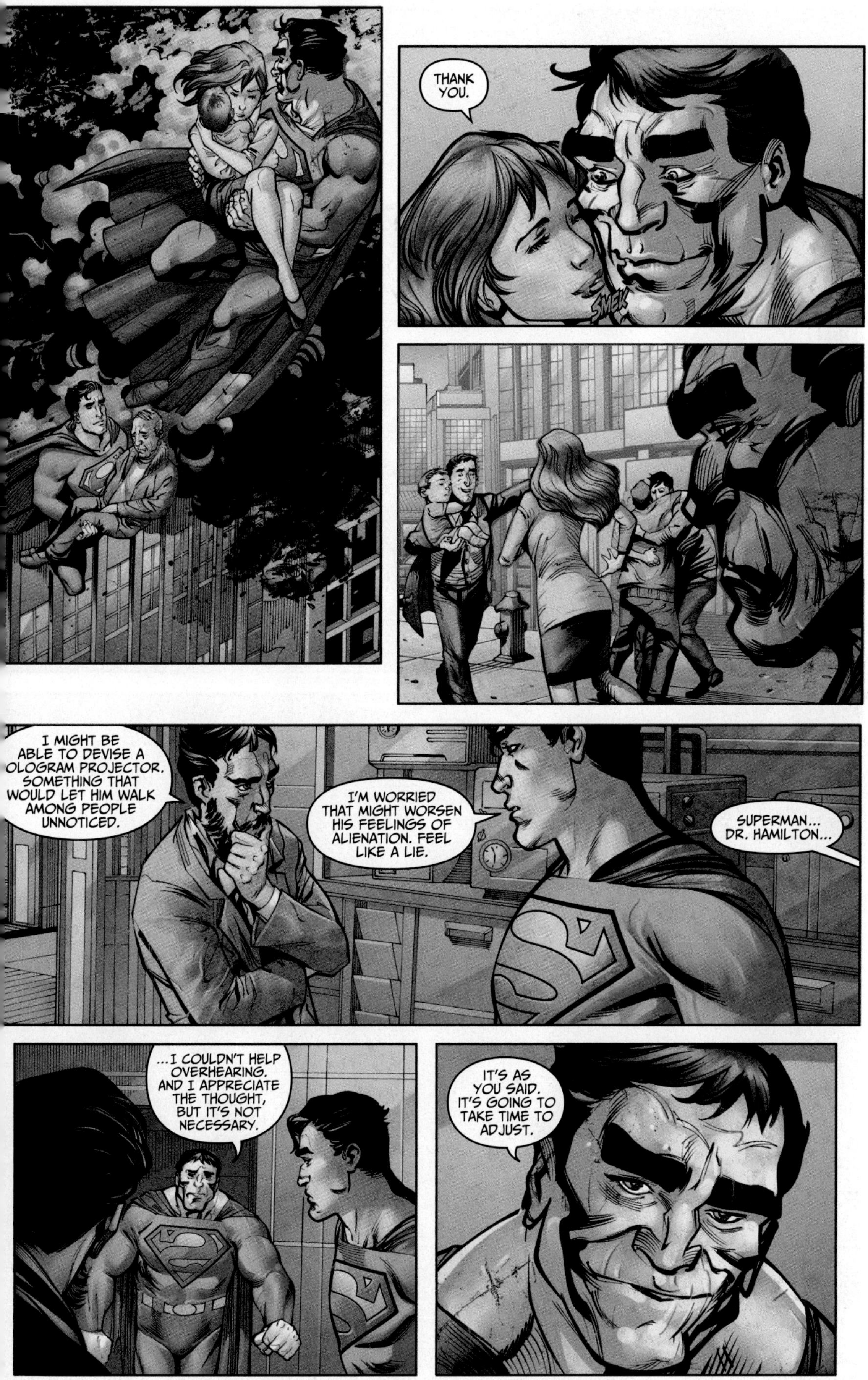
THANK YOU.
SMEK
I MIGHT BE ABLE TO DEVISE A OLOGRAM PROJECTOR. SOMETHING THAT WOULD LET HIM WALK AMONG PEOPLE UNNOTICED.
I'M WORRIED THAT MIGHT WORSEN HIS FEELINGS OF ALIENATION. FEEL LIKE A LIE.
SUPERMAN... DR. HAMILTON...
...I COULDN'T HELP OVERHEARING. AND I APPRECIATE THE THOUGHT, BUT IT'S NOT NECESSARY.
IT'S AS YOU SAID. IT'S GOING TO TAKE TIME TO ADJUST.

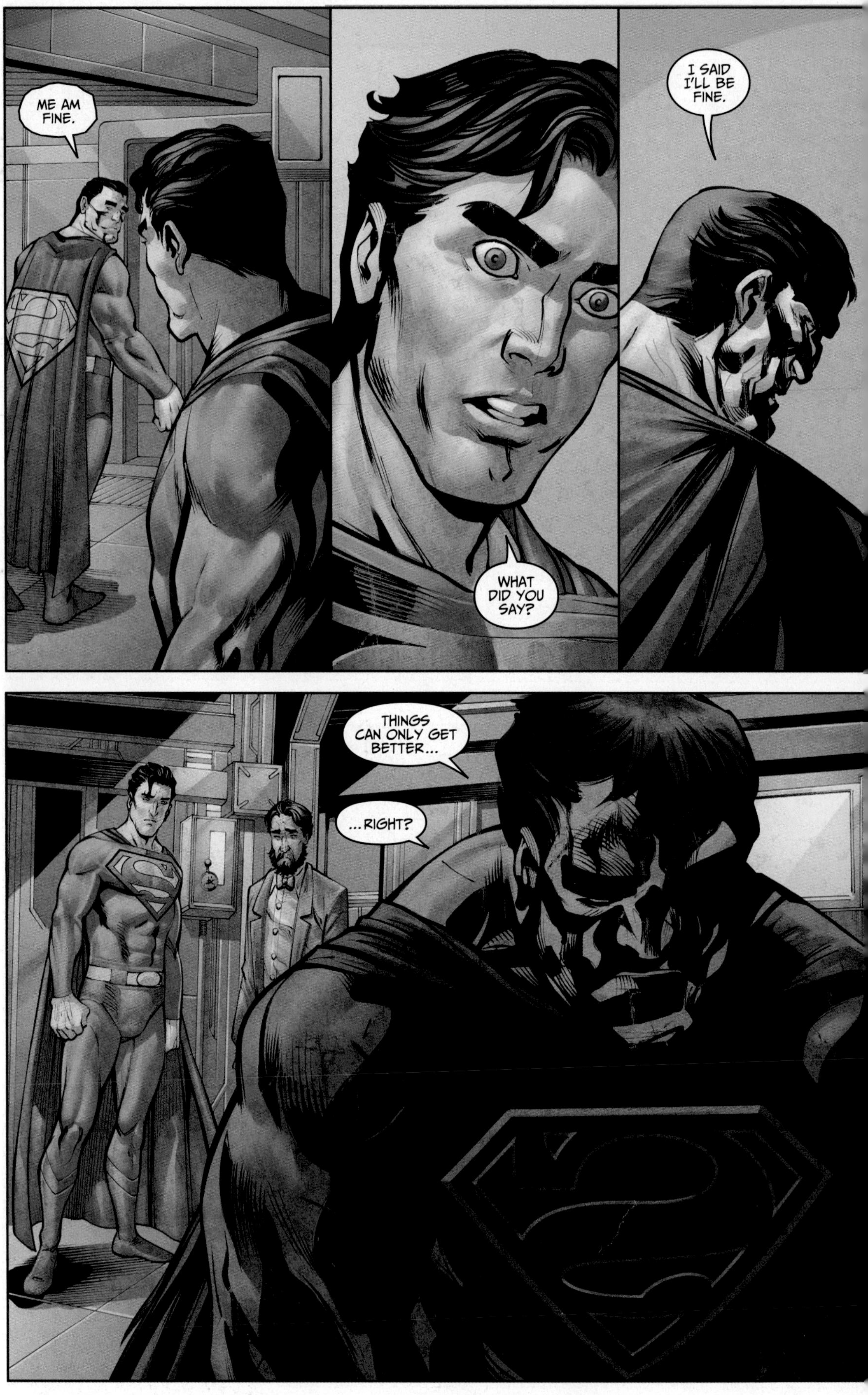

ME AM FINE.
WHAT DID YOU SAY?
I SAID I'LL BE FINE.
THINGS CAN ONLY GET BETTER...
...RIGHT?

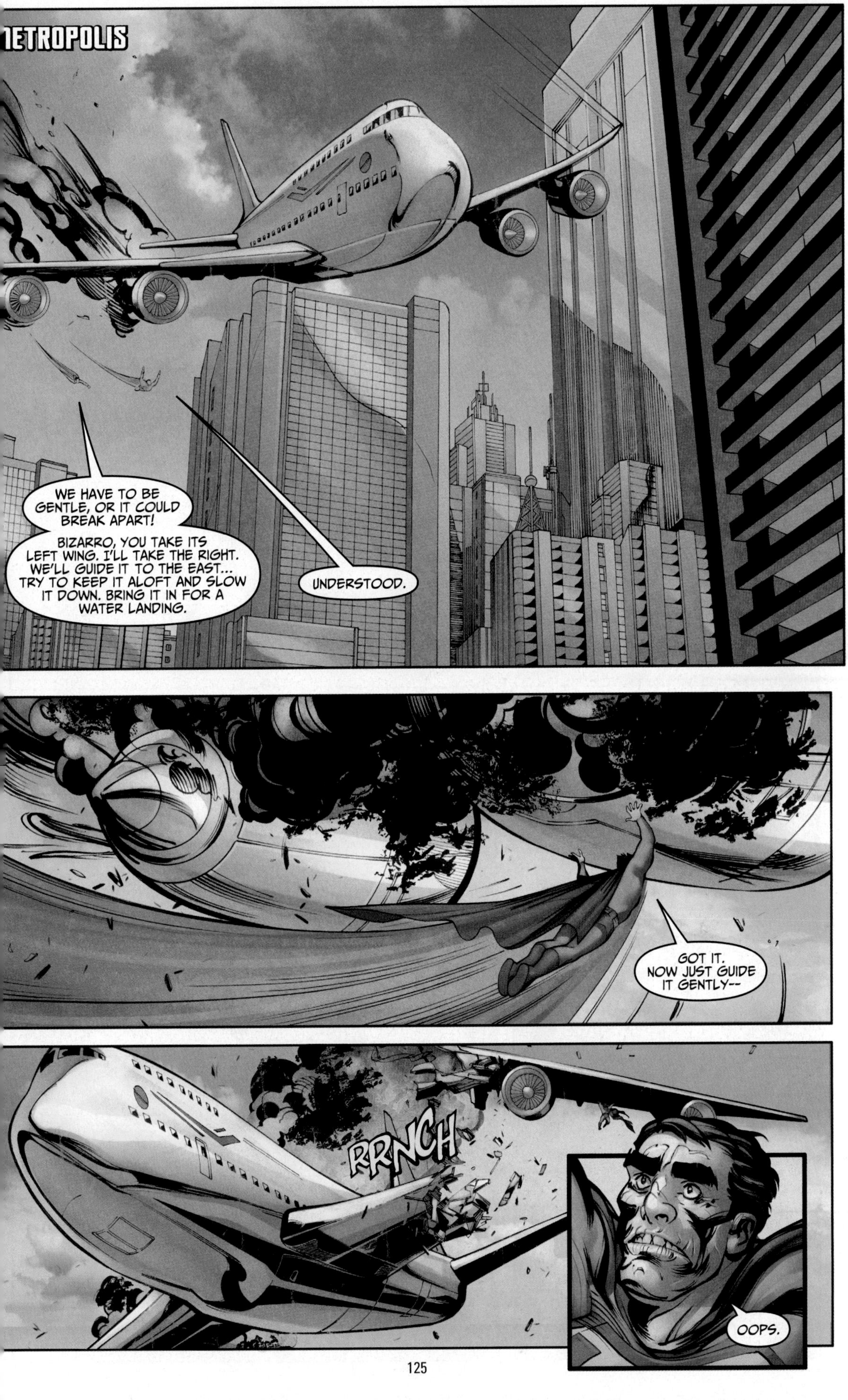
METROPOLIS
WE HAVE TO BE GENTLE, OR IT COULD BREAK APART!
BIZARRO, YOU TAKE ITS LEFT WING. I'LL TAKE THE RIGHT. WE'LL GUIDE IT TO THE EAST... TRY TO KEEP IT ALOFT AND SLOW IT DOWN. BRING IT IN FOR A WATER LANDING.
UNDERSTOOD.
GOT IT. NOW JUST GUIDE IT GENTLY--
RRNCH
OOPS.

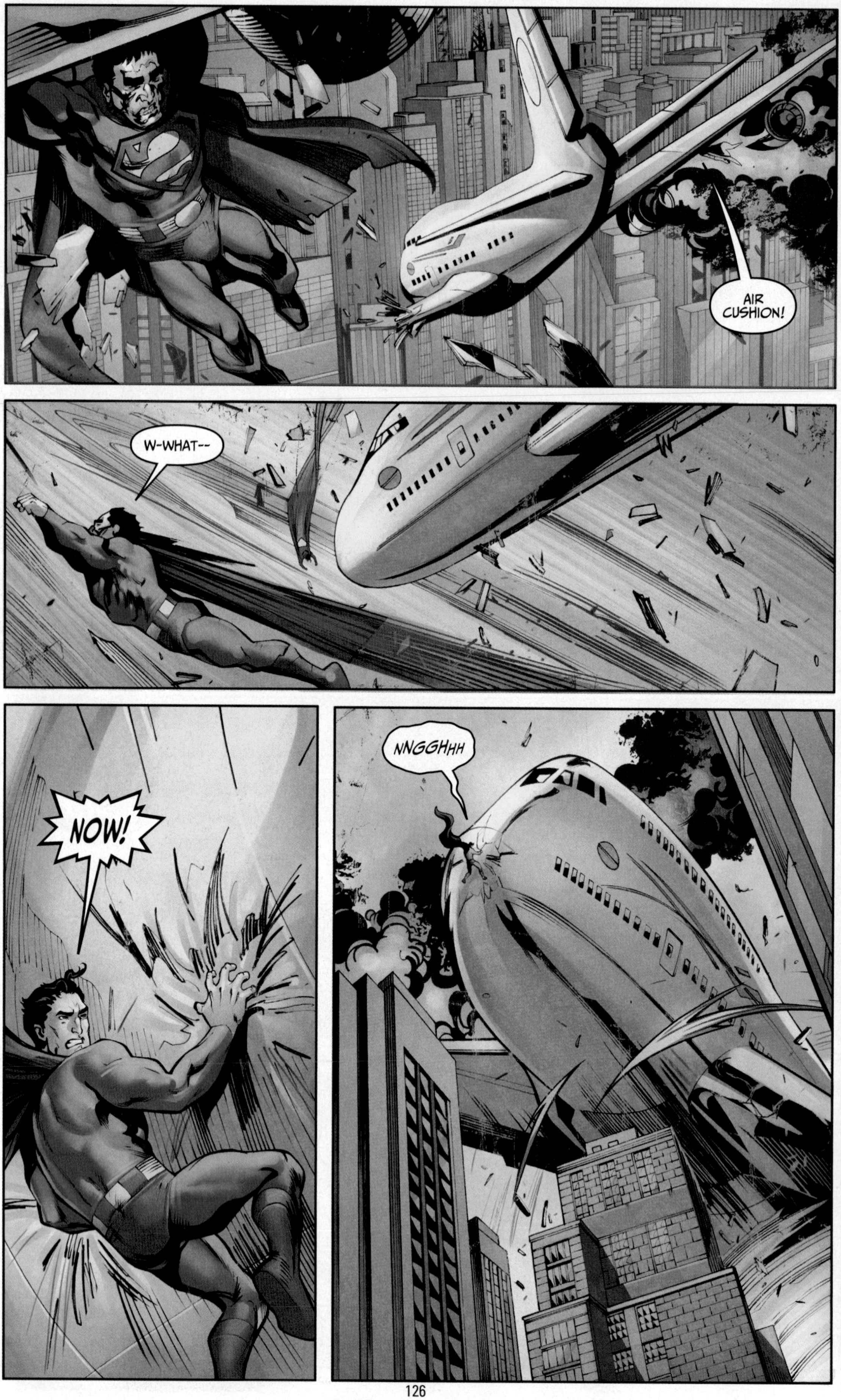
AIR CUSHION!
W-WHAT--
NOW!
NNGGHHH

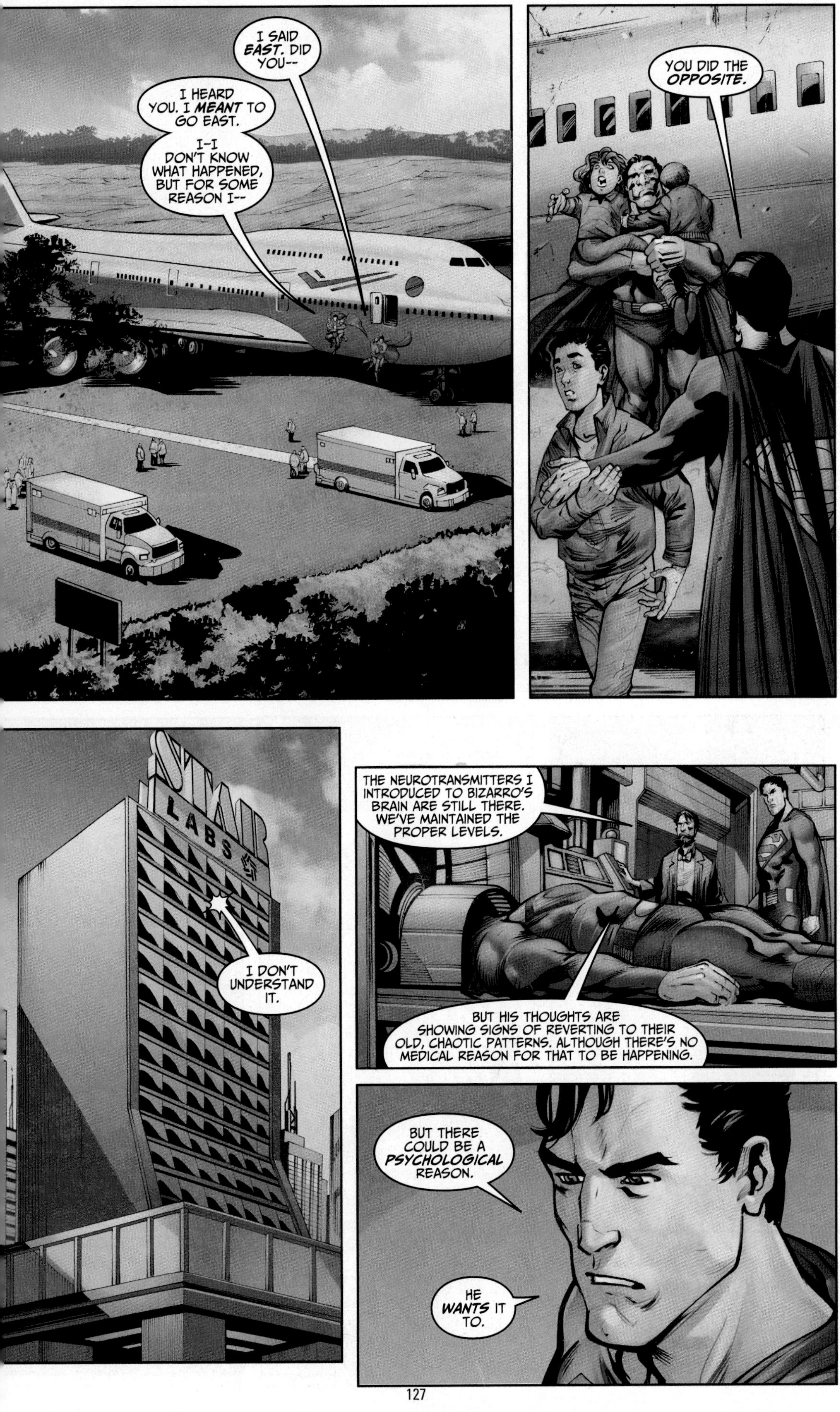
I SAID EAST. DID YOU--
I HEARD YOU. I MEANT TO GO EAST.
I-I DON'T KNOW WHAT HAPPENED, BUT FOR SOME REASON I--
YOU DID THE OPPOSITE.
STAR LABS
I DON'T UNDERSTAND IT.
THE NEUROTRANSMITTERS I INTRODUCED TO BIZARRO'S BRAIN ARE STILL THERE. WE'VE MAINTAINED THE PROPER LEVELS.
BUT HIS THOUGHTS ARE SHOWING SIGNS OF REVERTING TO THEIR OLD, CHAOTIC PATTERNS. ALTHOUGH THERE'S NO MEDICAL REASON FOR THAT TO BE HAPPENING.
BUT THERE COULD BE A PSYCHOLOGICAL REASON.
HE WANTS IT TO.

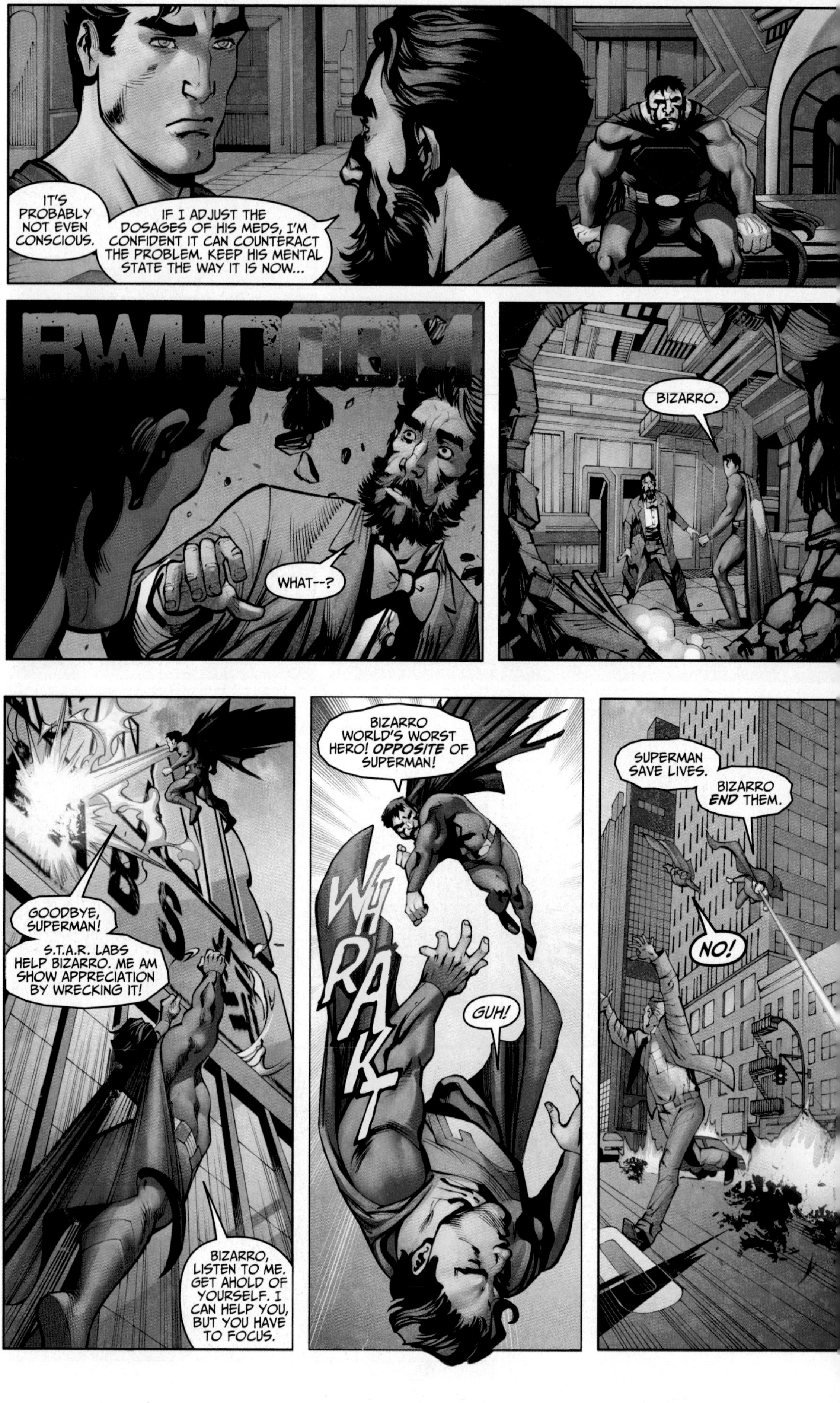
IT'S PROBABLY NOT EVEN CONSCIOUS.
IF I ADJUST THE DOSAGES OF HIS MEDS, I'M CONFIDENT IT CAN COUNTERACT THE PROBLEM. KEEP HIS MENTAL STATE THE WAY IT IS NOW...
RWHOOM
WHAT--?
BIZARRO.
GOODBYE, SUPERMAN!
S.T.A.R. LABS HELP BIZARRO. ME AM SHOW APPRECIATION BY WRECKING IT!
BIZARRO, LISTEN TO ME. GET AHOLD OF YOURSELF. I CAN HELP YOU, BUT YOU HAVE TO FOCUS.
BIZARRO WORLD'S WORST HERO! OPPOSITE OF SUPERMAN!
WHRAKT
GUH!
SUPERMAN SAVE LIVES.
BIZARRO END THEM.
NO!

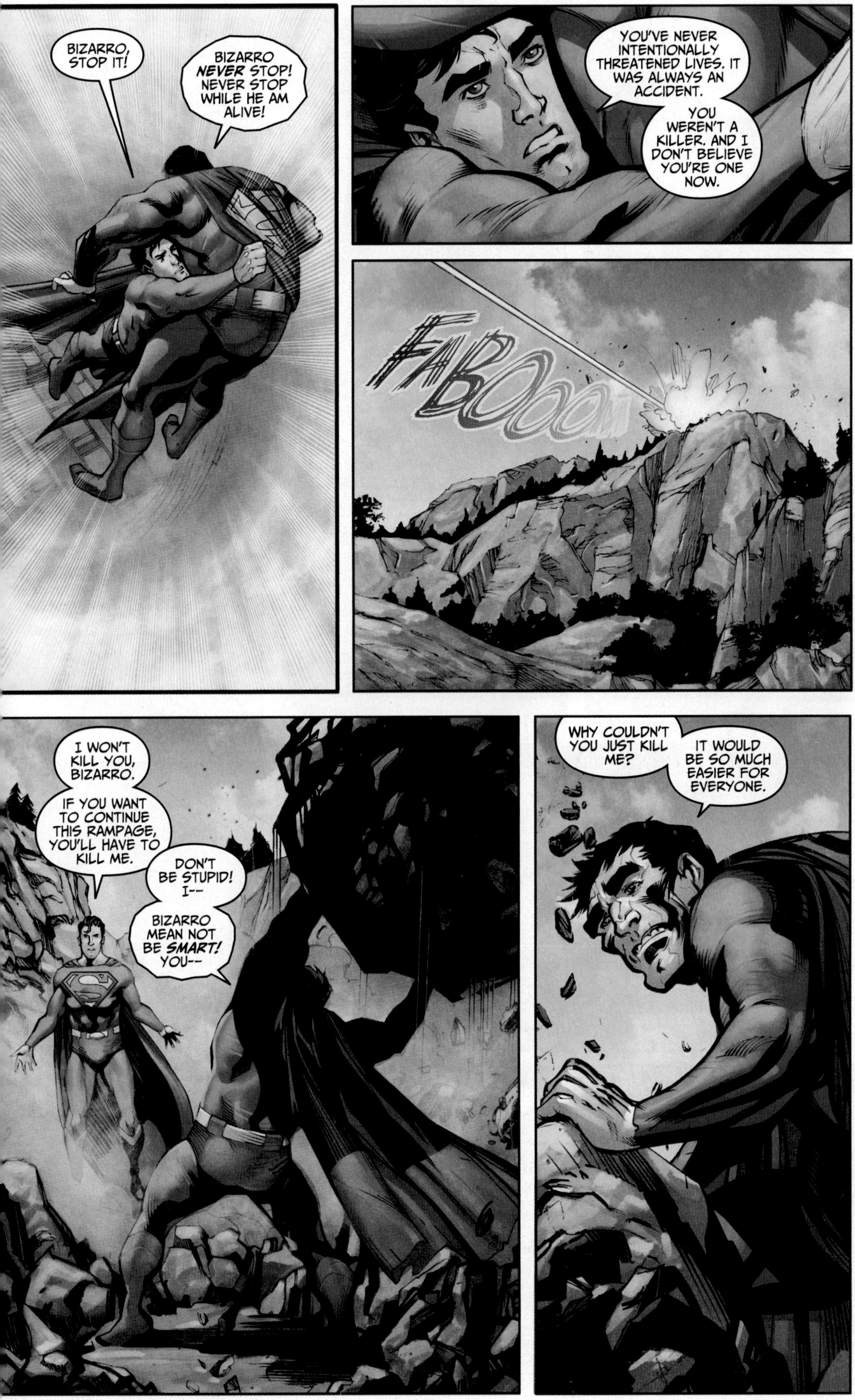
BIZARRO, STOP IT!
BIZARRO NEVER STOP! NEVER STOP WHILE HE AM ALIVE!
YOU'VE NEVER INTENTIONALLY THREATENED LIVES. IT WAS ALWAYS AN ACCIDENT.
YOU WEREN'T A KILLER. AND I DON'T BELIEVE YOU'RE ONE NOW.
FABOOOM
I WON'T KILL YOU, BIZARRO.
IF YOU WANT TO CONTINUE THIS RAMPAGE, YOU'LL HAVE TO KILL ME.
DON'T BE STUPID! I--
BIZARRO MEAN NOT BE SMART! YOU--
WHY COULDN'T YOU JUST KILL ME?
IT WOULD BE SO MUCH EASIER FOR EVERYONE.

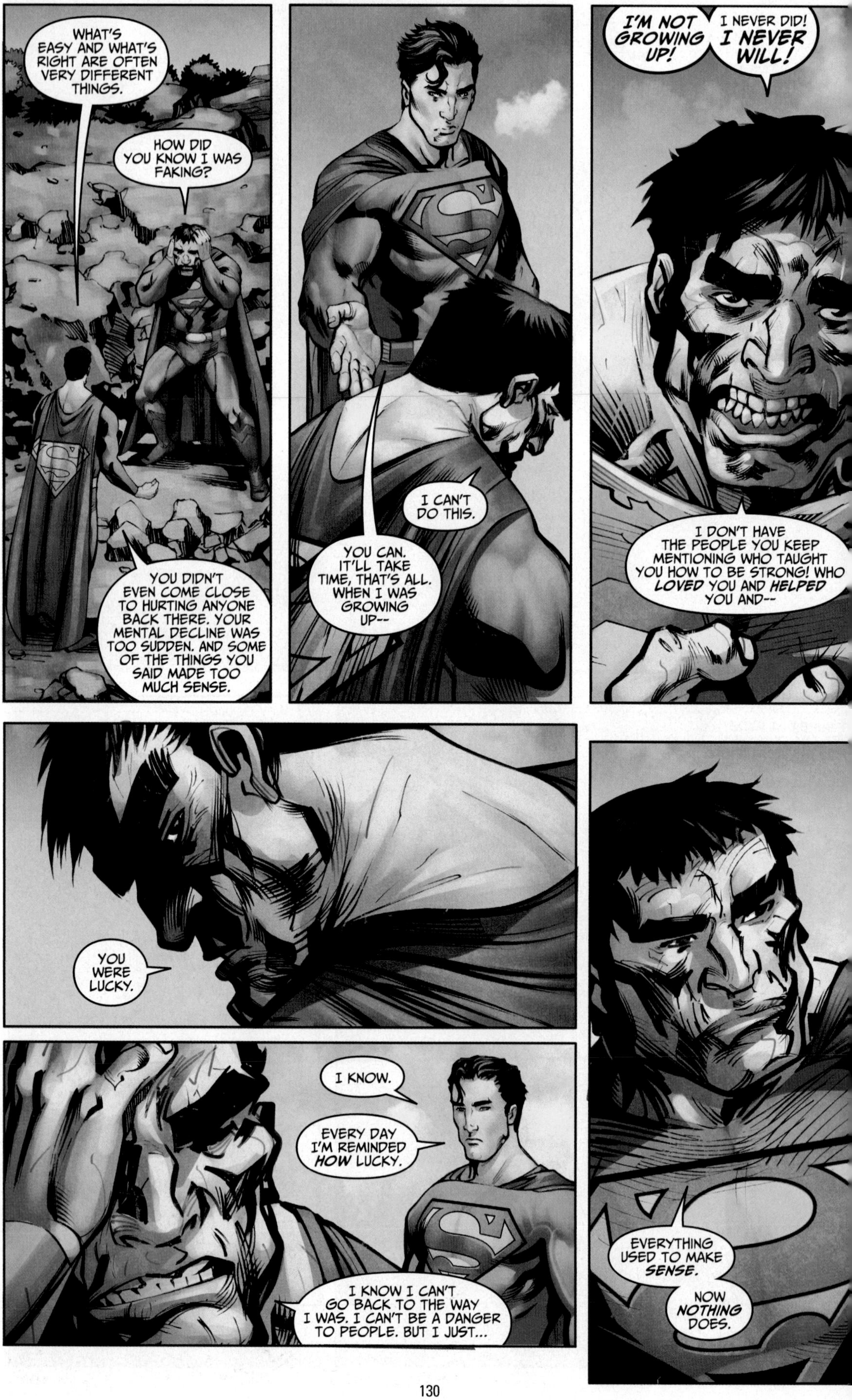
WHAT'S EASY AND WHAT'S RIGHT ARE OFTEN VERY DIFFERENT THINGS.
HOW DID YOU KNOW I WAS FAKING?
YOU DIDN'T EVEN COME CLOSE TO HURTING ANYONE BACK THERE. YOUR MENTAL DECLINE WAS TOO SUDDEN. AND SOME OF THE THINGS YOU SAID MADE TOO MUCH SENSE.
I CAN'T DO THIS.
YOU CAN. IT'LL TAKE TIME, THAT'S ALL. WHEN I WAS GROWING UP--
I'M NOT GROWING UP!
I NEVER DID! I NEVER WILL!
I DON'T HAVE THE PEOPLE YOU KEEP MENTIONING WHO TAUGHT YOU HOW TO BE STRONG! WHO LOVED YOU AND HELPED YOU AND--
YOU WERE LUCKY.
I KNOW.
EVERY DAY I'M REMINDED HOW LUCKY.
I KNOW I CAN'T GO BACK TO THE WAY I WAS. I CAN'T BE A DANGER TO PEOPLE. BUT I JUST...
EVERYTHING USED TO MAKE SENSE.
NOW NOTHING DOES.

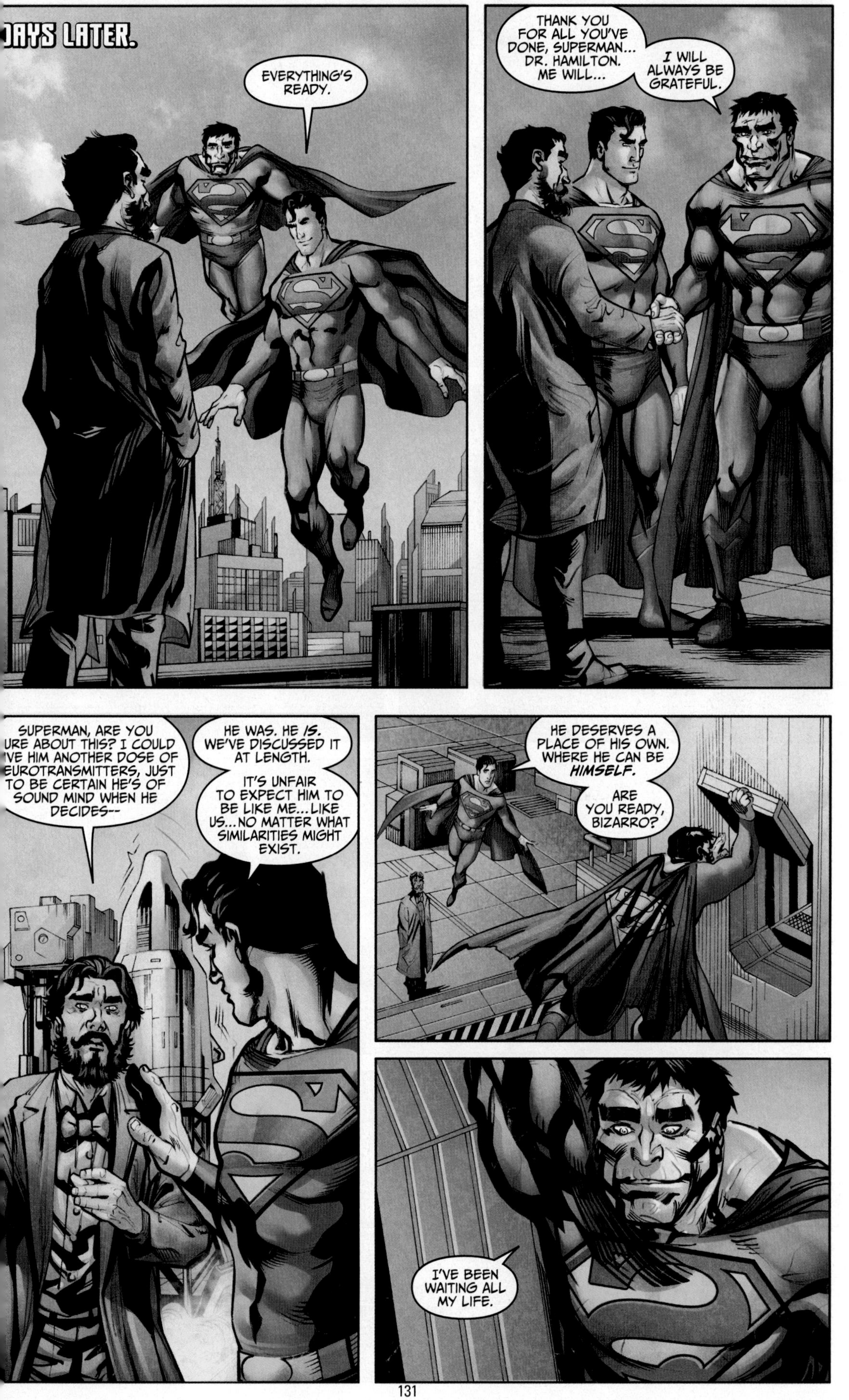
DAYS LATER.
EVERYTHING'S READY.
THANK YOU FOR ALL YOU'VE DONE, SUPERMAN... DR. HAMILTON. ME WILL...
I WILL ALWAYS BE GRATEFUL.
SUPERMAN, ARE YOU URE ABOUT THIS? I COULD IVE HIM ANOTHER DOSE OF EUROTRANSMITTERS, JUST TO BE CERTAIN HE'S OF SOUND MIND WHEN HE DECIDES--
HE WAS. HE IS. WE'VE DISCUSSED IT AT LENGTH.
IT'S UNFAIR TO EXPECT HIM TO BE LIKE ME...LIKE US...NO MATTER WHAT SIMILARITIES MIGHT EXIST.
HE DESERVES A PLACE OF HIS OWN. WHERE HE CAN BE HIMSELF.
ARE YOU READY, BIZARRO?
I'VE BEEN WAITING ALL MY LIFE.

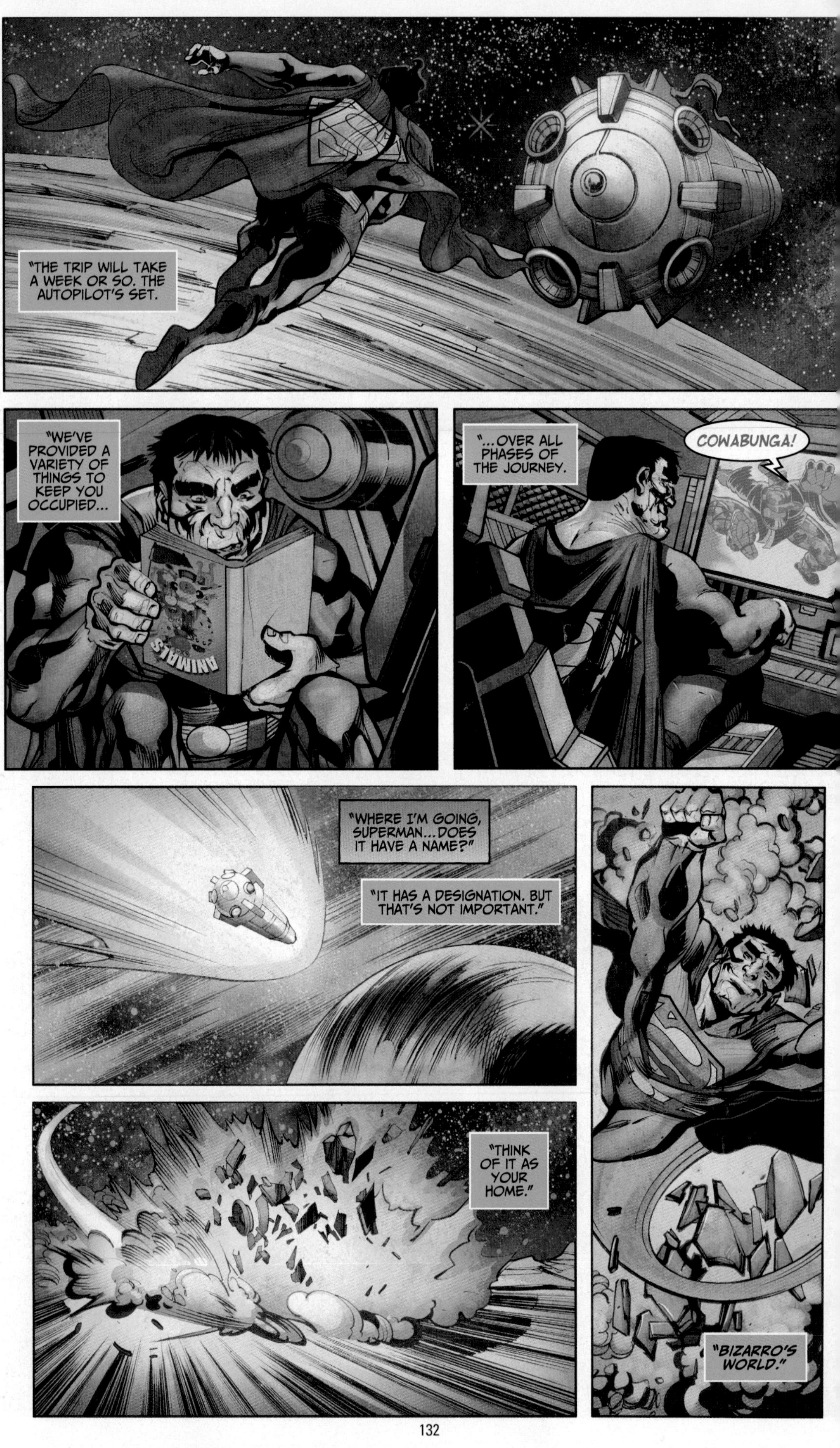
"THE TRIP WILL TAKE A WEEK OR SO. THE AUTOPILOT'S SET.
"WE'VE PROVIDED A VARIETY OF THINGS TO KEEP YOU OCCUPIED...
ANIMALS
"...OVER ALL PHASES OF THE JOURNEY.
COWABUNGA!
"WHERE I'M GOING, SUPERMAN...DOES IT HAVE A NAME?"
"IT HAS A DESIGNATION. BUT THAT'S NOT IMPORTANT."
"THINK OF IT AS YOUR HOME."
"BIZARRO'S WORLD."

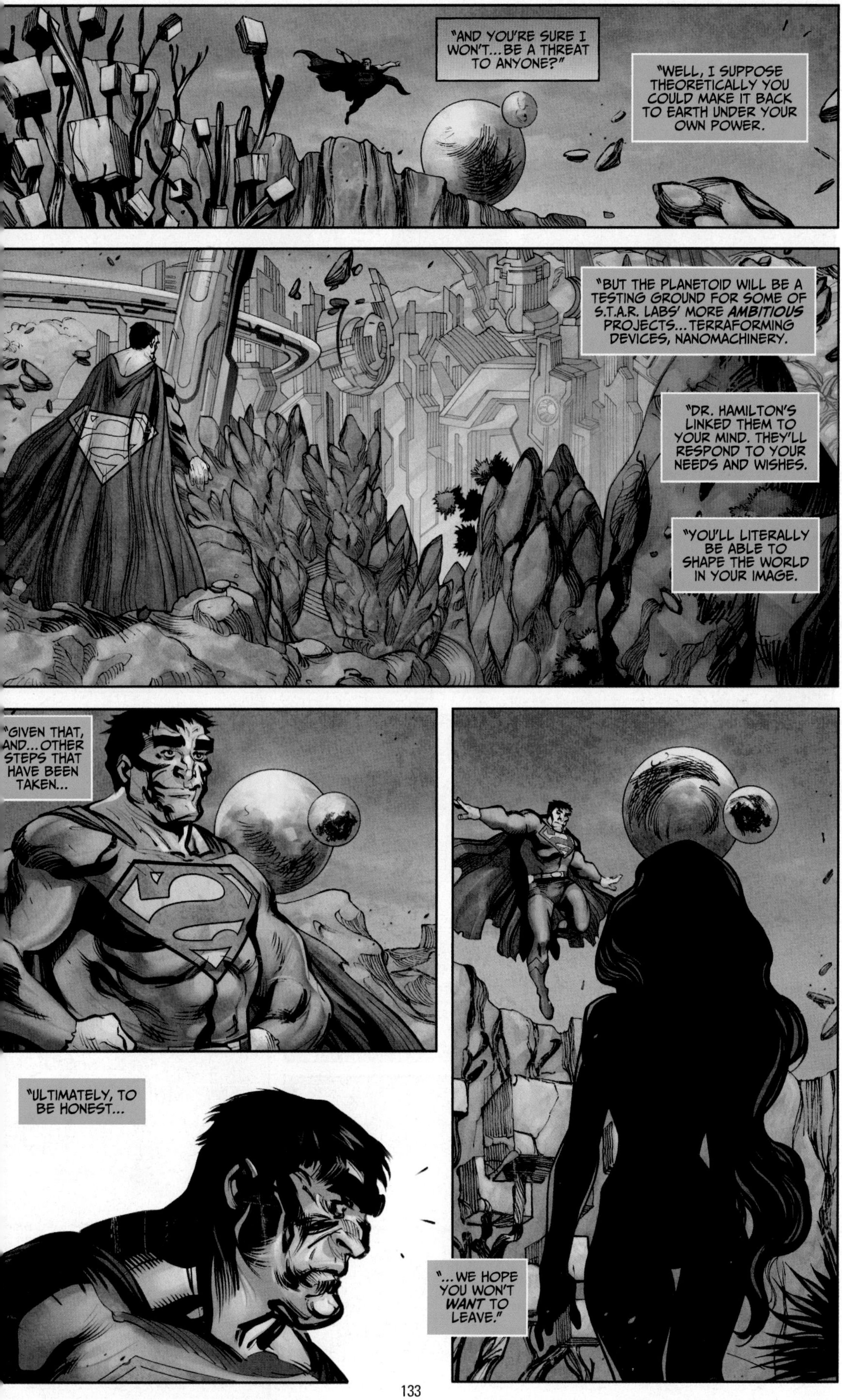
"AND YOU'RE SURE I WON'T...BE A THREAT TO ANYONE?"
"WELL, I SUPPOSE THEORETICALLY YOU COULD MAKE IT BACK TO EARTH UNDER YOUR OWN POWER.
"BUT THE PLANETOID WILL BE A TESTING GROUND FOR SOME OF S.T.A.R. LABS' MORE *AMBITIOUS* PROJECTS...TERRAFORMING DEVICES, NANOMACHINERY.
"DR. HAMILTON'S LINKED THEM TO YOUR MIND. THEY'LL RESPOND TO YOUR NEEDS AND WISHES.
"YOU'LL LITERALLY BE ABLE TO SHAPE THE WORLD IN YOUR IMAGE.
"GIVEN THAT, AND...OTHER STEPS THAT HAVE BEEN TAKEN...
"ULTIMATELY, TO BE HONEST...
"...WE HOPE YOU WON'T *WANT* TO LEAVE."

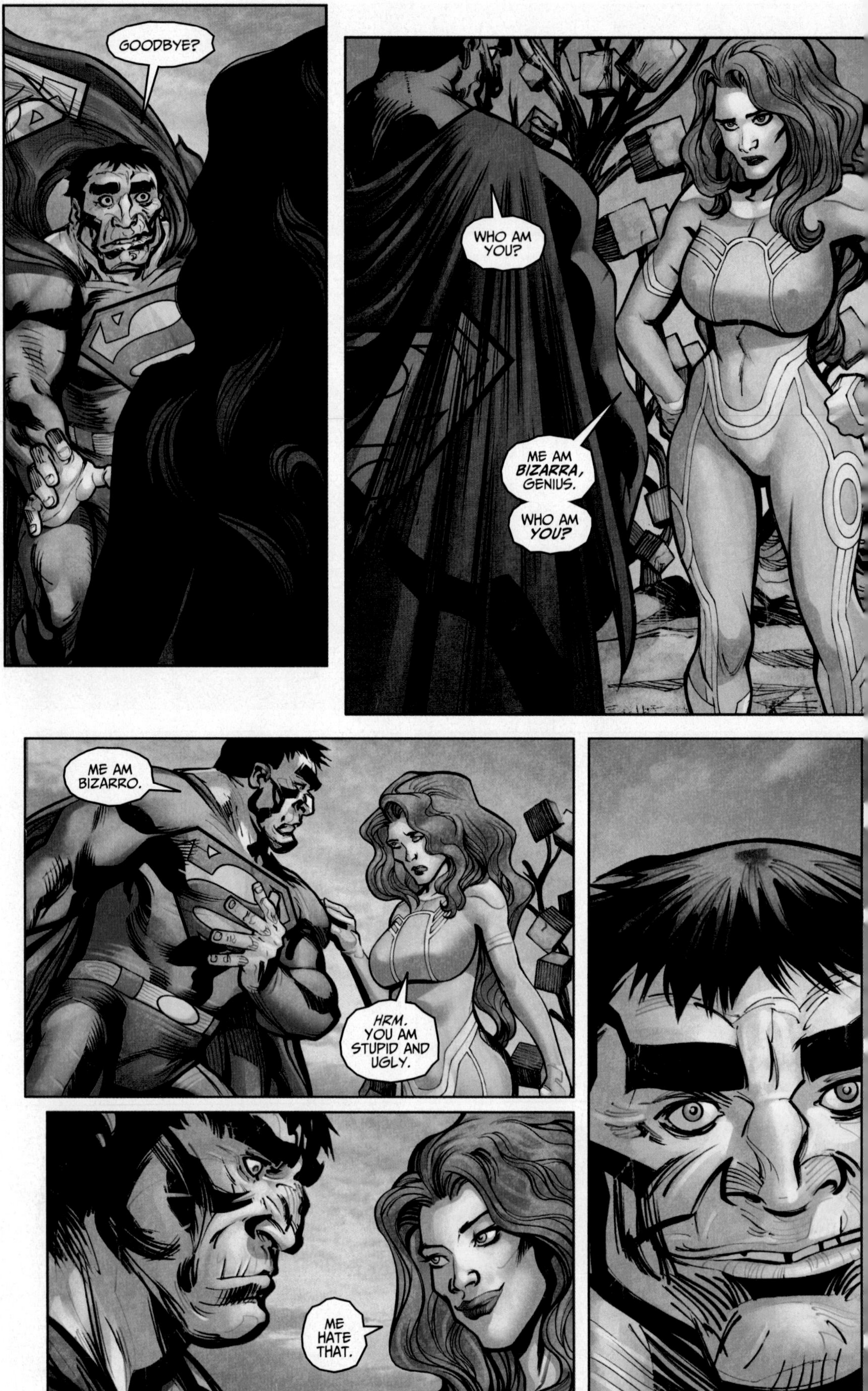
GOODBYE?
WHO AM YOU?
ME AM *BIZARRA*, GENIUS.
WHO AM *YOU?*
ME AM BIZARRO.
HRM. YOU AM STUPID AND UGLY.
ME HATE THAT.
END

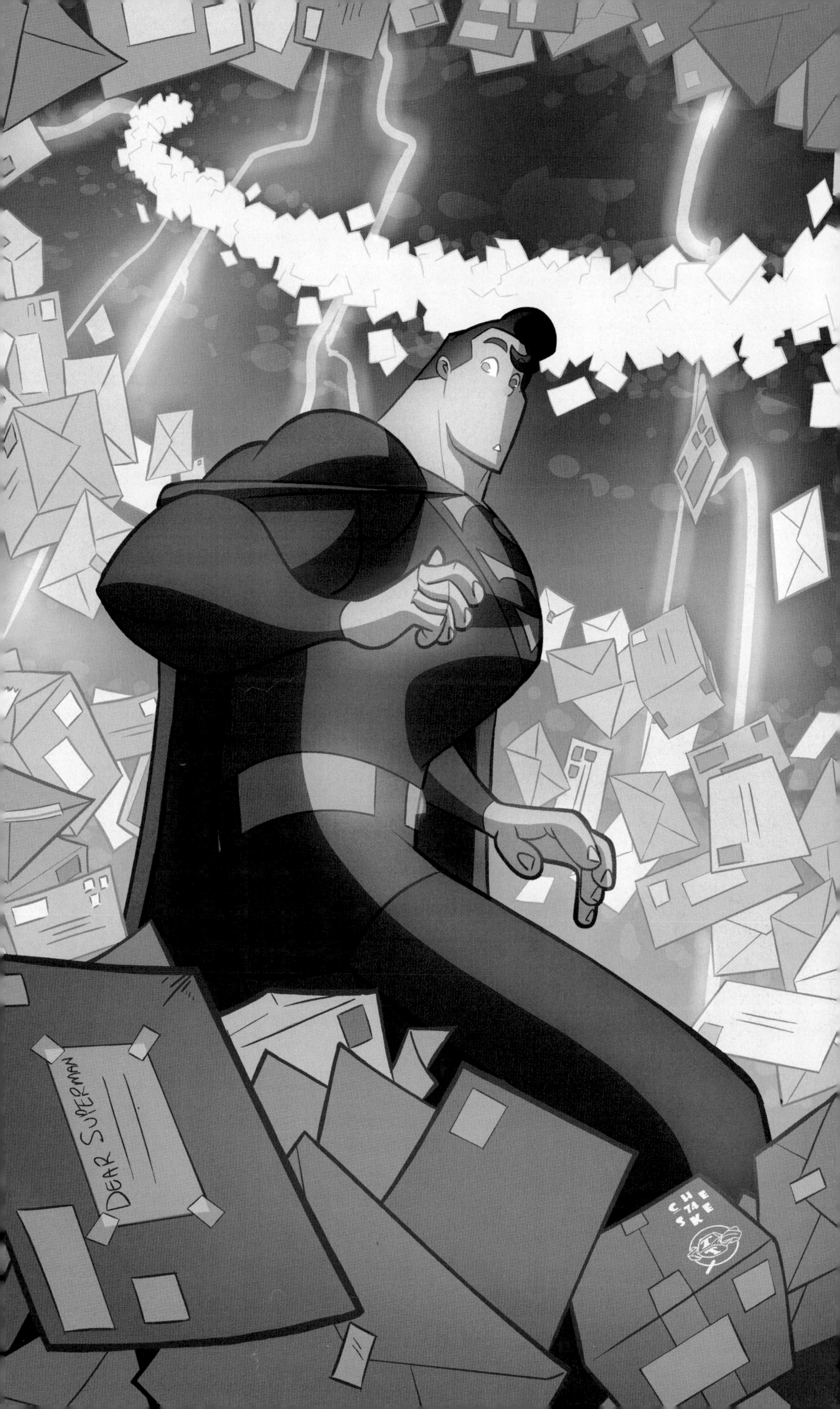
DEAR SUPERMAN

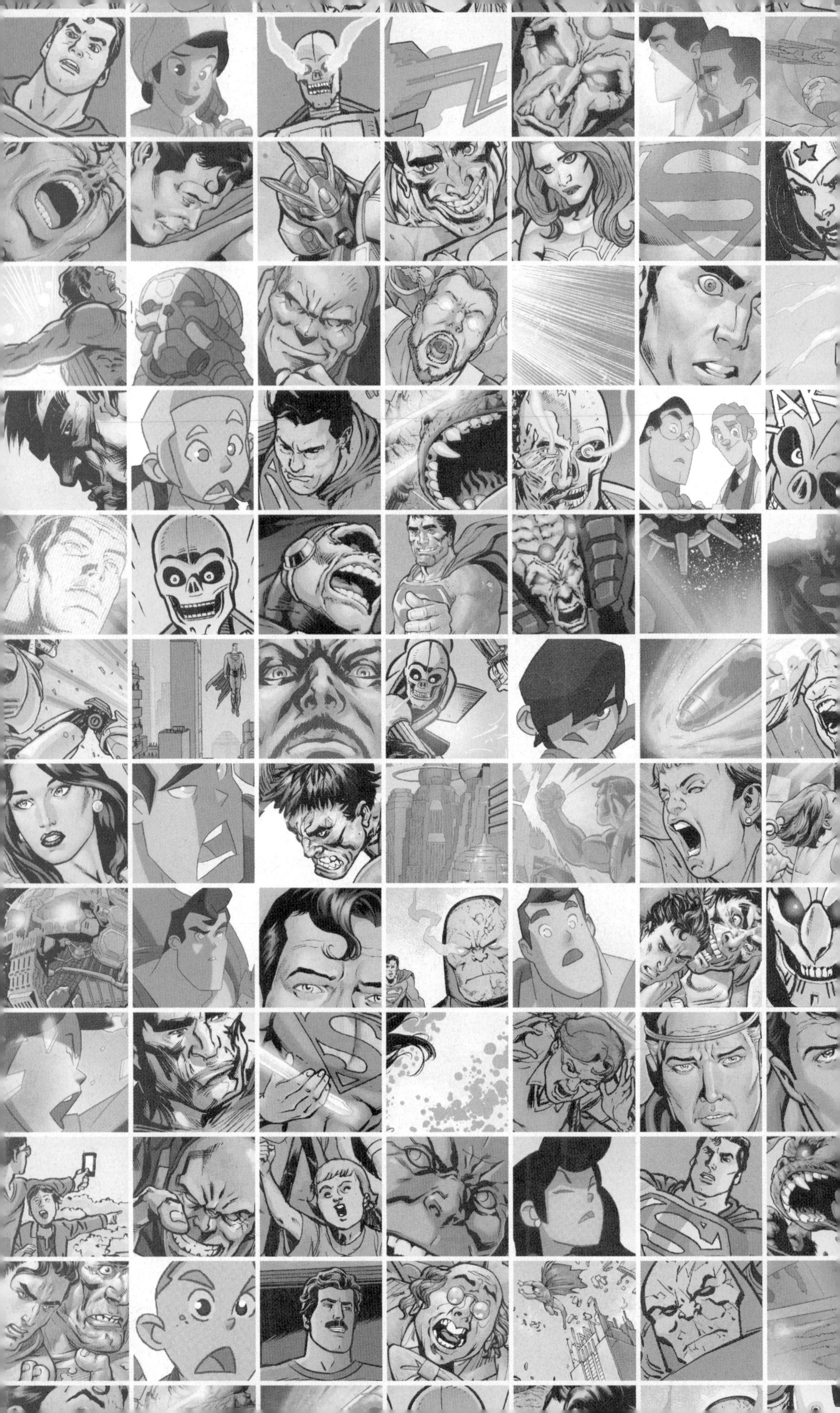

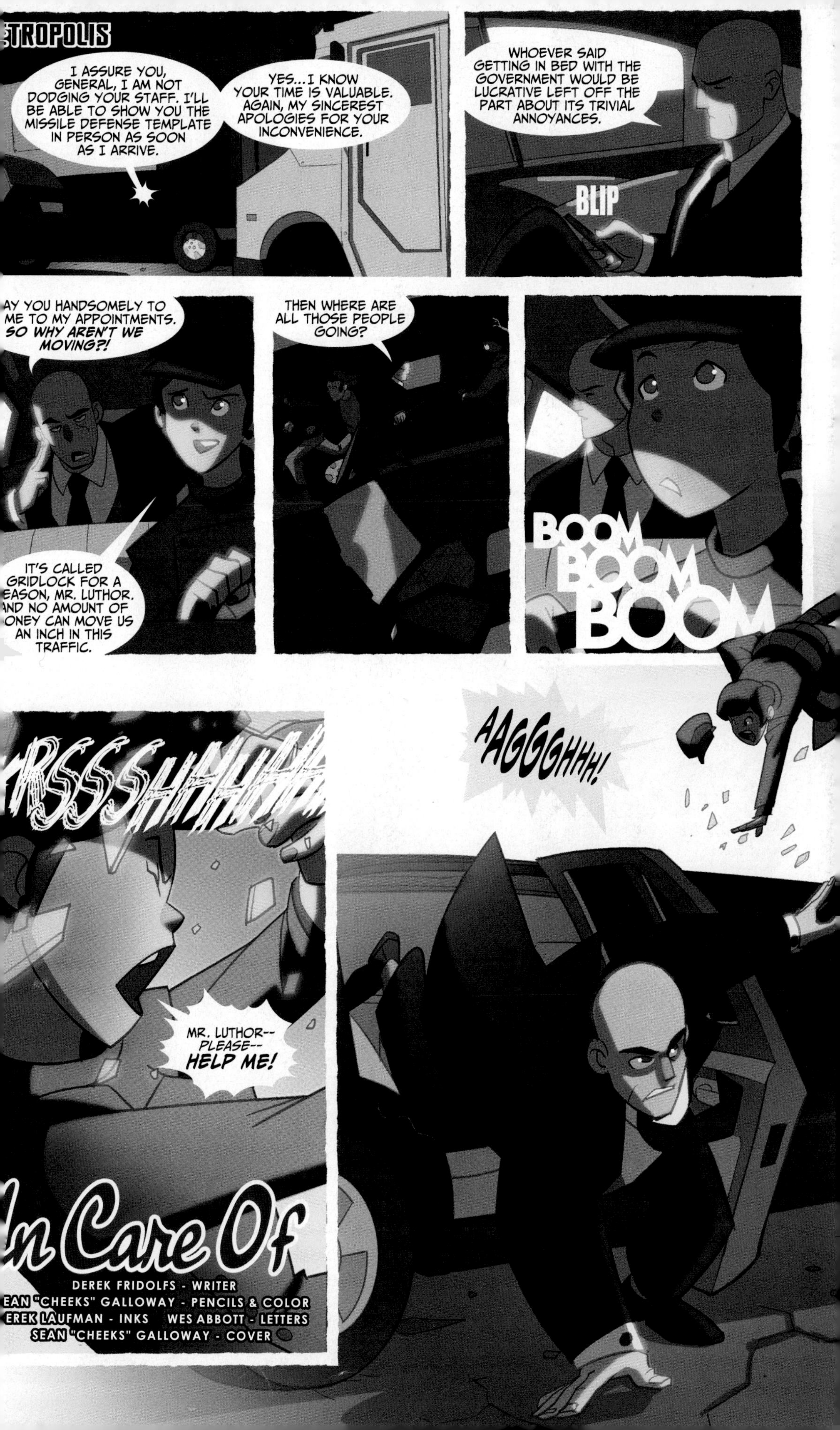
TROPOLIS
I ASSURE YOU, GENERAL, I AM NOT DODGING YOUR STAFF. I'LL BE ABLE TO SHOW YOU THE MISSILE DEFENSE TEMPLATE IN PERSON AS SOON AS I ARRIVE.
YES... I KNOW YOUR TIME IS VALUABLE. AGAIN, MY SINCEREST APOLOGIES FOR YOUR INCONVENIENCE.
WHOEVER SAID GETTING IN BED WITH THE GOVERNMENT WOULD BE LUCRATIVE LEFT OFF THE PART ABOUT ITS TRIVIAL ANNOYANCES.
BLIP
AY YOU HANDSOMELY TO ME TO MY APPOINTMENTS. SO WHY AREN'T WE MOVING?!
IT'S CALLED GRIDLOCK FOR A EASON, MR. LUTHOR. ND NO AMOUNT OF ONEY CAN MOVE US AN INCH IN THIS TRAFFIC.
THEN WHERE ARE ALL THOSE PEOPLE GOING?
BOOM BOOM BOOM
RSSSHHHH
AAGGGHHH!
MR. LUTHOR-- PLEASE-- HELP ME!
n Care Of
DEREK FRIDOLFS - WRITER
EAN "CHEEKS" GALLOWAY - PENCILS & COLOR
EREK LAUFMAN - INKS WES ABBOTT - LETTERS
SEAN "CHEEKS" GALLOWAY - COVER

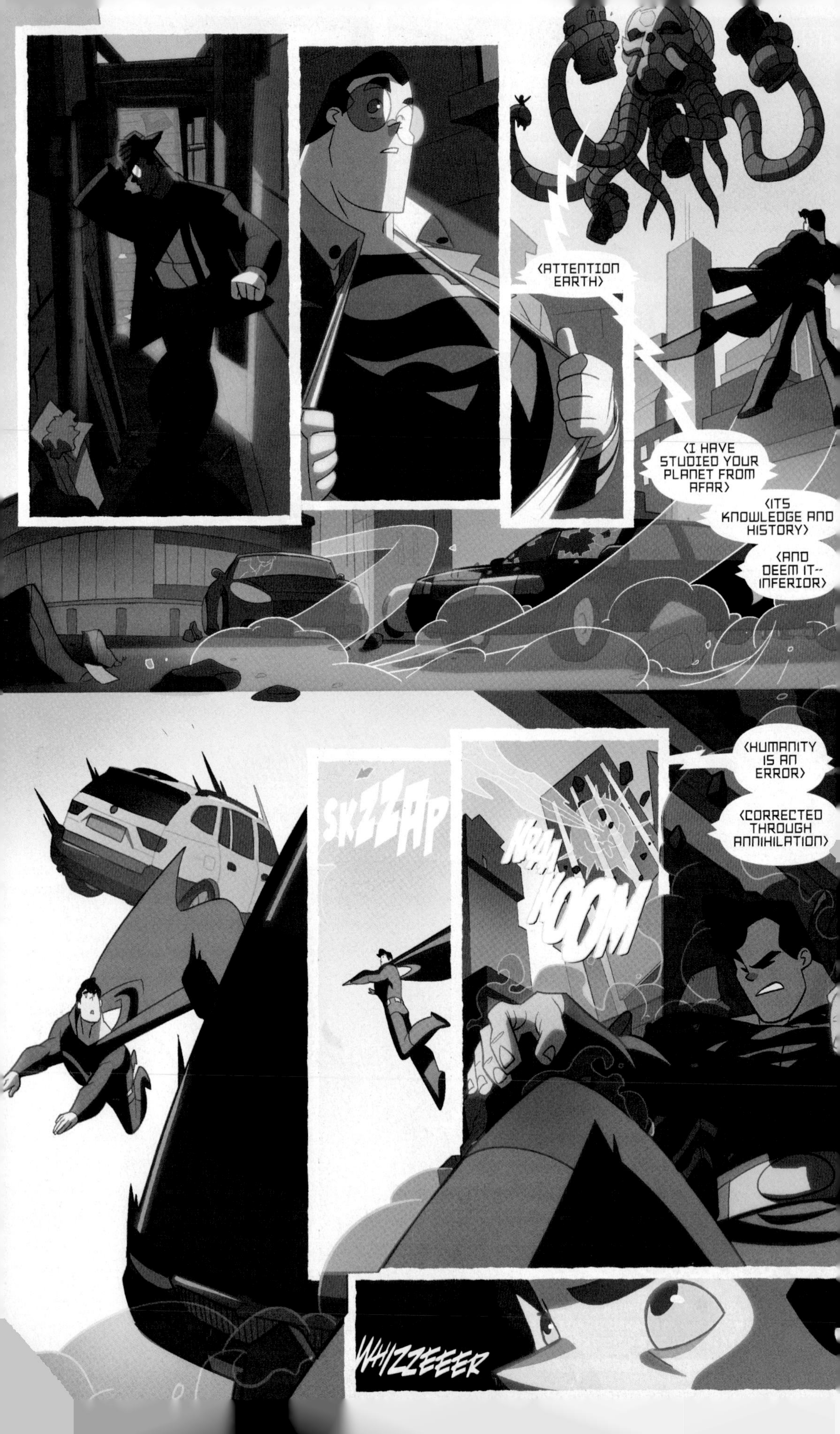

<ATTENTION EARTH>
<I HAVE STUDIED YOUR PLANET FROM AFAR>
<ITS KNOWLEDGE AND HISTORY>
<AND DEEM IT--INFERIOR>
SKZZAP
<HUMANITY IS AN ERROR>
<CORRECTED THROUGH ANNIHILATION>
KRAKOOM
WHIZZEEEER

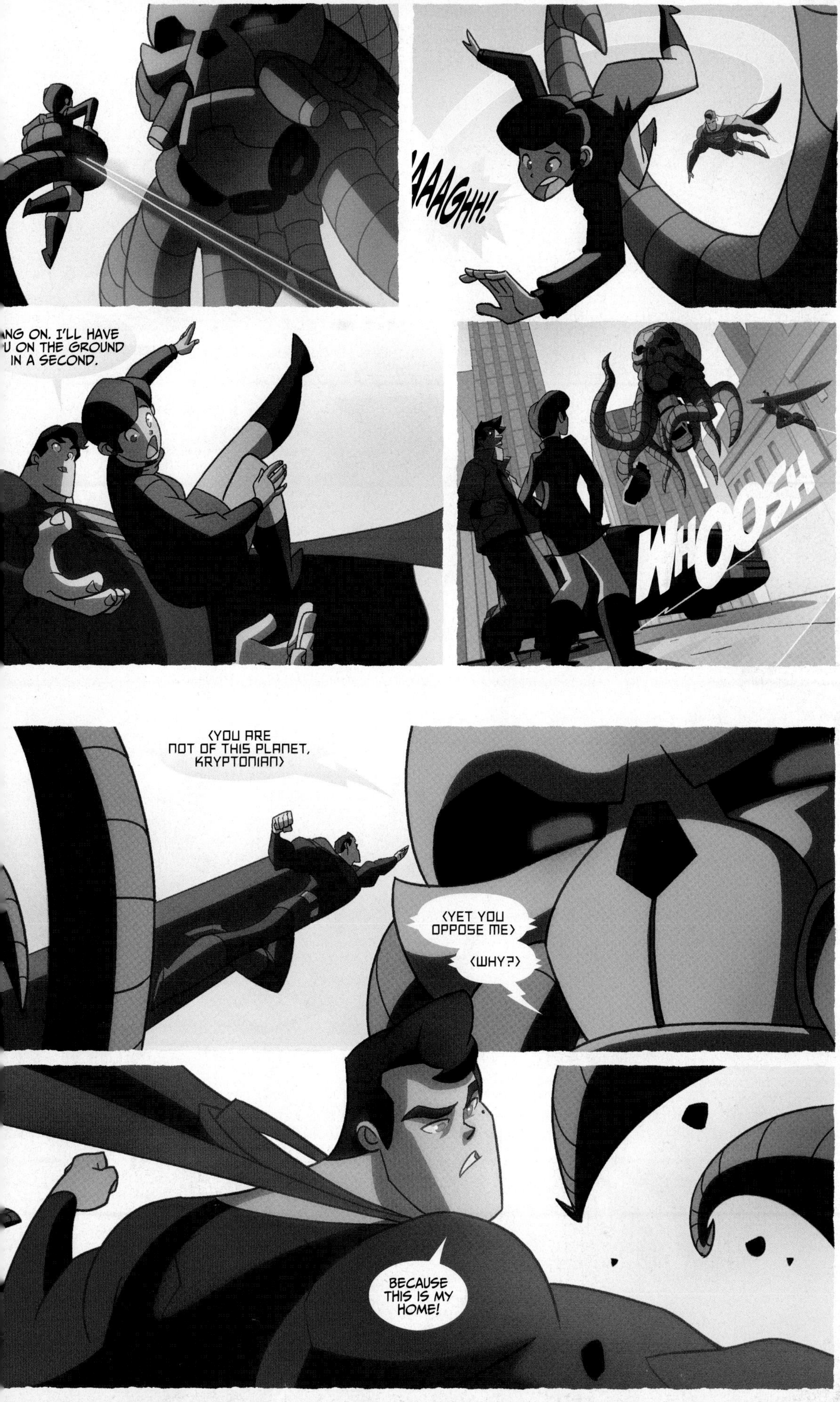

AAAAGHH!
NG ON. I'LL HAVE
U ON THE GROUND
IN A SECOND.
WHOOSH
<YOU ARE
NOT OF THIS PLANET,
KRYPTONIAN>
<YET YOU
OPPOSE ME>
<WHY?>
BECAUSE
THIS IS MY
HOME!

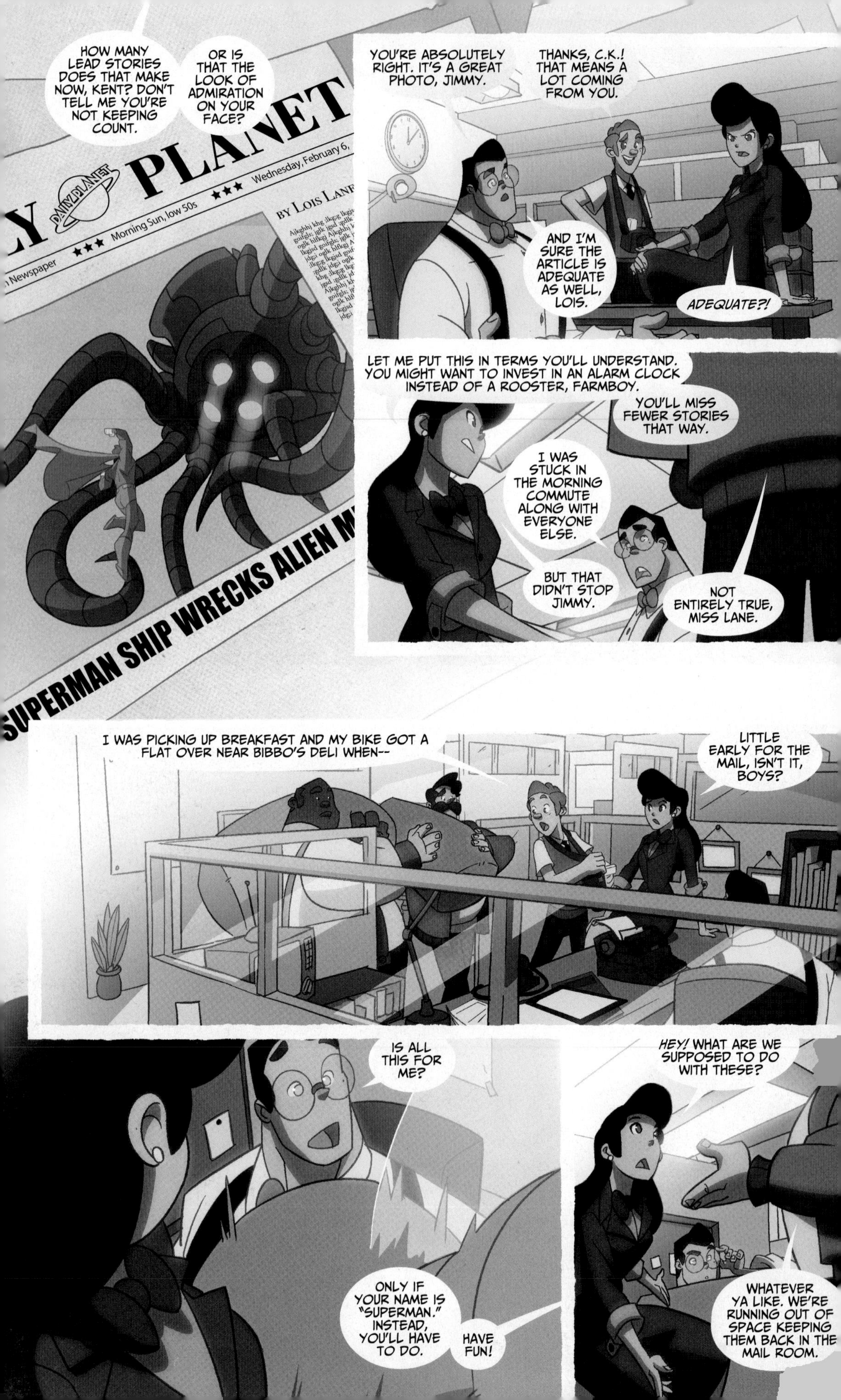
HOW MANY LEAD STORIES DOES THAT MAKE NOW, KENT? DON'T TELL ME YOU'RE NOT KEEPING COUNT.
OR IS THAT THE LOOK OF ADMIRATION ON YOUR FACE?
PLANET
Wednesday, February 6,
BY LOIS LANE
Morning Sun, low 50s
Newspaper
SUPERMAN SHIP WRECKS ALIEN M
YOU'RE ABSOLUTELY RIGHT. IT'S A GREAT PHOTO, JIMMY.
THANKS, C.K.! THAT MEANS A LOT COMING FROM YOU.
AND I'M SURE THE ARTICLE IS ADEQUATE AS WELL, LOIS.
ADEQUATE?!
LET ME PUT THIS IN TERMS YOU'LL UNDERSTAND. YOU MIGHT WANT TO INVEST IN AN ALARM CLOCK INSTEAD OF A ROOSTER, FARMBOY.
YOU'LL MISS FEWER STORIES THAT WAY.
I WAS STUCK IN THE MORNING COMMUTE ALONG WITH EVERYONE ELSE.
BUT THAT DIDN'T STOP JIMMY.
NOT ENTIRELY TRUE, MISS LANE.
I WAS PICKING UP BREAKFAST AND MY BIKE GOT A FLAT OVER NEAR BIBBO'S DELI WHEN--
LITTLE EARLY FOR THE MAIL, ISN'T IT, BOYS?
IS ALL THIS FOR ME?
ONLY IF YOUR NAME IS "SUPERMAN." INSTEAD, YOU'LL HAVE TO DO.
HAVE FUN!
HEY! WHAT ARE WE SUPPOSED TO DO WITH THESE?
WHATEVER YA LIKE. WE'RE RUNNING OUT OF SPACE KEEPING THEM BACK IN THE MAIL ROOM.

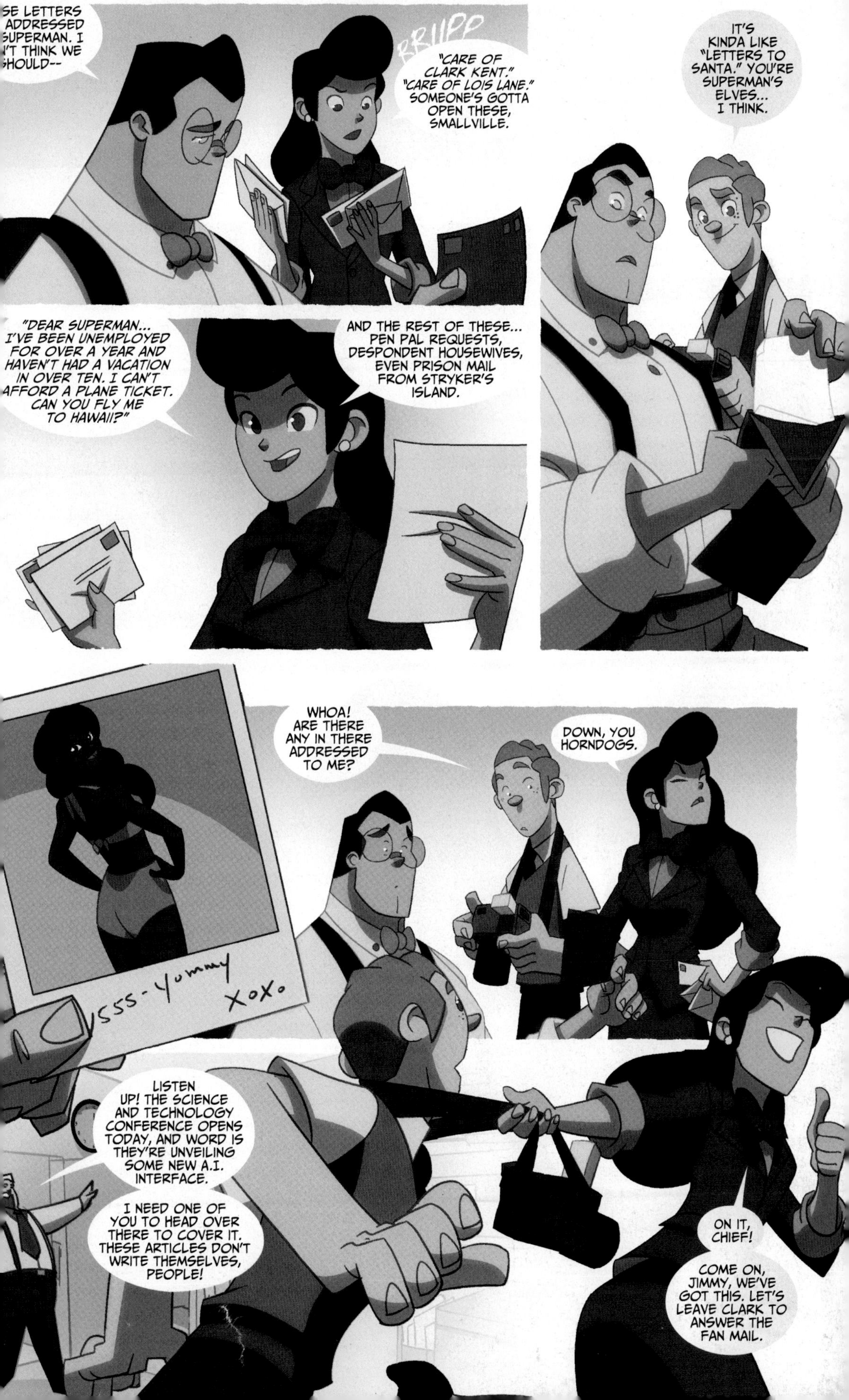
SE LETTERS ADDRESSED SUPERMAN. I 'T THINK WE HOULD--
BRUPP
"CARE OF CLARK KENT." "CARE OF LOIS LANE." SOMEONE'S GOTTA OPEN THESE, SMALLVILLE.
IT'S KINDA LIKE "LETTERS TO SANTA." YOU'RE SUPERMAN'S ELVES... I THINK.
"DEAR SUPERMAN... I'VE BEEN UNEMPLOYED FOR OVER A YEAR AND HAVEN'T HAD A VACATION IN OVER TEN. I CAN'T AFFORD A PLANE TICKET. CAN YOU FLY ME TO HAWAII?"
AND THE REST OF THESE... PEN PAL REQUESTS, DESPONDENT HOUSEWIVES, EVEN PRISON MAIL FROM STRYKER'S ISLAND.
SSS-Yummy XOXO
WHOA! ARE THERE ANY IN THERE ADDRESSED TO ME?
DOWN, YOU HORNDOGS.
LISTEN UP! THE SCIENCE AND TECHNOLOGY CONFERENCE OPENS TODAY, AND WORD IS THEY'RE UNVEILING SOME NEW A.I. INTERFACE.
I NEED ONE OF YOU TO HEAD OVER THERE TO COVER IT. THESE ARTICLES DON'T WRITE THEMSELVES, PEOPLE!
ON IT, CHIEF!
COME ON, JIMMY, WE'VE GOT THIS. LET'S LEAVE CLARK TO ANSWER THE FAN MAIL.

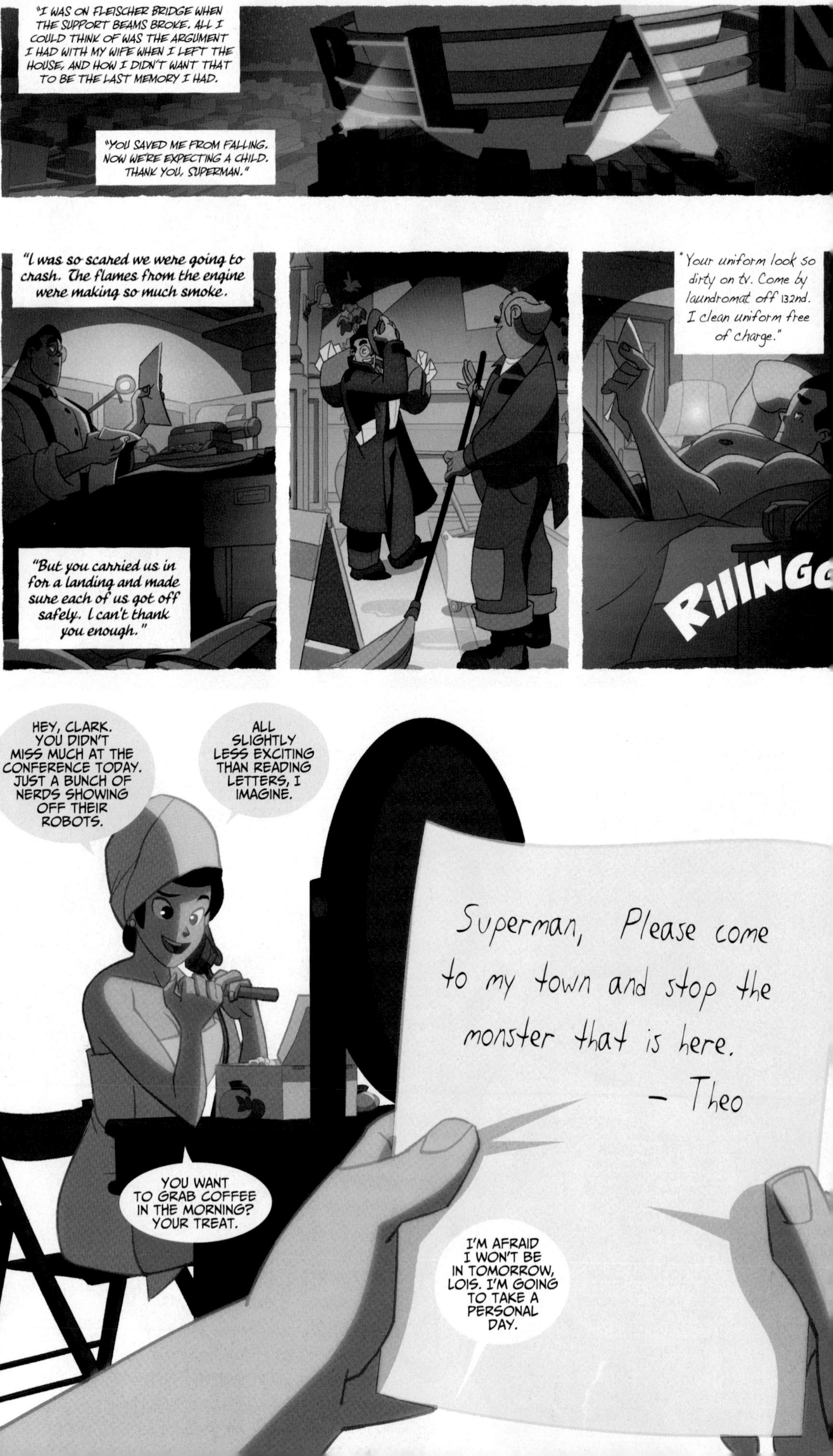
"I WAS ON FLEISCHER BRIDGE WHEN THE SUPPORT BEAMS BROKE. ALL I COULD THINK OF WAS THE ARGUMENT I HAD WITH MY WIFE WHEN I LEFT THE HOUSE, AND HOW I DIDN'T WANT THAT TO BE THE LAST MEMORY I HAD.
"YOU SAVED ME FROM FALLING. NOW WE'RE EXPECTING A CHILD. THANK YOU, SUPERMAN."
"I was so scared we were going to crash. The flames from the engine were making so much smoke.
"But you carried us in for a landing and made sure each of us got off safely. I can't thank you enough."
"Your uniform look so dirty on tv. Come by laundromat off 132nd. I clean uniform free of charge."
RIIINGG
HEY, CLARK. YOU DIDN'T MISS MUCH AT THE CONFERENCE TODAY. JUST A BUNCH OF NERDS SHOWING OFF THEIR ROBOTS.
ALL SLIGHTLY LESS EXCITING THAN READING LETTERS, I IMAGINE.
Superman, Please come to my town and stop the monster that is here. - Theo
YOU WANT TO GRAB COFFEE IN THE MORNING? YOUR TREAT.
I'M AFRAID I WON'T BE IN TOMORROW, LOIS. I'M GOING TO TAKE A PERSONAL DAY.

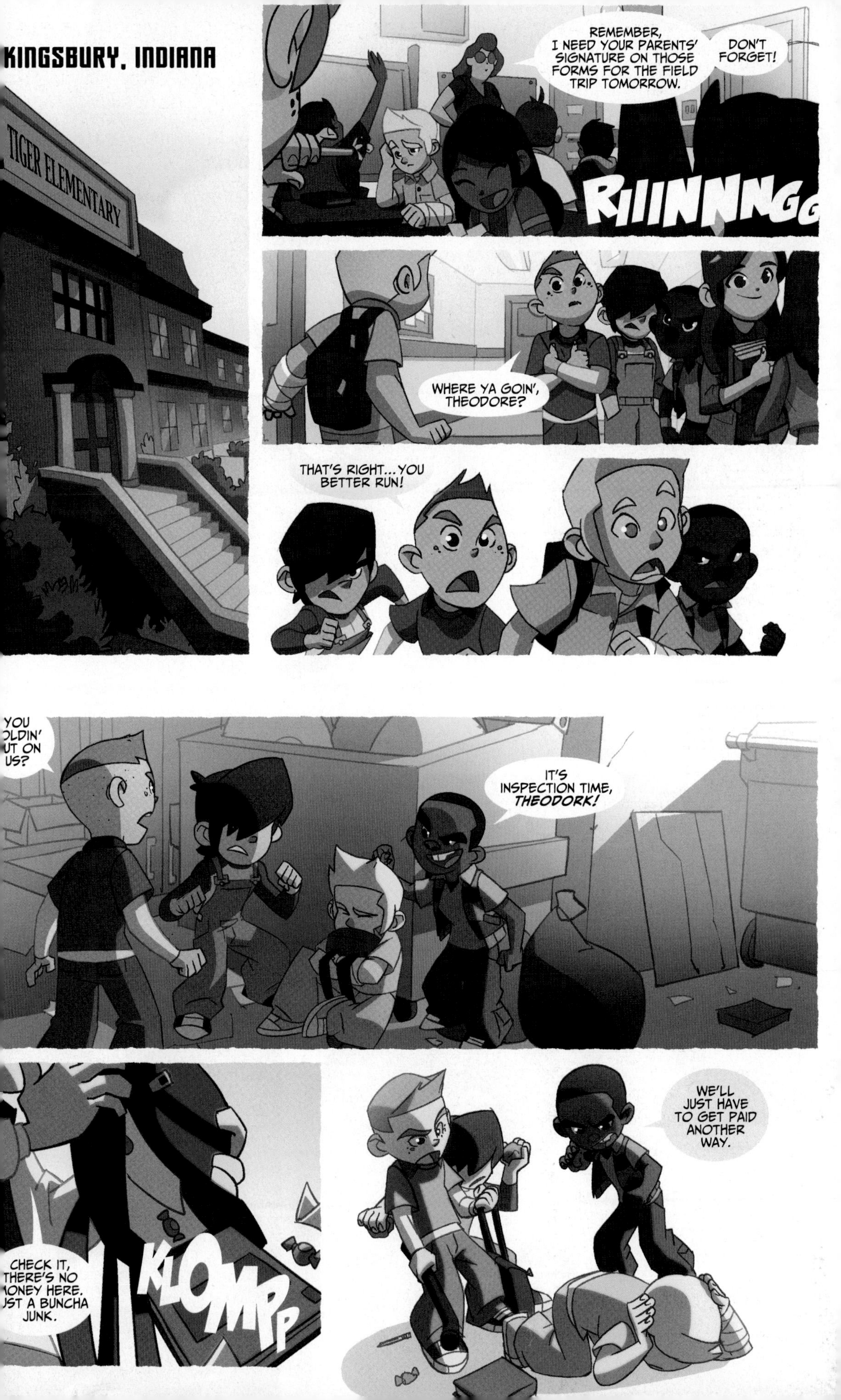
KINGSBURY, INDIANA
TIGER ELEMENTARY
REMEMBER, I NEED YOUR PARENTS' SIGNATURE ON THOSE FORMS FOR THE FIELD TRIP TOMORROW.
DON'T FORGET!
RIIINNNGG
WHERE YA GOIN', THEODORE?
THAT'S RIGHT... YOU BETTER RUN!
YOU OLDIN' UT ON US?
IT'S INSPECTION TIME, THEODORK!
KLOMPP
CHECK IT, THERE'S NO ONEY HERE. JST A BUNCHA JUNK.
WE'LL JUST HAVE TO GET PAID ANOTHER WAY.

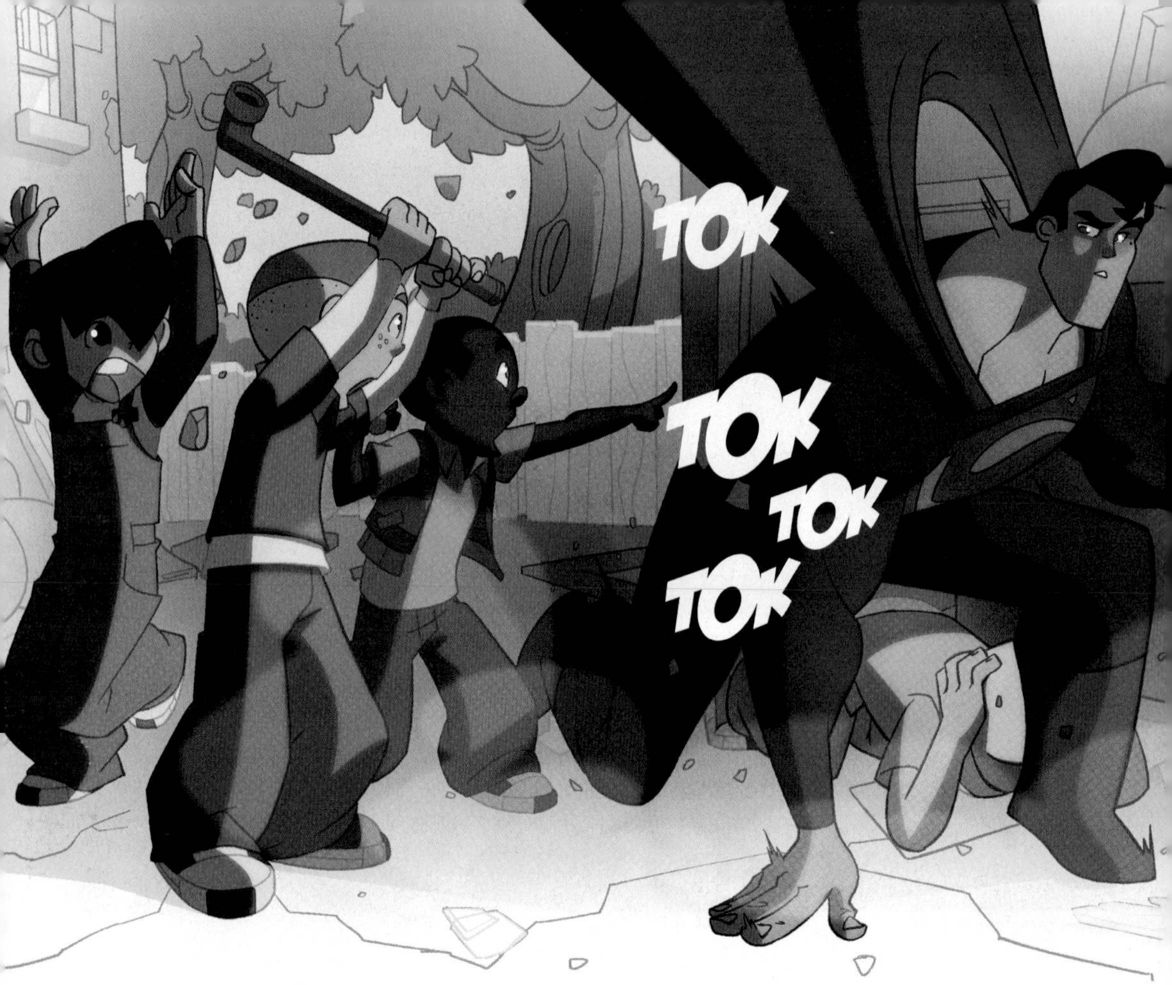
TOK
TOK
TOK
TOK

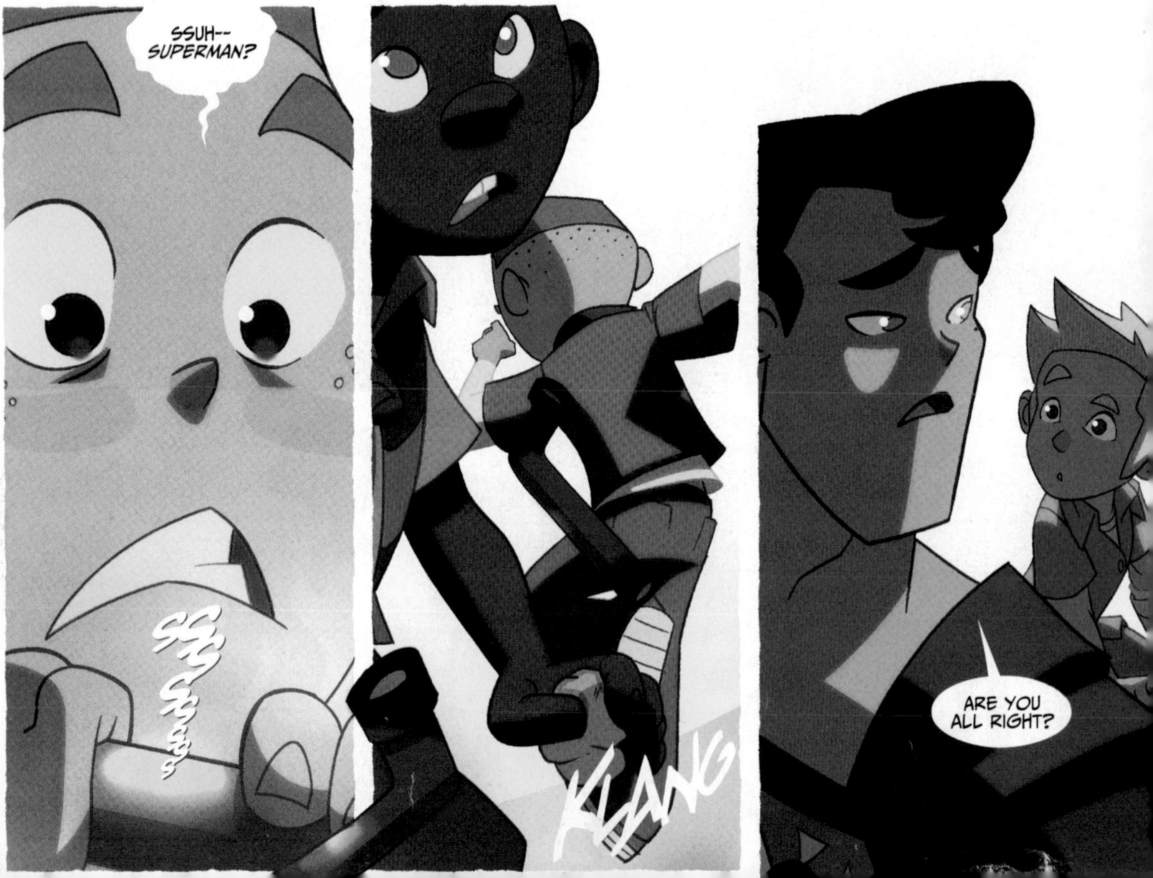
SSUH-- SUPERMAN?
KLANG
ARE YOU ALL RIGHT?

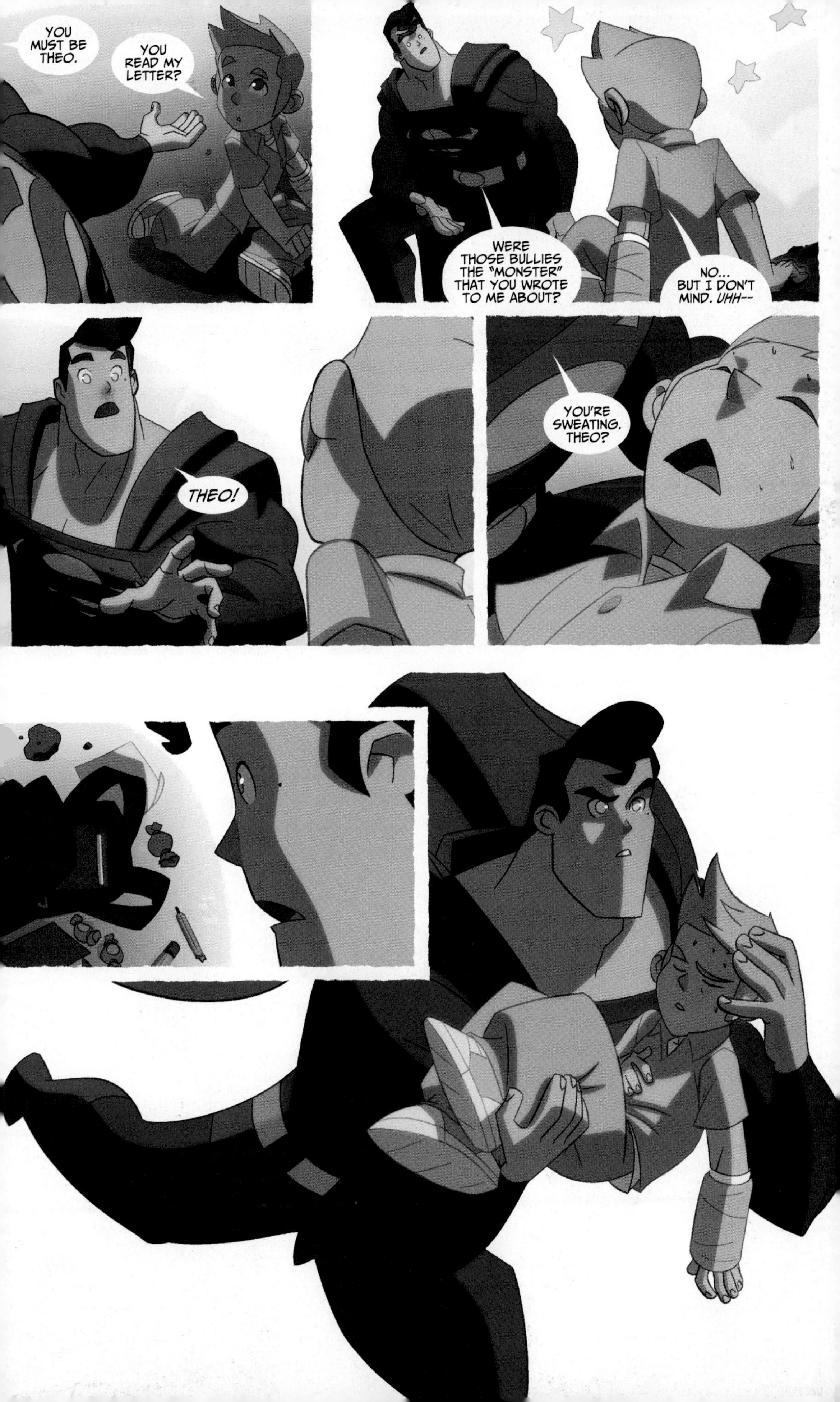
YOU MUST BE THEO.
YOU READ MY LETTER?
WERE THOSE BULLIES THE "MONSTER" THAT YOU WROTE TO ME ABOUT?
NO... BUT I DON'T MIND. *UHH--*
THEO!
YOU'RE SWEATING. THEO?

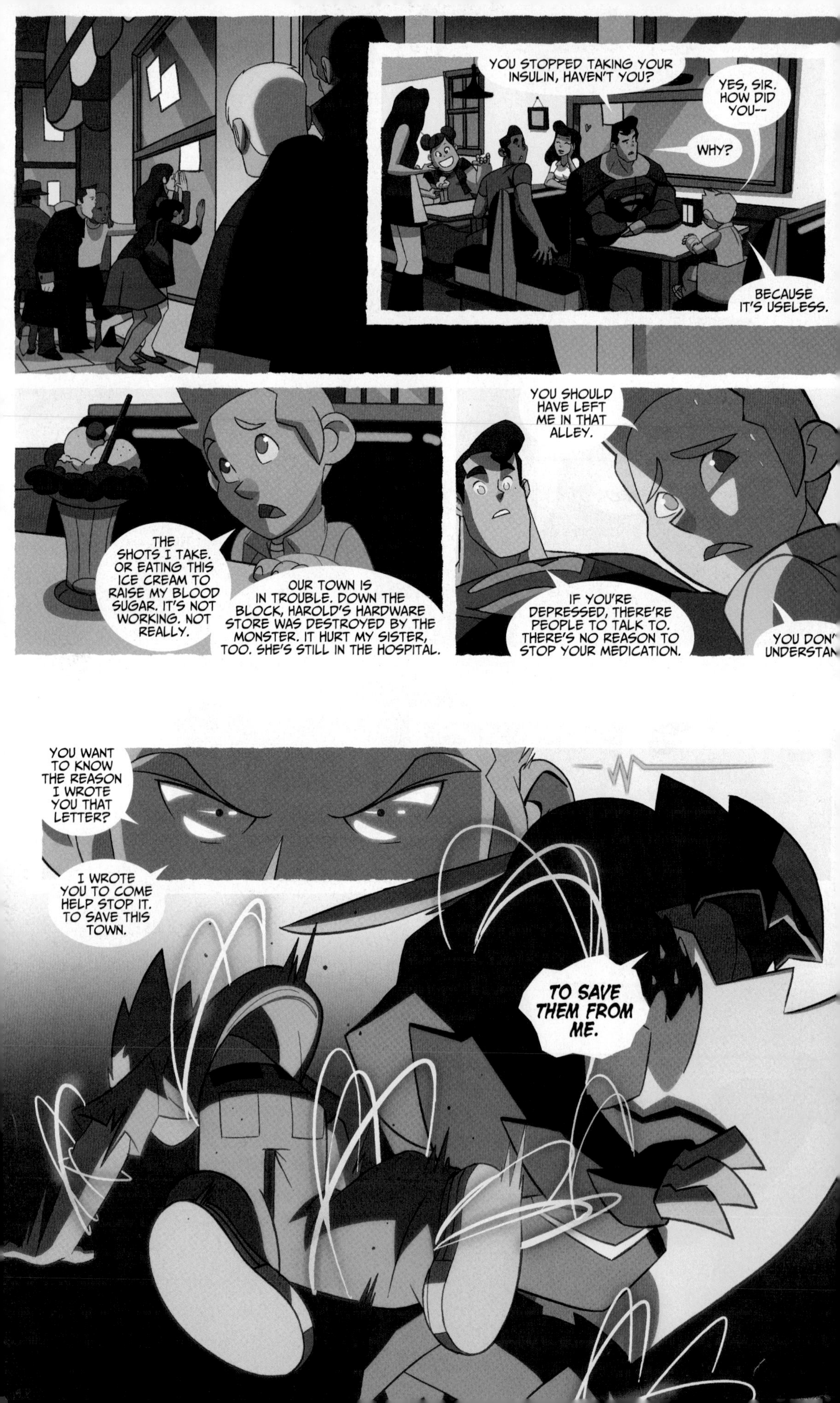
YOU STOPPED TAKING YOUR INSULIN, HAVEN'T YOU?
YES, SIR. HOW DID YOU--
WHY?
BECAUSE IT'S USELESS.
THE SHOTS I TAKE. OR EATING THIS ICE CREAM TO RAISE MY BLOOD SUGAR. IT'S NOT WORKING. NOT REALLY.
OUR TOWN IS IN TROUBLE. DOWN THE BLOCK, HAROLD'S HARDWARE STORE WAS DESTROYED BY THE MONSTER. IT HURT MY SISTER, TOO. SHE'S STILL IN THE HOSPITAL.
YOU SHOULD HAVE LEFT ME IN THAT ALLEY.
IF YOU'RE DEPRESSED, THERE'RE PEOPLE TO TALK TO. THERE'S NO REASON TO STOP YOUR MEDICATION.
YOU DON'T UNDERSTAN
YOU WANT TO KNOW THE REASON I WROTE YOU THAT LETTER?
I WROTE YOU TO COME HELP STOP IT. TO SAVE THIS TOWN.
TO SAVE THEM FROM ME.

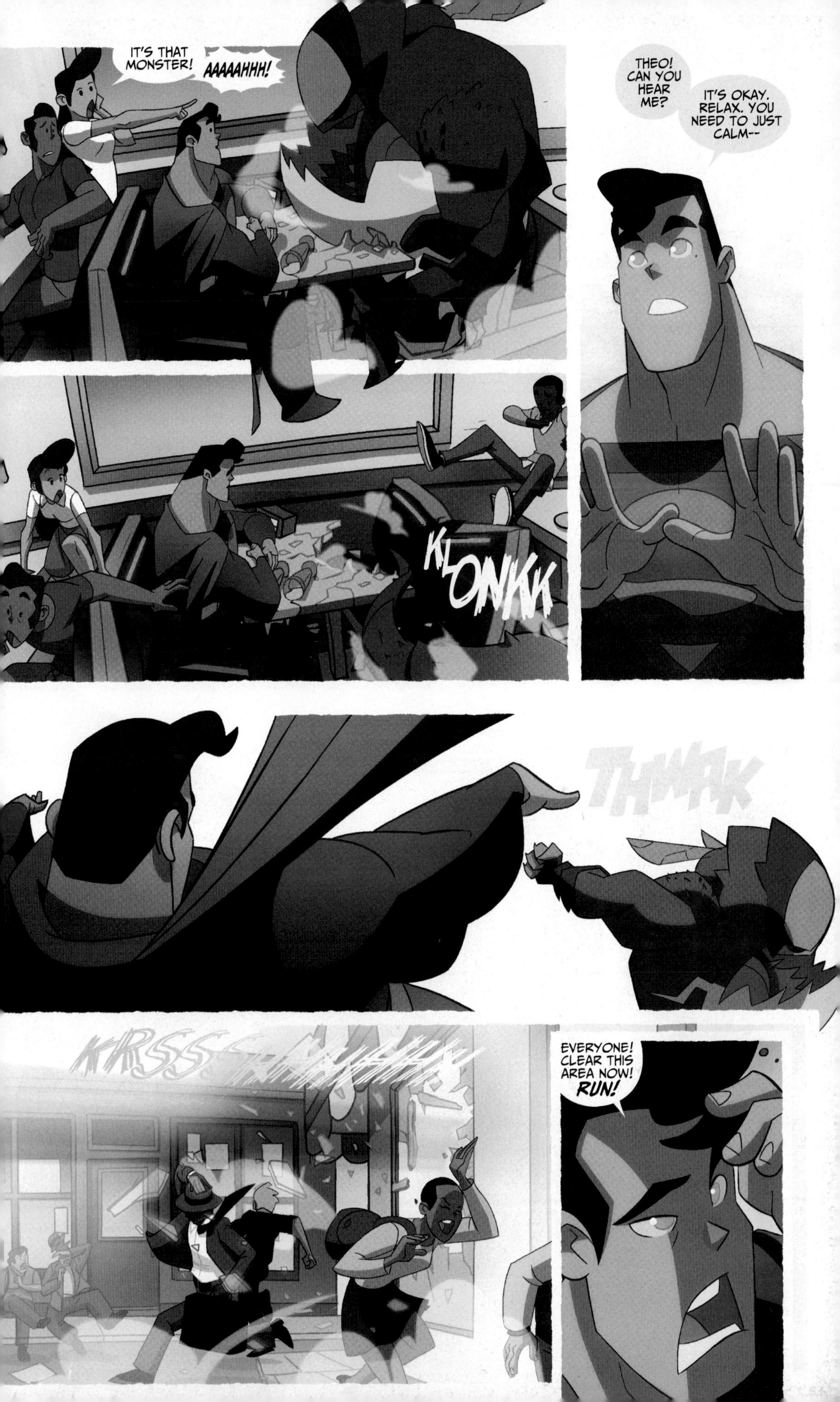

IT'S THAT MONSTER!
AAAAAHHH!
THEO! CAN YOU HEAR ME?
IT'S OKAY. RELAX. YOU NEED TO JUST CALM--
KLONKK
THWAK
KRSSSHHHHH
EVERYONE! CLEAR THIS AREA NOW! RUN!

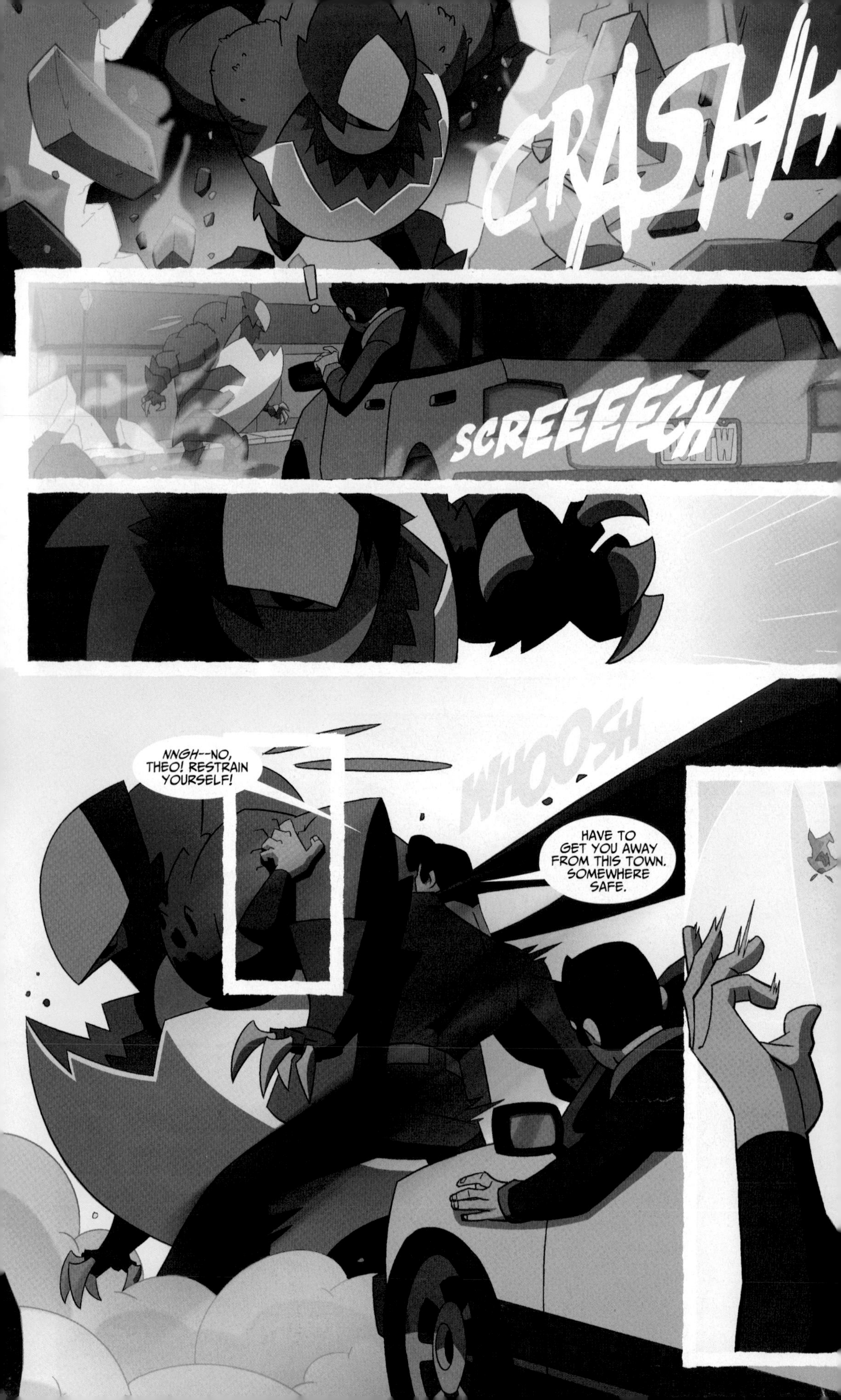
CRASHH
!
SCREEEECH
NNGH--NO, THEO! RESTRAIN YOURSELF!
WHOOSH
HAVE TO GET YOU AWAY FROM THIS TOWN. SOMEWHERE SAFE.

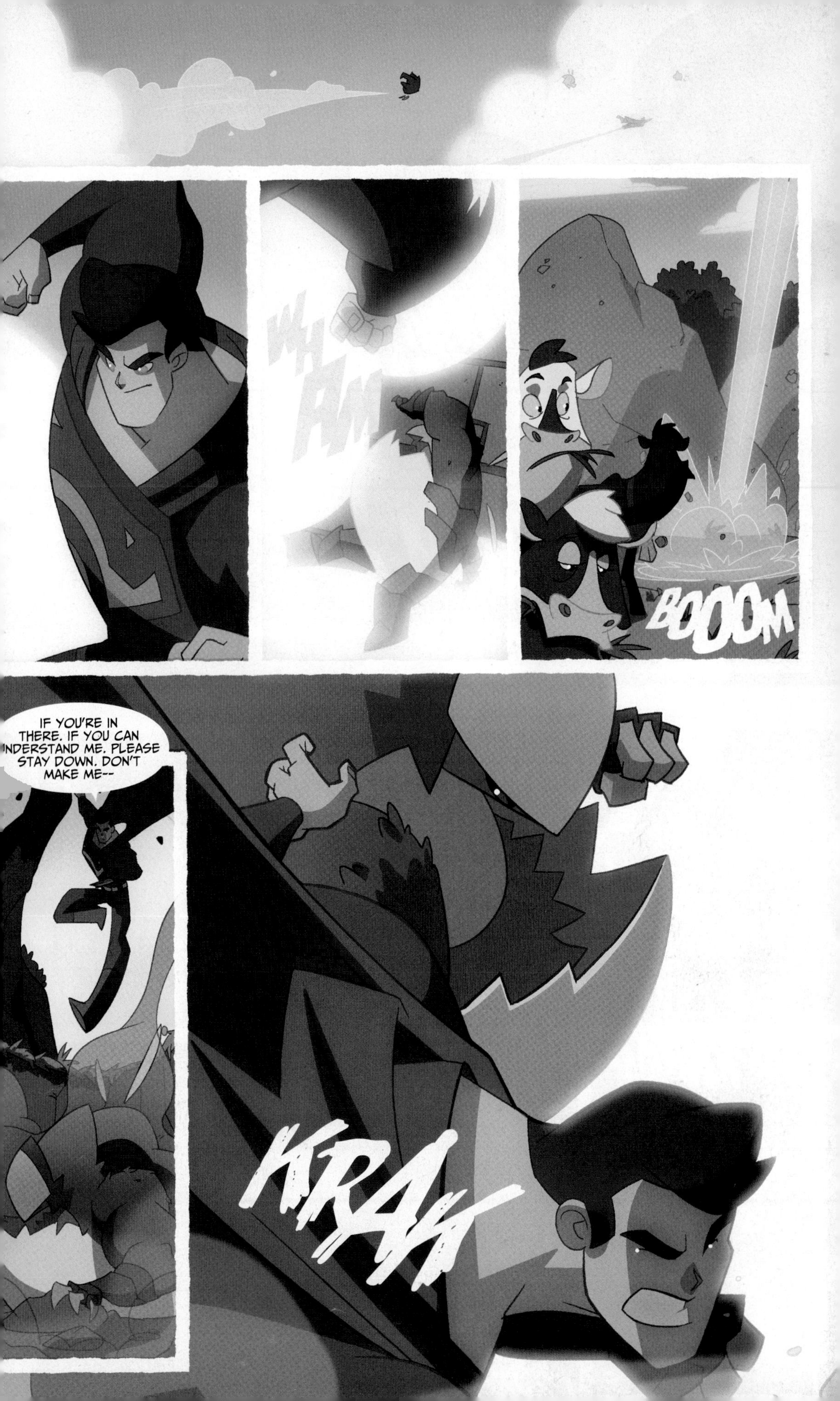
WHAM
BOOOM
IF YOU'RE IN THERE. IF YOU CAN UNDERSTAND ME. PLEASE STAY DOWN. DON'T MAKE ME--
KRAK

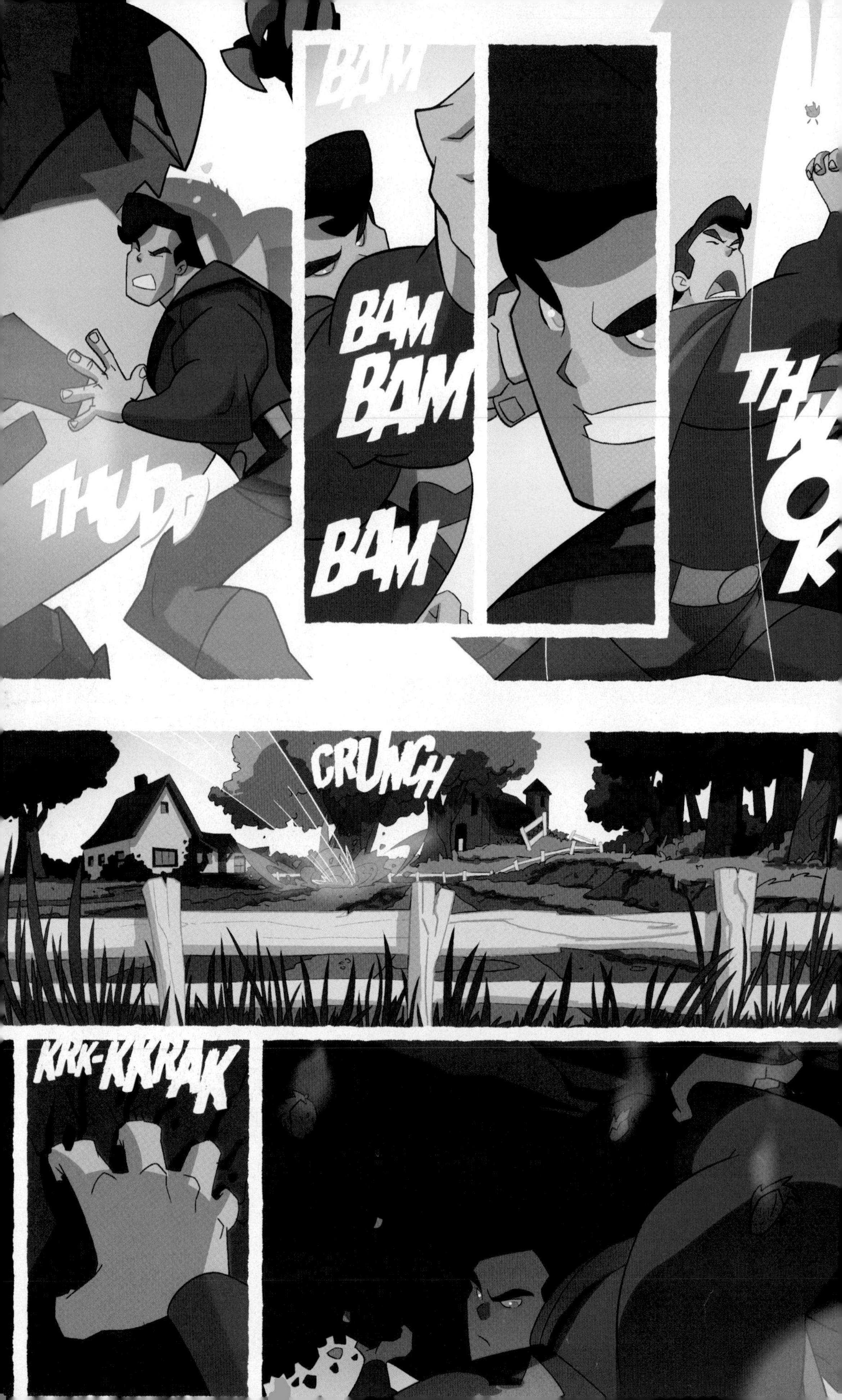
THUDD
BAM
BAM
BAM
BAM
THWOK
CRUNCH
KRK-KKRAK

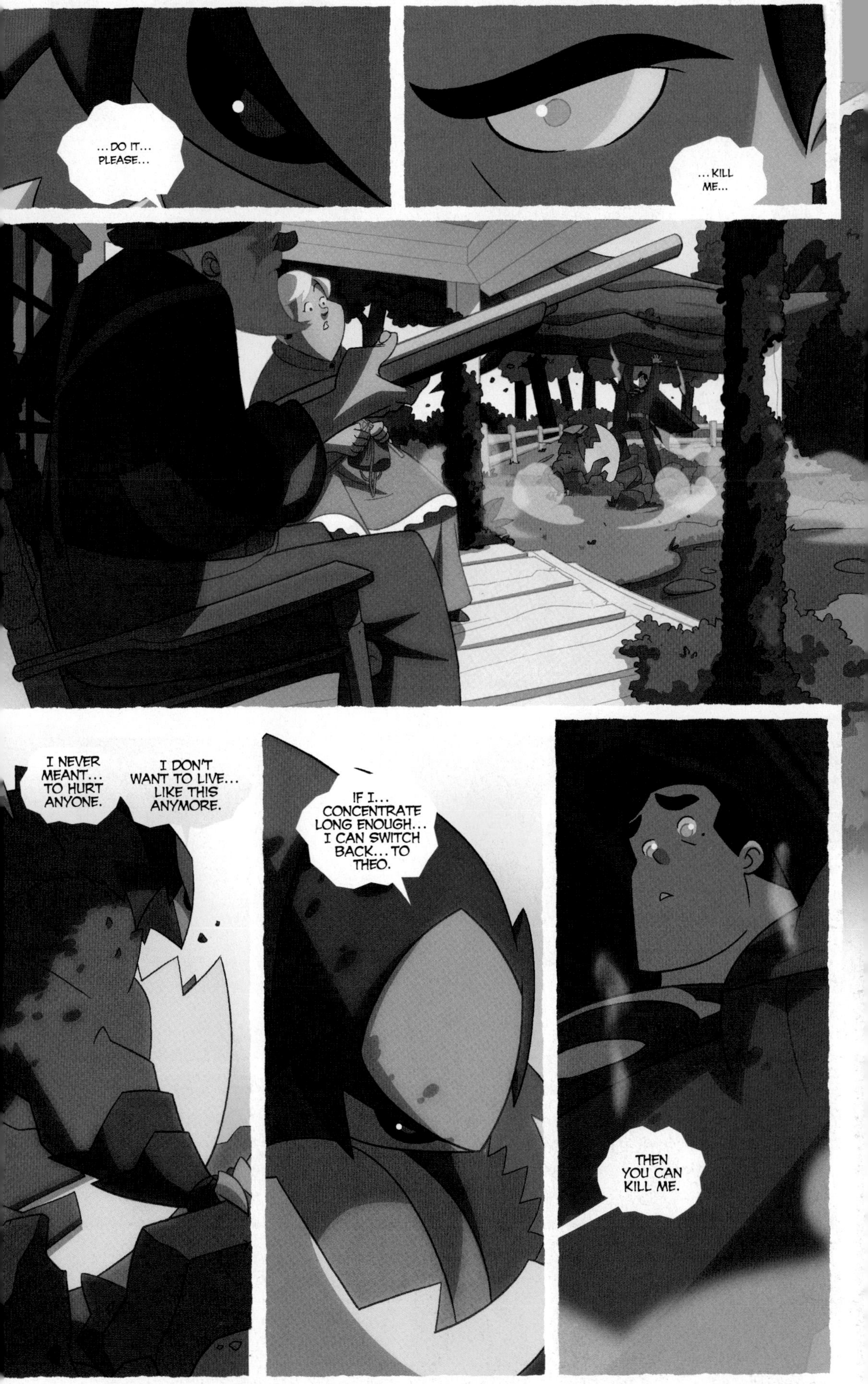
...DO IT...
PLEASE...
...KILL
ME...
I NEVER
MEANT...
TO HURT
ANYONE.
I DON'T
WANT TO LIVE...
LIKE THIS
ANYMORE.
IF I...
CONCENTRATE
LONG ENOUGH...
I CAN SWITCH
BACK...TO
THEO.
THEN
YOU CAN
KILL ME.

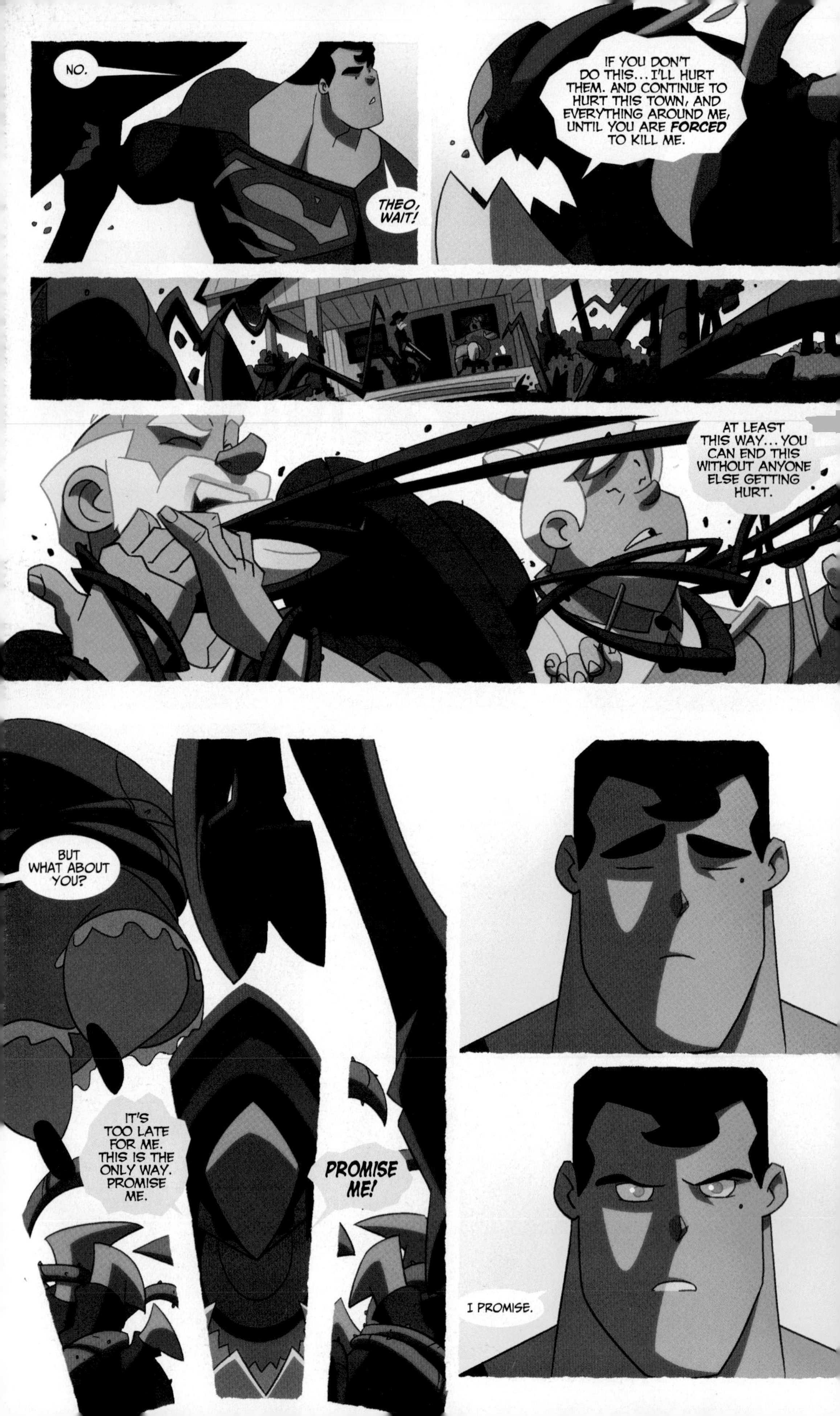
NO.
THEO, WAIT!
IF YOU DON'T DO THIS... I'LL HURT THEM. AND CONTINUE TO HURT THIS TOWN, AND EVERYTHING AROUND ME, UNTIL YOU ARE *FORCED* TO KILL ME.
AT LEAST THIS WAY... YOU CAN END THIS WITHOUT ANYONE ELSE GETTING HURT.
BUT WHAT ABOUT YOU?
IT'S TOO LATE FOR ME. THIS IS THE ONLY WAY. PROMISE ME.
PROMISE ME!
I PROMISE.

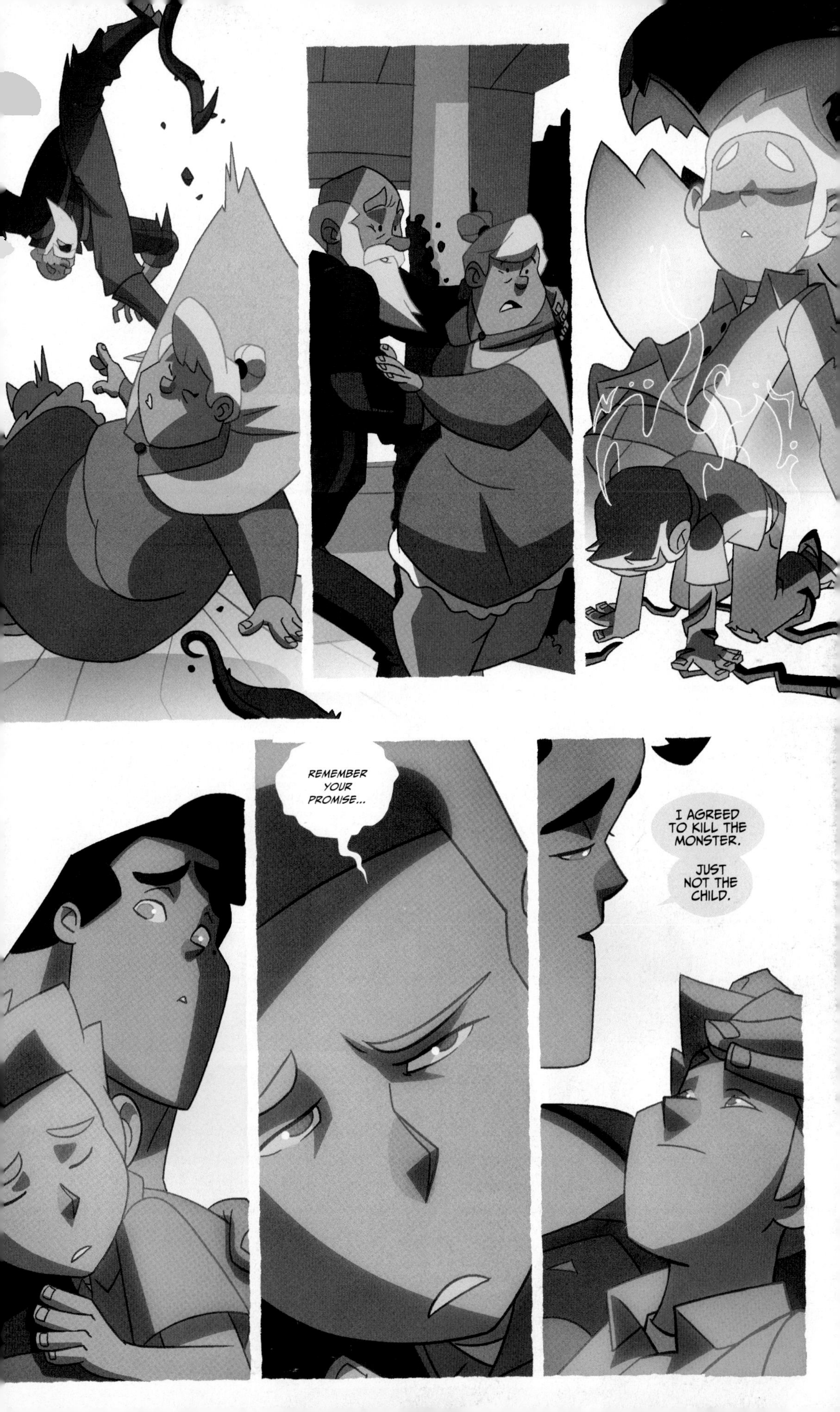
REMEMBER YOUR PROMISE...
I AGREED TO KILL THE MONSTER.
JUST NOT THE CHILD.

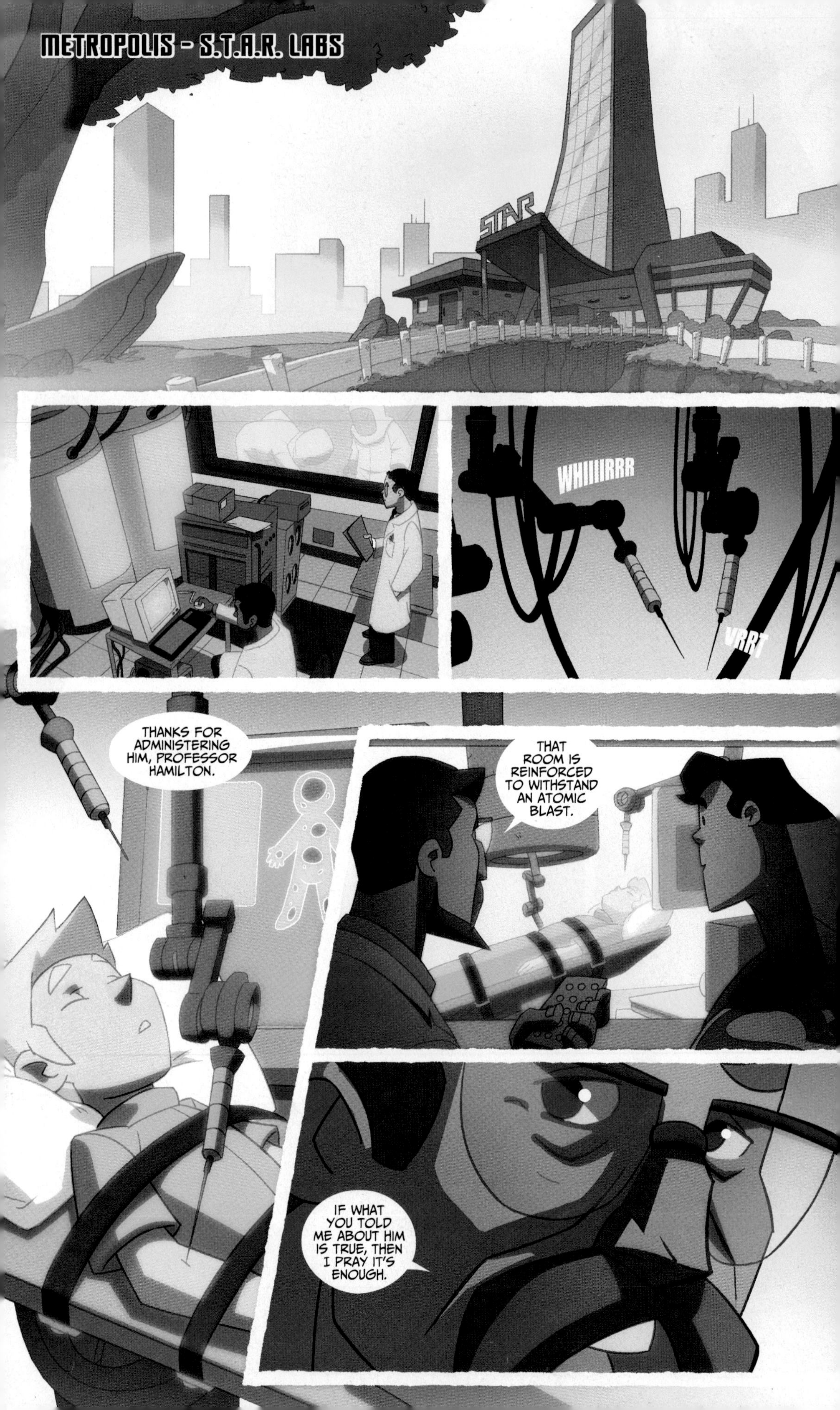
METROPOLIS - S.T.A.R. LABS
STAR
WHIIIIRRR
VRRT
THANKS FOR ADMINISTERING HIM, PROFESSOR HAMILTON.
THAT ROOM IS REINFORCED TO WITHSTAND AN ATOMIC BLAST.
IF WHAT YOU TOLD ME ABOUT HIM IS TRUE, THEN I PRAY IT'S ENOUGH.

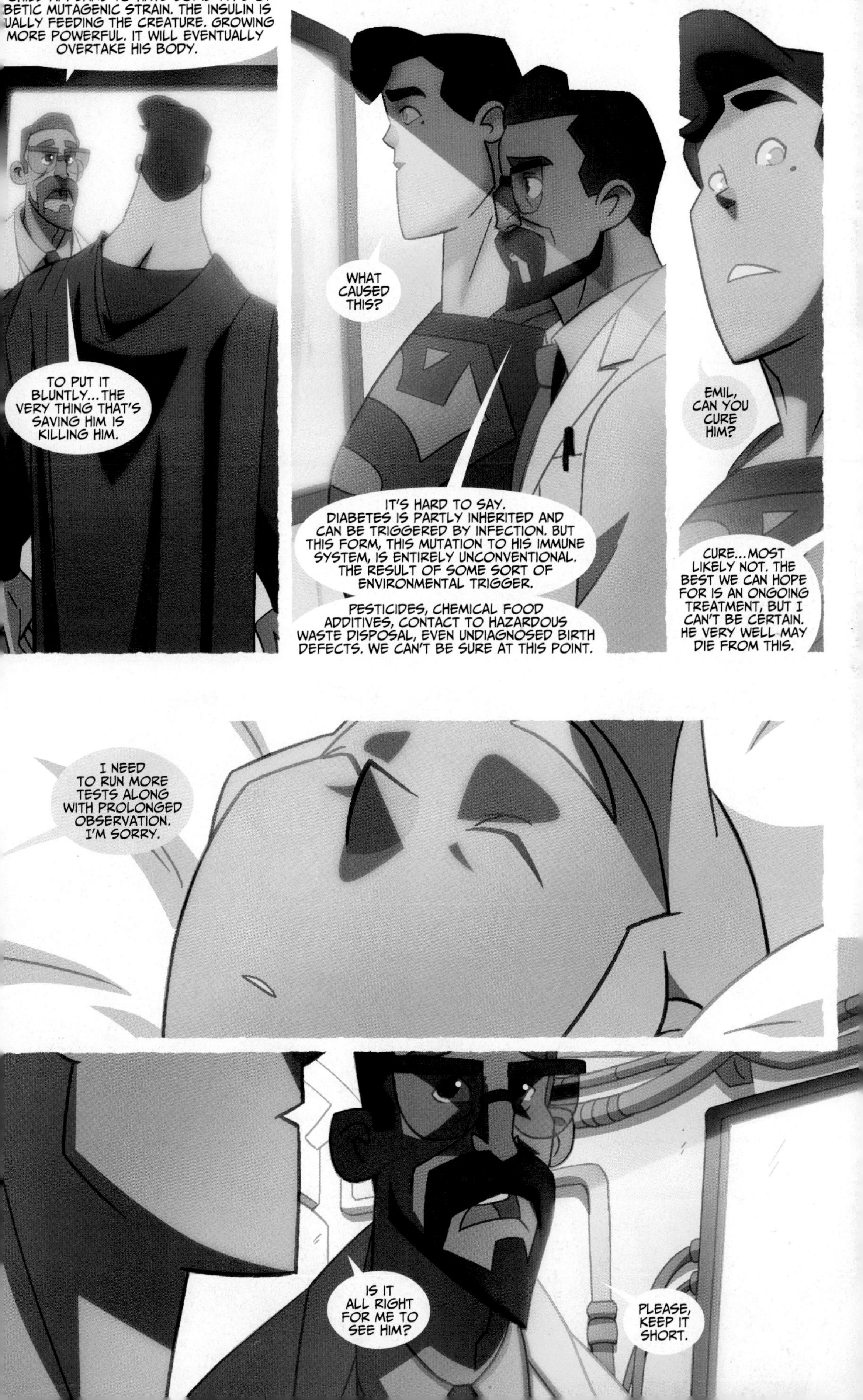
CHILD APPEARS TO HAVE SOME TYPE OF BETIC MUTAGENIC STRAIN. THE INSULIN IS UALLY FEEDING THE CREATURE. GROWING MORE POWERFUL. IT WILL EVENTUALLY OVERTAKE HIS BODY.
TO PUT IT BLUNTLY... THE VERY THING THAT'S SAVING HIM IS KILLING HIM.
WHAT CAUSED THIS?
IT'S HARD TO SAY. DIABETES IS PARTLY INHERITED AND CAN BE TRIGGERED BY INFECTION. BUT THIS FORM, THIS MUTATION TO HIS IMMUNE SYSTEM, IS ENTIRELY UNCONVENTIONAL. THE RESULT OF SOME SORT OF ENVIRONMENTAL TRIGGER.
PESTICIDES, CHEMICAL FOOD ADDITIVES, CONTACT TO HAZARDOUS WASTE DISPOSAL, EVEN UNDIAGNOSED BIRTH DEFECTS. WE CAN'T BE SURE AT THIS POINT.
EMIL, CAN YOU CURE HIM?
CURE... MOST LIKELY NOT. THE BEST WE CAN HOPE FOR IS AN ONGOING TREATMENT, BUT I CAN'T BE CERTAIN. HE VERY WELL MAY DIE FROM THIS.
I NEED TO RUN MORE TESTS ALONG WITH PROLONGED OBSERVATION. I'M SORRY.
IS IT ALL RIGHT FOR ME TO SEE HIM?
PLEASE, KEEP IT SHORT.

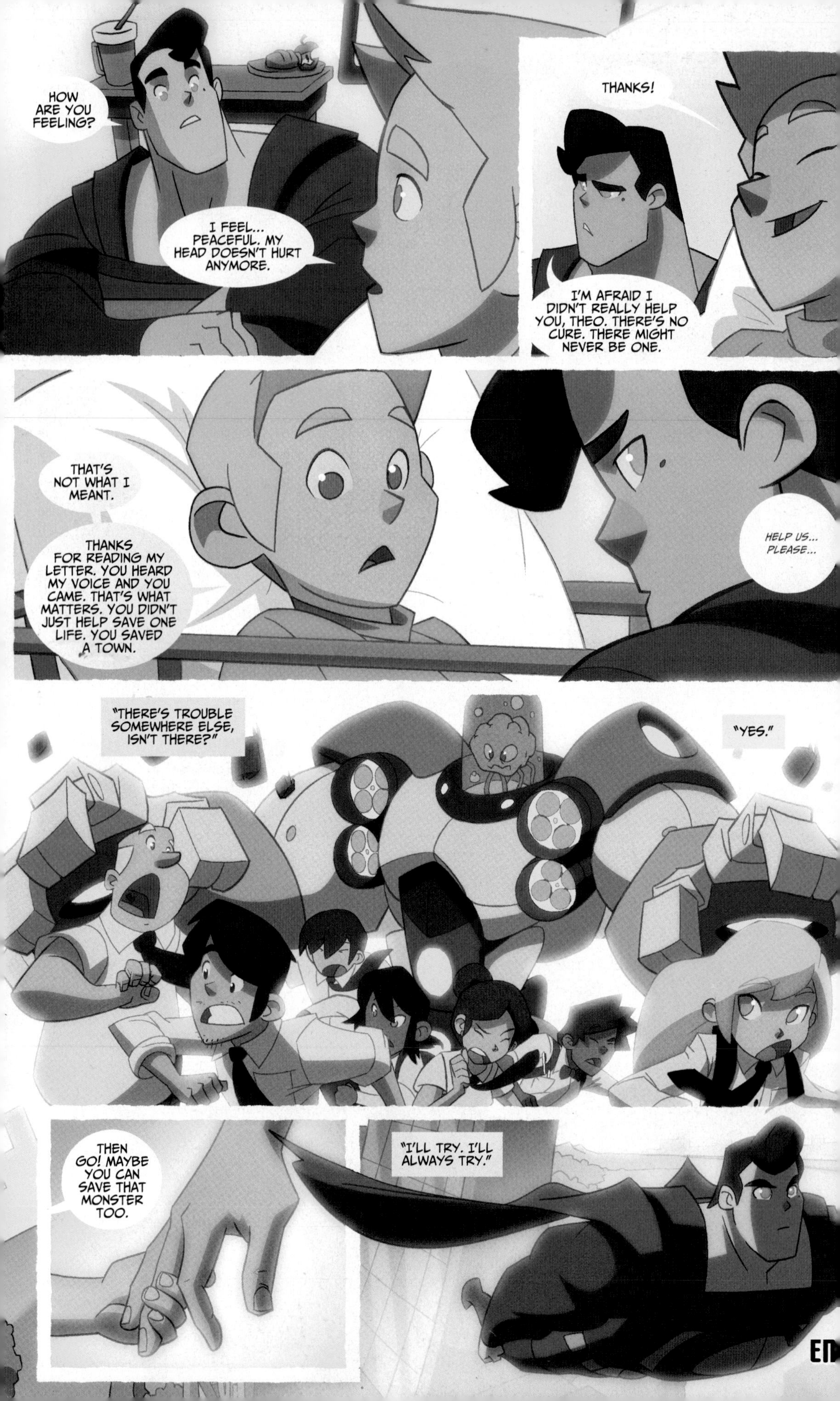
HOW ARE YOU FEELING?
I FEEL... PEACEFUL. MY HEAD DOESN'T HURT ANYMORE.
THANKS!
I'M AFRAID I DIDN'T REALLY HELP YOU, THEO. THERE'S NO CURE. THERE MIGHT NEVER BE ONE.
THAT'S NOT WHAT I MEANT.
THANKS FOR READING MY LETTER. YOU HEARD MY VOICE AND YOU CAME. THAT'S WHAT MATTERS. YOU DIDN'T JUST HELP SAVE ONE LIFE. YOU SAVED A TOWN.
HELP US... PLEASE...
"THERE'S TROUBLE SOMEWHERE ELSE, ISN'T THERE?"
"YES."
THEN GO! MAYBE YOU CAN SAVE THAT MONSTER TOO.
"I'LL TRY. I'LL ALWAYS TRY."
END

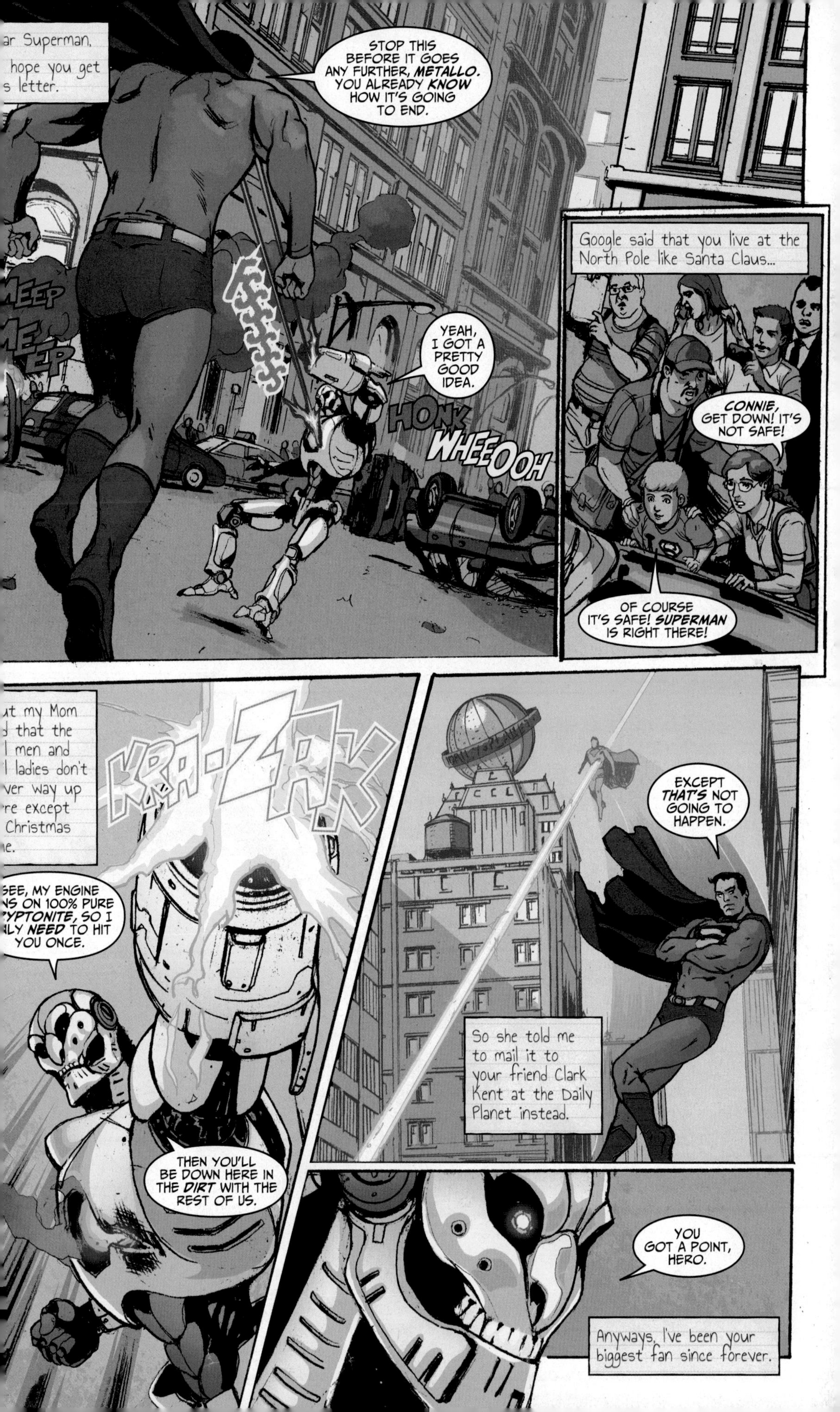
ar Superman,
hope you get
s letter.
STOP THIS BEFORE IT GOES ANY FURTHER, *METALLO.* YOU ALREADY *KNOW* HOW IT'S GOING TO END.
MEEP MEEP
FSSSS
YEAH, I GOT A PRETTY GOOD IDEA.
HONK
WHEEOOH
Google said that you live at the North Pole like Santa Claus...
CONNIE, GET DOWN! IT'S NOT SAFE!
OF COURSE IT'S SAFE! *SUPERMAN* IS RIGHT THERE!
ut my Mom
d that the
l men and
l ladies don't
ver way up
re except
Christmas
ne.
KRA-ZRAK
SEE, MY ENGINE
NS ON 100% PURE
YPTONITE, SO I
NLY *NEED* TO HIT
YOU ONCE.
THEN YOU'LL BE DOWN HERE IN THE *DIRT* WITH THE REST OF US.
EXCEPT *THAT'S* NOT GOING TO HAPPEN.
So she told me to mail it to your friend Clark Kent at the Daily Planet instead.
YOU GOT A POINT, HERO.
Anyways, I've been your biggest fan since forever.

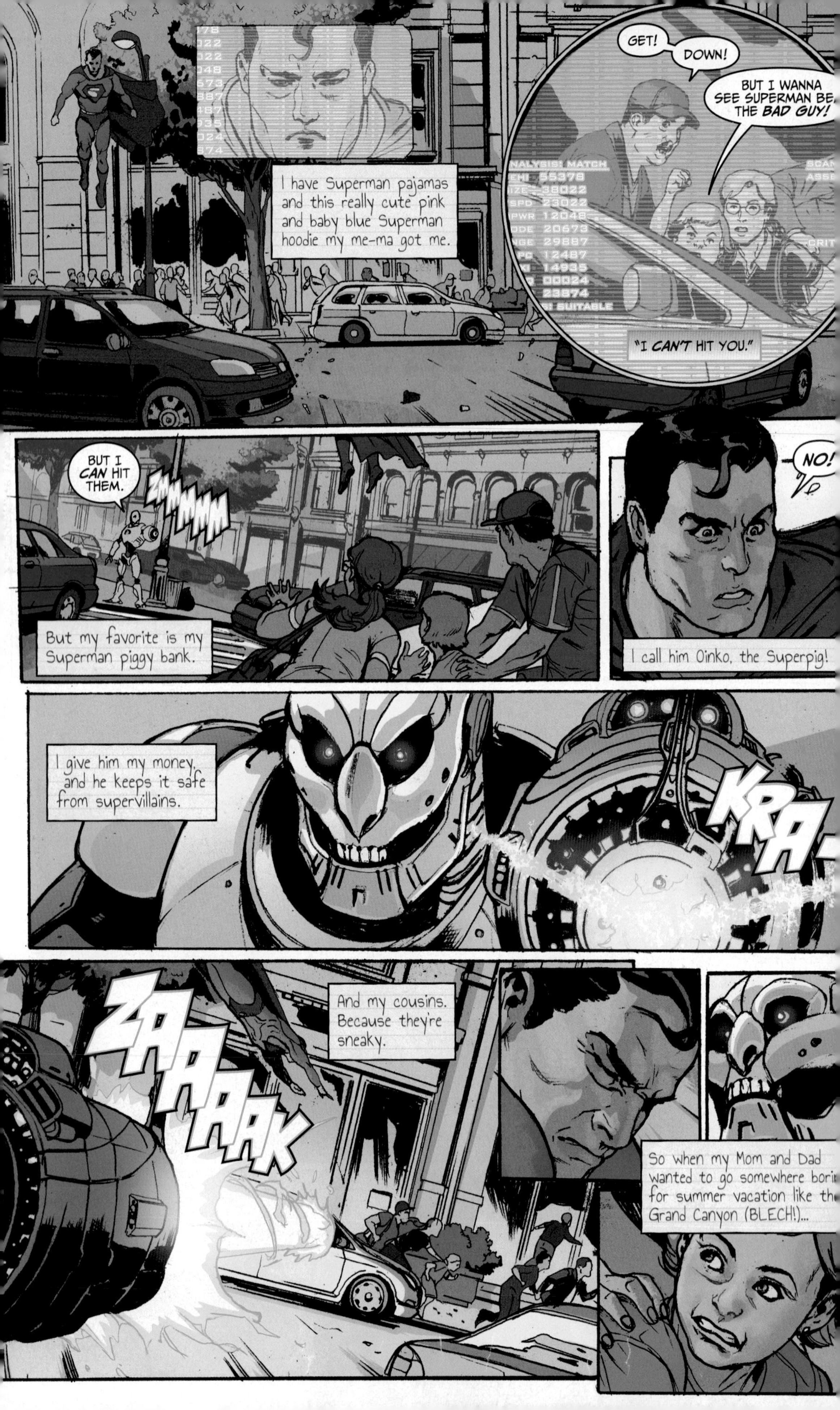

I have Superman pajamas and this really cute pink and baby blue Superman hoodie my me-ma got me.
GET!
DOWN!
BUT I WANNA SEE SUPERMAN BE THE BAD GUY!
"I CAN'T HIT YOU."
BUT I CAN HIT THEM.
ZMMMM
But my favorite is my Superman piggy bank.
NO!
I call him Oinko, the Superpig!
I give him my money, and he keeps it safe from supervillains.
KRA-
ZAAAAAK
And my cousins. Because they're sneaky.
So when my Mom and Dad wanted to go somewhere borin for summer vacation like the Grand Canyon (BLECH!)...

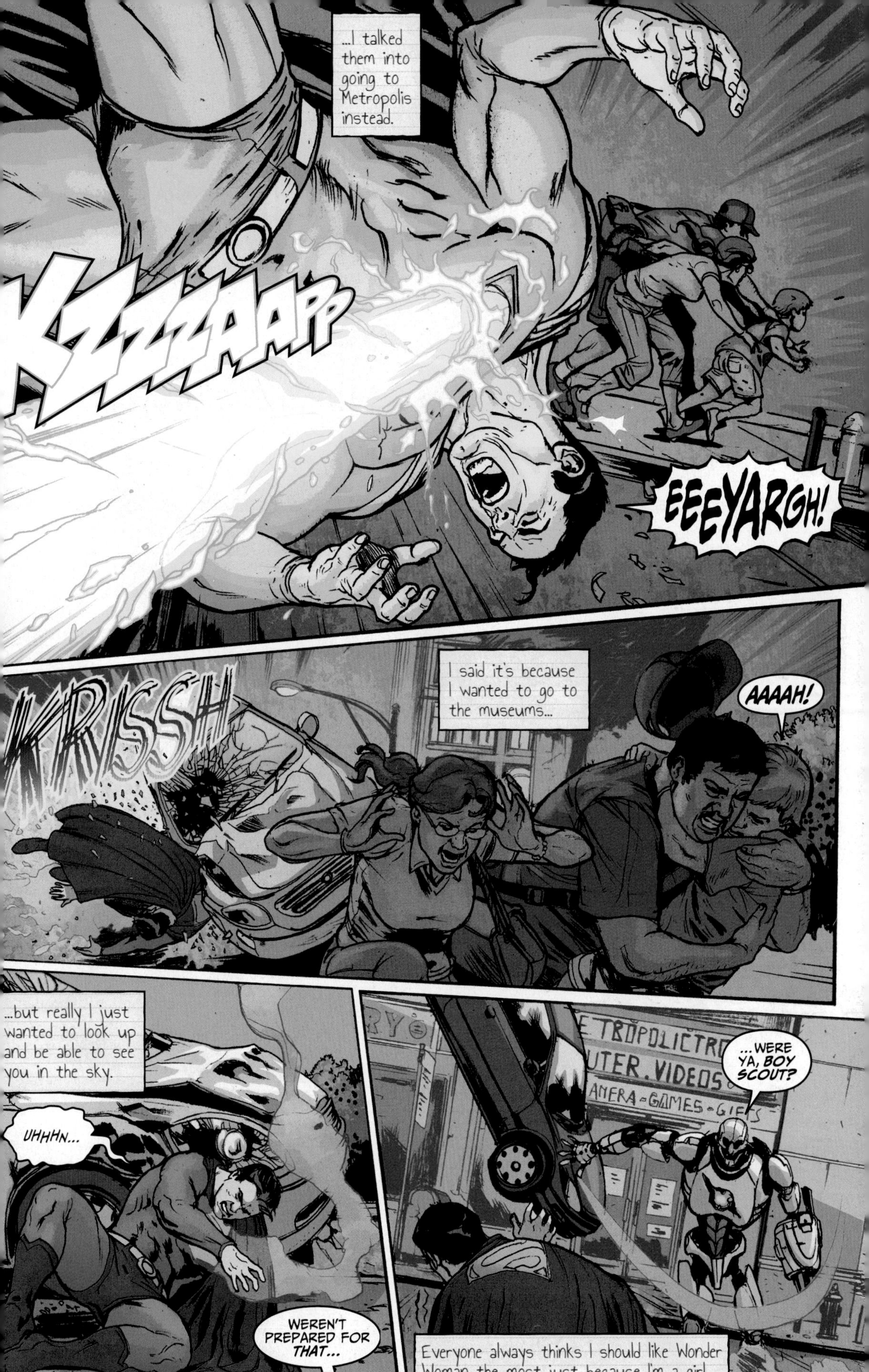
...I talked them into going to Metropolis instead.
KZZZAAPP
EEEYARGH!
KRISSH
I said it's because I wanted to go to the museums...
AAAAH!
...but really I just wanted to look up and be able to see you in the sky.
UHHHN...
WEREN'T PREPARED FOR THAT...
...WERE YA, BOY SCOUT?
Everyone always thinks I should like Wonder Woman the most just because I'm a girl.

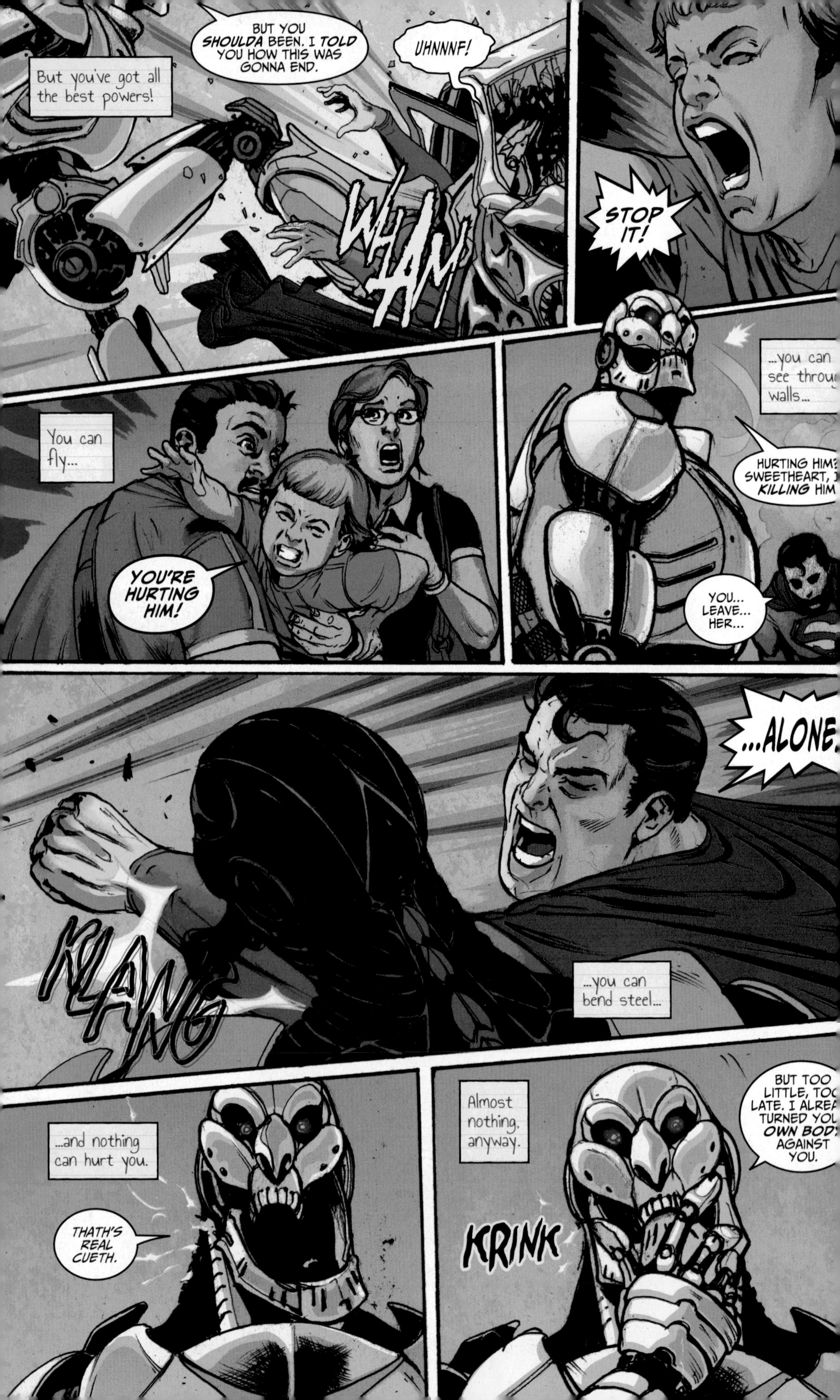
But you've got all the best powers!
BUT YOU SHOULDA BEEN. I TOLD YOU HOW THIS WAS GONNA END.
UHNNNF!
WHAM
STOP IT!
You can fly...
YOU'RE HURTING HIM!
...you can see throu walls...
HURTING HIM SWEETHEART, KILLING HIM
YOU... LEAVE... HER...
...ALONE.
KLANG
...you can bend steel...
...and nothing can hurt you.
THATH'S REAL CUETH.
Almost nothing, anyway.
KRINK
BUT TOO LITTLE, TOO LATE. I ALREA TURNED YOU OWN BOD AGAINST YOU.

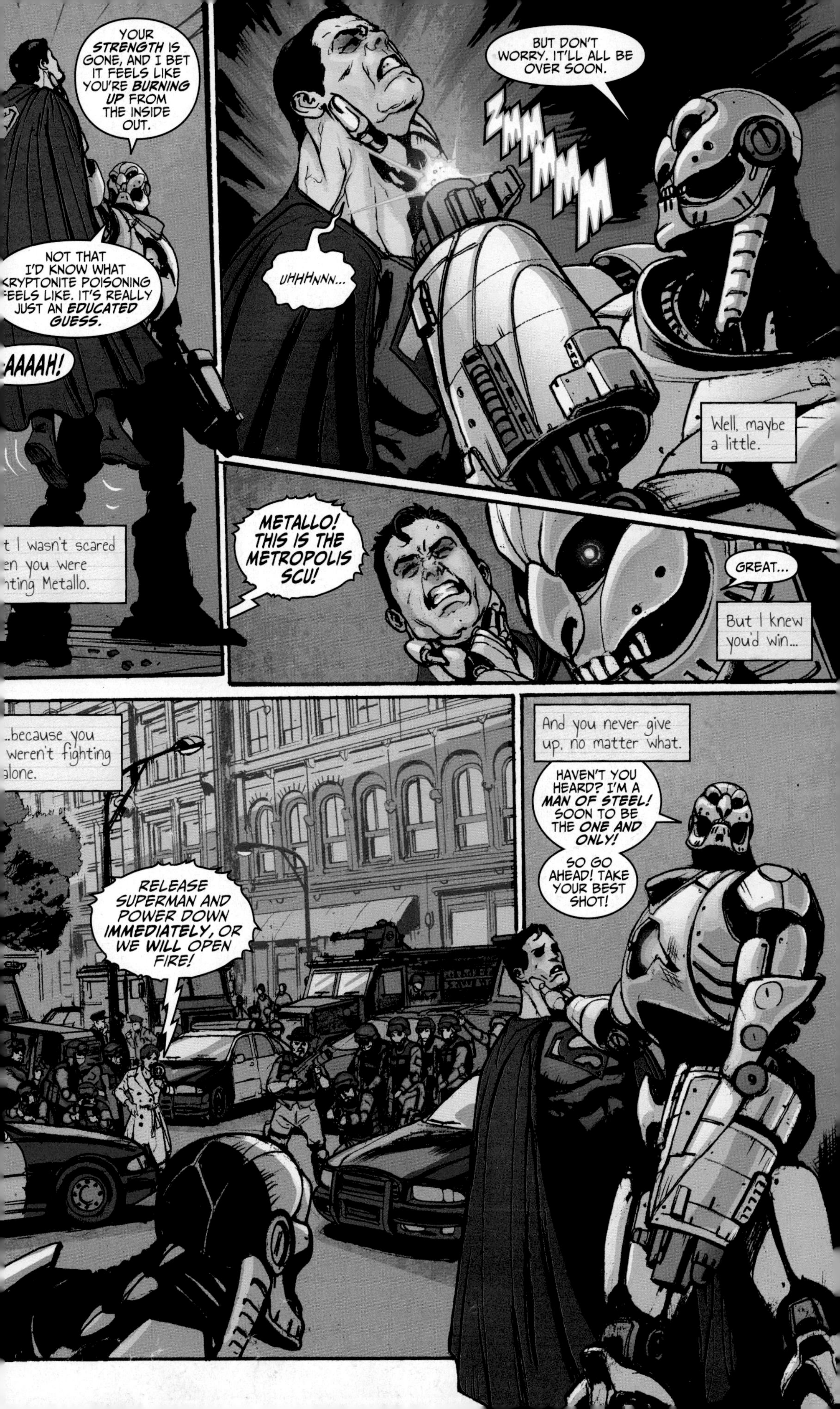
YOUR STRENGTH IS GONE, AND I BET IT FEELS LIKE YOU'RE BURNING UP FROM THE INSIDE OUT.
NOT THAT I'D KNOW WHAT KRYPTONITE POISONING FEELS LIKE. IT'S REALLY JUST AN EDUCATED GUESS.
AAAAH!
t I wasn't scared en you were nting Metallo.
UHHHNNN...
BUT DON'T WORRY. IT'LL ALL BE OVER SOON.
ZMMMMM
Well, maybe a little.
METALLO! THIS IS THE METROPOLIS SCU!
GREAT...
But I knew you'd win...
...because you weren't fighting alone.
RELEASE SUPERMAN AND POWER DOWN IMMEDIATELY, OR WE WILL OPEN FIRE!
And you never give up, no matter what.
HAVEN'T YOU HEARD? I'M A MAN OF STEEL! SOON TO BE THE ONE AND ONLY!
SO GO AHEAD! TAKE YOUR BEST SHOT!

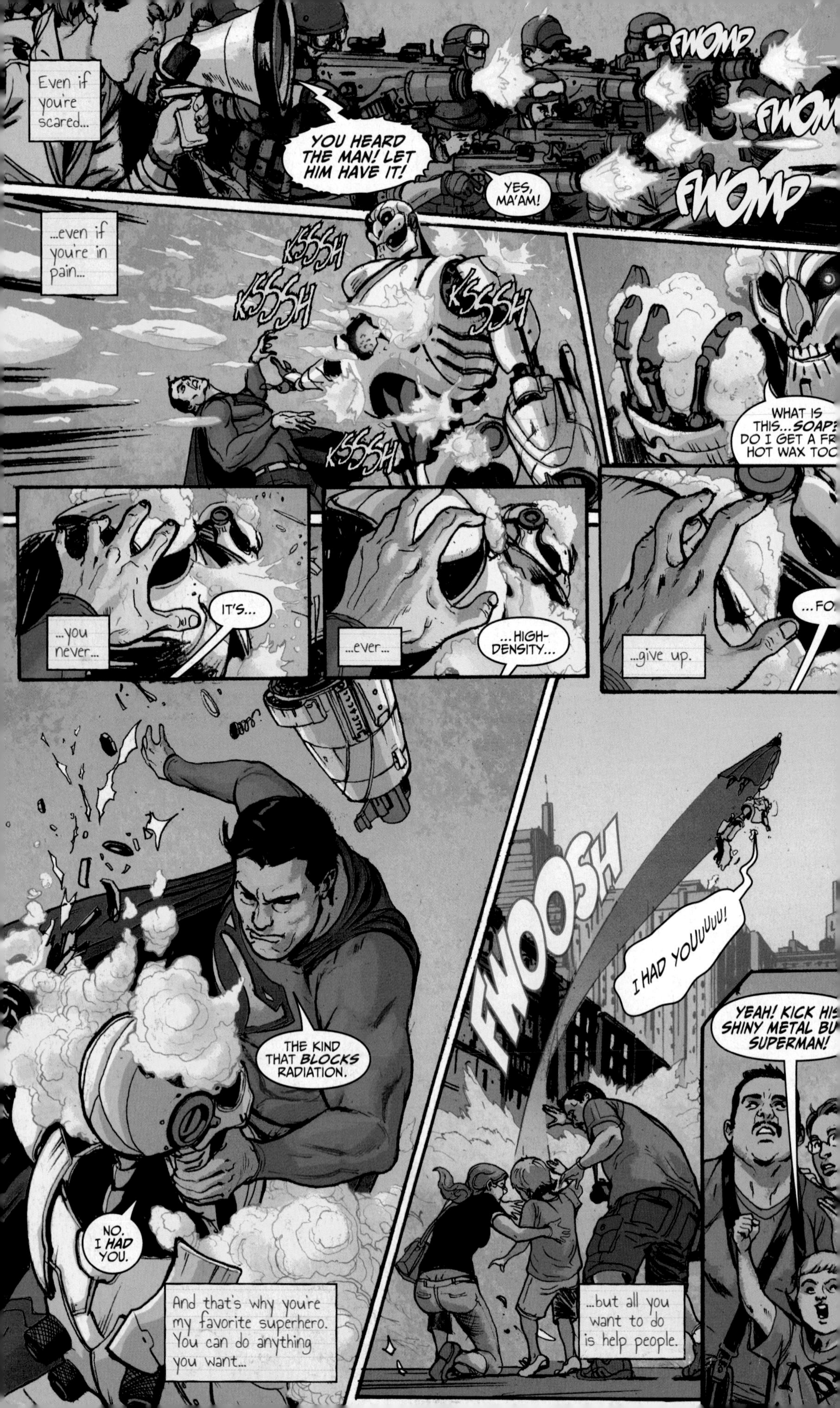

Even if you're scared...
YOU HEARD THE MAN! LET HIM HAVE IT!
YES, MA'AM!
FWOMP
FWOM
FWOMP
...even if you're in pain...
KSSSH
KSSSH
KSSSH
KSSSH
WHAT IS THIS...SOAP?
DO I GET A FR
HOT WAX TOO
...you never...
IT'S...
...ever...
...HIGH-DENSITY...
...give up.
...FO
THE KIND THAT BLOCKS RADIATION.
NO. I HAD YOU.
And that's why you're my favorite superhero. You can do anything you want...
FWOOSH
I HAD YOUUUUU!
YEAH! KICK HI
SHINY METAL BU
SUPERMAN!
...but all you want to do is help people.

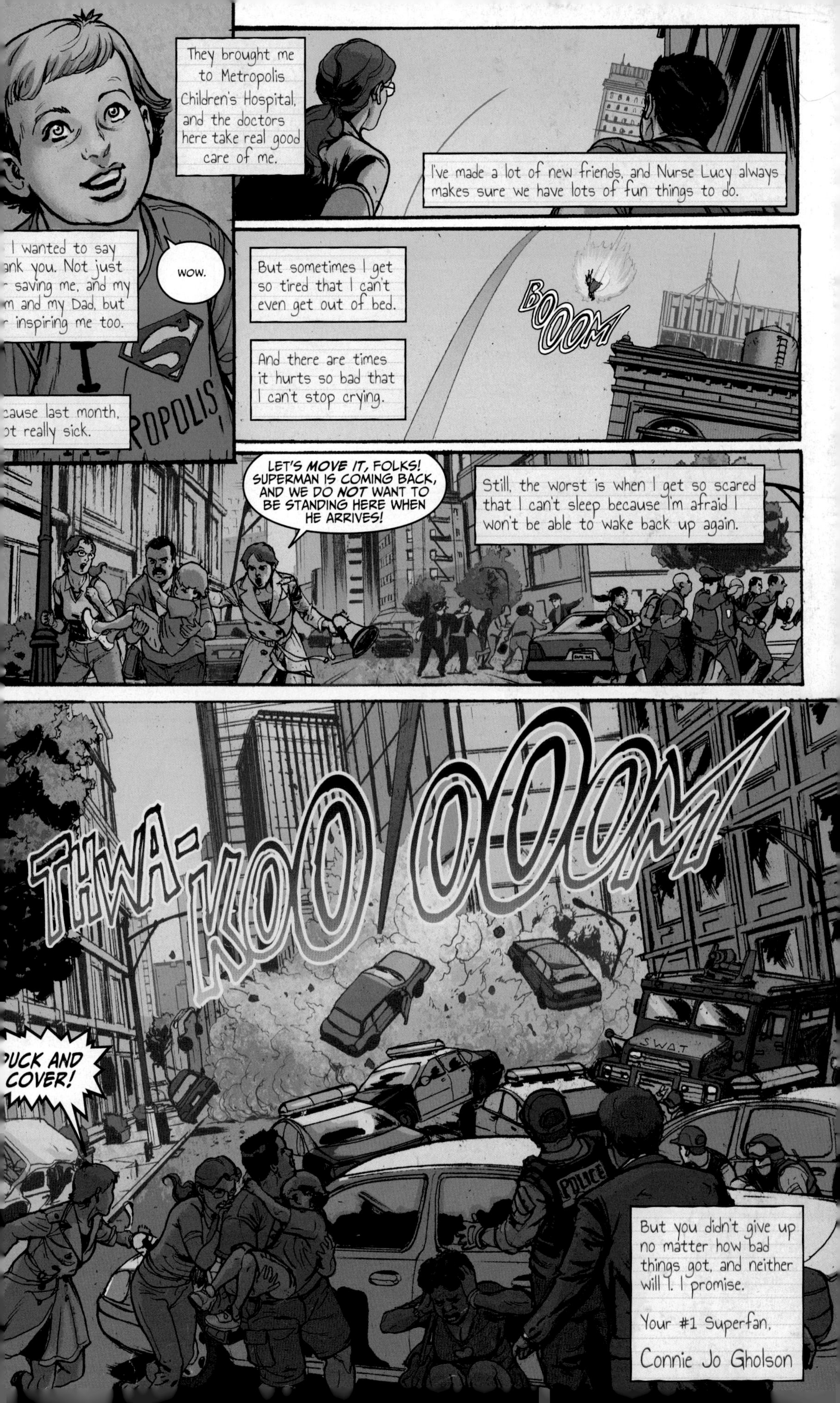

They brought me to Metropolis Children's Hospital, and the doctors here take real good care of me.
I've made a lot of new friends, and Nurse Lucy always makes sure we have lots of fun things to do.
I wanted to say
ank you. Not just
saving me, and my
m and my Dad, but
inspiring me too.
WOW.
cause last month,
ot really sick.
But sometimes I get so tired that I can't even get out of bed.
And there are times it hurts so bad that I can't stop crying.
BOOOM
LET'S MOVE IT, FOLKS! SUPERMAN IS COMING BACK, AND WE DO NOT WANT TO BE STANDING HERE WHEN HE ARRIVES!
Still, the worst is when I get so scared that I can't sleep because I'm afraid I won't be able to wake back up again.
THWA-KOOOOOOM
UCK AND COVER!
S.W.A.T.
POLICE
But you didn't give up no matter how bad things got, and neither will I. I promise.
Your #1 Superfan,
Connie Jo Gholson

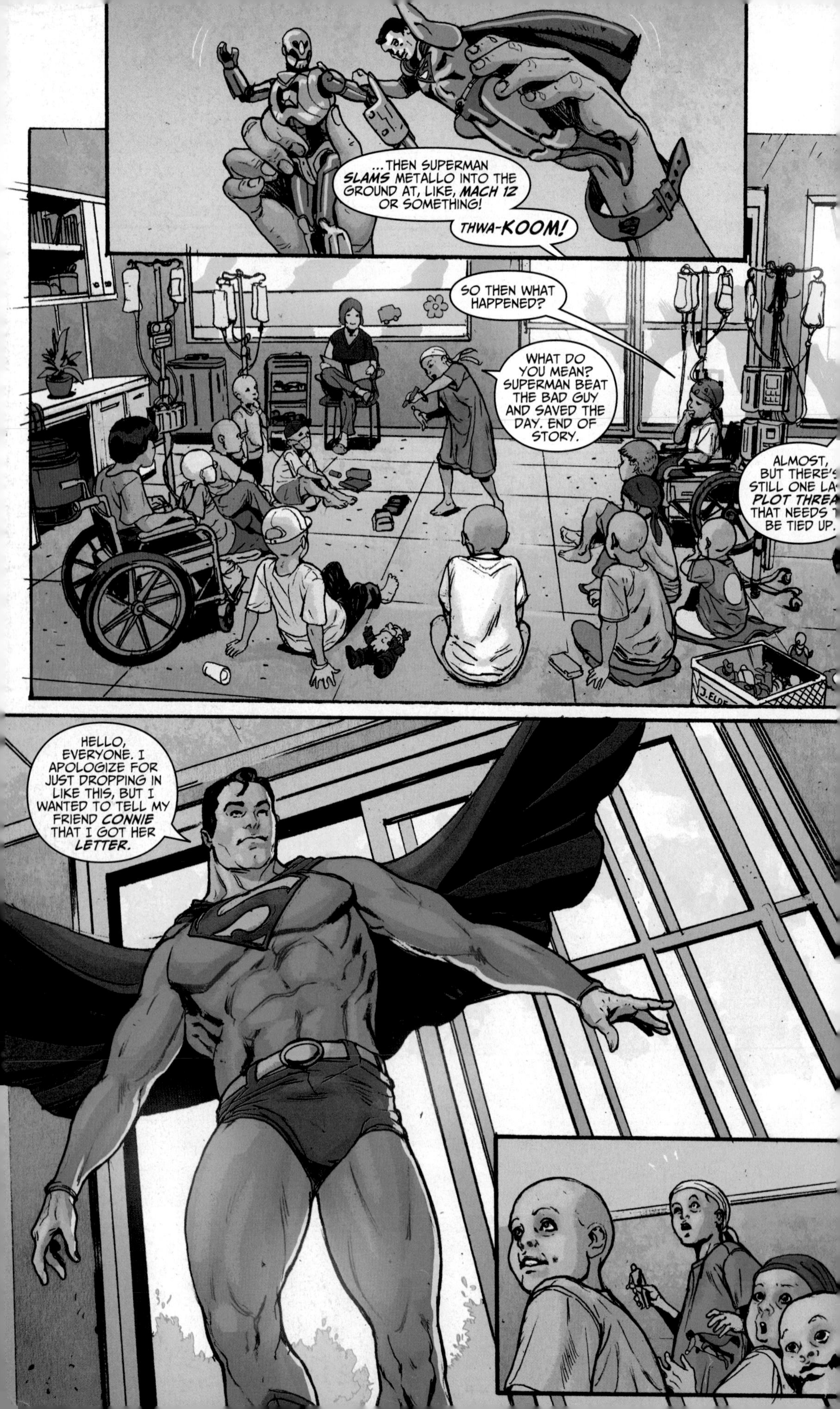
...THEN SUPERMAN SLAMS METALLO INTO THE GROUND AT, LIKE, MACH 12 OR SOMETHING!
THWA-KOOM!
SO THEN WHAT HAPPENED?
WHAT DO YOU MEAN? SUPERMAN BEAT THE BAD GUY AND SAVED THE DAY. END OF STORY.
ALMOST, BUT THERE'S STILL ONE LA PLOT THREA THAT NEEDS T BE TIED UP.
J. ELDE
HELLO, EVERYONE. I APOLOGIZE FOR JUST DROPPING IN LIKE THIS, BUT I WANTED TO TELL MY FRIEND CONNIE THAT I GOT HER LETTER.

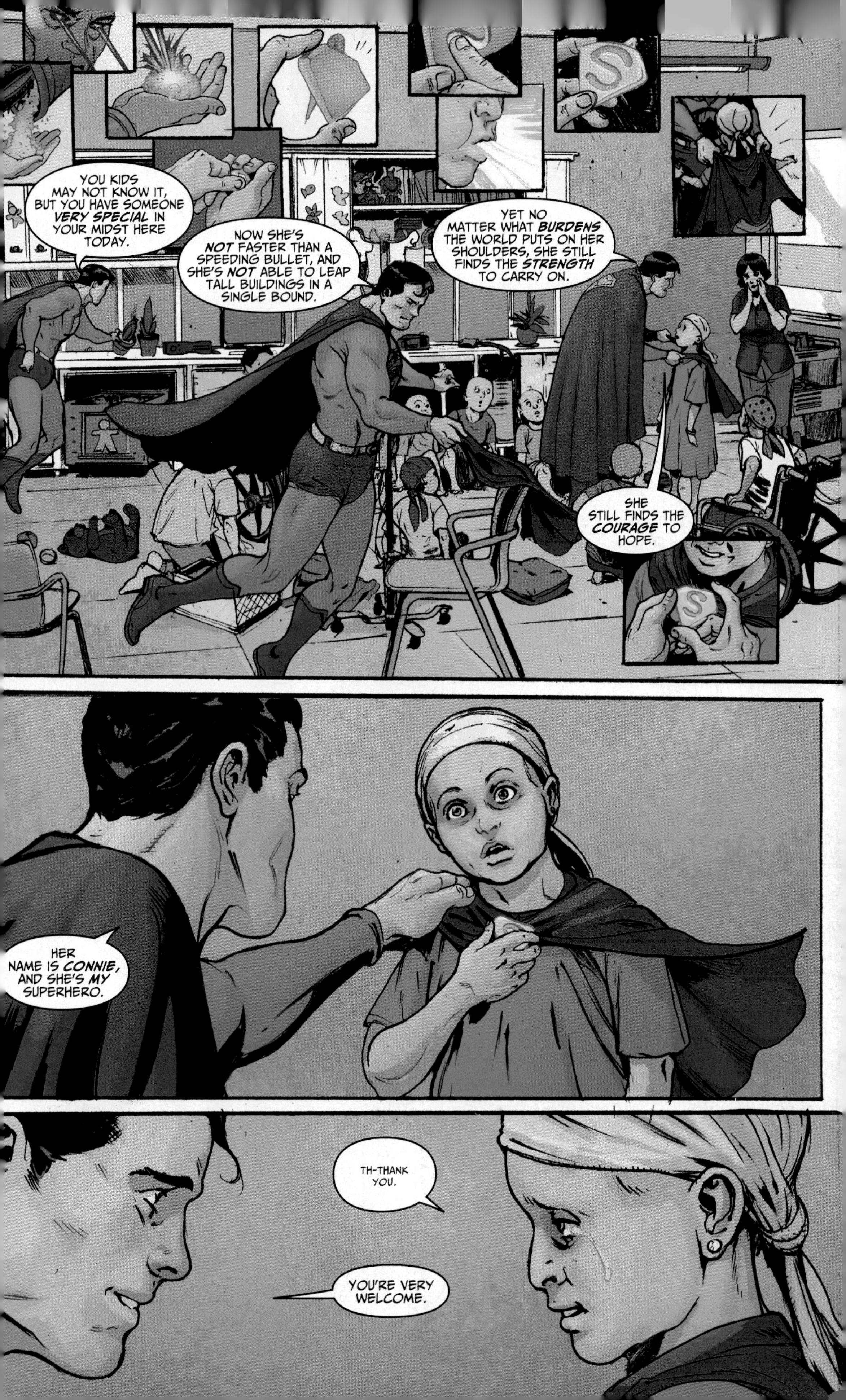

YOU KIDS MAY NOT KNOW IT, BUT YOU HAVE SOMEONE VERY SPECIAL IN YOUR MIDST HERE TODAY.
NOW SHE'S NOT FASTER THAN A SPEEDING BULLET, AND SHE'S NOT ABLE TO LEAP TALL BUILDINGS IN A SINGLE BOUND.
YET NO MATTER WHAT BURDENS THE WORLD PUTS ON HER SHOULDERS, SHE STILL FINDS THE STRENGTH TO CARRY ON.
SHE STILL FINDS THE COURAGE TO HOPE.
HER NAME IS CONNIE, AND SHE'S MY SUPERHERO.
TH-THANK YOU.
YOU'RE VERY WELCOME.

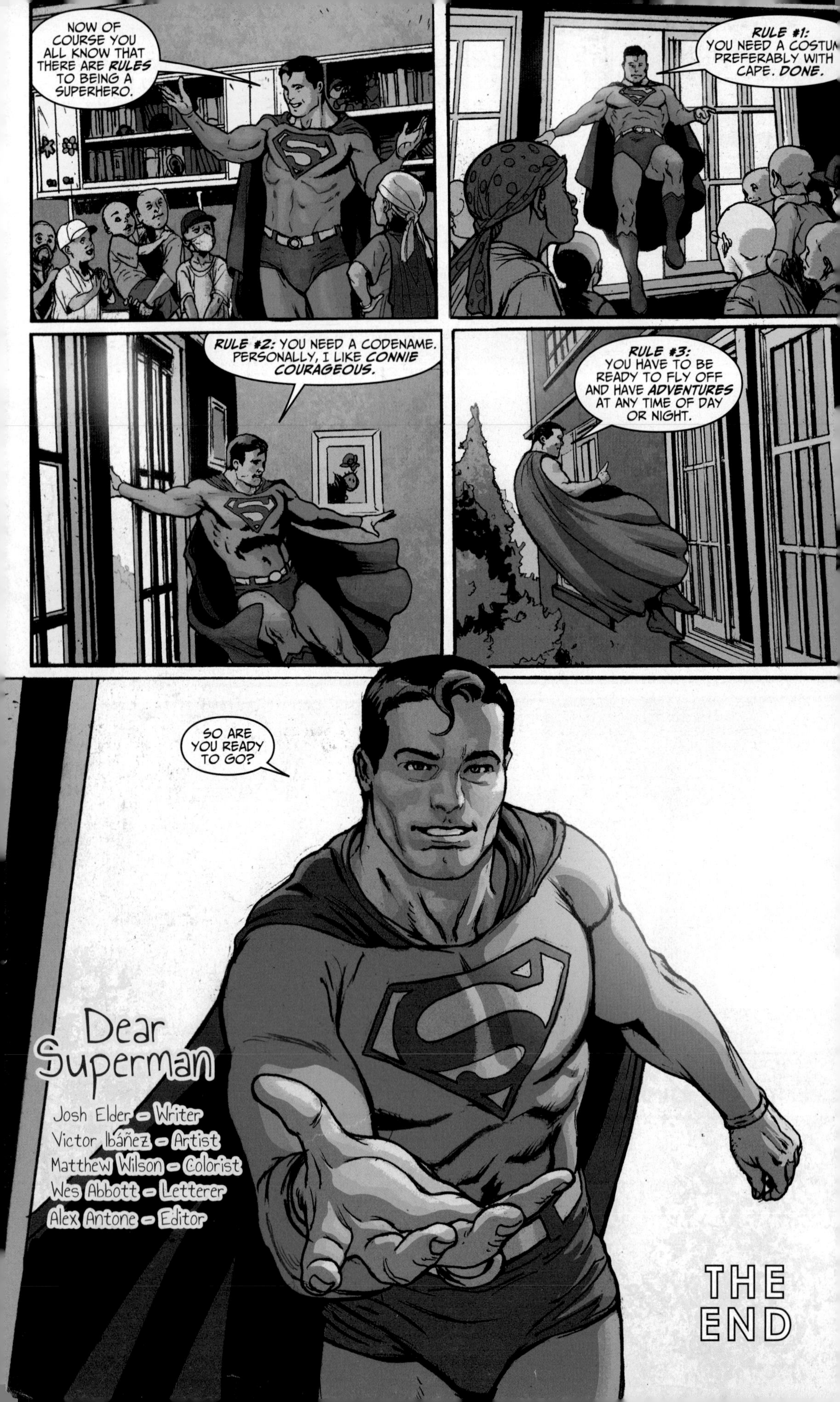
NOW OF COURSE YOU ALL KNOW THAT THERE ARE RULES TO BEING A SUPERHERO.
RULE #1: YOU NEED A COSTUM PREFERABLY WITH CAPE. DONE.
RULE #2: YOU NEED A CODENAME. PERSONALLY, I LIKE CONNIE COURAGEOUS.
RULE #3: YOU HAVE TO BE READY TO FLY OFF AND HAVE ADVENTURES AT ANY TIME OF DAY OR NIGHT.
SO ARE YOU READY TO GO?
Dear Superman
Josh Elder - Writer
Victor Ibáñez - Artist
Matthew Wilson - Colorist
Wes Abbott - Letterer
Alex Antone - Editor
THE END

"Excellent...From its poignant domestic moments, delivered in mostly warm, fuzzy flashbacks, to its block-buster battles, Straczynski's SUPERMAN: EARTH ONE renders like a feature film just waiting for adaptation."
—WIRED

FROM *THE NEW YORK TIMES* #1 BEST-SELLING AUTHOR
J. MICHAEL STRACZYNSKI
with SHANE DAVIS

SUPERMAN EARTH
ONE: VOL. 2

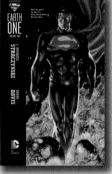

with SHANE DAVIS

SUPERMAN:
GROUNDED VOLS. 1-2

with EDDY BARROWS

WONDER WOMAN:
ODYSSEY VOLS. 1-2

with DON KRAMER and
PHIL HESTER

SUPERMAN

The #1
New York Times
Bestseller

EARTH
ONE

VOLUME ONE

J. MICHAEL
STRACZYNSKI

SHANE
DAVIS

"What do you get when you combine Twilight *and a classic superhero? The new Superman."*
—THE HOLLYWOOD REPORTER

DC COMICS™